NOTES ON
SOUTHSIDE VIRGINIA

By

Walter A. Watson

Edited by
MRS. WALTER A. WATSON

Under the direction of
WILMER L. HALL

CLEARFIELD

Originally Published as
Bulletin of the Virginia State Library,
Volume XV, Nos. 2-4 (September 1925)
Richmond, 1925

Reprinted
Genealogical Publishing Co., Inc.
Baltimore, Maryland
1977

Reprinted for
Clearfield Company, Inc. by
Genealogical Publishing Co., Inc.
Baltimore, Maryland
1990, 2003

Library of Congress Cataloging in Publication Data

Watson, Walter Allen, 1867-1919.
    Notes on southside Virginia.
    Reprint of the 1925 ed. which was issued in Richmond as Bulletin of
the Virginia State Library, v. 15, No. 2-4.
    1. Virginia—History, Local. 2. Virginia—Genealogy. 3. Virginia—
History, Local—Sources. I. Title. II. Series: Virginia. State Library,
Richmond. Bulletin; v. 15, no. 2-4.

F226.W33 1977   975.5   76-44245
ISBN 0-8063-0741-2

CONTENTS

Bulletin of the Virginia State Library

Edited by H. R. McILWAINE, State Librarian.

| Vol. XV. | SEPTEMBER, 1925. | Nos. 2-4 |

EDITORIAL NOTE.

It is one of the functions of the Board of the Virginia State Library to foster historical work in Virginia. From the time that the Board was entrusted with the management of the affairs of the Library it has had charge of the expenditure of a special publication fund and later of appropriations for publications that have been relatively generous. Out of these has been paid the cost of publishing the Library Bulletin and the Journals of the House of Burgesses and of the Council, while the general printing fund of the State has borne the expense of printing the Annual Report of the Library. First and last, the publications of the Library constitute a notable series.

In 1916 the General Assembly, because the right of the Library Board to print anything in its Annual Report other than an account of the actual work of the Library for the year had been questioned, passed an act specifically permitting it to print as a part of its report such special matter as its members thought of sufficient historical importance—provided the number of printed pages in any report should not exceed six hundred.

It was the intention for some time to have these notes printed as a part of the Annual Report, but this plan has given way to the plan to have them printed in the Bulletin, the Bulletin being for more reasons than one, which need not be detailed here, always a preferable vehicle of publication to the Annual Report; provided, money may be found in the Library appropriations to pay—as, fortunately, is the case at the present time.

The material appearing in the notes varies from hasty sentences jotted down in note-books and on scraps of paper, through carefully made abstracts from records in clerks' offices, to what appear to be completed biographical sketches (*vide* the sketches of George C. Dromgoole, William Branch Giles, and Dr. James Jones) which give an intimation of what Judge Watson's whole work would have been had he lived. The material, as he left it, however, is of sufficient value to justify publication. Others engaged in the co-operative work of setting forth the history of Southside Virginia will be much aided by his labors.

H. R. McILWAINE,
State Librarian.

FOREWORD.

My desire to make some valuable use of the labors performed through many years by Mr. Watson in collecting these notes decided me to have them published, fragmentary though they were. As the difficulty of their orderly arrangement was great and the extensive distribution of the finished work improbable unless through well directed channels, the opportunity afforded me for their present publication was accepted with genuine appreciation.

But for the untiring and efficient direction of Mr. Wilmer L. Hall, Assistant Librarian, these notes would have been a disordered mass of small value. To him I wish to express my deepest gratitude, and I wish also to express the hope that the publication may be of sufficient service to the historian and genealogist of the Southside to compensate Mr. Hall in some manner for his labors and to justify Dr. Henry R. McIlwaine, State Librarian, and the Library Board in the decision to send it out with the authority of the Virginia State Library.

CONSTANCE T. WATSON.

RICHMOND, VA., *July* 30, 1925.

INTRODUCTION.

That section of Virginia which lies south of the James River and east of the Blue Ridge Mountains is popularly known as the Southside; but the designation is often restricted to a smaller area, excluding the tidewater and upland counties, and sometimes also the northern counties of this region. This part of the State has been considered characteristically Virginian, and it still retains some of the traits which have tended to die out in other parts of the State. Always predominantly agricultural, it is a section which still has many large plantations, some of which are worked by tenant farmers on small holdings. It was the stronghold of slavery in Virginia. The climate is milder than in other sections of the State; some Southside counties along the North Carolina border raise cotton and peanuts as staple crops.

This region has produced some of the foremost men in Virginia history: John Randolph, William Branch Giles, George C. Dromgoole, William S. Archer. Patrick Henry, while not born here, made his home in Charlotte County. Besides these notables, hundreds of distinguished men have come from this section to serve the State and Nation.

Walter Allen Watson was, by birth, residence and temperament, a son of this fair section of Virginia. He had a passion to preserve from oblivion the traits of the people and the history of this region. For many years he spent much of his leisure time in making notes and storing his mind with information about people and things, which knowledge he purposed some day to embody in a history of the Southside. Possessed of indefatigable industry and endowed with an accurate memory and keen humor, he would doubtless have produced a valuable work, embellished with anecdotes and humorous sketches; but having died with his plans unfulfilled, it is left to others to compile his scattered notes, in the effort to preserve something of the local history which his labor had gathered. At the least it is to be regretted that he had not gone further in this work and had not made a more complete and definite written record; but it is believed that the historian and the genealogist of the Southside will find much matter of interest in these pages. It is probable, also, that many of these fragmentary notes will be suggestive of the course which investigators should pursue. There are, as yet, few local histories which deal with this section, and none of Nottoway or Amelia, the two counties which have a preponderant place in these notes.

The material has been derived entirely from the manuscript books and papers of Judge Watson, now deposited in the

Virginia State Library, with the exception that a few notes have been taken from private papers in the possession of his widow. It has been the aim to arrange this matter in some logical order without changing the original sense and wording. Many difficulties have attended the classification and co-ordination of this mass of heterogeneous, scattered and undigested material, as also the interpretation of fragmentary and obscure references, full of significance doubtless to the writer but conveying little apparent meaning to others. Inevitably there are errors. While much that was irrelevant or purely personal has been omitted, especially in the case of references to individuals in the diaries, effort has been made to preserve all pertinent data relative to the Southside and its people.

It was the purpose of Mrs. Watson to have these notes published as a memorial to her husband, and with the assumption by the library of responsibility for their publication, she has worked indefatigably in the arrangement and editing of them; her interpretation of a hasty and much abbreviated handwriting and her knowledge of personal and local allusions have been indispensable. To her, and to the many former friends of Judge Watson who have expressed an interest in this work, apology is made for the delay in publication; the pressure of library duties has permitted only brief periods of attention to the planning of the work and the supervision of its arrangement and editing.

Each of the biographical sketches of Judge Watson had been sent to Mrs. Watson by some one well acquainted with him at the period of which it treats. They, with a brief sketch written by herself, give an outline of his life and character.

WILMER L. HALL,
Assistant State Librarian.

SOUTHSIDE PUBLIC MEN[1]

CONFEDERATE STATES GENERALS.

Joseph E. Johnston, Henry Heth, Edward Johnson, Wm. Mahone, John Pegram, J. E. B. Stuart, J. R. Chalmers, W. L. Cabell, D. A. Weisiger, John R. Chambliss, P. St. G. Cocke, J. A. Early, T. L. Rosser, Samuel Jones, B. H. Robertson, Sterling Price, Sam Garland, R. E. Rodes, T. T. Munford, Wm. Terry, Roger A. Pryor.

FEDERAL GENERALS.

George Henry Thomas, Lawrence Pike Graham, Winfield Scott.

CABINET OFFICERS (FROM OTHER STATES).

G. M. Bibb, Prince Edward County, Va., Sec. of Treasury (Kentucky); A. V. Brown, Brunswick County, Va., P. M. General (Tennessee); W. T. Barry, Lunenburg County, Va., P. M. General (Kentucky; buried at Lexington, Ky.)

CHIEF JUSTICES (OF OTHER STATES).

A. G. Thurman, Lynchburg, Campbell County, Va., Ohio; W. T. Barry, Lunenburg County, Va., Kentucky; G. M. Bibb, Prince Edward County, Va., Kentucky.

UNITED STATES SENATORS (FOR VIRGINIA).

Henry Tazewell, Brunswick County; A. B. Venable, Prince Edward County; Wm. B. Giles, Amelia County; John Randolph, Prince George County; L. W. Tazewell, Norfolk County; B. W. Leigh, Chesterfield County; John Wayles Eppes, Chesterfield County; Wm. S. Archer, Amelia County; R. E. Withers, Campbell County; Wm. Mahone, Southampton County; John W. Daniel, Lynchburg City; Henry Tazewell, Brunswick County.

UNITED STATES SENATORS (FROM OTHER STATES).

George M. Bibb, Prince Edward County, Va., Kentucky; Walter T. Colquitt, Halifax County, Va., Georgia; Henry Chambers, Lunenburg County, Va., Alabama; Wm. Cocke, Brunswick County, Va., Tennessee; C. C. Clay, Sr., Halifax County, Va., Alabama; Jno. B. Henderson, Pittsylvania County, Va., Missouri;

---

[1]The following lists are not complete; they are given as compiled by Judge Watson.

Wilson Lumpkin, Pittsylvania County, Va., Georgia; Isham Talbot, Bedford County, Va., Kentucky; Waller Taylor, Lunenburg County, Va., Indiana; A. G. Thurman, Lynchburg, Campbell County, Va., Ohio; Jas. F. Trotter, Brunswick County, Va., Mississippi; Jas. Turner, Southampton County, Va., North Carolina; B. K. Bruce, Prince Edward County, Va., Mississippi; W. C. C. Claiborne, Sussex County, Va., Louisiana; Dixon H. Lewis, Dinwiddie County, Va., Alabama.

CONGRESSMEN.

We have been represented in Congress by Colonel Peterson Goodwyn, of Dinwiddie, 1803-1818; Thomas Saunders Gholson, Jr., of Brunswick, 1808-1816 (also in the Confederate Congress, 1863-1865); General John Pegram, of Dinwiddie, 1818-1819; Dr. James Jones, of Nottoway, 1819-1823; Wm. S. Archer, of Amelia, 1820-1835; John Winston Jones, of Chesterfield, 1835-1845; General George Coke Dromgoole, of Brunswick, 1835-1841 and 1843-1847; William Osborne Goode, of Mecklenburg, 1841-1843 and 1853-1859; Richard Kidder Meade, of Brunswick, 1847-1853; Roger Atkinson Pryor, of Dinwiddie, 1859-1861 (also in the Confederate Congress); Robert Ridgeway, of Cool Well, Va., 1869[2]; William H. H. Stowell (a carpet bagger), of Windsor, Vermont, 1874; Edward Carrington Venable, of Prince Edward, 1889-1890; and others.

Colonel Goodwyn died while a member of Congress in 1818 and was succeeded by General John Pegram, who appeared at the second session of the fifteenth Congress and was sworn in as representative (*Richmond Enquirer*, Nov. 20, 1818). General Pegram was previously Major General of the First Division of Virginia Militia in the War of 1812 (Journal, House of Delegates, 1813, table in back), and subsequently United States Marshal for the eastern district of Virginia. He represented Dinwiddie County in the House of Delegates many years and also served in the State Senate. He was a relative of General Winfield Scott.[3] It appears that Dr. James Jones was voted for in this election but was beaten. The following year, however, he beat General Pegram in the district (*Richmond Enquirer*, May 4, 1819). General Pegram, I think, lost his life by some accident on the Ohio River—the burning of a boat perhaps. In

[2]Of Amherst County. Editor of *Richmond Whig*, 1853-1865; became a candidate for Congress in 1865, but withdrew; elected to Congress, 1869; died Oct. 16, 1870. The fifth district, which he represented, consisted of Greene, Albemarle, Fluvanna, Nelson, Buckingham, Amherst, Appomattox, Bedford, Campbell, Prince Edward and the city of Lynchburg. Robert W. Hughes, in his address, "Editors of the Past," before the Virginia Press Association, June 22, 1897, spoke of Robert Ridgeway as having been "wonderfully efficient in his dashing peculiarities."

[3]His half sister, Martha P. Pegram, daughter by his father's second wife, Ann Harper Parham, married Colonel James Scott, of "Laurel Branch," Dinwiddie County, Virginia, brother of General Winfield Scott.

1823 Nottoway was transferred to Mr. Archer's district and Dr. Jones thus lost his seat. I think Nottoway was in the Chesterfield district when John Winston Jones represented it, but this is a matter of record and can be ascertained of course.[4] Mr. Freeman Epes recalls John Winston Jones, the congressman, as one of the most fluent men he ever heard before the people, and Colonel Jeffress recollects that he was a very effective speaker.

MEMBERS OF CONGRESS (OTHER STATES).

Charles Eaton Haynes, Brunswick County, Va., Georgia; Jos. Chappel Hutcheson, Mecklenburg County, Va., Texas; John Kerr, Jr., Pittsylvania County, Va., North Carolina; Wm. Lattimore, Norfolk County, Va., Mississippi; John William Leftwich, Bedford County, Va., Tennessee; Wm. Mallory Levy, Isle of Wight County, Va., Louisiana; Jas. Hamilton Lewis, Danville, Pittsylvania County, Va., Washington; Thos. Watkins Ligon, Prince Edward County, Va., Maryland; Wilson Lumpkin, Pittsylvania County, Va., Georgia; John H. Marable, Brunswick County, Va., Tennessee; Thos. Patrick Moore, Charlotte County, Va., Kentucky; Robert Page Waller Morris, Lynchburg, Campbell County, Va., Minnesota; Abner Nash, Prince Edward County, Va., North Carolina; Thos. Lawson Price, Pittsylvania County, Va., Missouri; Richard Clausell Puryear, Mecklenburg County, Va., North Carolina; Dixon Hall Lewis, Dinwiddie County, Va., Alabama; John W. Reid, Lynchburg, Campbell County, Va., Missouri; Thos. Bolling Robertson, Bellfield near Petersburg, Va., Louisiana; Alexander Dromgoole Sims, Brunswick County, Va., South Carolina; Martin Russell Thayer, Petersburg, Va., Pennsyivania; Allen Granberry Thurman, Lynchburg, Campbell County, Va., Ohio; Abraham Watkins Venable, Prince Edward County, Va., North Carolina; Thos. Williams, Greensville County, Va., Alabama; Henry Taylor Blow, Southampton County, Va., Missouri; Joseph J. Gravely, Henry County, Va., Missouri; Jas. Madison Gregg, Patrick County, Va., Indiana; John Henry Harmanson, Norfolk, Va., Louisiana; Robt. Anthony Hatcher, Buckingham County, Va., Missouri; Pressly T. Glass, Halifax County, Va., Tennessee; John Cocke, Brunswick County, Va., Tennessee; (General) Jas. Ronald Chalmers, Halifax County, Va., Mississippi; Thos. Claiborne, Brunswick County, Va., Tennessee; Seth Wallace Cobb, Southampton County, Va., Missouri; Walter Terry Colquitt, Halifax County, Va., Georgia; Henry W. Connor, Prince George County, Va., North Carolina; David Patterson Dyer, Henry County, Va., Missouri.

Richmond Enquirer, September 3, 1819: George M. Bibb appointed by the President United States attorney for the Kentucky district.

---

[4]At that time, the third congressional district comprised the counties of Powhatan, Amelia, Chesterfield, Goochland and Nottoway.

GOVERNORS (FOR VIRGINIA).

Beverley Randolph, Cumberland County; W. H. Cabell, Cumberland County; Wm. B. Giles, Amelia County; L. W. Tazewell, Norfolk County; P. W. McKinney, Prince Edward County; W. H. Mann, Nottoway County; Wyndham Robertson, Chesterfield County ("on the site of Manchester opposite Richmond").

GOVERNORS (OTHER STATES).

Wm. C. C. Claiborne, Sussex County, Va., Mississippi and Louisiana; T. W. Ligon, Prince Edward County, Va., Maryland; Wilson Lumpkin, Pittsylvania County, Va., Georgia; Abner Nash, Prince Edward County, Va., North Carolina; Sterling Price, Prince Edward County, Va., Missouri; James Turner, Southampton County, Va., North Carolina.

JUDGES.[5]

Among the judges of the superior courts were: Dabney Carr (about 1810[6]), Peter Randolph (about 1812-1821), Thomas Tyler Bouldin (1821-1825), John Y. Mason, James H. Gholson, John W. Nash, Thomas S. Gholson, E. C. Chambers.

Peter Randolph probably removed from Nottoway about 1820.

1843.	Circuit judge, James H. Gholson (Brunswick).
1845.	Circuit judge, James H. Gholson (Brunswick).
1848.	Circuit judge, James H. Gholson (Brunswick).
1854.	John W. Nash, circuit judge.
1856.	John W. Nash (Powhatan) circuit judge, second circuit court district, Nottoway, etc.
1861.	Thomas S. Gholson, circuit judge.
1867.	Thomas S. Gholson, circuit judge.

The Gholsons were brothers and lived in Brunswick; Thomas was a member of the Confederate Congress. John W. Nash lived in Powhatan.

---

[5]Judge Watson had compiled names of Virginians in Congress and in the higher State offices for various years of the nineteenth century. These names do not relate particularly to Southside men, are easily obtainable, and therefore are not given here. He had also listed a great many names of Southside members of the Virginia Legislature. These names are omitted here, being easily and more completely available in "A Register of the General Assembly of Virginia, 1776-1918," comp. by E. G. Swem and J. W. Williams. (Supplement to Annual Report, 1917, Virginia State Library.)

[6]In 1812, Dabney Carr was judge in the fifth circuit, which embraced the counties of Dinwiddie, Brunswick, Lunenburg, Nottoway, Amelia, Powhatan and Chesterfield.

Judge Peter Randolph lived at Nottoway Court House, at a place now owned by Herman Jackson. Randolph was elected judge of the circuit court in 1812 by the Legislature to succeed Judge William H. Cabell. Dabney Carr ran against him.

Richmond Enquirer, January 23, 1812: Peter Randolph, Esq., delegate from Nottoway, James Allen and Daniel Smith, Esq., judges of the circuit courts appointed by the Legislature yesterday—the first to supply place of Judge Cabell, the second of Judge John Coalter, the 3rd of Hugh Nelson, Esq. Dabney Carr was brought forward in opposition to the 1st, Allen Taylor to the 2nd, John G. Jackson, Esq., to the 3rd. Messrs. Randolph, Allen & Smith have been appointed by the Executive.

Petersburg Republican, April 3, 1821: Peter Randolph, Esq., having resigned the office of the judge of the general court for the 5th (Petersburg) district, the Governor appointed Samuel Taylor, Esq., of Chesterfield, but Mr. Taylor having declined, T. T. Bouldin, Esq., was appointed to succeed Colonel Randolph.

General Joseph Jones appointed collector of the port of Petersburg, vice Dr. Shore, deceased.—*Richmond Enquirer*, December 7, 1811.

Petersburg Republican, and *Richmond Enquirer* of May 4, 1821: Major General John Pegram has been appointed by the President U. S. marshal for eastern Virginia in room of General Andrew Moore, resigned.

In 1786, Patrick Henry moved to Prince Edward County, buying 1700 acres of land of Colonel John Holcombe. This place was near Venable's Ford on the Appomattox River. In 1792, he sold this land and bought of General Henry Lee a fine estate, "Long Island," in Campbell County, and moved there, December, 1792. In 1794, he bought "Red Hill" in Charlotte County and, living there in part, settled there permanently in 1796.

Richmond Enquirer, April 6, 1824: price John Randolph got for his tobacco that year.[7]

In *Richmond Enquirer*, December 7, 1811, an editorial under the title of "Gratitude to the Dead," in defense of Tom Paine against sneer of John Randolph contained in speech in Congress, Nov. 19, in which Randolph speaks of Paine as an "English staymaker."

George W. Crump, M. D., Powhatan; graduated Princeton College; member of Congress, 1826-27; chief clerk, Pension Bureau, 1832-50; died 1850.

Dixon H. Lewis, born Dinwiddie County, Virginia, 1802; eminent lawyer; member of Congress from Alabama, 1829-44; United States Senate, 1844-48.

Miss Martha Cocke saw Peter Francisco and remembered seeing him hold a grown man out in one hand.

---

[7]Refers to loss on tobacco sustained by John Randolph by the swamping of an old gunboat which was employed in transporting the tobacco from Petersburg to Richmond.

CABANISS.

Copy of a circular issued by P. W. Harper, of Dinwiddie, against Dr. John Cabaniss, of Nottoway, found among the papers of the late Judge Jas. Boisseau, of Dinwiddie, and sent to me by his son, Sterling Boisseau:

Departed this Life
in the
Form of A Circular Letter,
On the 13th inst., at his seat in Nottoway County,
Dr. John Cabaniss,
In the fourth year of his degree in Medicine.

This man, for more than twelve months, has been actively engaged in writing against me, during which time he has used every exertion in his power to exculpate himself from the charge of having made illiberal, ungenerous, and ungentlemanly remarks about me. His letters have been published in the form of a pamphlet and are now circulating among his friends and acquaintances. In the loss of this accomplished son of Hippocrates cowardice, falsehood and illiberality have lost one of their favorite sons, and they have now in common with each other to lament their irreparable loss. He was a coward; for his writing proves it—He was a violator of truth; for I have proven him so— He was illiberal; for he practiced illiberality. "On paper wings he takes his flight; with wax the father bound them fast; the wax is melted by the height, and down the towering boy is cast."

(Signed) P. W. HARPER.
Dinwiddie County, Jan. 25th, 1820.

NOTTOWAY PEOPLE.

Abraham Hatchett lived at old Mrs. Cochran's place on Jeffress' Store road. Very much respected and beloved. Father of John Archer Hatchett; high sheriff, 1820-1.

Richard Ligon lived back of John Watson's. Father of Mrs. Rather, who left her property to Dick Rather (Colonel), a member of the jury which tried Dr. Bacon.

Daniel Verser lived at Jesse Vaughan's place; father of Col. Buck and Dan. Verser and a member of the jury which tried Dr. Bacon, 1818. A soldier of the Revolution.

Sam Dunnavant lived at Dr. Royall's; tried Dr. Bacon.

Billy Dunnavant lived between Mrs. Jeter's and Burkeville. On jury of Dr. Bacon.

Wm. Fowlkes lived near Dr. Cabaniss's somewhere. Killed accidentally while crow-shooting. William Anthony tried for his murder but cleared. On jury of Dr. Bacon.

John Overstreet and Micajah Jennings lived in the Rocky Ford vicinity; Overstreet beyond the river and to the right of the road; Jennings on the Ray place (Rev. Geo. Ray). Jurors of Dr. Bacon. Sanney Baldwin lived at what we call "Baldwin's." Wash. Baldwin (same family) lived at John Harding's. Williamson Dickinson, son of Noten Dickinson, lived at old John or Ben Overton's place; high sheriff in 1844.

William Yates, who was commonwealth's attorney from about 1812 to 1818, lived about or at Wortham's place (now Goodwyn's) ; and Judge Peter Randolph, his kinsman, lived near the mill site (Fitzgerald's) which he first established, building a dam somewhat below the present one, with the statement that it was so strong and so secure that God Almighty himself could not break it. The rains are said to have taken it away very soon afterwards. (Statement of Mr. Freeman Epes.)

Major Anderson died in the woods near Abner Robertson's place. Mr. Cousins's boy, going down for the cows, found him lying in a dying condition after falling from his horse. No cause of death was ascertained. He then lived at Dr. Royall's place with a son-in-law, Owen, who moved to North Carolina. He won old Colonel Verser's last negro at cards.

Survivors[8] of Nottoway County made out by R. W. Oliver and myself, July 23, 1915: George Irby, Walter Irby, J. R. Foster ("Slab"), T. W. Epes ("Horse Shoe Tom"), P. H. Allen ("Rack"), George Hawkes, R. T. Jeter ("Turkey Tom"), G. T. Crawley, W. Macon Ingram, Peter Epes ("Peter Rusty"), Freeman Epes, L. H. Hayes.

GEORGE C. DROMGOOLE.

George C. Dromgoole was one of the most brilliant and original men ever produced by the Southside. He was born in Brunswick County, Virginia, May 15, 1797. Of his probable ancestry an article on the Dromgooles in Ireland in the *Richmond Enquirer* of May 24, 1847, states that they were originally Scandinavians and had acquired great estates about Dublin. His own account of his family in Virginia is found in the *Richmond Enquirer* of May 22, 1847, in a letter written by George C. Dromgoole to William L. McKenzie, and sent by him to the *New York Tribune*, from which it was copied. This letter is as follows: "My parents were not both natives of the Emerald Isle. My father, Edward Dromgoole, was born in Sligo. When a youth he came to America, a poor boy with religious impressions and a strong desire for religious freedom. He landed in Philadelphia in 1772; came to Baltimore and resided in that city, or its vicinity, with a Mr. John Haggerty, a tailor by trade and a man

---

[8]Hon. Louis S. Epes, of Blackstone, Va., states that this list refers to survivors of Nottoway cavalry in the Civil War.

of most exemplary piety. Edward Dromgoole had been brought up in Ireland to the trade of linen weaver. At Baltimore he assisted Haggerty at tailoring that he might not eat the bread of idleness. They both became disciples of John Wesley. In 1774 he commenced preaching and travelled extensively in Virginia and North Carolina as an itinerant Methodist preacher. He held the first Methodist class meeting in America. He settled in Brunswick County in the State of Virginia, where he resided until his death in 1835, in the 84th year of his age, having been a minister of the Gospel for more than sixty years. He intermarried with Rebecca Walton in said county, whose ancestors had early emigrated from England to America. Whether they descended from the family of the bishop, the author of the Polyglot Bible, or from old Isaac the fisherman, is not known, nor is it material. They lived happily together, raised and educated a family of children and left them a competency acquired neither by speculation nor extortion; it was the result of economy and honest industry. I am their youngest child."

George C. Dromgoole was rather below the average height and was inclined to stoutness. His picture exhibits most striking features, strong in expression and in outline. The mouth is of prodigious size, the forehead proportionately huge, like Mr. Webster's; his eye was most engaging and his hair was worn long after the Southern fashion of that day; altogether he must have been a man of prepossessing appearance, as we know him to have been of most prepossessing address. He dressed plainly, but well; a blue dress coat with grey trousers and slouch hat constituted his usual costume. He was a man of simple tastes and while a slave-holder of competent means never aspired to the ostentations of social life. His home was no doubt very quiet, as he never married, a choice to which, possibly, he was influenced by Lord Bacon's declaration that "the best works and of greatest merit to the public have proceeded from unmarried or childless men." At one period he gave some attention to military affairs and became brigadier-general of the State militia.[9] He was educated at the University of North Carolina and at William and Mary College, and had as contemporaries at William and Mary William O. Goode, of Mecklenburg County, Judge Clopton, of New Kent County, and Alexander Brodnax, of Brunswick County. He left Williamsburg in 1818, and retired to his native county.

I am not aware that he ever practiced law to any extent and assume that at this period he lived a retired and studious life upon his estate. In 1823, however, he was called to public life by an election to the Virginia House of Delegates and three years later to a seat in the State Senate from the district of Brunswick,

---

[9] Of the Fifteenth Brigade; he resigned in 1838 and was succeeded by James W. Pegram.

in which body he early took high rank and became for several years the presiding officer of the Senate.   When the question of the Constitutional Convention of 1829-1830 came up for discussion before the Legislature, John Randolph came from Washington to Richmond to attend the debate.   It was upon this occasion that he declared the speech delivered by Dromgoole against the reform convention to be the ablest plea in behalf of conservative institutions he had ever heard.   Notwithstanding his great effort on that occasion, the journal of the convention that soon afterwards assembled shows the remarkable fact that Dromgoole took no part in its proceedings and did not speak on a single question.   John Randolph, in one of his speeches before the convention, complained of Dromgoole's silence; saying he deeply regretted the indisposition to participate in the debates evinced by the delegates from his congressional district, an indisposition arising not from lack of ability, or from a lack of confidence in displaying that ability; that he had looked to Brunswick for a display of the talent that he knew it to possess, but had looked in vain.

In the convention Dromgoole represented the district of Dinwiddie, Brunswick, Mecklenburg and Lunenburg counties; his colleagues were Gen. William H. Brodnax, of Dinwiddie, Mark Alexander and William O. Goode, of Mecklenburg.   William O. Goode was a rather thin-visaged, wiry man and a good talker upon the hustings, while not quite eloquent; he indulged a good deal in platitudes, with some of the aggressive thoughts of bolder speakers.   *Niles' Register* of May 1, 1847, says; "Mr. Dromgoole was distinguished for prompt eloquence, extensive experience in public affairs and great parliamentary knowledge."   In politics George C. Dromgoole ranked democratically.   Indeed, he was born a democrat and continued one of the most pronounced type throughout his entire career; he not only believed in Jeffersonian, but perhaps, also, in the Athenian type of democracy.   He was emphatically a man of the people, acknowledging allegiance to them and them only, holding firm faith in their capacity to govern themselves.   His opposition to the Convention of 1829 was the only reactionary tendency he ever exhibited.   Inside the Democratic Party he was not a Calhounite, probably not as much wedded to slavery as those who shared the feelings of that illustrious senator.   His beau-ideal of a statesman was Silas Wright, who was the head of the "Barnburners" or anti-slavery faction of the New York Democracy.

In 1833 Dromgoole was a candidate for Congress for the first time, against Alexander Knox and William O. Goode, of Mecklenburg, and James H. Gholson, of Brunswick; the first three Democrats and the last a Whig.   The result was as might have been foreseen.   Gholson was returned, and the Whig Party strongly intrenched itself in the district.   The ensuing election (1835) was a contest between Dromgoole and Gholson alone, and the former was elected over his able competitor and never after failed at an election. So completely did he break down the Whig Party in the district that generally he had no opposition. Years after Gholson's disastrous defeat by Dromgoole in 1835, Gholson was asked by a friend what he meant by making a canvass when the odds were so overwhelming. He replied that he had arranged to move to Petersburg to practice law and ran against Dromgoole simply as an advertisement of himself, which step he had never regretted.

The *Richmond Enquirer*, May 30, 1845, under caption, "A Portrait of a Politician," paints an interesting sketch of General Dromgoole and his mental characteristics, personality, etc. Says he was the leader of the Democrats in the House of Representatives on all trying occasions, no matter who had been chosen nominal leader; as a parliamentary tactician, unrivalled in this country.

No man ever enjoyed or merited to a greater extent the confidence of his people than did George C. Dromgoole, but in the latter years of his public career his habits were not of the most fastidious character and his liberal libations to Bacchus came to be the subject of criticism, even by his friends; political enemies were, of course, ready to seize upon such vulnerable features of a public character, and in the election of 1847 they made them the ground of vehement attack, hoping with the disaffection among his friends to unite the opposition and break down their hitherto invincible foe. They brought out against him Colonel George E. Bolling, of Petersburg, a Whig leader of courage and character, who had achieved distinction in the Legislature. As designed by the Whigs from the outset, the contest became largely one of personalities between the two candidates and, as was natural, it assumed an acrimonious and sometimes unpleasant spirit. Joint discussions took place throughout the district, and the opponents of "Old Drum," as they called him, thought they had at last made sure of their prey; "the eagle was quarried in his eyrie, the wounded lion was hunted to his lair." Bolling, while respectful, was earnest in his personal assaults and boldly criticised what he thought delinquencies in his opponent. At Nottoway Courthouse he exhibited the "Journal of Congress," by which he showed that Dromgoole had been very inattentive to his duties in Washington and really absent from his seat the greater part of the time. "Here," said he, "on ——— day of ——————— an important vote was taken, and Mr. Dromgoole was not recorded as voting on either side; the question was vital to your interests, fellow citizens; where was your representative at that time? And so, examining all the pages of this Journal, I find your representative during all that long session of Congress was in his seat and voted only eleven times. Fellow citizens, can you afford to have your interests so neglected?" Pursuing this line of argument, supported by documentary evidence, Bolling seemed to have the command of the situation, and Dromgoole's friends began to despair of his defense. His opening sentence, however, dispelled all fears and immediately reassured his followers. He said: "Fellow citizens, Colonel Bolling has read you the Journal of Congress," and I presume he states the facts as they are; it may be true that I voted as he asserts, but every time I did vote I represented you and your interests. Should you elect Colonel Bolling to Congress I have no doubt in the world that if the session continued through every day in the year there he would be, in his seat every day, and every day vote against you and your interests. One of us two must be returned, and the question for you to determine, my friends, is whether you would rather have a man to represent you eleven times or one to misrepresent you three hundred and sixty-five times." From this the old war-horse went on to defend his record and expose the pretentions of his opponent until Whigs themselves hung their heads in shame. His splendid ability prevailed upon the hustings, as seen by the following vote for Congress in the Brunswick district:

	Dromgoole	Bolling
Petersburg	190	381
Dinwiddie	217	317
Brunswick	226	140
Nottoway	120	174
Greensville	99	63
Prince George	129	115
Mecklenburg	415	259
Amelia	235	161
	1631	1610

Dromgoole's majority, twenty-one.   (From *Richmond Enquirer,* April 30, 1847.)

The *Richmond Whig* of April 27, 1847, said: "General Dromgoole has long been the acknowledged leader of the old Hunker division of the Locofoco party in Virginia—a post for which he was peculiarly qualified by his fine talents as a debater and his singular adroitness as a party and parliamentary tactician."

Dromgoole's friends allowed Bolling to run him such a close race as a rebuke to his intolerable habits, but his feelings were so deeply wounded that after this exciting canvass, though he had prevailed over all the efforts his enemies had made for his political destruction, he never appeared again before the people. His health declined and he died in the quiet seclusion of his estate in Brunswick County, on April 27, 1847, at the early age of 49. He sleeps with his ancestors and "may his faults lie gently on him."

Richmond Enquirer, May 22, 1847, contains editorial on Dromgoole from the *Memphis Monitor,* pays high tribute to his memory and says he had by will left his estate to the children of Daniel Dugger.[10]

The *Washington Daily Union,* April 29, 1847, stated: "One of. the first men in Virginia, occasionally the strongest man in the House of Representatives. Everyone admitted the extent of his powers and the stability of his principles,—few who knew him but will lament his fate."

The *National Intelligencer,* May 3, 1847, said of him: "He died of bilious pleurisy on Wednesday night last. Mr. Dromgoole was a distinguished politician, endowed by nature with the sagacity to plan and courage to execute. He was the ablest debater of his party and unequalled as a legislative tactician. His death will be sincerely regretted by those who have always known him, as we have done, as a decided political opponent, it is true, but also as a courteous and kind-hearted gentleman."

The *Richmond Enquirer,* April 16, 1847, in detailing the services of Dromgoole in Congress, stated that he was the first parliamentary lawyer in Congress.

The *Richmond Enquirer,* April 30, 1847; editorial on the death of General Dromgoole, headed, "Died in Harness": "General Dromgoole was a giant in mind, and his honor and character were never impeached. Faults he had like other men, which in the language of the Pennsylvanian, somewhat 'impaired the usefulness of one of the brightest intellects in the Union'."

Niles' Register, May 1, 1847, said: "The Hon. G. C. Dromgoole, the late distinguished and talented representative of the State of Virginia in the United States Congress, and generally recognized as the administration leader in the House at the last session . . ."

Richmond Whig, of April 30th, 1847, said: "Tho' opposed to him politically, we have always felt profound respect for his fine endowments and an admiration of many traits in his personal character—qualities which enabled him to wield a powerful influence over public sentiment—particularly in that portion of the State where he resided and where he was best known."

The *Richmond Enquirer,* December 24, 1847, contains a brief speech made by James M. Mason in the Senate of the United States on Dromgoole. It paid high tribute to the deceased, concluding thus: "Virginia and the Union may both regret the death of one of the most able and practical legislators that ever rendered valuable service to either."

Richmond Enquirer, May, 12, 1847: "The late George C. Dromgoole": "Not only in Virginia, but throughout our whole country the solemn tidings of the death of this distinguished statesman have been received with the deepest regret. The *New York Globe* pays the following well merited tribute to the mem-

---

[10]See Dromgoole-Dugger Duel, p. 55.

ory of this brilliant light, whose name will ever stand enrolled with the first of Virginia's sons." Then follows the editorial from the *New York Globe*. Obituary notices, comments and resolutions are also contained in the following issues of the *Richmond Enquirer*:
May 7, 1847, quotes editorial from the *New York Globe*; June 2, 1847, republishes from the March number, 1839, of the *Democratic Review*, a sketch of Dromgoole; May 15, 21, June 15, 1847 contain various resolutions.

WILLIAM BRANCH GILES.

Probably the most notable man of the Southside was William Branch Giles, Democratic leader of Congress during Jefferson's administration and one of the ablest politicians the country has produced.

William Branch Giles was born in 1762, of respectable parents in comfortable circumstances, according to Judge Nash in *Richmond Enquirer*, 1830. Dr. Richard F. Taylor says he was born in Powhatan and Dr. Theodorick Pryor says he came from Hanover to Amelia at the same time with his own (Dr. Pryor's) grandfather.

Giles lived near Giles's Bridge (from whence the name) at a place now owned by a Mr. Blair, of Richmond. He resided at one time at "Wigwam," Amelia County, and subsequently at "Elk Hill." Dr. Richard F. Taylor showed me Giles's study chair, which is now in Dr. Taylor's possession (1890). He was the youngest child of William Giles, of Amelia County. His elder brother, John Giles, was an officer in the Continental Army and died in Charleston. One of his nephews, Samuel Jones,[11] lived in Powhatan County. His son, Thomas Tabb Giles, was a lawyer of considerable repute; of great care and accuracy in chancery cases (so Judge Farrar says); a member of the State Democratic Committee in 1854. He lived near Mannboro facing the Namozine Road, until a few years preceding the Civil War. He died in Richmond about 1880 and was, until about 1875, a partner of·Judge Farrar. Peyton Giles, son of William B. Giles, died in St. Louis, Mo., 1854, in the forty-second year of his age. He was a lawyer of extensive information, but modest demeanor.

Giles had a varied and singular career. He was educated at Hampden-Sidney College and Princeton, going from Hampden-Sidney to Princeton as a member of the family of Dr. Smith. He left Princeton before graduating and went to Williamsburg to study law under George Wythe. Later he settled in Peters-

---

[11]The *Richmond Enquirer*, January 16, 1812, has an account of the burning of the dwelling house of Mr. Samuel Jones. Speaks of Miss Nancy Bass and Mr. Edward Bass, brother and sister of Mr. Jones. Miss Bass perished. "Mr. Jones and Miss Bass are the nephew and niece of William B. Giles, Esq."

burg, where he practiced law five or six years and evinced astonishing powers as an advocate; but he was never a sound and learned lawyer. It is said that he was an attendant at Grub Hill church at Paineville, in Amelia County, though a great infidel and gambler. Together with Burk, an Irish refugee, he founded the Paineville Infidel Club at Paineville. (According to Dr. Theodorick Pryor). He married, in 1795, Martha Peyton Tabb, eldest daughter of John Tabb, of Amelia County, who had a splendid fortune. His own paternal inheritance came to him about the same time and he thus had the command of wealth. His first wife died in 1805 or 1806, and he married then a widow Graham, *née* Frances Ann Gwynn, of Prince William County, who was the mother of Gen. Lawrence Graham, of Washington, and Miss Hartley Graham. She was a lady much younger than himself. There were children of both marriages. He was a great invalid. In 1816 he was attacked by a disease which undermined his health for the remainder of his life.

While living in Petersburg, Giles ran for Congress, 1790, to succeed Theodorick Bland, who died before the expiration of his term. He was opposed by a Colonel Edmunds, of Sussex County, an anti-Federalist, who had been an officer in the Revolution and had lost a limb in battle. The canvass was an animated one. Giles was elected, but did not take his seat, as Congress adjourned before he reached the capital. He was re-elected without opposition until 1798, when he resigned. He was elected as a Federalist, but soon became a Democrat and an ardent follower of Jefferson. He was elected to the Virginia House of Delegates from Amelia in 1798, for the purpose of championing the Virginia resolutions against the Alien and Sedition laws, in procuring the passage of which he co-operated with Madison. In 1800 he was again elected to Congress and declined re-election in 1803, at which time John W. Epes was returned. He was appointed to the United States Senate by the Virginia Council in 1804 to succeed A. B. Venable and was elected by the Legislature to succeed W. C. Nicholas the same year. He was one of the ablest supporters of Jefferson and Madison until 1811-12, when he joined the opposition. He was re-elected to the Senate in 1811 and resigned in 1815. He was again in the House of Delegates, 1816-1817, and was defeated for election to the United States Senate by John Randolph in 1825. He became Governor of Virginia in 1827. He was one of the four delegates who represented the district comprising Amelia, Chesterfield, Cumberland, Nottoway, Powhatan counties and the town of Petersburg, in the Virginia Constitutional Convention of 1829-30.

During the War of 1812 he was confessedly the leader of his party in the Senate, and during his encumbency was second only to Jefferson and Madison in developing the principles of the Constitution and giving that instrument a practical operation. Returning from a visit to Amelia County, Giles voted for the

declaration of the War of 1812, which declaration passed the
Senate by a vote of 19 to 13. The *Richmond Enquirer*, of May
22, 1812, has: "Letters from the Simple to the Great, to Honorable William B. Giles, now at home." This was a letter bearing
severe strictures on Giles for going home from the Senate when
the question of war was to be voted on in that body; saying, that
all along he had cried up the war, and then had retired behind
the woods and vales of Amelia, and calling upon him to resign
and let Virginia have some other person to represent her.
Dr. Richard F. Taylor thinks Giles was defeated for Congress in 1826 by William S. Archer; Mr. Harvie says he was not.
William Pope Dabney, in a letter dated December 22, 1892,
states: "William Archer never beat Giles for Congress.[12] He
and John Randolph when first candidates got every vote in this
[Powhatan] County. I never heard that William S. Archer,
who, when he was a candidate for the reform convention of
1850-51,[13] was called by John M. Daniel[14] a 'political shite-poke
whose speeches read as well backward as forward,' ever had the
temerity to antagonize William Giles. I have heard that he said
of Archer that when in Congress 'he never stormed a political
rat-trap.' The general tradition is that Giles was born in Amelia
and that he was of very obscure education and was the son of a
shoemaker. Did you ever know that he contributed more than
any one man in Virginia to prevent emancipation in 1830-1? He
and Professor Thos. R. Dew[15] first taught that slavery was a
positive blessing."

For Giles's personal appearance, see Hugh Blair Grigsby's
"The Virginia Convention of 1829-30, p. 23; *Southern Literary
Messenger*, vol. 17, p. 297, article by Hugh R. Pleasants; "William Branch Giles," by Dice R. Anderson. For Jefferson's personal relations with Giles, see the "Writings of Thomas Jefferson," Collected and Edited by Paul Leicester Ford, 10 vols.,
passim.

Giles has been the object of bitter abuse by Northern
writers. Henry Cabot Lodge pays his respects to him in the following elegant language in his "Alexander Hamilton": "A rough,
brazen, loud-voiced Virginian, fit for any bad work, no matter
how desperate." Henry Adams says, in his "John Randolph":
"Giles, whom no man ever trusted without regret." William W.
Story's "Life and Letters of Joseph Story," Vol. 1, p. 158, has
the following: "Giles exhibits in his appearance no marks of
greatness; he has a dark complexion and retreating eyes, black
hair and robust form. His dress is remarkably plain and in the
style of Virginia carelessness." Fred Scott Oliver's "Alexander

---

[12]But see D. R. Anderson, "William Branch Giles," p. 218.
[13]Virginia Constitutional Convention of 1850-51.
[14]The brilliant and versatile editor of the *Richmond Examiner*.
[15]Thomas Roderick Dew, professor in William and Mary College, author of influential works in support of slavery.

Hamilton" states: "The hero of this period was Giles, of Virginia, a preposterous pugilistic character, to whom notoriety was much and failure in calumny merely failure and not disgrace. Behind him we have always a vision of Madison with sponge and basin and a towel. He was a squat, untidy, black-a-vised little man with prodigious vitality, a quick eye and a shrewd oratorical gift in a *mêlée;* a stout fellow with loud lungs; in combat entirely without scruples.

As a man of talent, Giles stood in the front rank and was unrivaled in many of the attributes of his mind. His genius was of the first order, but his judgment, though good, bore no proportion to his genius. Patrick Henry was on the opposite side of a case with him in early life and predicted his eminence; so did George Mason, who met and talked with him in a hotel in Richmond. He was great in colloquy, and of his readiness in debate Dr. Southall relates the story told him by an old citizen of Amelia who was present when Giles, in his last days and in enfeebled condition, met at Amelia Courthouse, on the old tavern court, William S. Archer, then in his prime, for joint discussion, and completely swept Archer away.

From his entrance into Congress in 1790 his mind became a great storehouse of all history, national and state. Giles was a great debater; he had no superior in the American Congress in his time, a time including the best days of Madison, Bayard and Dexter. Hugh R. Pleasants, in *Southern Literary Messenger* of May, 1851, compares him to Charles James Fox, who was regarded as perhaps the greatest debater the world has ever seen. Giles said that Gallatin was the strongest and Bayard the next strongest man he ever met in Congress.[16]

Giles was always ready, never needed any preparation. He possessed the faculty of being able to reply at all times and without notice. He had no rant or vociferous declamation in delivery. A calm, though animated, conversational style was used by him; he indulged in no frantic gesticulation, never sweated like a carthorse in giving birth to his ideas. His words were full of thought, but not to overflowing. His character and tastes eminently qualified him for a great debater. Controversy was the element in which he lived. In private life this was a very marked trait. His public speeches resembled in delivery private conversation; his conversation had much the character of public speaking.

Sometime in John Adam's administration, Madison prepared to answer a speech of some Federal leader. The night before his speech was to be delivered he was taken sick, and as it was of the utmost importance that a reply be made, he sent for Giles and, placing his notes in the latter's hands, entrusted the

---

[16]Mr. Watson states that the greater part of this and the following paragraph is taken from the "Sketches of the Convention of 1829-30," by Hugh R. Pleasants in *Southern Literary Messenger,* 1851.

cause to his care. Giles made, with the little time allowed, one of the ablest speeches ever heard in Congress.

Giles amused his later years by re-printing some of his speeches, but he has left nothing that can throw any general light on the stirring scenes through which he passed. He was the author of the celebrated letters in the *Richmond Enquirer* about 1820, on the tariff and "Hard Times." They were written at the "Wigwam." His literary remains are scanty, and materials for his biography are sadly small. He was less qualified as a writer than is common in the case of men of his talent. It is deeply to be lamented that in this country the collection of the opinions of our own wise, good and great men should so often be largely lacking. Statesmen most deeply skilled in political science, and especially in the principles of democratic government, have sunk into oblivion as their bodies have sunk into the grave. The voice of our fathers is heard by our children only in the murmur of indistinct tradition. That voice which might have ministered light to our minds, harmony to our opinions, stability to our principles and veneration for our institutions is silent.

Giles died at "The Wigwam" in Amelia, in the 69th year of his age, and is buried at that place.[17]

JAMES JONES.

Dr. James Jones was one of the leading men of Nottoway County. He was born on the eve of the Revolution in Nottoway Parish, Amelia (now Nottoway) County, Virginia. His paternal ancestors were of Welsh lineage and of honorable fame in the fatherland. A grandfather with two brothers came from Wales to America. One of the latter was Major Peter Jones, the old friend and fellow traveller of Colonel Byrd, of Westover, so well known to Virginia history. In his native parish, James Jones's parents were among the wealthiest and most reputable, and his education was unstinted. At Hampden-Sidney and the University of Pennsylvania he mastered the learning of his own country. He graduated from Hampden-Sidney College in 1791. Among his fellow students were many destined to much distinction in the various walks of life: William H. Cabell and Dabney Carr, so distinguished in the judicial annals of Virginia; Moses Waddell, the distinguished Georgia educator and sometime president of Franklin College. George Bibb, of Kentucky, famous in so many stations—as the colleague of Henry Clay in the Senate, the author of the great speech in reply to Mr. Webster, and not less as Governor of his native State—was another classmate.

The college, then as now, was a great seat of Calvanism, and could not fail to awaken the religious sentiment of our stu-

---

[17]Dr. Joseph W. Eggleston, of Richmond, states that Giles is buried at the "Jeter (once Cadwell) place, cut off from the Wigwam plantation."

dent, who mainly for this gratification became, for a season, a student in the family of the celebrated Devereux Jarratt, an Episcopal clergyman and scholar of Dinwiddie.

From Philadelphia he repaired to the University of Edinburgh, at that date the principal center of medical learning in Europe, where he graduated with signal honors, returning to his native State and county a physician, whose education and talents soon placed him at the head of his profession.

It is worthy of remark that in colonial days the medical art seems to have suffered much neglect in Virginia, and doubtless the colonies generally. Among the first to espouse its study was Col. Theodorick Bland, of Prince George, subsequently so prominent in the Revolutionary struggle, and a brother of Richard Bland. He preceded Dr. Jones some years at Edinburgh, and from his diligence in seeking to improve the medical craft at home is justly considered a pioneer of the profession.

Shortly upon his return from Europe, Dr. Jones was wedded to Miss Catherine Harris, of Surry, a lady whose high qualities of heart and head well enabled her to promote his happiness and to grace domestic comfort.

The religious principles of his early life were not fostered at Edinburgh. The atmosphere of the university was decidedly skeptical, and he came back indoctrinated with the tenets of free thought and the infidel philosophy of Europe.

The Nottoway community was far from devout. The Jacobinic policy of Mr. Jefferson had prostrated the traditional church. Its prestige was struck down, and its creed was no longer a fruitful inspiration for men's daily lives. The disregard of historic precedent in the subversion of long standing political and ecclesiastical systems was working its logical effect upon the public mind. Men grew speculative and became revolutionary. Tom Paine's "Age of Reason" appeared in 1794 and was widely read in America. In Virginia its influence was particularly fruitful.

A number of wealthy and highly educated gentlemen of the Nottoway vicinity organized a "Tom Paine's Infidel Club," a philosophic society for study and debate. They erected a hall in the little hamlet of Paineville, still extant and preserving the name. Dr. Jones was the foremost counsellor of its proceedings, though not a founder of the society, as has been asserted. It originated with William B. Giles and an Irish refugee named Burk. Giles had come over to Amelia from Hanover County in early life; his disbelief dated back many years.

The society flourished for several years, and it is hard to over-estimate the influence of such an institution, combining as it did social and intellectual prestige. To this day, I am credibly informed, the locality is not infrequently racked with religious controversy and schism.

Meanwhile Dr. Jones had established his home at "Mountain Hall," and fortune and fame seemed to smile upon him in generous plenty. Children had risen up to bless him and complete the measure of domestic happiness untouched by time. But the picture changed. The weight of human hours came at last. Death stripped away the first offspring of his love, and in turn bereaved him of a beautiful and only daughter. Prostrate with sorrow, in the seclusion of his study he sought comfort of heathen and skeptical philosophy. But reason, unassisted by revelation, could offer no solace. Vain was the thought! Yet in the sacrifice of Calvary he found the peace this world's wisdom could not bestow, and it is said soon thereafter assembled his infidel club and delivered before it a Christian address, whereupon it was at once disbanded and never met again. This occurred about 1810.

In after years Dr. Jones became an elder and pillar in the Presbyterian Church, and it was owing in large part to his instrumentality that a people steeped in luxury and irreligion succumbed to the great moral reformation which swept the Southside counties in 1825 and so materially altered the life of the population.

But it is as a politician that Dr. Jones will be chiefly remembered. Like Colonel Bland again, he could not remain an indifferent spectator of public affairs. Repeatedly his county sent him to the General Assembly, which body in 1809 elected him to the Privy Council of State, where he served with W. W. Hening, Peyton Randolph and others well remembered in the Old Dominion.

In reporting his resignation to the General Assembly, Governor Smith referred to him as "a member so highly esteemed and truly estimable."

I pass over his important services in the War of 1812, which are a matter of record, and on to the election of 1819, when he stood for Congress in the Petersburg district against General John Pegram, of Dinwiddie.

They both belonged to the Jeffersonian school, and the issue was as much "men" as "measures." The race was close and animated. Pegram brought to his aid large social influence and the prestige of a seat already occupied in Congress. The great question of the hour was the arbitrary execution of Arbuthnot and Ambrister under martial law in the Seminole War of the previous year. On this ground Pegram arraigned "Old Hickory" and shared the fate of the United States Bank in later times.

The succeeding elections returned Dr. Jones to Congress without opposition. During all the stormy scenes which ushered in the Missouri agitation, notwithstanding his own emancipation and colonizing sympathies, Jones stood with his party resolutely against any Federal encroachment upon local rights.

The fact of his anti-slave convictions being well-known and accepted in a strong slave community is one of the many circumstances going to establish the historical truth that the Southern people were not originally bent upon perpetuating slavery; and that had no outside irritation inflamed their motives and feelings, they might finally have solved the problem of bondage in gradual manumission. In the breaking up of the old party lines in 1824, under the lead of the *Richmond Enquirer*, Dr. Jones supported Mr. Crawford for the presidency and stood upon his electoral ticket. He served his party in this capacity for five successive elections and completed the roll of his public offices as an elector for Van Buren in 1840.

Having related the chief facts of Dr. Jones's life, a task remains to draw the man—his character and abilities. Some now living remember the stately, dignified appearance of this old Virginia gentleman; his portrait hangs in illustrious company on the walls of the State Capitol. It is the work of St. Memin and an excellent example of that artist's peculiar style. In the visage we discern nothing of that personal charm and symmetry of feature which so often accompanies mental excellence, nor any of those bold outlines which stamp forever upon the memory the lineaments of a great man. There is only the modest dignity of countenance, the grace and the fixedness of purpose so character-istic of the original.[18]

In Dr. Jones the social faculty was largely developed. His domestic relations were eminently happy. Fifty years of his life he mingled freely with the gayest and most fashionable circles of society. Accordingly, his manners and habits were those of elegance and well-bred repose,—yet grave and reserved to a degree which sometimes approached austerity toward those not accorded a place at his fireside. In Washington his household held influential social connection with President Monroe and with lesser lights of renown.

Dr. Jones's extreme modesty alone is said to have prevented his becoming distinguished as a debater in Congress. But he was not a leader among men in the truest sense. None was stronger in his convictions or more inflexible in his principles; but of that self-confidence nearly always found in strong natures and of that domineering temper which characterizes men fit for leadership he knew nothing. His moral character as exhibited to the public was of the Roman stamp,—stern, inflexible, elevated.

---

[18]The State Library was housed in the Capitol when Mr. Watson wrote the above. In its collection of portraits there is one by St. Memin, claimed to be that of William H. Cabell, but this claim is questioned and it is possible it may be the portrait referred to by Mr. Watson as of James Jones. Effort to establish the certain identity of this portrait, by comparison with the Dexter Catalogue of the St. Memin Collection of Portraits and through investigation of sources of more recent study of the work of this artist, has been unavailing.

He survived the age the Psalmist says is allotted to man, and, decorated with the honors of his country, died at "Mountain Hall" full of days and of wisdom. Amid the rush and greed of the present day, the "fierce competition" and "fiercer bribery" of wealth, we cannot comprehend the worth of a character so disinterested and unassuming. There is a wealth of soul more to be coveted than silver or gold,—a higher spirit than that which fills the market place; the soul that animated the old South before the pig iron philosophy of Birmingham and Pittsburgh came to crush out the poetry of the nation. We now fail to understand that mere beauty has its value; that the beautiful and the good has its use, as well as the practical and the profitable.

Posterity will delight to remember this scholarly citizen and dignified gentleman as the completed type of a social order now extinct but unsurpassed in the life of nations,—as a man beloved of his generation, than whom few were wiser and none more just.

If in the foregoing sketch aught has been recorded to rescue a worthy name from time's effacing finger and also to add a faithful page to the neglected annals of this Commonwealth, my purpose is more than fulfilled.

"I remember that Dr. James Jones in his latter years traveled in a carriage and drove two shabby old sorrel mares. The team always stood at Nottoway Courthouse in front of Bob Roberts's store, near Archer Robertson's present site."—Related by Colonel W. C. Jeffress.

Dr. Jones, when he first settled at "Mountain Hall," lived in the house next the garden, which he afterward kept as a lodging for guests.

The visiting cards and dining invitations among Dr. Jones's private papers are curious relics of the time and bear the names of many celebrities. Particularly unique is the style employed by John C. Calhoun; that of William Wirt is the most characteristic and attractive.

Exact Copies of two Invitations sent to Dr. Jones when a Member of Congress in 1820.

Address on outside of invitation.

Address:
  Hon'ble
    Mr. Jones
      at Miss Hayes's
        Capital Hill

Invitation:

Mr. Calhoun requests the favour
of Mr. Jones's company on Tuesday
next to dinner at 5 O'Clock.   The favour of
an answer is requested.

Thursday
10 feby 1820

Address:

To

The Honble James Jones

H. Re

Invitation:

Mrs. Decatur requests the
favor of Mr. & Mrs. Jones's company on Thursday evening the 17th
of February.

These invitations were written in small, flowing handwriting on plain note-size paper, folded and sealed, without envelope and delivered by courier. They are in marked contrast with the ornate invitations of the present and demonstrate the unostentatious simplicity of one hundred years ago. It is interesting to note the use of abbreviations in both address and body of the invitation.

Privy Council of Virginia, Jan., 1809: McRae, Stuart, W. W. Hening, Geo. Wm. Smith, Peyton Randolph, Wm. Munford, John Heath.

May 29, 1809, (Rec. Privy Council) Dr. Jones and Wm. B. Hare were admitted to the Council on their certificates. They took the prescribed oath before Daniel Hylton, a justice of the peace of Henrico County.

Richmond Enquirer, Dec. 5, 1811. Communication from Lieut. Gov. Geo. Wm. Smith, acting as Governor, dated Dec. 2, 1811, announces to the General Assembly Dr. Jones's resignation in the following words: "and a very unpleasant duty is that of communicating the resignation of James Jones, Esq., who was also a member of the Privy Council or Council of State. The cause of this resignation, which will be seen in the accompanying document (No. 10), has added much to the regret felt by the remaining members, and in which the General Assembly will doubtless participate for the loss sustained in this department of a member so highly esteemed and so truly estimable."

Dr. Jones resigned his seat in the Privy Council a few weeks past.—*Richmond Enquirer*, Nov. 27, 1811.

Virginia House Journal, 1811-12: House on Jan. 7, 1812, elected a successor in the Executive Council to James Jones, who had previously resigned. In this Council with him were Peyton Randolph and Geo. Wm. Smith, who while a member was elected Governor. Dr. Jones, then, must have served under Smith and the preceding Governor. Barbour was then Governor (1812) The Council then had such men as George William Smith and Peter V. Daniel, who was elected to the Council the year after under Governor James Barbour.

Virginia House Journal, 1813: Dr. James Jones was director general of hospital and medical stores and rations from 17 April to May 22, 1813.[19]

Idem., 1813: An account for services as director general of the hospitals, inadmissible; no such officer provided for in the U. S. laws. Claim $75.00 presented at the accountant's office, War Dept. U. S., 1812.[20]

Richmond Enquirer, Dec. 17, 1814: A letter from Col. R. E. Parker, dated Dec. 5, 1814, from Westmoreland Co., to the Adjutant General states that Captain Shackleford[21] was severely wounded in a skirmish in that county some days before—a ball in the leg—and that Dr. Jones was in attendance upon him.

In the Legislature which met in Dec. 1818 Dr. Jones was in House of Delegates from Nottoway on Committee for Courts of Justice.

House of Delegates, 1827-8: Dr. Jones served on Committee of Finance and of Schools and Colleges.

Dr. Jones Elector for 3rd. district, Virginia, on the Van Buren and R. M. Johnson ticket in 1840. Virginia went Democratic.

Richmond Enquirer, May 12, 1848, contains Dr. Jones's obituary. Also published by the *Watchman and Observer*.

DR. LEFTRIDGE.

Dr. Leftridge, a French doctor of education and skill, lived in old William Jennings's house (Nottoway County) near the graveyard and probably died here. He married a young lady who had been his adopted child, and reared a family here.

He wrought some marvelous cures in the community, especially in the case of Captain Joseph Fowlkes about 1805, whose family physicians, Dr. James Jones and Dr. Josh. Fitzgerald, had given him up for dead. Dr. Jones had left in the evening and gone over to Captain Dupuy's to spend the night, and, on riding

---

[19]"Journal of the House of Delegates of the Commonwealth of Virginia, Begun and Held at the Capitol, in the City of Richmond, 17 May 1813," p. 35.

[20]*Idem.*, p. 23.

[21]Possibly Captain Vincent Shackleford, of Richmond, Va.

by the next day and seeing several people out in the yard, he inquired, "At what time did Captain Jo. die last night?" He was told that Mr. Fowlkes was much better after Dr. Leftridge came in the night from "Miller Hill," where he then lived, and doctored him. Leftridge's family removed to the West somewhere.

BENJAMIN WATKINS LEIGH.

Born in 1781 in Chesterfield County. His father, who died in Leigh's infancy, was a minister of the Episcopal Church.

He attended school under the Rev. Needler Robinson, completing his education at William and Mary College, where he stood high. He was in the class with Chapman Johnson, Henry St. George Tucker and Robert Stanard. These great lawyers succeeded Marshall and Wickham at the head of the profession. Chapman Johnson and Leigh were great friends.

Leigh escaped in early days the infidelity which obtained in circles of fashion in his section of the Virginia of that date.

He was a man of very striking and handsome appearance. The breaking of a leg in early life gave a limp to his walk, which was, nevertheless, most graceful. A thick-soled shoe partly compensated the difference in the length of his limbs. He had black hair and very effeminate features, was small in statue, and had a hand that would have made a study for Kneller.

His first law case was at Petersburg in defense of a boy who had slain his father for beating his mother. Leigh won a great success.

He was the author of papers under the name of Algernon Sidney, in the *Richmond Enquirer*, about 1819, on the execution by Andrew Jackson of Arbuthnot and Ambrister. See *Richmond Enquirer*, December 22, 1818.

For his refusal to take the anti-duelling oath, the Court of Appeals attempted in 1810 to exclude him from the bar upon the ground that as a lawyer he was an officer of the court and commonwealth and hence bound to take the official oath. Leigh's argument against this exactment, upon the ground that a lawyer is not an officer of the court, was very able and full, leading the court to set aside the oath and admit him.

Leigh was the compiler of the Virginia Code of 1819.

With the exception of John Randolph, he was the most remarked man in the Constitutional Convention of 1829-30. Instead of Giles, who was too old and feeble to take his wonted place, Leigh was selected to lead the eastern side of the Convention in that "great battle of the giants."

He was a close friend of General Winfield Scott.

Leigh was sent to Kentucky to arbitrate the celebrated Virginia-Kentucky dispute.[22] Clay and Bibb represented the latter State.

---

[22]In regard to military land claims.

Leigh went as mediator to South Carolina in 1833, at the time of the nullification controversy. He served in the Legislature. Was United States senator. Author of an able paper on the "Right of Instruction." (See *Richmond Enquirer*, February 1, 1812) In favor of the proposition.[23] There is a eulogy of him in the *Southern Literary Messenger* of February 1851, by William H. McFarland.

PHIL. T. SOUTHALL.

In the *Richmond Enquirer*, June 15, 1814, Dr. Phil. T. Southall in a card explains his absence from professional duties and states that he has returned to make Cumberland County (at Raine's Tavern) his home. He promises advice and medicine free to those unable to pay for services.
He was the father of Dr. Joseph Southall, of Amelia.

RICHARD KIDDER MEADE.

Richard Kidder Meade, of Petersburg, succeeded George C. Dromgoole in Congress. He was a good-looking man of rather dark complexion and weighed about two hundred pounds; very courtly in manner and conversation but not upon the whole so good a speaker as talker.

POLITICAL NOTES.

Memoranda of the poll returned by the sheriffs for the Congressional election in Brunswick district, July 26, 1790.

	William Branch Giles	Thos. Edmunds	Sheriff
Brunswick	280	110	
Cumberland	256	36	
Powhatan	160	17	
Nottoway	119	58	P. Lampkin
Dinwiddie	179	84	
Pr. George	53	185	
Sussex	5	266	
Mecklenburg	131	275	
Lunenburg	151	169	
Amelia	186	7	
Greensville	41	94	
	1561	1301	(260 majority)

Another poll for same office, in September 1790, and between same candidates in the whole district: Giles 2097, Edmunds 1435; 662 majority for Giles.

[23]*i. e.*, the right of a Legislature to instruct the U. S. Senators of its State.

Nottoway delegates 1811 (April election): Peter Randolph and Richard Epes.

Joseph Goodwyn elected State senator from the district of Dinwiddie, etc., April 1812.

Corresponding Committee for the Madison electoral ticket in 1812 for Nottoway County were: Wm. C. Greenhill, Edward Bland, Richard Epes, John D. Royal, Tyree G. Bacon, John Hewitt, Edmund Irby.

Presidential Election, 1812: Madison & Ward, 150; King, 1. In another report, later, Nottoway is quoted, 159 for Madison and 0 for King.

House of Delegates, election, April, 1814: Tyree G. Bacon and Thomas Wells [for Nottoway Co.]

Richmond Enquirer, April 2, 1819, quotes notice from *National Intelligencer* of the April Congressional elections without correction; one clause is this: "In the Dinwiddie district, the re-election of John Pegram is opposed by Dr. J. Jones, both of same politics." This of course is wrong.

Richmond Enquirer, April 6, 1819, records under Virginia elections: Nottoway, Jones 243, Pegram 13.

Richmond Enquirer, April 9, 1819, records Nottoway, Jones 246, Pegram 13; Jones's majority, 233. Dr. Jones ran against General Pegram last election and Nottoway voted less than this time for him. The message states that in the last election the vote was 166 to 7, 159 majority for Jones.

Richmond Enquirer, April 20, 1819, speaks of that election of 1819 as a very quiet and smooth one in Virginia.

Same contest: Prince George County, Dr. Jones 162, Pegram 65. Jones went to Greensville with 390 majority. Greensville gave Dr. Jones 86, Gen. Pegram 105. Dr Jones came to Petersburg with a majority of 301. In Petersburg Jones received 87 votes, Pegram 50. (Not all, I reckon).

Richmond Enquirer, April 23, May 4, 1819; Dr. Jones elected in place of General Pegram by 76 majority.

The Congress of 1819: John Randolph returns, beating Archibald Austin in the poll. Halifax, Geo. Tucker, place of Wm. J. Lewis (declined). Mecklenburg, Mark Alexander, in place of Thomas M. Nelson.

Among the Presidential electors, 1820, on the Republican ticket (Monroe and Tompkins) are found the names of—

1st District	William Holt	Norfolk
2nd "	Dr. Chas. W. Graves	Surry
3rd "	John Pegram	Dinwiddie
4th "	Robt. B. Starke	Greensville
5th "	John Purnall	Pr. Edward
6th "	Dr. Branch T. Archer	Powhatan
8th "	Charles Yancey	Buckingham
10th "	William Brockenborough	Richmond

(The above taken from the *Petersburg Republican,* 1820, by F. R. Lassister.)

Petersburg Republican, April 13, 1821, states Knight and Ward elected to House of Delegates, Nottoway. April election, 1821: *Richmond Enquirer,* April 13, Dr. James Jones, of Nottoway, is reelected to Congress without opposition.

Richmond Enquirer, July 20, 1821: Fourth of July celebrated at a spring near Miller's Tavern (Prince Edward Co.). The Declaration of Independence read by William Branch, Jr. Present, also, Col. Samuel D. Burke, Col. John H. Knight, Dr. William J. Dupuy, John Foster, John M. Ligon. Col. Burke's toast: "The members of the Virginia Legislature, may they have longer heads and shorter tongues."

A legislative caucus convened in the House of Delegates, Feb. 21, 1824, to frame an electoral ticket in favor of William H. Crawford for President. In the 7th (Amelia, Nottoway, etc.) Dr. James Jones of Nottoway, Mark Alexander of Mecklenburg. The *Richmond Enquirer* supported Crawford. Also as members of the Corresponding Committee of Nottoway, Richard Jones (brother of Dr. Jones), Tyree G. Bacon, Richard Epes, Samuel Morgan, John H. Knight, Austin Watkins, Edmund Wills.

Richmond Enquirer, March 12, 1824: Nottoway, Amelia, Powhatan, Chesterfield, Cumberland composed the 7th congressional district (W. S. Archer).[24]

Richmond Enquirer, April 13, 1827, records: House of Delegates, 1826-27, H. R. Anderson, Capt. Nathan Ward. House of Delegates, 1827-8, James Jones, 146; H. R. Anderson, 132; John H. Knight, 122; Samuel G. Williams, 48. Jones and Anderson elected.

Richmond Enquirer, Dec. 15, 1827: A legislative caucus favorable to the formation of a Jackson electoral ticket was held in the Capitol and adjourned until January 14, 1828. Dr. Jones, of Nottoway, attended.

Richmond Enquirer, Jan. 17, 1828: Legislative convention reconvened Jan. 14 and nominated Jackson and Calhoun. The electoral ticket held Dr. Jones elector for the 6th district.

In this campaign, 1828, the corresponding committees for Jackson's ticket included Dr. A. A. Campbell, Capt. Richard Jones, Capt. Nathan Ward, Archer Robertson, John H. Knight, John P. Dupuy, William Taylor Wills, L. Jones, Samuel B. Jeter, Edmund Irby, Austin Watkins, Edward Bland.

Richmond Enquirer, April 11, 1828: Elections for House of Delegates annually; Nottoway, April 1828, James Jones and H. R. Anderson. For Convention 1829-30, 8 for and 83 against.

In the presidential election of 1828, Nov. 3, Dr. Jones, the Jackson elector, carried Nottoway by 208 to 2 for Adams.

---

[24] W. S. Archer served as a Representative in Congress from January 18, 1820, to March 3, 1835.

Richmond Enquirer, April 10, 1829, gives vote of Nottoway for House of Delegates: Dr. A. A. Campbell, 88; Dr. Austin Watkins, 79; A. Hatchett, 64.

Richmond Enquirer, March 17, 1832: Legislative caucus met in this month in the Capitol favourable to Gen. Jackson. They declined to make a specific nomination for Vice-President. The Jackson electoral ticket consisted among others, in 1832, of James Jones of Nottoway and Archibald Austin of Buckingham. Dr. Jones was elector of 3rd. district this time. He was nominated by Mr. Old. There were twenty-three electors this year, twenty-two elected by the people and the twenty-third appointed by the Legislature.

In this campaign the Corresponding Committee for Nottoway was: Lewis Jones, Capt. Richard Jones, Dr. A. A. Campbell, Bartelote P. Todd, Col. Samuel B. Jeter, Col. John H. Knight, John P. Dupuy, Col. E. T. Jeffries, Maj. H. R. Anderson, Dr. Austin Watkins, Anthony Webster, Col. Travis H. Epes, William B. Green, Capt. William B. Irby, Peter Epes, Robert Fitzgerald, Jr., Col. Wm. C. Greenhill, Capt. P. O. Lipscomb, George N. Seay, John Fitzgerald, William Thomas, John W. Connelly, Nathan Ward, Maloye W. Robertson, Asa Hawkes, Nathan H. Jones, Frank L. Moseley, Robert H. Booth, William Taylor Wills, William B. Wilson. In this campaign a great effort was made in Virginia to pledge the Jackson electors to P. P. Barbour for Vice-President. They, however, remained uncommitted, to cast their ballot for whom it might be most judicious.

The electoral ticket of Jackson was elected. It appears that Nottoway cast 200 votes for "Old Hickory" and none for Clay.

Nottoway County Republican Campaign Committee elected at Richmond convention which nominated Van Buren, Feb. 22, 1840: Dr. Campbell, Robert Fitzgerald, Timothy Wortham, William A. Scott, Wm. B. Smith, Wm. Thomas, Thomas Howson, B. W. Fitzgerald, Putnam Stith, James J. Verser, Thomas Dickinson, W. W. and Albert A. Bass, Col. John H. Knight, Col. Edward T. Jeffries, Maj. Wm. C. Knight, George W. Oliver, Chas. H. Carter, Sam Cary, Jas. M. Taylor, Paschal J. Fowlkes, Sharpe Carter, Grief T. Cralle, Wm. R. Jennings, Col. Sam B. Jeter, John Wilson, Jr., John Bland, Williamson Tucker, Wm. Atkins, Wm. W. Webster, Thomas Dean, Wm. B. Irby, Archer Worsham, George A. Cralle, Capt. Thomas Jackson, Capt. Thomas Jones, Asa Crenshaw, George Prosize, William Watkins, Daniel J. Jackson, Capt. Nathan Ward, Robert W. Roberts, B. C. Jones, R. T. Ward, John P. Dupuy, George C. Ingram, Stith A. Ingram, Anderson J. Fowlkes, Peter J. Grigg, George N. Seay, Williamson Dickinson, Col. Tilman E. Jeter, Thomas Nelson, Col. William Verser, Wm. Perkinson.

In the vote of April, 1840, for House of Delegates, in Nottoway, Booth was the Whig candidate and William Fitzgerald the Democrat. There were upwards of 400 votes cast. On the face of the poll Capt. Ward writes Booth had 209 and Fitzgerald 207. On the back of the poll lay eight contested votes, two for Booth and six for Fitzgerald. Total: Booth, 210; Fitzgerald, 213; one vote thrown out. This was the subject of considerable contest. See Booth's letter in the *Richmond Enquirer*, May 1, 1840; also Capt. Ward's letter in the *Richmond Enquirer*, May 12, 1840. · The Booth *vs.* Fitzgerald election case discussed in *Richmond Enquirer*, Aug. 14, 1840. The matter referred to Chapman Johnson, of Richmond.

At Nottoway Court House Thursday (Court Day) Oct. 1, 1840, a meeting of the Democratic Party was held for the purpose of district organization for election purposes. Dr. Campbell, chairman, Sharpe Carter, Sec. Louis C. Bouldin submitted the resolution to appoint eight sub-committees to wait personally upon all Republican voters in their sections and notify them of the day, place, and manner of holding presidential elections; and to furnish every facility which their years or infirmities may require to bring them to the polls. At Jennings Ordinary the committee was: Peter J. Grigg, Antony W. Crowder, Joel Motley, Robert Ward, John P. Dupuy, Wm. R. Jennings.

Nottoway vote in 1844: Clay, 187; Polk, 182.

Presidential electors, 1844, on the Democratic ticket (Polk and Dallas) : 1st Dist. John S. Millson, M. C., Norfolk; 2nd Dist. Thomas Wallace, Petersburg; 3rd Dist. Wm. R. Baskerville, Mecklenburg County; 5th Dist. Archibald Stuart, M. C., Patrick County; 9th Dist. Wm. H. Roane, (Judge, Court of Appeals), Henrico County.

Presidential Electors, 1844, Republican Whig ticket (Clay and Frelinghuysen) : 1st Dist. Robert H. Whitfield, Isle of White County; 2nd Dist. John E. Shell (Member Virginia Convention of 1850-51), Brunswick County; 3rd Dist. Henry P. Irving, Cumberland County; 5th Dist. George H. Gilmer, Pittsylvania County; 9th Dist. Raleigh T. Daniel, Richmond.

Richmond Enquirer, February 2, 1847: Democratic Convention at Farmville, January 27, 1847, nominated Thomas S. Bocock for Congress in place of E. W. Hubbard, who declined standing for re-election.

Richmond Enquirer, April 4, 1848, gives account of a Democratic mass-meeting at Amelia Courthouse, in which Peter F. Boisseau beat Lewis E. Harvie for nomination for House of Delegates.

Richmond Enquirer, September 5, 1848: Amelia County; meeting of the Democracy; Democratic Republican Party of Amelia meeting held in courthouse August 24, that being court day; Fabius Lawson, Esq., chairman; Dr. Thomas W. Neale, secretary; Thomas T. Giles submitted resolutions; debate by Lewis E. Harvie, T. Edgar Bottom, Hon. R. K. Meade.

Nottoway Democratic Meeting at courthouse, September 7, 1848: Col. John H. Knight presided and B. C. Jones, Sec. Appoint delegates to Lynchburg convention September 20, 1848. Delegates: Roger Pryor, Dr. Campbell, Thomas H. Campbell, Dick Irby, W. C. Knight, Thomas Hamlin, W. C. Jeffress, Charles H. Carter, William Fitzgerald, W. A. Scott.

Nottoway vote in 1848: Cass, 143; Taylor, 117.

Democratic State Convention at Staunton, Nov. 30, 1854. Animated contest soon arose among the friends of Henry A. Wise and Shelton F. Leake; lasted three days; Wise nominated on third day. Roger A. Pryor was there in the interest of Wise. Mr. James H. Gilmore, of the University, was a Wise delegate and told me Pryor did not take active part upon the floor but was doing the wire-pulling behind the scenes. Pryor put up in rooms at same hotel, I think.

The campaign of the Democratic Party in Virginia in 1855, or Henry A. Wise against "Know Nothingism."

Perhaps political excitement never ran higher in any State than in Virginia in 1855. Wise opened the campaign at Ashland Hall, Norfolk, Jan. 5, 1855. Stephen A. Douglas also made a powerful speech in Richmond on March 27 (see speech in Hambleton's Life of Wise[25]). R. M. T. Hunter also made a great argument in Richmond against the American party soon afterwards (*vide* Hambleton's Wise).

The State Democratic organization was perfect that year.

The district elector for 4th congressional district was Richard Kidder Meade, of Petersburg.

Senatorial elector for Nottoway, Lunenburg and Prince Edward, 9th senatorial district, W. Cabell Flournoy; 7th, Lewis E. Harvie; 10th, Wm. B. Baskerville, Mecklenburg.

County electors: Amelia, William Gregory; Nottoway, Thomas Rowlett; Brunswick, Robert D. Turnbull; Buckingham, E. W. Hubbard; Powhatan, H. L. Hopkins; Sussex & Richmond, F. Dillard; Lunenburg, William J. Neblitt; Mecklenburg, Mark Alexander, Jr.; Prince Edward, Samuel C. Anderson; Surry, Dr. M. G. Holt.

Know Nothing ticket put up at Winchester, 14th March 1855: Governor, Thomas Stanhope Flournoy, of Halifax; Lieutenant Governor, James M. H. Beale, of Mason; Attorney General, John M. Patton, of Richmond.

Among distinguished Southside Democratic orators of the canvass: Roger A. Pryor, editor of *Richmond Enquirer;* A. D. Banks, editor of *Southside Democrat;* R. K. Meade, of Petersburg; Henry L. Hopkins, late Speaker of House of Delegates; Wm. M. Treadway; Cabell Flournoy, of Prince Edward.

In the 4th Congressional district the candidates for Congress were William O. Goode, who had already served two terms in Congress, and "Mr. Tazewell, of Mecklenburg, a young gen-

[25]Hambleton, James P. "A Biographical Sketch of Henry A. Wise, with a History of the Political Campaign in Virginia in 1855 . . ." Richmond, Va., J. W. Randolph, 1856.

tleman of great facetiousness, whose anecdotes during the canvass were exceedingly entertaining and pleasing to his auditors."[26] Goode was elected by about 2000 majority.

The elector of the district was Richard Kidder Meade, formerly a prominent member of Congress and a distinguished leader of the states' rights party.

The *Southside Democrat*, of Petersburg, was edited with signal ability during the campaign by Messrs. Banks and Keiley.

Third district: for Congress, Democrat, John S. Caskie, of Richmond; Know-Nothing, Wm. C. Scott, of Powhatan. Major Scott beat John Minor Botts and A. J. Crane for the nomination. He was distinguished for the accuracy of his political information; was of good education and unblemished private character. Scott carried Richmond City by considerable majority but was beaten in the district.

First congressional district: Democrat, Thomas S. Bocock (elected) ; Know Nothing, N. C. Claiborne, of Franklin. The result: H. A. Wise, 83,000+ ; Flournoy, 73,000+. Bocock ran ahead of his ticket by some 1,000 or more.

	Wise	Flournoy
Amelia	309	234
Buckingham	496	551
Prince Edward	427	355
Mecklenburg	874	480
Petersburg City	783	747
Richmond City	1166	2144
Halifax	1163	587
Lunenburg	465	201
Nottoway	228	187

The Legislature of 1855, senatorial districts: Lunenburg, Nottoway and Prince Edward, Thos. H. Campbell, Dem.; Campbell and Appomattox, Thos. H. Flood, Know Nothing; Powhatan, Cumberland and Chesterfield, Wm. Old, Dem.; Mecklenburg and Charlotte, L. W. Tazewell, Know Nothing.

House of Delegates: Amelia and Nottoway, Wm. F. C. Gregory, Democrat; Brunswick, Edward Dromgoole, Democrat; Buckingham, Thos. M. Bondurant, K. Nothing; Cumberland and Powhatan, W. P. Dabney, Democrat; Essex, and King and Queen, M. R. H. Garnett; Lunenburg, Geo. W. Hardy, Democrat; Prince Edward, T. T. Treadway, Democrat; Richmond, H. K. Ellyson, K. Nothing; H. B. Dickinson, Know Nothing; R. C. Stanard, Know Nothing.

The election took place May 24, 1855.

Roger A. Pryor's majorities in the congressional election in the fourth Virginia district against Thomas F. Goode, Novem-

---

[26]Hambleton, "Biographical Sketch of Henry A. Wise," p. 345.

ber 1859: Nottoway, 131; Petersburg, 393; Dinwiddie, 232;
Charlotte, 171; Cumberland, 164; Brunswick, 245; Powhatan,
34 (not fully reported); Prince Edward, 80; Amelia, 163 (not
fully reported); Lunenburg, 30 (not fully reported). Goode's
majority: Mecklenburg, 877. Colonel Goode lost only 160 votes
in Mecklenburg, so Mr. Atkins told me.

Election Ticket[27]

OPPOSITION TICKET

(Seal of Virginia)

ELECTION MAY 26th

For Governor:
Wm. L. GOGGIN

For Lieut. Governor:
WAITMAN T. WILLEY

For Attorney General:
WALTER PRESTON

For House of Delegates:
WARNER W. GUY

For Representative to Congress:
JOHN T. THORNTON

For Board of Public Works:
AUGUSTUS HOPKINS

Note: The last name is written in by hand in pencil.

Blackstone, Sept. 27th, 1889.
Sidney Epes introduced George C. Cabell as the grandson
of Nottoway. Mr. Cabell said: First time he had the pleasure
of addressing the people of Nottoway. Bones of his people for
six generations lie in the graves of Nottoway (his grandfather
and grandmother lie in Nottoway)[28] Referred to the record of
Nottoway in the War. . . (Reviewed the history of our affairs
since the war). William Mahone was elected as Democratic Re-
adjuster. The race issue is all coming right. Blessed be God,

---

[27]Whig Party, 1859. Goggin was from Bedford County; John T.
Thornton, from Prince Edward County; Warner W. Guy was nominated
at an "Amelia and Nottoway district convention," at "The Junction" (Burkeville), in Nottoway County. Evidently electoral ticket used in Amelia and
Nottoway.

[28]Evidently maternal lines, bearing other names than Cabell.

the Anglo-Saxon race is sticking together. Negroes go to "ole master" and "ole mistress" for comfort, for bread and meat, but he stands with the scalawags at the polls. Negroes don't get enough offices in the Republican Party; they get nothing save a few offices which don't pay enough to get the salt to pickle a jay bird. Mahone a traitor worse than Judas Iscariot, because Judas was poor and wanted money; worse than Arnold, because he was led astray by his Tory wife.

Mahone and in hell holding a negro between him and the fire.

William Mahone—Widow Malone—Alone[29]

Democratic Ticket[30]

Election, Tuesday, Nov. 5th, 1889

For Governor,
P. W. McKinney,
Of Prince Edward.

For Lieutenant-Governor,
J. Hoge Tyler,
of Pulaski.

For Attorney-General,
R. Taylor Scott,
of Fauquier.

For the House of Delegates,
J. A. Taylor

Election, November 3rd., 1891.

For House of Delegates,
From Amelia and Nottoway,
Sidney P. Epes.

For Senate,
Nottoway, Lunenburg and Brunswick,
Walter A. Watson.

[29]Political gibe of the time.
[30]This ballot is very small (2¼ x 1½ inches) and is printed on very thin paper. These were sometimes called "tissue ballots" or "kiss-verse" tickets, the latter name being derived from the little slips of thin paper on which were printed sentimental verses, and which were contained in the wrappers of a popular candy of that day. It seems these tickets were, on account of the difficulty of separating them, found very useful in situations in which skilful manipulation of the ballot was deemed necessary.

Regular

Democratic Ticket.

Election, November 8th, 1892.

For President,
Grover Cleveland,
of New York.

For Vice President
Adlai E. Stevenson,
of Illinois.

Electors at Large,
Robert C. Kent, of Wythe.
Holmes Conrad, of Frederick.

District Electors

1st	Wm. A. Little, Jr.,	of Spotsylvania.
2nd	Robert R. Prentis,	of Nansemond.
3rd	Meade Haskins,	of Richmond City.
4th	F. R. Lassiter,	of Petersburg.
5th	E. W. Saunders,	of Franklin.
6th	J. Thompson Brown,	of Bedford.
7th	A. Moore, Jr.,	of Clarke.
8th	R. Walton Moore,	of Fairfax.
9th	J. C. Wysor,	of Pulaski.
10th	H. D. Flood,	of Appomattox.

For Congress,
Fourth District,
James F. Epes.

State Democratic Ticket

Election, 7th of November[31]

For Governor,
Charles T. O'Ferrall,
of Rockingham.

For Lieutenant-Governor,
Robert C. Kent,
of Wythe

[31]1893; another ticket was identical with one above except caption
which reads "People's Party of Virginia."

For Attorney-General,
R. Taylor Scott,
of Fauquier.

For House of Delegates,
Amelia and Nottoway,
Robert G. Southall.

SOUTHSIDE IN VIRGINIA CONSTITUTIONAL CONVENTIONS.

CONVENTION OF 1788.

Brunswick: John Jones and Binns Jones. Colonel John Jones (probably a descendant of Captain Peter Jones, of Petersburg, according to Grigsby), burgess from Dinwiddie, 1757-1758; State senator, 1776-1787; speaker of Senate, 1787-1788; county-lieutenant of Brunswick, 1788 and later. He was the grandfather of the Honorable John Winston Jones,, through his son Alexander Jones and Mary Ann Jones, daughter of Peter Winston.

Charlotte: Thomas Read and Paul Carrington. Read, son of Colonel Clement Read; William and Mary College; clerk of Charlotte County; died at his seat, "Ingleside," in 1817. Carrington, son of Col. George Carrington; burgess (1765-1775); member of all the Revolutionary Conventions; judge, General Court of Virginia; chief justice, 1780; Court of Appeals, 1789; died in the 86th year of his age.

Dinwiddie: Joseph Jones and William Watkins. Jones, member House of Delegates, 1784-1787; postmaster of Petersburg, Virginia; general of militia; married Jane, daughter of Roger Atkinson, of "Mansfield."

Surry: John Hartwell Cocke and John Allen.

Lunenburg: Jonathan Patteson and Christopher Robertson.

Mecklenburg: Samuel Hopkins, Jr., and Richard Kennon. General Kennon was appointed Governor of Louisiana territory by Jefferson, and died there.

Prince Edward: Patrick Henry[32] and Robert Lawson. General Robert Lawson was a gallant and meritorious officer of the Revolution.

Amelia: John Pride and Edmund Booker. Pride was in the Virginia Senate and speaker of that body in 1789. The Bookers have frequently been prominent in local politics.[33]

---

[32]Judge Watson probably considered that Patrick Henry required no comment.
[33]See Booker genealogy, p. 156.

Buckingham: Charles Patteson and David Bell. Patteson on Committee of Safety of Buckingham, 1776; House of Delegates, 1776, 1777, 1781-82, 1782, 1784-1785, 1787-88. Bell, son of David Bell and Judith Bell (sister of Archibald Cary, "Ampthill.")

Campbell: Edmund Winston, member for Campbell, Convention of 1788, was from "Hunting Tower," Buckingham; judge, General Court; first cousin of Patrick Henry, whose executor he was and whose widow he married; died 1813. Descendants in Missouri.[34]

Halifax: Isaac Coles and George Carrington. Col. Isaac Coles, son of Major John Coles, an Irish immigrant to Henrico who is buried at St. Johns; married a Thompson of New York, and brother-in-law to Elbridge Gerry. Coles Ferry, Halifax, perpetuates the name and seat of Col. Coles. Congress 1789-91, 1793-97. Carrington, lieutenant in Revolution and son of George Carrington of Barbadoes.

CONVENTION OF 1829-1830.

(See *Southern Literary Messenger*, March and May 1851, sketches by Hugh R. Pleasants, Esq.)

This convention has been called "the great council of the giants." It was said to have comprised the ablest talent that ever assembled in a single convention in the United States. An eminent jurist of New York said that he doubted if any other State in the Union could have arrayed in council so great intellects as Virginia then assembled, or whether the Revolutionary times beheld so many intellects of such high order. John Randolph said that the convention was the grave of many a local reputation.

From the *Richmond Enquirer* I learn the following, which I quote from memory: The candidates for the convention in this district (Nottoway, etc.) were John W. Jones, B. W. Leigh, W. S. Archer, Samuel Taylor, William B. Giles, Branch T. Archer, William R. Johnson, William Old. The *Richmond Enquirer* of March 20, 1829, contains a call from a citizen of Nottoway for Dr. James Jones to stand for the convention and advocating his election. He was voted for by a few in Nottoway but was not a candidate.

The *Richmond Enquirer* of April 17, 1829, gives an account of a public meeting in Nottoway on April 2: Edward Bland, chairman, H. R. Anderson, secretary; endorsed for the convention William B. Giles, B. W. Leigh, John W. Jones and W. S. Archer.

Jones led in the district; Leigh was second; Taylor came next. The real contest was between Giles and Archer. Amelia was the last county to vote, and they entered this county nearly

---

[34]Robert Alexander was the other delegate from Campbell County.

even. It being known that Amelia would decide the election, a hot contest developed there. Giles won by a small majority. Nottoway gave very few votes to Taylor, Johnson, and Branch T. Archer.

Vote in the district, by counties. (From the *Richmond Enquirer*, May 8, 1829).

Nottoway:

B. W. Leigh	157	W. R. Johnson	15
J. W. Jones	121	Wm. Old	10
Wm. B. Giles	102	Dr. Jas. Jones	8
W. S. Archer	92	B. T. Archer	1
Sam Taylor	58		

Chesterfield:

Jones	351	Giles	146
Leigh	329	W. S. Archer	93
Johnson	246	B. T. Archer	17
Taylor	245	Old	87

Powhatan:

Old	161	Taylor	89
Jones	143	W. S. Archer	88
Leigh	109	B. T. Archer	81
Giles	98	Johnson	12

Petersburg:

Jones	111	W. S. Archer	91
Leigh	104	B. T. Archer	9
Taylor	85	Johnson	44
Giles	53	Old	2

Cumberland:

Jones	179	Archer	124
Leigh	172	Giles	122
Taylor	150		

Amelia:

Jones	203	Giles	173
Leigh	188	Archer	128
Taylor	107		

Total: Jones, 1111; Leigh, 1031; Taylor, 737; Giles, 695; W. S. Archer, 618.

Some Southside members of the Convention who served in Congress: William B. Giles, Amelia, senator, the then Governor of Virginia; George C. Dromgoole, Brunswick; W. O. Goode, Mecklenburg; Mark Alexander, Mecklenburg; John Y. Mason, Southampton; James Trezvant, Southampton; John Randolph, Charlotte; William S. Archer, Amelia, senator; Benjamin Watkins Leigh, senator; L. W. Tazewell, Norfolk, senator; Archibald Stuart, Patrick; George Loyall, Norfolk; John Winston Jones, Chesterfield, Speaker House of Representatives.

William B. Giles was in very feeble health but his intellect was unimpaired. He spoke but rarely in the Convention. Pleasants, in his "Sketches of the Virginia Convention," says that if Giles was not equal to Charles James Fox, the most powerful debater the world ever saw, he certainly had no superior in the American Congress during his time, and that time embraced the best days of Madison, Bayard and Dexter.

The Convention met in the Capitol at Richmond on October 5, 1829. Madison nominated Monroe for president (on account of the latter's pecuniary misfortunes, probably), and he was elected and escorted to the chair by Madison and John Marshall. George W. Munford was clerk, and William Randolph sergeant at arms, defeating Peter Francisco. Thomas Ritchie was elected printer over J. H. Pleasants and T. W. White. Dr. Calvin H. Read, of Northampton, died before taking his seat and the remaining delegates from the district elected William K. Perrin, of Gloucester. Most of the work of the Convention was done in committee of the whole, where P. P. Barbour presided. On November 7, General Robert B. Taylor addressed a letter to the president of the Convention resigning his seat in consequence of instructions from his constituents in behalf of the mixed basis of whites and blacks for representation; Hugh Blair Grigsby succeeded him. The only motion made by Dromgoole was one to lay on the table the application of Elisha Bates (Society of Friends) to hold religious services before the Convention. John Taliaferro, of King George, resigned and was succeeded by Judge John Coalter of the Court of Appeals. Richard Morris represented Hanover, and an orator he was, says Pleasants.

CONVENTION OF 1850-1851, AS RELATED BY COLONEL W. C. JEFFRESS.

The candidates before the people of the district were Robert Turnbull, of Brunswick, John E. Shell, of Brunswick, Scoggin,[35] of Prince Edward, and Weisiger and Thomas Campbell, of Nottoway. Scoggin was a farmer and the others were lawyers. The first three were elected and Campbell was left at home. He was the only conservative in the field and the only point of difference between the candidates was the elective judiciary, which

---

[35] James L. Scoggin.

he opposed and the others advocated. Groundhog democracy was so rampant in the district that even this modest conservatism was snowed under. Shell was a man of considerable ability. As he was speaking from the steps of the courthouse old Charles Smith remarked to Colonel Jeffress that he knew Shell intimately and that he spoke not a word of his true sentiments but was one of the most thorough aristocrats going. Scoggin subsequently opposed Tom Campbell for the Senate but was defeated by Nottoway, which gave Campbell every vote polled except five.

SOUTHSIDE EDUCATIONAL INSTITUTIONS.

Of course our people have patronized various institutions of learning more or less liberally; but the chief association and interest have centered around old Hampden-Sidney and Charlottesville. Nottoway's names at Hampden-Sidney make up a long and honorable list. Many of them appear upon the graduate rolls and many more on the list of under-graduates.

The Nottoway graduates of Hampden-Sidney down to 1852 were Dr. Jones (1791), Dr. Theodorick Pryor (1826), Dr. George Fitzgerald, Dr. R. B. Tuggle, Hon. A. D. Dickinson, James H. Fitzgerald, W. H. Anderson, A, H. Robertson, Roger A. Prayor (1846), John H. Knight (1848), E. O. Fitzgerald (1850), W. R. Carter (1852).

Dr. James Jones's class at Hampden-Sidney in 1791 contained William M. Watkins, Moses Waddell, President of Franklin College, now Georgia University, and George Bibb, Governor of Kentucky and U. S. senator.

At Hampden-Sidney our students generally united themselves with the Phip. Lit. Society,[36] organized in 1805, Dr. John Peter Mettauer being one of the organizers; in fact, almost to a man save Dr. Theodorick Pryor and Gen. Roger A. Pryor, who joined the Union Hall. The Phip. Hall turned out all the lawyers and speakers, while the Union furnished the preachers and teachers. The name of W. Henry Anderson mentioned above claims a word further. , The figure of this young man loomed considerably above the level of average ability, and his premature death in Georgia ended a career brilliant in its span and assured of higher renown. He was a son of Maj. H. R. Anderson, and after leaving Hampden-Sidney in 1839 studied law and removed to Georgia. His brother, the Hon. Clifford Anderson is now a distinguished member of the Macon Bar. It is of interest to know that W. H. Anderson was the teacher who formed part of the subject of Johnny Reb's[37] famous lecture "The Old Field School."

---

[36] Philanthropic Literary Society.
[37] Pseudonym of Judge Fernandino R. Farrar.

Richmond Enquirer, July 3, 1821: Hampden-Sidney College and the civilization of Southside Virginia.
Hampden-Sidney students raised $93.87½ in aid of the Greeks in 1827.—*Richmond Enquirer,* April 20, 1827.
By April 19, 1861, the students of Hampden-Sidney College had organized themselves into a company under the supervision of Col. Womack and had elected Rev. President Atkinson captain. A report in the *Richmond Dispatch* of that date says: "A secession flag now floats over the old college. When the question was asked where shall ge get a pole? David Ross, the old college servant, said: 'I'll go and cut one and carry the big end.' David wants to go as cook. The State will accept their services, which have been offered to the Commonwealth."

JEFFERSON DAVIS TO THE PHILANTHROPIC LITERARY SOCIETY.

As one of the many tokens of the high regard the late President Davis always entertained for Virginia, I have in my possession a letter, written in his own hand and in his last years, which contains a most graceful tribute to the people of this Commonwealth and also to one of its colleges. The letter, dated 1885, was addressed to an officer of the Philanthropic Literary Society of Hampden-Sidney College, in response to his election as an honorary member of that body.[38]

Beauvoir, Miss., April 13, '85.
My dear Sir:
I thankfully accept the honor conferred by the Philanthropic Literary Society of Hampden and Sidney College.
Venerable by long and useful existence, illustrious by the patriots, heroes and sages, whose names grace your rolls, I am grateful that you have deemed me worthy to be numbered among them. It has given me much pleasure to receive your assurance of kind regard, and especially to know that you of Hampden and Sidney emulate the example of your sires, whose dauntless maintenance of principle gave to them such fair claim that it was a matter of just pride to be a Virginian.
Please present my cordial good wishes to your associate members and believe me yours
Faithfully,
JEFFERSON DAVIS.

UNIVERSITY OF VIRGINIA.

The catalogues of the University of Virginia credit us with the following graduates and undergraduates down to 1867: Colonel T. H. Epes (1826), Dr. Theodorick Pryor (1827), Peter

[38]The letter was written to Mr. Watson and is still in Mrs. Watson's possession.

B. Jones, T. Freeman Epes, Colonel W. C. Knight, W. B. Smith, Dr. J. M. Hurt, Dr. John C. Watkins, Samuel P. Fowlkes, Roger A. Pryor, John A. Morgan, William B. Taylor, Dr. Joseph D. Eggleston, John H. Knight, A. H. Robertson, E. O. Fitzgerald, Samuel Hardy, Judge Branch J. Epes, Thomas H. Fuqua, Charles A. Jones, Dr. Joseph A. Jones, L. H. Crenshaw, Captain John E. Jones, John E. Shore, Orlando Smith, Robert T. Carter, T. Lafayette Jackson, William H. Perry, John W. Wilson, J. P. Fitzgerald, H. P. Fitzgerald, John K. Jones, Thomas W. Ford, E. G. Booth, T. E. Royall, James F. Epes, F. S. Williams, John S. Hardaway, Richard H. Harris, John Clarke Howard.

Class of 1826. A distinguished class: T. H. Epes, R. E. Scott, Lewis E. Harvie, R. M. T. Hunter, Edgar Allan Poe, John B. Magruder, Hugh Pleasants. Nottoway had but one student at the University.

JEFFERSON LITERARY SOCIETY.

Some of the members, 1829-30.

Major William C. Scott, Powhatan County, Va.

1830-31.

Thomas Scott, Powhatan County, Va.
Charles S. Trueheart, Powhatan County, Va.
Dr. John B. Harvie, Powhatan County, Va.
Henry M. Bentley, Powhatan County, Va.
J. T. and G. L. Hairston, Henry County, Va.
Thomas W. Ligon, Prince Edward County, Va.
William H. Harrison, Amelia County, Va.

HARRISON'S ACADEMY.

Located at "Wigwam," Governor Giles's home. It was operative as early as 1826. In that year Dr. Richard F. Taylor, Sharpe Carter and Freeman Epes were students there. Old "Goat" Harrison[39] was then a teacher there.

WASHINGTON ACADEMY, AMELIA COUNTY.

Organized about 1840. Bridgeforth and Archer[40] were among the trustees.

---

[39]William H. Harrison.
[40]The act incorporating the Washington Academy of Amelia, March 14, 1840, mentions, among the trustees, the names of Miles Archer and William Archer; Bridgeforth (probably Benjamin Bridgeforth) is not mentioned.

JEFFERSON COLLEGE, AMELIA COUNTY.

Jefferson College, in Amelia County, was formally incorporated by act of legislature, Dec. 26, 1800, with the following trustees: William Merewether, John Archer, Peterfield Archer, Daniel Hardyway, John Burke, David Meade, Everard Meade, Sr., James Henderson, Bennett Brown, Joshua Chaffin, Thomas Randolph, John Royal, John Randolph, Jr., William Daniel, James Jones, M. D., Peter Randolph, John Shore, Joseph Jones, Thomas Read, Sr., and John H. Foushee, gentlemen. The original petition to the legislature for incorporation, dated December 5, 1800, is in the Virginia State Library; it bears the names of the above trustees, and gives their residence as Amelia County with the exception of John Randolph, Jr., and William Daniel, of Cumberland County; James Jones, M. D., and Peter Randolph, of Nottoway County; John Shore and General Joseph Jones, of Dinwiddie County; Thomas Read, Sr., of Charlotte County; and John H. Foushee, of the City of Richmond.

RELIGIOUS DENOMINATIONS.

EPISCOPAL.

Vestry books of Southam Parish, Powhatan County: January, 1746, 1267 tithables; November, 1747, 1360 tithables.

Inventory of the estate, real and personal, of the Episcopal Church in Nottoway Parish, taken by Stephen Cocke and Peter Lamkin, May 3, 1785: 340 acres of land, with glebe and houses thereon; rent, six pounds; personal effects, one cup and plate, etc.; two churches with three and a half acres of land; one chapel of ease.[41] (Amelia Will Book 3, p. 441.)

In 1796 there were 3371 tithes in Nottoway; in 1797, 3412 tithes. The county levy for this year was 7d per tithe, or $331.73.

Vestry Book, Southam Parish, Goochland County.[42]

July 1747. p. 16. Thomas Watson appointed one of the processioners for the lands beginning "at Ham Chapel, thence by the new road near Mr. Scotts to Muddy Creek, up the same

---

[41] A supplementary chapel to ease or relieve the mother church and serve distant parishioners.

[42] In his "Old Churches, Ministers and Families of Virginia," (1861) Vol. 1, p. 456, Bishop Meade states: "Goochland County was cut off from Henrico in 1727. In the year 1744 the parish of St. James Northam was restricted to the north side of the river, and that on the south side was called St. James Southam, both of them being in Goochland, which still lay on both sides of the river, and extended from the Louisa line to Appomattox River."

to Barnets Road to Pruets Path, along the same to Ham Chapel."
Merriman and Bond [Other processioners?]
p. 25: part of Watson's land marked.
p. 44: 1325 tithables in the parish, 1748.
1751: William Watson appointed processioner by vestry
on Farewallet Creek and Guinea Road.
1755: William Watson appointed processioner for the
lands on Little Guinea Creek, etc. He signed report with his
mark in April 1756. Report shows he was then land owner.
Report of other processioners shows his land adjoined one
Samuel Meredith and that one Christopher Watson attended as
witness upon processioners.
1759: William Watson appointed a processioner for land
on Little Guinea. William and Christopher Watson named as
witnesses to report, etc.
1763: Ordered that William Watson and others procession
land between Jones's Creek, King William Parish lines, James
River, Fire Creek to the Middle Road, the Middle Road to Mrs.
Mayo's Road, thence to Buckingham Road. This report was
made and signed by William Watson, 1764.
1765: William Watson's land processioned, Daniel Watson
present.
Chesterfield Deed Book 4, p. 163, shows deed from vestry-
men of Dale Parish, 1760, conveying one half acre of glebe land,
laid off in town, Gatesville, to Peter Eppes, gentleman, of Prince
George.
Under the architect Robert Mills was laid the corner-stone
of the Monumental Church, Saturday, Aug. 1, 1812.
Richmond Enquirer, July 27, 1814: Pew no. 3, Monumental
Church, advertised for sale to highest bidder on Saturday, 30
July, at Mr. Lynch's Coffee Room; by order of the vestry. De-
linquent pew holders also reminded that thirty days delinquency
forfeits the pew.

THE THEATRE OF 1811.[43]

A resolution of condolence was moved in eloquent words
in the U. S. Senate in January following by Wm. B. Giles, then
a senator of the State. See *Richmond Enquirer*, Jan. 14, 1812.

PRESBYTERIAN CHURCH.

The First Presbyterian Church was founded in Richmond
about 1812[44] by Dr. John Holt Rice. Until then he had preached
in the old Capitol or Mason's Hall.

---

[43]The Richmond Theatre, which burned December 26, 1811, with the
loss of seventy-two lives. The Monumental Church was erected on its site.
[44]1812; cf Richmond. First Presbyterian Church. "Proceedings of
the Celebration of the Eightieth Anniversary of Its Organization, May 1,
1892." Richmond, Va., Whittet & Shepperson [1892].

THE PRESBYTERIAN CHURCH IN NOTTOWAY COUNTY.[45]

As far back as the days of the Reverend Samuel Davies, there were in Nottoway County (then a part of Amelia County known as Nottoway Parish) several families composed wholly or in part of Presbyterians. One of these families, named Wilson, lived at "Mountain Hall," near the line of Amelia and eight or ten miles from Paineville; another family, named Tanner, lived near-by on a part of the "Mountain Hall" tract; and a third family lived some two miles away. These people attended upon the sacramental seasons at old Pole Green Church in Hanover under the Reverend Samuel Davies. Jack Stewart, "the African preacher," used to relate to Dr. Jones (the words are repeated varbatim in the record) how they used to get ready and go off on horseback in these periodical journeys. Tanner afterward attended Briery Church, and his funeral, which took place after Dr. Jones had settled at "Mountain Hall," was preached by the Reverend Drury Lacy, one of the faculty of Hampden-Sidney.

Captain Robert Smith, who resided in the fork of the Nottoway, was also a Presbyterian and attended Briery. Dr. Archibald Alexander preached at Captain Smith's house when he visited Nottoway as a missionary from Hanover Presbytery. A man named Chambers, of Captain Smith's neighborhood, died about 1790 and requested in his will that Rev. Drury Lacy should preach his funeral; so it is probable that he was a Presbyterian. With the extinction or emigration of these families, every vestige of Presbyterianism in the county was destroyed.

Many years afterward, James Henderson and Robert Fitzgerald, who had commenced the mercantile business as co-partners near the courthouse soon after the Revolution, connected themselves with the College Church of Hampden-Sidney, then under the pastoral charge of Dr. Hoge.

In 1823 or 1824 there were only three Presbyterians in the county, the venerable Mrs. James Henderson, of Nottoway Courthouse, the venerable Mrs. Shore, widow of Dr. John Shore, of Petersburg, and her son, Dr. Robert Shore, who had removed to and settled in the county a few years previously.

A church was organized at Green's Church the third Sunday in September, 1824, by Dr. J. H. Rice. Robert Shore, Philemon Holcombe and John C. Hill were elected and ordained ruling elders. Robert Shore was the first delegate from the church to Hanover Presbytery, which met at Buckingham Courthouse on May 5, 1825.

---

[45]Records of Nottoway Presbyterian Church, V. 1.

EARLY MEMBERS OF THE CHURCH.

John C. Hill, elder, dismissed and recommended to the Amelia church.

Robert Shore, elder.

Philemon Holcombe, elder, dismissed and removed to Tennessee.

Mary Henderson, died October 1829.

Rebecca M. Shore, dismissed to Petersburg church.

Ann Shore, died December 1830.

Mary L. Lampkin, dismissed to Lunenburg church.

Andrew Mc Quay, dismissed to Lunenburg church.

Amelia Mc Quay, dismissed to Lunenburg church.

Jane L. Dupuy, dismissed to Petersburg church.

John R. Robertson, removed to Alabama.

Ann E. Caruthers, removed.

Peter R. Bland, removed to Tennessee.

Richard Jones and Elizabeth Jones.

Sarah Bland, removed.

George Foster, died in 1837.

Robert Dennis.

Sarah D. Brodnax, removed to Tennessee.

Elizabeth Dennis, removed.

Harry, a colored slave.

Elizabeth B. Jones (afterward Mrs. Epes).

Frances Epes (afterward Mrs. Pryor).

Martha Campbell (afterwards Mrs. Patterson).

Ann Augusta Bland (afterwards Mrs. S. F. Cocke).

Thomas F. Ward, elder, died in 1836.

L. C. Bouldin, certificate from Petersburg church.

Old Mrs. Bland, who was an Episcopalian, and lived in the lower end of Nottoway.

Old Mr. Hawkes, who was a Methodist, and also lived in lower end of County.

INFANTS.

James Jones White, baptised April 18, 1829.

Mary Virginia Hawes, [?] baptised December 18, 1831.

William Henry Anderson, baptised 1832.

Clifford Anderson, baptised 1834.

MARRIAGE REGISTER.

Dr. R. Shore to Mrs. Martha A. Hardaway, September 11, 1827.

Miss Frances Epes to Dr. Pryor, December 21, 1832.

Miss Ann Augusta Bland to Reverend S. F. Cocke, November 5, 1833.

Dr. James Jones seems to have been one of the founders of the Presbyterian church in Nottoway. Dr. Ruffner said of this church that soon after his conversion this Dr. Jones wrote to the Reverend J. H. Rice, asking him to send him a young minister. The minister sent was the Reverend W. S. White, who, a short time before, had been licensed to preach. Dr. Jones took him into his home and gave him all possible assistance in his work. Soon afterward a church was organized and Dr. Jones was made the first elder. The church referred to by Dr. Ruffner as organized under the ministry of Dr. White, with Dr. Jones as elder, was the Presbyterian church of Nottoway, later presided over by the venerable Theodorick Pryor.

Dr. Jones said it was in 1823 or 1824 that Dr. Hoge and the Reverend J. H. Rice called at his house and spent the night. After much conversation on the state of religion in the community, they concluded that a missionary could do good among the people. Reverend Robert Roy was procured from Princeton Theological Seminary and after a year's labor, with the aid of Dr. John H. Rice, he succeeded in organizing a church in 1825.

Dr. Jones relates that the bigotry and ill-begotten zeal of the then existing denominations did much to oppose the progress of the Presbyterian church. This he attributed to ignorance and sectarian jealousy; they finally became co-workers in a movement that proved to be one of the greatest reformations that ever occurred in the history of any community.

The county was irreligious throughout its length and breadth. Periodical jockey club meetings, revelling, balls, parties, barbecues, card and drinking parties, with a host of other dissipations of the most grossly immoral tendencies, obtained everywhere; but after this reformation all this disappeared. This account was penned by Dr. Jones in 1844.

The next elder elected was Peter R. Bland, 1827.

William S. White came to Nottoway as licentiate in 1827.

August 2, 1828, Dr. James Jones elected ruling elder.

November 1828, William S. White ordained evangelist.

John C. Hill belonged to the Amelia church.

Dr. William J. Dupuy and Samuel P. Hawes were elected elders in 1830.

Thomas F. Ward and Phil B. White were elected ruling elders in 1830.

William S. White was elected pastor in 1829.

William Taylor Wills was elected elder in 1832.

William S. White's resignation was accepted at Upper Church on May 13, 1832.

Reverend Theodorick Pryor was installed pastor in November 1832; the sermon was preached by Dr. Wm. S. Plummer; the charge was delivered by Dr. Burwell.

Dr. Pryor was moderator of East Hanover Presbytery at Mt. Carmel Church, Powhatan County, in September, 1834.

Susan Moore was expelled from the Church in 1834 for "the awfully aggravated sin of uncleanness."

SUBSCRIPTIONS TO BUILD THE BRICK CHURCH.

Dr. Jones,	$200.	Colonel Isham G. (Sundy		
Captain Ben Ward,	100.	or Lundy?),	$ 50.	
Colonel John H. Knight,	100.	Colonel T. H. Epes,	50.	
Major John L. Morgan,	100.	Reverend Stephen F. Cocke,	25.	
Dr. George Fitzgerald,	100.	Major H. R. Anderson,	20.	
Ed G. Booth,	100.	Asa Oliver,	20.	
Robert Fitzgerald,	100.	Captain Nathan Ward,	20.	
B. C. Jones,	75.	Albert D. Fuqua,	25.	
Dr. Robert Shore,	50.	Dr. Austin Watkins,	20.	
William Taylor Wills,	50.	Colonel B. P. Todd,	10.	
Asa Dickinson,	50.	Dr. Josephus Carter,	10.	
		and many others.		

NEWSPAPERS.

The *Petersburg Intelligencer* was started about 1785. John Dickson, editor, died in 1814. The paper was advertised for sale in the *Richmond Enquirer*, August 10, 1914.

In 1819 the papers of Petersburg were the *Petersburg Intelligencer* and *Petersburg Republican*.

The *Richmond Enquirer* of October 5, 1814, records the death of Samuel Pleasants, editor of the *Virginia Argus*. He was public printer of Virginia at the time.

The *Richmond Enquirer*, September 14, 1814, contains the following: "We respectfully request our subscribers to avail themselves of the opportunity afforded by the members of the General Assembly to transmit the arrearages due to this office. Notes of the Virginia and Farmers' Bank will be received in payment."

The *Richmond Enquirer* in 1814 was five dollars a year in advance.

In 1819 the editor of the *Norfolk and Portsmouth Herald*, James O'Connor, died. With his death the paper suspended. About this time the Norfolk *Beacon* was started.

The organ of the Democratic Party in Petersburg and for the fourth district in 1859 was *The Press*.

In 1819, the *Petersburg Republican* was edited by Edward Pescud who married a daughter of Peter Francisco.

ROADS.

The road from Jeff's store[46] to Nottoway Courthouse was in years gone known as "Dudley's Road"; the one to Miller's old store, as the "Raccoon Track." (Information from Colonel Jeffress.[47])

---

[46]Jeffress's store.
[47]William C. Jeffress.

The Namozine Road runs from Jennings Ordinary down past Fergusonville and Dennisville.
The road crossing Lazaretta Creek just below Royall's and Jeter's Mill seat (Dyson's) shown to have been called Yarborough's Road, 1792. (Nottoway Deed Book 1, p. 275.)

MAIL ROUTES.

In 1818 there was no mail route to Jennings Ordinary. The two lines in that district were: From Richmond via Chesterfield Courthouse, Spring Hill, Colesville, Holcomb's, Dennis, Amelia Courthouse, Perkinsonville, Paineville, Deatonsville and Jamestown, to Farmville, once a week; 105 miles. The other route was from Petersburg via Dinwiddie Courthouse, Darvills, Village Hill, Morgansville, Blacks and Whites,[48] Hendersonville, Nottoway Courthouse, Hungarytown, Brydie's Store, Double Bridge, Pleasant Grove, Haleysburg, Wylliesburg, Bibbs Ferry, and Scottsburg, to Halifax Courthouse, once a week; 123 miles.

In 1819 there was a mail route from Perkinsonville by Jennings Ordinary, Millers Tavern, Moores Ordinary, and Keyes', to Charlotte Courthouse, once a week; 45 miles. The mail left Perkinsonville every Friday at 4 P. M. and arrived at Charlotte Courthouse on Saturday at 5 P. M. (Return J. Meigs, Postmaster-General).

SLAVERY.

The emancipation of negroes with a view to their settlement in Africa received the support of conservative opponents of slavery, the sympathy of the churches, and the patronage of leading men among the slave holders of the border states, 1831-1840.

Richmond Enquirer, 1854: "A Nut for Abolitionism." A bill, reported by Mr. Campbell[49] to the Virginia Senate and passed, to allow certain free negroes in Nottoway the privilege of selling themselves into slavery again. They had been manumitted by a gentleman of the county and desired to be sold to their master's next of kin. A large number of respectable citizens of Nottoway added their recommendations to the aforesaid object.

Pass issued to a slave: "Branch has leaf to pass to Francis M. Watson in Lunenburg County and return home tomorrow, March the 4 1862.

R. A. A. Watson."

Two negroes sold in 1790 at £ 25 _ _ _ on twelve months credit.

---

[48]Now Blackstone.
[49]Thomas H. Campbell, of Nottoway County.

Huguenots in Southside Virginia.

Vide Southern Literary Messenger, April 1841: Letter from Charles Campbell.

INDIANS.

Indian relics and sites are found on Sweathouse Creek; stones for grinding purposes, it is thought, on the southeastern hill. Many bowls and pots were in possession of Mr. Ely Craddock at Mannboro in 1890. Dr. Southall wants to know if Flat Creek was not called Wyanoke by the Indians.

DUELS.

THE DROMGOOLE-DUGER[50] DUEL.

Dr. Pryor related to me the Dromgoole-Duger duel. The latter kept a hotel at Lawrenceville and it was for some insulting allusion to this[51] by Dromgoole at his (Duger's) table that Duger smacked his face. Thereupon General Dromgoole's military subordinates told him that if he took the affront they would throw up their commissions and refuse to serve under him longer. Dromgoole was drinking. Tucker,[52] of Brunswick, was Duger's second. He made a mistake in giving orders, saying, "One, two, three—fire!" instead of "Fire" first. Duger was killed; Dromgoole, a poor shot, killed him accidentally, perhaps.[53]

MASON-McCARTHY DUEL.

On February 6, 1819, General A. T. Mason,[54] United States senator, was killed at Bladensburg, Md., by John McCarty. For particulars see the *Richmond Enquirer* of February 9, 1819. In the Senate, James Barbour, who was Mason's colleague, spoke in an eloquent manner, on a resolution on Mason's death. It seems that McCarty was an officer in the navy and this resolution was to authorize the President to strike his name from the rolls of the government. Barbour asserted, in his speech, that he was the author of the first law against duelling upon the statute books of Virginia.

---

[50]Also spelled Dugger.

[51]It has been stated that the allusion was to Duger's mother having been a midwife, a more likely explanation.—cf "The Public Life of George C. Dromgoole," by Edward James Woodhouse (*The John P. Branch Historical Papers, of Randolph-Macon College,* No. 4, June 1904, p. 270).

[52]Thomas Goode Tucker.

[53]cf account of duel in *William and Mary College Quarterly Historical Papers,* Vol. 1, p. 270.

[54]Armistead Thompson Mason, senator from Virginia, 1816-1817, in place of William B. Giles, resigned.

Richmond Enquirer April 7, 1854: Account from Charlottesville of the rencontre between Edgar Garth and David W. Flournoy, a student of the University on the court green. Bowie knives and pistols used. Mr. Garth shot and terribly cut. Flournoy but slightly wounded. Took place at the Monticello House.

CRIMES AND TRIALS.

Charles Knight was referred to as a Tory and harborer of Tarleton. He was at one time apprehended, together with a man named Burke, in counterfeiting money. Their apparatus was kept in a fodder stack, or at least a pen with stack of tops over and around. They were raided one night while at work in their covert by some dozen citizens of whom Captain Fowlkes was one, tied to a tree and severely whipped.

My grandmother thinks the first white man hung in Nottoway was named Wicks (or Weeks), who killed old Mr. Hood, a blacksmith, at or near the courthouse about 1824. She attended the hanging, and a thousand or more people were present.[55]

Peter Kendal, tried in 1809 for the murder of his wife, lived at Newman's Old Field between Mrs. Newman's and Fowlkes's. He was cleared on the evidence of Dyce Hardaway, a woman living in the house.

TRIAL OF THOMAS WELLS.

On May 29, 1816, Captain Thomas Wells, a militia officer, a member of the House of Delegates at the time, and owner and keeper of a tavern at the court house, shot and dangerously wounded Peter Randolph, judge of the Fifth Circuit of the Superior Court, and Colonel William C. Greenhill, commander of the militia regiment of Nottoway. He shot them after sunset for entering his yard. They both fell in the open space north of the courthouse square, in front of the tavern, which stood where Fuqua's Tavern stood, and may have been in part the same. Judge Randolph was carried to William Verser's, somewhere between the present Dean's store and Goodwyn's house, where he lay for six weeks. Colonel Greenhill, after falling, got up and walked to the tavern of C. D. George (Dr. B. B. Jackson's house).

The *Richmond Enquirer* of June 1, 1816, gives an account of this affair. This paper on June 5 printed an extract from

---

[55] A hanging in that time and section was an event of importance which gave opportunity for a public gathering. Many of those who attended, especially ladies, were not spectators of the hanging itself. It is said that they attended as a protest against crime and to uphold the laws.

a letter of Dr. James Jones to a gentleman in Richmond, giving a brief diagnosis of Judge Randolph's condition. Dr. Jones was the attending physician. On June 10, this paper printed a letter from Thomas Wells explaining in detail his view of the tragedy, the actual shooting and attendant circumstances. He said that the judge fell fourteen yards from his door and that when he came from the garden to the house he found the servant holding three horses (two of Judge Randolph's and one of Colonel Greenhill's) within seventeen yards of his piazza and in front of his dining-room door. The trial was held before the county court (sitting as an examining court only) at the August term, 1816. The commonwealth was represented by William Yates, commonwealth's attorney, and Peter Bland; the defense by Major James Robertson, State senator, and Edward Bland. The trial lasted several days and the prisoner was discharged.

Thomas Wells was subsequently hung for the murder of Captain Perry in Georgia. The *Petersburg Republican* of November 14, 1820, contains in full the sentence passed upon him, Judge Clayton presiding.

THE MUIR MURDER.

The trial of William Dandridge Epes for the murder of Francis Adolphus Muir is given in a pamphlet published by J. M. H. Brunet, 1849.[56]

BACON-HARDAWAY AFFAIR.

This affair occurred some time in July, 1818. A short notice of it is in the *Richmond Enquirer* of July 21, 1818; an editorial on it is in an earlier issue of the same month. This paper stated, on October 13, 1818, that "the case has caused considerable interest throughout the globe."

Colonel William C. Greenhill and Colonel Tyree G. Bacon were prominent citizens of Nottoway. Greenhill lived in the lower end of the county, I think, a place called "Greenhill" on Cellar Creek. He was a man of education.

Colonel Greenhill and Colonel Bacon, who had been a delegate in the Legislature, had some personal or political differences, it seems. Randolph, when elected judge of the General Court about 1812, was colonel of the militia regiment and Bacon was the major. To the vacancy Greenhill, a cousin of Randolph, was elected by the officers of the regiment, being pro-

---

[56]"Trial of William Dandridge Epes, for the Murder of Francis Adolphus Muir, Dinwiddie County, Virginia . . ." Petersburg, Va., J. M. H. Brunet, 1849. 76 p.
Mr. Watson had compiled a general account of this case, taken from the above work; it is not reproduced here.

moted over the head of Bacon. This was probably the beginning of the feud which led to the unfortunate affair.

Colonel Bacon's son, Dr. Bacon, was at the time living in Charlotte or Mecklenburg county. Dr. John S. Hardaway bore a challenge of some sort to Colonel Bacon for Colonel Greenhill, and it was this that gave offense to Dr. Bacon. They met at Nottoway court afterwards and got into a stabbing match, in which Hardaway was killed.

The trial of Dr. Bacon for the murder of Dr. Hardaway occurred in the autumn of 1818 at Nottoway Court House. The Nottoway records are as follows:

Superior Court Order Book, No. 1.

At a Superior Court held at Nottoway Court House on the 8th of September 1818, Peter Randolph, Esq., Judge, a Grand Jury, of which James Dupuy was Foreman, presented Wm. C. Greenhill and Tyree G. Bacon and Wm. C. Greenhill and Roland Ward for fighting each other at Nottoway Court House on June 4th last, on information of Robt. Dickinson and Joseph B. Ingram. An indictment was presented against Geo. S. G. Bacon for the murder of John S. Hardaway—a true bill.

George S. G. Bacon, who stands bound by a recog. entered into before an examining court, held for the County of Nottoway to appear this day to abide trial for murder of Dr. Hardaway, appeared in discharge of his recog. and on motion of Com. Atty. was committed to jail.

Sept. 29th.—George S. G. Bacon, late of the County of Nottoway and parish of Nottoway in county aforesaid, who stands indicted of the murder of John S. Hardaway, was led to the Bar in custody of the Jailer, etc., whereupon came the Jury, John Robertson, Richard Ligon, Daniel Verser, Samuel Dunnavant, William Dillon, Henry Jennings, William Dunnavant, William Fowlkes, Micajah Jennings, John Overstreet, Hampton Waller and Nathan Depriest, partly heard evidence and adjourned.

The case occupied the day, September 30, and on October 1, the jury brought in a verdict of "not guilty."

PETITION TO THE GENERAL ASSEMBLY OF VIRGINIA FOR PAY.

A petition of James Borum, constable for Nottoway, and Jos. H. Fowlkes, James Jackson, Basset Watson, Jennings Robertson, William Vaughan, Polaski B. Bell, Henry H. Cook, Peter Ellington, Lygnol [?] Moore and Peter R. Bland, representing that about the month of April 1810, by virtue of a warrant issued by a justice of the peace in Nottoway, they were employed three days and two nights in Prince Edward County in apprehending and bringing to Nottoway Jos. Watson and others charged with forcible entry, or housebreaking, in Nottoway, for which service they ask the Legislature pay, as Nottoway refuses allowance.

INCIDENTS OF THE REVOLUTION AND WAR OF 1812.

TARLETON'S RAID.

Cornwallis's order to Lieutenant-Colonel Tarleton, dated Cobham, July 8, 1781, directed him to set out the next day on his raid of Southside Virginia. The force consisted of "the corps of cavalry and mounted infantry under your command" and the destination was "Prince Edward Courthouse, and from thence to New London in Bedford County." The object was the destruction of military stores, to cripple the subsistence of Greene's army in Carolina. The order set forth, "all public stores of corn and provisions are to be burned, and if there should be a quantity of provisions or corn collected at a private house . . . destroy it, leaving enough for the support of the family," etc.; "all persons of consequence, civil or military, brought to me before they are paroled."

Tarleton's force consisted of the British Legion and eighty mounted infantry (the returns of the surrender at Yorktown show 241 men in the Legion). A detachment was left at Suffolk to receive him on his return; also to intercept any American light troops on the way northward from Carolina, or any British prisoners. The command left Cobham on July 9 and made long movements in the mornings and evenings, thus avoiding heat and darkness. The troops soon reached Petersburg and advanced to Prince Edward Courthouse, and from there toward the Dan River. The stores, which were the principal object of the expedition, had been sent from Prince Edward and all that country to Hillsboro and Greene's army about a month before. Tarleton halted two days in Bedford. He returned by a different route, completing an expedition of 400 miles in fifteen days, and rejoined the troops at Suffolk.[57]

Tarleton's dragoons captured old James Cooke (Fred Cooke's father) at Jennings Ordinary. He lived there at the time and was perhaps the first resident of the Ordinary. A dragoon made Cooke mount behind him on the horse and carried him to Tarleton's headquarters, which were then at the home of old Charles Knight, who lived at Burkeville or a little above (at Billy Horner's, it is thought). On the way, the soldier took Cooke's silver shoe and knee buckles. At headquarters, Tarleton made the man restore them and sent Cooke home. The soldier, however, waylaid him on the return and got the buckles, anyhow.

[57]The foregoing information is found in Tarleton, Sir Banastre, "A History of the Campaigns of 1780 & 1781, in the Southern Provinces of North America." London, 1787, p. 358-359.

Mrs. Ward (wife of Col. Ben Ward) was captured just above Burkeville in her carriage, endeavoring to escape to relatives in Charlotte with her fine equipage and personal effects. She was pillaged by some dragoons. Captain Fowlkes's brother witnessed the act from a tree top near by. On leaving the Ordinary, after deploying toward what is now Jetersville, they flushed Colonel William Craddock (my great-great-great grandfather maternally). He lived near, if not upon, Dr. George Scott's place. The British pursued him from his home in hot haste until he was forced to take shelter, with his horse, in a barn on the road to Jetersville. Here the troops passed him, but he was fearful lest his horse should neigh to those passing and so reveal his presence. He escaped. The British encountered Peter Francisco at "West Creek."[58] They burned Daniel Jones's mill at "Mount Airy" on West Creek and old Amelia Courthouse, together with part or all the records, I think.[59] They also burned a granary on the Richmond road near Mannboro. Charred wheat from it is still preserved, and some, I understand, was exhibited at the Philadelphia Centennial Exposition in 1876. The British followed the Namozine road toward Petersburg and Chesterfield Courthouse. house.

My grandmother thinks Tarleton behaved, in the main, generously towards the inhabitants during the raid. He visited Captain Jo Fowlkes's mother, a widow, who lived in Prince Edward a few miles above old Burkeville, and turned a chair down for a pillow and lay on the floor to rest. He set guards to watch and did not allow anything to be molested. He would always rebuke his men for depredations and in many instances showed a kind spirit.

Journal of the Virginia House of Delegates.

1793, p. 36, names petition of James Dupuy, Jr., asking compensation for loss of horse, etc., stating that during the invasion of Cornwallis he had commanded a volunteer company of horse and been taken prisoner, etc.

Idem., 1797, page 30: Petition of Thos. Griffin Peachy of Amelia for relief for house (dwelling and store) at Rocky Run in Amelia, destroyed by Tarleton, July 12th, 1781. 600 or 700 bushels of wheat destroyed—public property.

Petition of Daniel Jones for building of mill and granary destroyed by Tarleton, 1781.

WAR OF 1812.

In the War of 1812, many men of Amelia were attached to the First Regiment.

---

[58]The home of Benjamin Ward.
[59]No evidence has been found of any such destruction at the court-

The *Richmond Enquirer* of Oct. 20, 1814, printed Judge Peter Randolph's charge to the grand jury of Powhatan (Thomas Miller, foreman) in which he made an appeal for the prosecution of the War.

An editorial in the *Richmond Enquirer*, Sept. 3, 1814, states that the army around Richmond for the defence of the capital was assuming excellent organization. 1st and 4th brigades were present. Maj. Maurice, of Norfolk, was Adj. Genl.; C. W. Gooch, Deputy Adj. Genl.; Maj. C. Fenton Mercer, Inspector Genl.; Dr. James Jones, Hospital Surgeon Genl.; Lt. Col. Cargill, Q. Master Genl. Gov's Staff Aids: B. W. Leigh, Phil. N. Nicholas, and Hugh Nelson. Col. T. M. Randolph was also organizing an independent *élite* corps.

Washington had fallen, it seems, already. Volunteers from all over the Commonwealth rushed to defend the city. A fine corps of horse under Capt. Carr, of Albemarle, Capt. Archer, of Powhatan, Lieut. H. Watkins, from Prince Edward, and Capts. Jeter and Tanner (Towns),[60] from Amelia.

Mr. Madison in view of the condition of the country called Congress to meet Sept. 19, 1814. Peterson Goodwin was then a member from the Dinwiddie district.

CIVIL WAR.[61]

HISTORIC HOMES AND PLACES.

AMELIA COUNTY.

"Dykeland" on Flat Creek, the home of Lewis E. Harvie; "Farm Hill," home of Dr. Richard F. Taylor; "Wigwam," Governor Giles's home.

"Clay Hill." John Randolph used to be an intimate visitor at this mansion. He always stopped there on his way to the capital, also stopping with Judge Farrar's grandfather near Deatonville. Mrs. Farrar, he declared, cooked the best biscuit on the continent. He would come there from "Bizarre" and go to "Clay Hill" the next night.

Mrs. Farrar (Judge Farrar's mother) kept a female school for many years at his present residence.

William J. Barksdale lived at "Clay Hill," where he died shortly prior to the war, about 1860. A writer in the *Richmond Enquirer* of that date says that he was more distinguished looking than any man he had ever seen except Henry Clay. On the boulevards of Paris he always attracted attention.

---

[60]The *Richmond Enquirer* of this date has it "Towns."
[61]Judge Watson's notes contain a roll of Company (Troop) E, Third Va. Cavalry, in Civil War, showing names of men from Nottoway Co. This information, with additional data, is available in Confederate records in Virginia State Library and is not reproduced here.

Paineville or Painesville, Amelia County.

Paineville is the site of old Union Church. That was one of the finest congregations in Virginia in its hey-day. Old Dr. Phil Southall said Paineville was named for a man who lived at Paineville years since.

Alexander Campbell and Dr. Thomas (founder of the Thomasites) [62] had a great and protracted debate here on the virtue of their respective creeds. Campbell had first inducted Thomas into his faith and liked his intelligence; but subsequently Thomas split off, and it was on this that Campbell came back to argue at Paineville. Campbell is said to have completely crushed Thomas.

Thomas published his denominational paper at Paineville, so Dr. Joseph Southall says.

In Grandpa Horner's boyhood days, the tavern at Paineville was kept by a Mr. Jeter. A race-track was here. It was a muster point also for the militia and one of the two voting places in Amelia, the courthouse being the other. Card tables were kept upstairs in the hotel. Brookin Enroughty shot Hardaway, his brother-in-law, at Rodophil near here. Another man had been killed at Rodophil years before.

The old house (presumably the Paine Club House) was very old, but standing in Grandpa Horner's recollection. It was a good frame, two-story, long house and was called, he thought, the old Masons' Hall. No Masons, though, had ever met there in his day, he said.

Paineville was once a great place for Fourth of July celebrations. Grandpa Horner relates that two men were wounded here once by the discharge of a cannon, and one died subsequently from the effects.

The speakings on such occasions would be held in Union Church.

Paine Club: Dr. Pryor says it was organized by an Irish refugee named Burke; that Governor Giles was a member, but never heard that Dr. Jones was, nor heard him speak of it.

Fergussonville.

The old people called Fergussonville "Fargussez." Clerk Epes told me when he was a boy the people sometimes spoke of it as "Robert Jennings's Store." This man [Robert Jennings] went South.

Jetersville, Amelia County.

Grandma Eliza [63] says in her childhood she was in the habit of visiting this place, which then had no such name. Colonel

---

[62] John Thomas, founder of the sect of Christadelphians or Thomasites.
[63] Great-grandmother, Mrs. Eliza Robertson.

Jeter lived there and probably kept a tavern. Grandma stayed with her Uncle Abram Jackson, who was a store-keeper. Old Tom Perkinson (father of Capt. John E. Perkinson) also kept store here. Perhaps place was then called Perkinson's. According to tradition Jetersville was named for "Black Jack" Jeter, John Jeter, son of Rodophil Jeter. Dr. William J. Holcombe (M.D.), father of James P. Holcombe, lived and died near Jetersville and was buried near Dr. Joseph Bass Anderson's.

Old Dr. Meigs,[64] of Philadelphia, Mrs. Royall says, was born here, too. Dr. William Thomas Warriner says so too.

Richmond Enquirer, July 17, 1816: Advertisement of Tilman E. Jeter for boarders at "Mill Grove" very convenient to the mineral Springs in Amelia.

Richmond Enquirer, May 12, 1848: Amelia Springs will be opened 1st July for visitors and can accommodate 75 or 100 persons. Terms—Board: Single meal 50c; $1.25 per day; $6.00 per week; $20.00 per month. Children and servants half price. Horses 50 cents per day.—Thomas C. Willson.

LUNENBURG COUNTY.

Hungary Town.

In old times, some Hungarians settled on the site of Hungary Town and that is how the name originated.[65] Old Bob Scott, father of Ned, built the house there. Ned Scott married —————— Chambers.

David J. Williams went security for Bob Scott, a brother Methodist, who pleaded usury on him, and David afterwards used to say that he was as good a Methodist as ever cracked a whip until Bob Scott cheated him out of $1,000. (As given me by R. W. Oliver, July 23, 1915.)

NOTTOWAY COUNTY.

Barebones.[66]

"Your letter was most welcome and more especially that it called me back to the Namozine Road and put me off at Ellett's. Before the woods were cut, this place, "Barebones," on the south side at the falls of the creek, was one of the most sequestered and picturesque spots in our county. There was a short time back, and may be still, if the "d— saw mills" have had any heart left, a beech tree on the north bank bearing in plain letters an

---

[64]Possibly Dr. Charles Delucena Meigs or Dr. J. A. Meigs both at one time professors in the Jefferson Medical College, Philadelphia.

[65]Spelled also as Hungrytown in early post office directories.

[66]From a letter written by Mr. Watson, August 6, 1916, to Mr. Thornton Jeffress, Rochester, N. Y.

inscription cut by my step-grandfather, Horner, in 1853. The isolation of Barebones and the silence of its woods attracted me in early life and the place always seemed to me to have a mystic meaning, which I could not unravel. I have but few sentimental associations with it. It is true I have raised many a fox from its cover,—now and then—not often—I have collected about 2-½ barrels of nubbins from its soil,—the annual rent of "free niggers." But I can't let Barebones go without telling you a curious speculation I drifted into respecting this place. Some time back I saw in a Richmond bookstore a little book styled 'The True Nancy Hanks,' as well as I remember by Caroline Hitchcock of New York. She was a lady of means connected with the Hanks family and sorely grieved at the damage tradition had done the reputation of the mother of Lincoln; and resolved to clear up the record of this lady of the wilderness. Turning its pages I came across the statement that Nancy Hanks was born in Amelia County and emigrated with her father to Kentucky in 1785. The next time I went to Amelia Court House, I got the old deed books and looked up her father's moderate realty holdings. I had not the time to make an exhaustive examination, but the only land owned by him seemed to be immediately on Barebone Creek (then Amelia now Nottoway) and, as far as I could see without retracing the line, in the vicinity of Ham's and Ellett's. If personal association may invest material things with spiritual life, why may it not be that the memory of Nancy Hanks—the vicissitudes of fortune which came to her after life and to that of her son—is the spirit which still broods over the wild waste of Barebones?"[67]

"Glenmore" in Nottoway County owned (1906) by Landon P. Jones; it was sold to him from the estate of my father (Meredith Watson) by court in suit, Leath and others *vs.* Watson, adm. It was the old seat of the Watsons in Nottoway. Since 1860 there have lived at "Glenmore" Captain Giles A. Miller, James Asa Eggleston, Dr. William H. Robertson and John Thursfield (an Englishman).

"Mountain Hall" is near the line of Amelia, eight or ten miles from Paineville.

Jones's Mill, Nottoway County: Crawley Fitzgerald says Jones's Mill, southeast of Blackstone, was in old times Lallard's Mill.

---

[67]Mr. Watson had preserved a newspaper clipping, dated Nottoway Court House, Feb. 10, 1891, showing Abram Hanks as one whose deposition was to be taken in a case between Letty Jenkins and Pryor Jenkins. Presumably he was interested in the survival of the name Hanks in Nottoway.

BOUNDARIES.

AMELIA COUNTY.

At a Quarterly Court held for Amelia County on Thursday the 26th day of March 1789, present: Edmund Booker, Henry Anderson, Peter Lamkin, and Edmund Booker, Jr., Gentlemen. Peter Randolph, Richard Jones, William C. Craddock, and Richard Ogebly (Ogilby is the name) gentlemen, or any two of them (one being from each Parish) are appointed Commissioners to attend the County Surveyor (or in case he cannot attend, any other surveyor that may be approved of by the said Commissioners) in running the dividing line between Amelia Co. and Nottoway Co., and for them to employ such necessary [help?] that may be wanting and the Commissioners to make their report to the Court of Amelia and the Court of Nottoway.

April 24th, 1789, at a Court, the report of the Commissioners was made and ordered to be recorded. At same Court, ordered that William Cross Craddock be paid £2.20 for expenses in running the dividing line between the county of Amelia and Nottoway; Peter Randolph 8s. 3d.; Richard Jones £1.16.10; To Joseph Woodson, John Blankenship and James Craddock, £2.8.0 for eight days service as chain bearers at 6s per day; John Craddock £2.8 [?] for provider of rations.

To John Dejernatt for running the county line, £40.7½ and for him to account to amount of 76 or sixteenth part to Sherwood Walton for use of the Colage.[68] Order Book 1788-91, p. 145-6.

NOTTOWAY.

The eastern boundary of Nottoway was defined by an act of the House of Burgesses in 1734, the purpose of which was to divide the then county of Prince George in two and to fix the limits of the new county of Amelia. The act was to take effect in 1735. (Hening, "Statutes at Large," Vol. 4, page 467.)

The line fixed as the east boundary of Amelia (which has since become that for Nottoway as far as that county extends) begins "at the mouth of Namozain Creek, up the same to the main or John Hamlin's fork of the said creek; thence up the south or the lowest branch thereof to White Oak Hunting Path; and thence by a south course to strike Nottoway River."

The west line of Nottoway was defined by an act of the House of Burgesses separating Prince Edward from Amelia in 1753 (Hening, "Statutes at Large," Vol. 6, p. 379) and was

---

[68]Probably refers to fees required of surveyors to be paid to William and Mary College. Surveyors at that time were commissioned by the Governor on recommendation of the college.

"to run from Ward's Ford on Appomattox River to the mouth of Snail's Creek on Nottoway River."

The northern county line was defined by an act of the House of Delegates, 1788, to take effect, 1789, (Hening, Vol. 12, p. 723) separating Nottoway from Amelia and describing the former as "all that part of said county (Amelia) lying south of a line to begin at a place called Well's bridge on Namozene Creek, which divides said county from the county of Dinwiddie, thence running through the county of Amelia so as to strike the line of Prince Edward County, five miles west of a place called Ward's Ford on Appomattox River," etc.

By a subsequent act, 1792 (Hening, Vol. 13, p. 561), this line was changed and it was enacted "that the county line shall in the future be considered as the line of separation of said parishes (Raleigh and Nottoway)."

N. B. It will be seen that you will have to get the act defining Raleigh and Nottoway Parishes (somewhere in Hening between 1734 and 1776) to ascertain the exact line for Amelia and Nottoway. I have no reference to this in my papers.[69]

COUNTY RECORDS.

AMELIA COUNTY.

Amelia County Court Order Book, No. 1.

1735: Charles Irby one of the justices. Stephen Dewey qualified as attorney. Abraham Burton appointed surveyor of the road from Flatt Creek to Sappony Ford and Deep Creek lower bridge. William Green surveyor ye aforesaid bridge to Namozeen Road. John Ferguson surveyor of the road from Flatt Creek and down Anderson's Road. Lewis Tanner ordered to clear road from the bridge below Mrs. Anderson's quarter to Buckskin. Robert Tucker surveyor of that road from Namozine Bridge to Sweat House Creek. John Nance appointed surveyor from Butterwood to the coming in of the race paths near Mr. Irby's. Christopher Robertson surveyor from Bagley's order [ordinary?] to Captain Stark's quarter. Francis Man surveyor of road across Beaverpond branch into Anderson's Road. Christopher Hinton surveyor road over the Sweathouse Creek below Abraham Jones's Quarter into the Main Road. David Lyles surveyor of a bridle way from the Rattle Snake ford to the church on Flatt Creek. William Clark surveyor of road from West Creek to the fork of the road near Captain Peter Jones's quarter. William Crawley surveyor from Captain Peter Jones's fork where Clark lives off to Wintercomake. William Watson, Gent., county surveyor. Robert Taylor surveyor from Mrs. Anderson's Bridge to Deep Creek Bridge. John Benson

---

[69]Not given in Hening's "Statutes at Large"; cf Meade, "Old Churches, Ministers and Families of Virginia" (1861) V. 2, p. 23.

appointed to clear a bridle way from West Creek to the Court House. John Winingham appointed to clear a bridle way from West Creek to the Chapell on Nottoway. Row surveyor from Dabney's to the Cuttbanks. Edmund Franklin surveyor of the road from the bent creek into Booker's Road. James Anderson appointed surveyor of the highways where Christopher Robertson was surveyor. George Bagbey (or Bagley) surveyor of the highways from the Celler to Dandys Race paths.

County Levy: Robert Bolling, Gent., for running the line between Prince George and this county, 1196 (I don't know whether tobacco or what); Richard Jones for 2 old wolfs 320; William Moses 5 young wolfs 400; other wolfs 960—1680; 588 tithables @ 16 per poll (lbs. of tobacco), 9408.

1736: Samuel Pincham surveyor of the Road from Flatt Creek to Smax Creek in room of Abraham Burton (deceased). James Clark licensed to keep ordinary near Namozine. Thomas Bevill licensed to keep ordinary. John Ferguson surveyor of the road·from Flatt Creek to Court House. Negro slave returned to Isham Epes, of Prince George. Ferry established on Appomattox to be kept by Thomas Bevill. John Burton, sheriff. Three thousand four hundred and thirty allowed in bounty for twenty-nine wolf heads. Tithables, 649 at twelve pounds of tobacco per head.

1737: Richard Booker to contract for a boat to be kept by Thomas Bevill, who is to set over [free] all persons inhabiting this county and all others having tithables therein and charge others, four pence for man and horse, eight pence for a cart, four pence for chair to two wheel chaise. Charles Burkes surveyor of a Road to be cleared from the Court House to Anderson's Road near the race paths, etc. Robert Vaughan surveyor of Road to be cleared to Thomas Bottom's on West Creek to the Old Ponds of Flatt Creek along or near the Old Ridge Path. William Echols surveyor of road to be cleared from the White Oak on Flatt Creek to John Hurt's near the fork of Stock's Creek. John Dawson surveyor of road to be cleared from Flatt Creek to or near the fork of Saylor's Creek. Thomas Bevill, ordinary license renewed. Samuel Jordan is appointed surveyor of the Nottoway Road in room of John Nance and he is ordered to clear and keep same in repair. Charles Irby, gent., appointed to take list of tithables from Deep Creek downwards the extent of the county. Henry Anderson, gent., to take list between Deep and Flatt creeks. John Dawson, gent., to take list from Flatt Creek to the extent of the county upwards. Upon petition, John and Thomas Jackson, Harper and others, leave is given them "to clear a road from the county line between Tomahitton and the Birchen Swamps to the Chappel on Nottoway the most convenient way, etc. Lawrence Brown and Field Jefferson allowed to condemn one acre land on north side West Creek, belonging to Thos. Tabb, gent., for a mill, Brown and Jefferson owning on opposite side. William Marshall surveyor of the High Waies from Deep Creek to Knibbs Creek to clear the same and keep in repair. Samuel Hudson surveyor of the High Waies from Craddock's on Flatt Creek to Bush River, clear and keep the same in repair. Thomas Covington surveyor of the High Waies from Tanner's to Craddock's—clear, etc. County levy for bounty on thirty-six wolfe heads. Thomas Bevill for keeping the Ferry, 520 (pounds tobacco, I reckon). Leave granted to clear a road from the county line between Tomahitton and the Burchen Swamp to the chappell on Nottoway. Henry Robertson petitioned for condemnation of 1 acre on Little Nottoway, property of William Yarbro, for a mill. 759 Tithables at eighteen per poll (pounds of tobacco per poll), 13662.

    1738: Clement Read qualified attorney. Henry Robertson's petition for one acre for a mill on Little Nottoway belonging to William Yarbro, and the latter summoned. William Baldwin licensed to keep Ordinary at Court House. Richard Bowker, gent., to clear a road from his mill to Flatt Creek bridge. County levy for twenty-three wolves. 870 tithables at ten pounds tobacco per poll. On motion Joseph Morton, ordered that road be cleared from George Walker's plantation to Buffalo River—to be cleared by "the people above Bush River together with Joseph Morton their surveyor." Ordered that Mr. Walker's people clear from said Walker's plantation into the road from Col. Randolph's Quarters so down as far as before appointed but not above where Walker's Road runs into Col. Randolph's.

    1739: Charles Irby qualified as sheriff. William Hudson surveyor of West Creek Road in place of William Clarke. John Leverett appointed surveyor of the road from Letbetter's low grounds on Nottoway River the nearest way to Butterwood road. Edward Booker, gent., to take tithables between Deep and Flatt creeks. Francis Anderson, gent., to take tithables above Flatt Creek. William Watson, gent., to take tithables below Deep Creek. Joseph Morton, Jr., appointed to mark out and clear a road from Colonel Richard Randolph's Quarter to the ridge which divides the county from Brunswick, the nearest and best way, etc. Richard Jones, gent., appointed to meet Commissioner from Prince George and agree to let a bridge over Namozain Creek, and reported that it had been let to Daniel Coleman. Petition of sundry inhabitants in this county for a ferry at the Cut banks—mouth Flatt Creek. Matthew Talbot surveyor, road from Flatt Creek to the Church, and that it be cleared soon as convenient. William Yarbro appointed surveyor of a road to be cleared from the head of James Anderson's road to the head of Cold Water Run upon the ridge between Nottoway River and the Lazaretta Creek. The persons to do the same, Henry Yarbro, Christopher Robertson, Jr., Edward Robertson, Robert Rowland and Richard Hix. Edward Booker, gent., surveyor of road to be cleared most convenient way from his house to the

Church. John Burton appointed to continue his road from Flatt Creek to the Court House. Henry Anderson surveyor of the road in place of William Marshall. Ordered that a road be cleared from Booker's Mill into Lyle's road to the Court House. County levy, Nov. 1739: 3710 (lbs. tobacco, I reckon) for wolf heads. 800 to Thomas Bevill for keeping Ferry. 3786 levied to build a bridge over Appomattox River. 943 tithables at twenty-two pounds tobacco per head.

1740: Richard Jones proved his importation in order to take up land, and that he came from Bristoll in 1732. Ordered that road whereon Arthur Leigh is surveyor be continued to Nottoway River and that Mr. Thomas's hands be employed thereon and that the road whereon Leverett is surveyor be neglected. A petition, Thomas Foster and others, that road from the Church to Stock's Creek may be continued to Sandy Creek, filed, and Commissioners appointed. Abraham Cocke, gent., to take list of tithables below Deep Creek. Thomas Tabb, gent., to take list of tithables between Deep and Flatt creeks. John Burton, gent., to take list of tithables above Flatt Creek. Ordered that Mr. Walker's road be cleared from Saylor's Creek to Crawford's and from thence into Burton's Road to Court House. Petition for bridge over Appomattox where road is already cleared at or near Jenneytoe. Richard Booker and Joseph Scott appointed to confer with Goochland Court. Arthur Leigh appointed to clear a road as Abraham Cock and Samuel Jordan shall direct from Mr. Cock's Mill into the Church road, the same people employed as on the road Leigh was before surveyor of. Richard Booker, Thomas Tabb and Joseph Scott, gents., appointed Commissioners with Goochland Commissioners to let the bridge over Appomattox at Jenytoe. John Thomas appointed to clear a road from Jordan's Bridge the best way into Mr. Cock's Road; the persons to be employed thereon, Thomas and James Anderson, John Thomas, Thomas Taylor and all other male tithables. Matthew Cabiness surveyor of a road to be cleared from James Anderson's road into Jordan's road and so to Nottoway Chapell. Stephen Dewey, attorney for King.

County levy: Edward Booker, gent., his allowance as Burgess, 1900; Richard Jones, gent., his allowance as Burgess, 1845; Fifteen wolves; Thomas Bevill, for keeping Ferry, 1000; 1094 tithables at twenty-one lbs. tobacco per head. Total levy 23,394.

1741: John Burton, gent., fined for not keeping in repair road from Stock's Creek to Sandy Creek. William Barnes, surveyor of the road from Stock's Creek to Saylor's Creek, and the hands above Stock's Creek formerly employed on Burton's Road to assist. Henry Tartoe (?) surveyor road from Stock's Creek to the Court House—all hands below Stock's Creek to assist. Ordered that the bridle way from Robert Vaughan's to the Court House be kept open where the path now is. Commissioners report that Goochland Court refuse to join in building bridge at

Jennytoe. Daniel Coleman, surveyor of road from Captain Jones's Quarter to Wintercomake in room of Robert Coleman. William Jackson surveyor of the road in place of John Leverett. On petition, Samuel Jordan, that the bridge near Nottoway formerly built by him being on a public road and out of repair, etc., ordered that Charles Irby let it to bidder, etc. Henry Anderson surveyor from Anderson's Road into Mr. Booker's Road to the River Bridge and naming persons, etc. Lodwick Tanner appointed surveyor of road to be cleared from Granger's path into the road to the Bridge and hands named, etc. Robert Ferguson surveyor of the road from the Harricane into Jordan's Road in the room of Jackson. Ordered a road to be cleared from a little below John Winn's into Fisher's cart path and from there to Jordan's Bridge.

County levy: 16 wolf heads; 1185 tithables at fifteen lbs. tobacco per head.

1742: George Avery surveyor of the road from Ward's Quarter into Anderson's Road; Ward's, Mrs. Anderson's and Wilkerson's hands to do the same. Thomas Covington to clear the road from Ward's Quarter to the foot of the hills the other side Flatt Creek at Craddock's Bridge. Petition for a bridge over Appomattox at Captain Hudson's Quarter where David Lyle lately dwelt, granted, and Commissioners appointed to consult Goochland. Petition, William Westbrook, to erect mill on Lee's Creek (opposite land owned by Richard Dennis). Samuel Jordan appointed surveyor of the road from Nottoway Chapel to Prince George County Line; John Thomas from Jordan's Branch to Cock's Road; Arthur Leigh from Nottoway Road to the fork of Nottoway; William Evans from Jordan's Bridge to Great Nottoway; Charles Irby from his house to West Creek; John Benson from West Creek to the Court House; William Jackson from Great Nottoway to the county line of Prince George and the Church Road up to the Harry Cain; Robert Ferguson from the Harricane to the Chappell; James Anderson from Dandy's Race Paths to Captain Starke's new Quarter; William Yarbro up to the ridge of Nottoway; George Bagley from Spinner's to Dandy's Race Paths; Major Richard Jones from Spinner's to Wintercomake; Daniel Coleman from Wintercomake to Namozain Bridge; William Dunifant from Knibb's Creek to the bridge over Appomattox River; Thomas Brooks from Anderson's Road down to bridge over the River; Robert Ferguson from Comb's Bridge over Flatt Creek to Court House; Samuel Cobbs from fork Burton's Road to Knibb's Creek; Henry Anderson from Knibb's Creek to Mrs. Anderson's Bridge [?] and to Booker's Road. Christopher Robertson, old and infirm and hardly able to support himself, made levy free. Bathol. Archer surveyor of road to be cleared from Appomattox River near Colonel Richard Randolph's Quarter up to Hill's Fork on Vaughan's Creek. Henry Dawson surveyor of road to be cleared from Echols Road on Stock's Creek up to the ridge at fork of Sandy Creek. Bridge ordered to be let over Deep Creek at Green's and that a road be cleared from said bridge into the main road the best way to Burton's Bridge, and Abraham Green, gent., appointed surveyor of same. Ordered Edward Robertson and Robert Rowland be paid for building bridge over Deep Creek at Peter Jones's Quarter. Frederick Ford surveyor bridle road from Nottoway Road to Rocky Run Chappell. John Childrey surveyor from Saylor's to Sandy Creek. County levy: 1120 pounds tobacco for wolf heads at 140 pounds each. 1394 tithes at nine pounds tobacco per head.

1743: Christopher Hinton surveyor of a road from said Hinton's into the main road below Rocky Run Chappell. Thomas Markham surveyor from Lyle's Ford in room Thomas Burton. Abraham Cock, gent., surveyor of the road from John Thomas's to the bridge from Nottoway and to the ridge path near the race paths and has agreed it shall be through the field by his peach orchard,—the persons to clear are Henry and William Batts, Edward Cox, Laugh. [?] Flyn, William Cross and said Cox's male tithables. Arthur Leigh surveyor from Thomas's to Main Nottoway; the same hands as before excepting those on Cock's and others convenient. Commissioners report that a bridge from William Booker's [?] land in this county to George Williamson's land in Goochland near Jennytoe is the most convenient place for a bridge above Flatt Creek and were authorized to confer with Goochland. Ordered a road to be cleared from the Ridge Road to the place where it is believed a bridge will be built at Bass's. John Nash, gent., appointed surveyor of a road from Bush River Branch across Saylor's Creek into Walker's Road. William Marshall surveyor from the Lawyer's Path into Anderson's Road; the persons employed, Roger, Davis, and Stephen Neale, Josiah Tatum, Robert Thompson, Peter Thompson, John Osborne, William Clarke, William Hatchett, John Pride, William Marshall and Hugh Chambers. Josiah Motley with his gang is ordered to clear a bridle way out of Bush River Road above Mr. Read's into Nottoway Road. Anthony Griffin surveyor of the road from Watson's musterfield along the ridge to the first branch of Snale's Creek; the persons employed, Sell Johnson, Henry Johnson, Daniel Dejarnett and Captain Watson. Abraham Green surveyor from the fork of Booker's Road to lower bridge over Appomattox, the persons employed, Francis, Robert and Samuel Mann, Samuel Morgan, Thomas Reams, John Perdue, Abraham Burton, Essex and Thomas and Daniel Bevill, Mr. Botts, Ralph Perkinson and Samuel Pitchford—and they are also to clear a road from Deep Creek Bridge to the River Bridge as near Burton's and Bevill's lines as possible. John Blanchett surveyor of the road from Booker's Fork to the fork of the road leading to the upper River Bridge. Report of Commissioners that Goochland Justices refuse to join in building bridge near Jennytoe and directing suit against them. Lewis Vaughan surveyor from West Creek into Bush River Road in room of William Mayes; the persons employed, Robert Vaughan, Jeremiah Childrey, William Baldwin's Quarter, Edmund Covington, William Mayes, John Ellis. Watson's Road comes into Flatt Creek; Jackson's Road comes into Church Road at Nottoway Road from Yarbrow's to Woody Creek, crossing Irby's Road.

County levy: 23 wolves, bounty for. 1558 tithables, twelve pounds tobacco per head.

1744: Order letting bridge over Nottoway River in conjunction with Brunswick. Mr. John Hull to have liberty to clear a road from Deep Creek into the road near James Anderson's. Edward Thweatt apponted surveyor of road to be cleared beginning at James Anderson's and so into Butterwood Road at or near Leith's Creek. Petition of Richard Jones, Jr., for one acre of land on West Creek for Mill,—land opposite side himself belonging to George Steegal. Commissioners appointed to agree with Henrico to let to "build or rebuild a bridge over Appomattox River at Abraham Burton's." Major Richard Jones surveyor of road over the head of his mill in room of George Bagley. Thomas Bevill surveyor of road in place of Abraham Green. Robert Rowland authorized to open a bridle way out of Anthony Griffin's Road to Sandy River Chappell. Petition of Francis Anderson to have road cleared to Clement's Mill, etc.

Co. levy: 1766 tithables at twelve pounds tobacco per poll. 9 wolf heads paid for.

1745: Commissioners report they have let Burton's Bridge to be built by Thomas Anderson and kept in repair seven years. Commissioners appointed to view a cart way from Henry Robinson's house to his mill. On motion of William Watson, gent., it is ordered that a bridleway be opened from the New Road at head of Lazaretto to Nottoway Chapple and that said Watson, Matthew Cabiness, James Olive, Edward and Nathaniel Robertson and Isham Vaughan and their tithes clear the same and that Matthew Cabiness be surveyor thereof. James Olive surveyor of the New Road from Mallory's Creek to the Race Paths below Watson's and that Peter Jones's tenants, Watson's and all others convenient to said road clear the same. Robert Vaughan surveyor of the Fork Road from Irby's Courthouse Road into Bush River Road. Richard Hix ordered to clear the road from where Irby's Road crosses the road to Mayes's down to Deep Creek. Ordered that a road be cleared from Rev. Mr. John Overby's to Dandy's Race Paths. William Dandy, William Short, Thomas Williams, Ephrim West, John West, John Clark, William Hardwrarthe [?] and their tithes work same and William Dandy be surveyor. John Mayes surveyor of road from Dandy's Race Paths into Thomas Jones's Road. Ordered a road be cleared from Mallory's Creek along the Ridge to Randolph's Road at the head of Bush and Meherrin rivers, and that Anthony Griffin, hands of Colonel Richard Randolph's Quarter where Harding is overseer, and Captain John Nash's Quarter, etc., etc., open and clear the same. Order granting Henry Robertson leave to clear the cart path applied for before. Order appointing surveyors to clear Appomattox River mentions that there were below Flatt Creek an upper and lower bridge (the former must have been at Goode's). Ordered that a road be cleared beginning against Edward Jones and to cross West Creek near Tully's Branch and from there between Wilkinson's Quarter and Ward's the best and nearest way to the Court House. Edward Jones, John Osborn, Stephen Bentley and their tithes—both the Wilkinson's, Ward's and Mr. Hardaway's tithes to clear the same, and Mr. Hardaway be surveyor. Thomas Anderson reports he had built the bridge over Appomattox at Burton's and Commissioners authorized to receive the same and pay him fifty pounds, Amelia's proportion. William Barnes ordered to clear road from or near Whitworth's in Saylor's Creek Road below the Race Paths, and the tithes of Mr. Meredith and Thomas Whitworth, Jr., to be employed. William Yarbrough permitted to clear a road from his house into Captain Irby's Road to the Court House. John Tally surveyor road from Namozain Bridge to James Coles's Spring Branch and Robert Tucker from that point to Wintercomake. Daniel Coleman surveyor from Wintercomake to Rocky Run; Thomas Booth from Rocky Run to Spinner's Branch. Abraham Green, gent., granted leave to clear bridleway from his house to Rocky Run Chapple.

County levy: 17 wolf heads allowed. 1886 tithes at nine pounds tobacco per poll.

1746: Bridge on Flatt Creek near William Craddock's and Comb's Bridge on Flatt Creek ordered repaired. Report that the bridge over Appomattox is much out of repair and Commissioners appointed to confer with Henrico on subject of rebuilding said bridge (Goode's probably?) Ordered a road be cleared from Stock's Creek to Sandy Creek and John Moulden surveyor. Orderer to let the rebuilding of the bridge over Appomattox at Goode's. 2056 tithables.

1747: Order to clear a road from Henry Robertson's mill path to Crenshaw's Ford over Little Nottoway into Jordan's Road below the chappell.

1748: Bridge ordered on Little Nottoway where Yarborough's Road crosses it. Petition for dividing Raleigh Parish presented in court and ordered certified. John LeNeve[70] recommended for deputy clerk.

1749: Raleigh Parish had been divided in two by April Court, but I find no order of division. John LeNeve qualified as deputy clerk.

---

[70]Now spelled Leneave.

Amelia Order Book [no number given]

1780:   John Howson applied for water grist mill on Deep Creek opposite Stephen Johns's. P. 30, John Howson got order to build grist mill on Deep Creek opposite Stephen Johns's. James Anderson surveyor road from Watson's Old Ordinary to the county line in place of Bagley; Dickerson Jennings, from Jennings Ordinary to Watson's Old Ordinary in place of Richard Bradshaw.

1782:   William Bell got permission to erect his mill on Flatt Creek. P. 99, Peter Stanback granted ordinary license at the Court House of this County. P. 163, Petition of John and Joseph Jennings to build water grist mill on Deep Creek below mouth Cabin Branch, they having lands on both sides creek. P. 98-100, Divides the county into several districts for overseers of the poor, naming many roads, creeks, etc.

1792:   Edwin Booker, Sheriff.

1795 [?]:   Richard Ogilby, Coroner [?] of Amelia, 1790.

Land Book, Amelia, 1787.[71]

Francis Epes charged with 993 acres; Francis Epes charged with 816 acres; Francis Epes charged with 1738 acres; Francis Epes charged with 400 acres; Peter Epes charged with 1175 acres; Robert Fitzgerald charged with 277 acres; William Fitzgerald charged with 1098 acres; William Fitzgerald charged with 218½ acres; Francis Fitzgerald charged with 766 acres; Francis Fitzgerald charged with 218½ acres; James Oliver's Est. charged with 150 acres; Isaac Oliver charged with 548 acres; Richard Oliver charged with 100 acres; Richard Oliver charged with 450 acres; Richard Pryor charged with 150 acres; Luke Pryor charged with 150 acres; Philip Pryor charged with 324 acres; John Royall charged with 1370 acres; John Royall charged with 110 acres; Little B. Royall charged with 535 acres; Little B. Royall charged with 167 acres; Benjamin Ward, Jr., (heir or heirs) charged with 527 acres; Benjamin Ward, Jr., (heir or heirs) charged with 705 acres; William Watson charged with 1556 acres; Sherwood Walton charged with 400 acres.

[71]See Land Book, no. 5, Amelia, 1782-1801 (Archives Dept., Virginia State Library).

CHESTERFIELD COUNTY.

Chesterfield County Court Order Book, No. 1.

1749:   Among the first justices to hold first court were Richard Eppes, Seth Ward, Richard Royal, John Baugh, William Eppes, etc.

1750:   Edward Watson, a witness, paid for attendance upon March Court—p. 92.

1751: Ordered that Ann Watson, widow and relict of Joseph Watson, deceased, be summoned to appear at the next court to declare such things as shall be then and there demanded of her—p. 117.

1752: County Court ordered Alexander Gordon to let the repair of the bridge over the Appomattox near his house (Index to Order Book names it "Goodes at Gordon's Bridge").

1753: Commissioners appointed to confer with Amelia to let the rebuilding of bridge over Appomattox at Goodes.

1754: Alexander Gordon granted ordinary license at his house "near Goodes Bridge in this county," etc.

NOTTOWAY COUNTY.

The first deed recorded in Nottoway bears date of 1789: an indenture for 746 acres of land, in which John Worsham was one of the parties.

Nottoway County Court Order Book 1.

Feb. 5, 1793. William Greenhill, Samuel Pincham and Richard Dennis ordered to let and keep in repair for seven years Spain's Bridge over Deep Creek, and Parham's Bridge over Cellar Creek. Commissioners appointed to let Batte's Bridge over Little Nottoway River.

County court held Thursday, April 4, 1793. Present: William Greenhill, Freeman Epes, William Fitzgerald, Francis Fitzgerald, William Watson, Robert Fitzgerald, John Doswell, Richard Bland, Richard Dennis, Samuel Pincham, James Dupee, Hamlin Harris, and Peter Robertson, gents, justices.

Isaac Holmes, clerk of this county, being dead, the court proceeded to appoint a clerk, and named Peter Randolph, gent. Randolph gave bond, with Francis Muir and Samuel Pincham as sureties.

Vivian Brooking qualified as executor of Isaac Holmes, with Freeman Epes as surety.

On April 5, 1793, the court, under Act of General Assembly, proceeded to appoint officers of militia, as follows: Freeman Epes, lieutenant colonel (and commandant) ; Edward Wells, 1st major; Samuel Pincham, 2nd major; Moses Craddock, 1st captain, 1st battalion; Samuel Watkins, 2nd captain, 2nd battalion; William Sydnor, 3d captain, 2d [?] battalion; William Cabiness, 4th captain, 2d battalion; John Lampkin, 5th captain, 1st battalion; Charles Wilson, 6th captain, 2d battalion; James Dupee, 7th captain, 1st battalion; George Green, 8th captain, 2d battalion; Abraham Hatchett, 9th captain, 1st battalion; John Epes, 10th captain, 1st battalion, Robert Winfree, 1st lieutenant, 1st battalion; Henry Fowlkes, 2d lieutenant, 1st battalion; John William Connally, 3d lieutenant, 2d battalion; James Cook, 4th lieutenant, 1st battalion; James Wilson, 5th lieutenant, 2d battalion. (The first three named were members of the county bench—the appointing power.)

James Dupuy, Jr., was Commissioner of Revenue in 1793; worked eighty days.

May, 1793, Thomas Molley (Motley?) allowed to practice law.

In June 1793, the Court recommended to the Governor and Council, for appointment as sheriff for the ensuing year, William Greenhill, Freeman Epes and Abner Osborne, gents. The same recommendation was made in June 1794.

County Court held July 4, 1793. Edmond Wills, William Watson, Francis Fitzgerald, James Dupuy, justices present. Peter Lampkin, Stith Bolling, and John Doswell appointed to let and keep in repair for seven years the bridge over Little Nottoway River at Shelton's. Ordinary license to Peter Stainback at the Court House. Bridge over Nottoway River near Mrs. Cross's let. Application of John Cocke to erect mill on Little Nottoway opposite James Gunn, etc. James Gunn on south side Little Nottoway opposite John Cocke applies for mill dam,—competitor of Cocke. Freeman Epes, surveyor of the road from the Church Road by Mrs. Jeter's to Watson's Point Road at Cocke's plantation to be worked by hands of Mrs. Wilkinson and said Epes. Samuel Morgan, surveyor of the road from Cocke's Road at the corner of Drinwater's [Drinkwater?] old field to Jordan's Road near Green's Church. Edward Weeks surveyor of the road from Cocke's Road along the Parsons Road to the sign board,—hands of David Tucker, Robert Tucker, Abner Osborne's Quarter, Daniel Stone, Edward Bass, William Cousins, John Wilson's Quarter and Thomas G. Peachy's Quarter to work on it.

Grand Jury present: surveyor of the road from Francis White's to Jordan's Bridge, the surveyor of the road from Francis White's to the Burnt Ordinary, surveyor of the road from Francis White's to Battses Bridge, surveyor of the road from Battses Bridge to Cross Bridge, surveyor of the road from the county line near Owen Smith's to John Mann's Mill and from Mann's Mill to Jenning's Ordinary, surveyor of the road from the county line near Piller's Ordinary to the County line near John Davis's store, and the surveyor of the road from Herrikin Creek to Green's Church for not keeping in repair, etc. Ordered that the hands of * * * * be taken from Jackson's Road and added to the hands that work on Crenshaw's Road.

"William Bell's Ordinary" at Bell's Old Field.

County levy, December, 1793:

George Craghead, Deputy Attorney	$	25.
Peter Randolph, Clerk		25.
" " "		14.
Rawleigh Carter, former Sheriff		25.

William Parrot, for building and keeping
in repair seven years the Falls Bridge
over Great Nottoway River_____ 51.33
John Doswell, for building and keeping in
repair seven years Battses Bridge___ 218.00
To John Doswell, for building and keeping
in repair seven years Shelton's Bridge
over Great Nottoway _____ 57.80
Hugh Wallace, for building and keeping in
repair for seven years Cross's Bridge_ 66.66
Henry Hastings, for building and keeping
in repair seven years bridge over Deep
Creek at Spain's _____ 50.00
Peter Stainback, for keeping the Court
House _____ 16.16
3265 Tithables at 17cts. per tithe_____ 754.25

April 1794. Peter Lampkin, William Cryer and Rawleigh
Carter, late sheriff, ordered to settle their accounts as such before a committee. May, 1794. Undertaker of Maye's Bridge
over Deep Creek presented. License granted William Bell to
keep ordinary at his house, 1794. Edward Bland asked license
to practice law, in June, 1794. Grief Green recommended as
attorney, 1794. John Garland Jefferson qualified attorney,
June [?] 1794. Joseph Jennings, Sr., got license to keep ordinary at Jennings Ordinary, with James Cook, surety, June 1794.
William Bell and Joseph Jennings granted ordinary licenses for
one year at their houses in this county. Edward Bland granted
certificate of good character to apply to examiners for license to
practice law. Inventory and appraisement of estate of Gabriel
Fowlkes, deceased, recorded. Richard Oliver surveyor of the
road from Joseph Jennings's Ordinary to Henry Ferguson's, to
be worked by his hands and those of Joseph Jennings, Sr. and
Jr., Joseph Woodson, John Mann, James Mann, Thomas Cook,
Charles Stewart, Thomas Powell, Free Julius, and Free Charles.[72]
W. Peter Robertson asks lief to erect mill on Little Nottoway,—
he owning land on both sides. Uriah Lipscombe surveyor of the
road from James Henderson's to Rowland's Church. (This date
there was a Maye's Bridge on Deep Creek). Henry Farley
overseer of the road from William Bell's Ordinary to the county
line near George Baldwin, with the hands of himself, Robert
Winfree, William Watson, Langly Jennings, Williamson Piles,
James Farley, Sr., Jacob Belcher, Benjamin Ward's Estate,
Henry Smith, Anna Harper and John Ellington. Petition of
John Beadel and others for a road beginning where the county
dividing line ends to Prince Edward line, thence along between
William Kennon's and Thomas Jackson's to John Beadel's mill,

---

[72]The two latter were evidently free negroes.

thence by William Mitchell's into the great road; thence across the same to Bell's Mill. Daniel Marshall surveyor of road from the old bridge to Rowland's Church.

1795: Grief Green qualified as attorney.

1796: Peter Bland recommended and qualified as attorney. Commissioners appointed to meet Commissioners from Amelia and Dinwiddie to let bridge for seven years on Namizine Creek at place called Wills's Bridge. Roads mentioned for work, etc.— The road from Rowland's Church to the County line; the road from Rowland's Church to Watson's Road. County levy, 1796: Tithables 3460[73] at 1s 9d per tithe, $1009 & 16 cts.

Nottoway County Court Order Book 2.

1797: Samuel Morgan granted license to keep an ordinary at his house. Overseers of roads appointed: "Road from Lamkins old store to William Sneeds to be worked by the hands of Didimus [?] Valentine, Griffin Lamkin, the estate of William Smith, Zach. Hooper and Hannah Crute." The road from Stephen Jones's Bridge to the county line near his house. License to Joseph Wells to keep ordinary at his house, Peter Stainback, Sr., his surety. License to Sterling Lewis to keep ordinary at the Court House. Joseph Jennings (son of Joseph) appointed constable. Overseer of the road from the road opposite Francis Fitzgerald's to Winnegram's Creek,—hands of James Henderson, Robert Fitzgerald, Richard Jones, Jr., the estate of Henry Robertson and others to work it.

Court Quarter Session, August, 1797.

Roads presented: From Francis White's to Batt's Bridge. From Batt's Bridge to Cross's Bridge, etc. Thomas V. Brooking surveyor of the road from Woody Creek Bridge to the road leading by Asa Davis's store. Duncan Cameron qualified as attorney. George Craghead deputy attorney for the Commonwealth. Thomas Epes surveyor of road from Jordan's Bridge on Nottoway River to the fork of the road near John Andrew Schwartz's in the room of William Irby. Daniel Verser commissioner of the taxes in this county. Freeman Epes, Gent., sheriff, succeeded by Edmund Wills (Oct. 1797). License to John Robertson to keep an ordinary at the house formerly occupied by Henry Fergusson. County Levy: 3412 Tithes at 7d per tithe $331.73.

1798: Appraisement of Estate of Thomas Epes, deceased, returned and recorded. Ordered that Stith Hardaway's hands that work on the plantation which he purchased of Freeman Epes work on the road from Jordan's Bridge on Nottoway River

---

[73]Another note, referring to Nottoway Deed Book No. 1, gives the number of tithes in 1796 as 3371.

to the fork of the road near John A. Schwartz's instead of Freeman Epes's hands. Hands of Woodlief Thomas and others to work on the road from Batte's Bridge to John A. Schwartz's, etc. Jerman Baker qualified as attorney. [John A. Schwartz was one of the surviving partners of Cocke, Schwartz and Co. (Case of Schwartz in Court of Appeals, see Virginia Reports).] John Bass, Jr., qualified as surveyor. Ordinary license to Joseph Jennings, Sr., at his house. June, 1798—Twelve months more time allowed Peter Randolph "to rebuild the mill formerly John Winn's on the Lazaretta Creek in this county with a dam to stagnate the same water which said Winn was formerly entitled to." A marriage contract between William H. Robertson of one part and Susanna Winn and Freeman Epes of the other recorded. Commissioners report upon a view of the clerk's office built by Peter Randolph under contract, that it be received, June 7th, 1798, and then ordered by the Court that the public records be kept therein. Election for overseers of the poor in "the lower district" on May 30th appointed "at the Burnt Ordinary" (2 districts in the County). The other was held at Jennings Ordinary. Road surveyors: "for the road from Pulliam's old field to county line," Stephen Roberts; the road from Jennings Ordinary to Pulliam's old field, Peter Dupuy, surveyor. Samuel Morgan indicted for selling liquor at "the Burnt Ordinary on Cox Road." Luke Pryor, a Juror. Richard Bennett, Sr., given under county seal a certificate of good character by the Court "he being about to remove out of the State." Petition of John Epes for leave to turn the road from Celler Creek to the south near the said Epes's grainery, etc., filed and commissioners appointed to view the proposed route. John and William Doswell and Elisha Jeffress appointed commissioners to meet with Lunenburg and let the building of a bridge over Nottoway River at Wade's Bridge. Application of Hamlin Harris to open the road called Winnegam's Creek Road leading from his house through the lands of Uriah Lipscombe. Barbee Miller appointed surveyor on Pulliam's Road from his house to Jennings Ordinary, and the hands of said Miller, James Dupuy, Sr. and Jr., Peter Dupuy, William Hundley, Daniel Jones, John White and Ambrose Beasley to work same. Shadrack Holt surveyor of Pulliam's Road from said Miller's to Prince Edward line. Hands of Shadrack and John Holt, Edward Jones, Thomas Womack, William Singleton, William Harper and Silas Fore to work it. John Anthony Fowlkes and Thomas B. Robertson qualified as attorneys. Application of John White for leave to turn the road called Pulliam's leading to Bell's Mill upon his line, and commissioners appointed. Road from John A. Schwartz's to the fork above the Burnt Ordinary, etc. Basebeech [?] surveyor.

1799: Daniel Verser, commissioner of revenue, produced his account and showed that 140 days were requisite to perform his work. Daniel Justice, surveyor of the road from Cross's to

Batte's Bridge in place of John Cocke. William Watson qualified as sheriff. Langley B. Jennings appointed surveyor of the
road from Bell's Tavern by Jennings Ordinary to Amelia line
near George Baldwyn's to be worked by hands of William Watson, Wilson Piles, L. B. Jennings, Henry Farley, Benjamin
Ward's Estate, John Gilliam, Henry Smith, James Farley, Sr.
and James Hayes. James Cook, surveyor of road from Roland's
Church to Jennings Ordinary, to be worked by hands of James
Cook, Jesse Walton, Henry Baldwyn, Pleasant Walton, James
J. Fowlkes and Joseph Jennings. Peter Bland asks lief to turn
the road leading by his house to Comer's Mill. Richard Dennis,
Jr. surveyor of the road from Cellar Creek Bridge to Woody
Creek Bridge,—hands of Peter Bass, Nathan and James
Fletcher, John Royall, Eliza Williams, Matthew Ward, William
Pincham, Daniel Hardaway's Quarter, Richard Dennis, Jr. and
James Sturdivant to work same. County Levy: 353 tithes at
10 cts per tithe.

Nottoway County Court Order Book 3.

1801: Bridge across Nottoway River called Dudley's leading to Lunenburg. Grief Green appointed by the County Court
deputy attorney for the commonwealth. Lief granted William
Fitzgerald and Catherine his wife to erect dam on one of the
branches of West Creek for grist mill,—water to be dammed
twelve feet high—they owning the land on both sides. Commissioners report that only one-half acre of James Wingo would be
flooded. (Ward's Mill at West Creek). Rack-Coon Track
Road: Dabney Morris applied to open a public road by the above
name, turning out of the main road leading from the Court
House to Dudley's Bridge above said Dabney Morris's store and
running through the land of Rawleigh Carter, Obediah Dowdy,
James Borum, Claiborne Chandler, Elias Dejarnett, Austin
Fowlkes, John Fowlkes, Jr. and Thomas Green to the county
line of Prince Edward. Daniel Verser, commissioner of the
revenue, paid for fifty-two days service. Grand Jury present
John Robertson, surveyor of the road from Nottoway Meeting
House to Rowland's Church.

1802: Lief asked by Daniel Hardaway to turn the road
leading from the old bridge on Cellar Creek called old Court
House Road to Deep Creek Bridge called Spain's Bridge.
Joseph I. Fowlkes granted ordinary license at his house. Grand
Jury presented Uriah Lipscombe, surveyor of the road from Henderson's Store to Rowland's Church. Lief granted Casimer
Cabiness to turn the road leading from Rowland's Church to
Smith's Meeting House. Lief given Samuel Morgan to turn the
road at the intersection of Stoker's [?] and Cocke's Road on his
land—the roads cutting his land in two. William Jones surveyor
of the road from Amelia County line to the fork of the road near

Ferguson's old tavern. Lief granted Noten Dickinson to erect dam on Flat Creek. Lands of James Cooke "overflown." Edward Jones, surveyor of the road (called Pulliam's Road) from Barbee Miller's to the County line in place of Shadrack Holt. John Doswell, sheriff. Peter Randolph, clerk.

1803: County Court nominates to Governor and Council Edmund Wills for colonel of the militia in place of Freeman Epes resigned; John Epes for major in lieu of Wills promoted; Grief Green for major in lieu of William Cabiness resigned; Francis Epes for captain in lieu of John Epes promoted. They were appointed (at least first two). Lief granted Dabney Morris to erect dam for grist mill on Great Nottoway River. Richard Bland, sheriff. 3539 tythes at twenty-five cents per head.

1804: Lief given John Hurt to erect dam on Ellis Fork for grist mill for ten feet water. Nicholas Vaughan and Curtis Jackson given small damages. Mary Robertson (*alias* Wilkinson) *vs.* James Robertson, John Robertson, Elizabeth Comer, John and Elizabeth Royall (children of John Royall) Elizabeth, James, Mary Epes, Martha Ann and Caroline Jones (children of Richard Jones, Jr.) Mary Robertson, daughter of James Robertson, Mary Robertson, daughter of John Robertson, and Richard Jones, Jr., Defendants. John Roberts surveyor of the road from the Bridge across Little Nottoway near Randolph's Mill to the sign board near this place. Tyree G. Bacon surveyor of the road leading from his house to Rowland's Church from his spring branch into the road leading by Rowland's Church with his own hands. Asa Davis surveyor of the road leading from T. G. Bacon's to Rowland's Church beginning at the said Bacon's Spring Branch and from thence into the road leading by Jennings Ordinary, with the former hands together with his own. James Chambers is appointed surveyor of the road leading from Winningham's Creek to Francis Fitzgerald's lane in the room of Asa Davis, with the hands of Polly Anderson, Joseph Friend, William Richardson, Brightwell Rather, Francis Epes, Richard Jones and Roberth Fitzgerald. County Levy, 3555 tithes.

1805: Commissioners appointed to view the old way proposed to be opened by Archer Robertson from Jennings's Mill leading by Mrs. Wilkerson's to Smith's Meeting House and report, etc. Commissioners appointed to divide estate of Francis Epes, deceased, between his children Woodley, Irby, Francis, and Joshua, after giving dower to widow Mary Epes. Commissioners appointed to view the way proposed to be opened by Gabriel Fowlkes leading from said Fowlkes's mill into the ridge way from Nottoway Meeting House to the main road near Robert Dickerson's. Anthony Gills appointed surveyor of road in place of Barbee Miller, deceased, to be worked by his own hands and those of Benjamin Ward (home plantation), James Dupuy (home plantation), Peter Leflett, Josiah Hundley, Eliza Overton,

John Philips, Josiah Forest, James Dupuy, Sr., William Hundley
and Estate of Barbee Miller. William Smith appointed surveyor
of the Church Road leading from Rowland's Church to the main
road above Smith's Store in place James Cooke (deceased), to
be worked by his own hands and those of James Cooke's Estate,
James Dupuy, Jr., at Deep Creek plantation, George Smith,
Joseph I. Fowlkes and Miller Ellington.

Nottoway Superior Court Order Book.

Superior Court, April 24, 1809. Present, William H. Cabell,
judge; Francis Fitzgerald, clerk. The latter's bondsmen were
Thomas Epes, Richard Epes, Francis Fitzgerald. The following
attorneys qualified to practice in the court: Peter Johnston
(father of General Joseph E. Johnston), Peter Bland, Edward
Bland, John Lane, Peter Randolph, Jr. (afterwards judge),
Peter R. Bland, and Peyton Doswell. (This was then the Fifth
Judicial Circuit.) David Robertson was appointed prosecutor
for the commonwealth. In 1810, William Yates became attorney
for the commonwealth. Among the cases tried at the term was
an ejectment brought by Don Carlos against Napoleon Bonaparte. Peter Kendal was tried for murder and acquitted.

1810: John Royall, John D. Royall, William Greenhill,
William G. C. Greenhill, William Pincham, Nathan Ward
and Stephen Beasley appointed commissioners to let rebuild-
ing of the bridge across Cellar Creek, near Conrade Webb's.
Lewelling Jones, Peter Perry, William Wills, and Jas. H.
Munford appointed commissioners to meet commissioners
from Dinwiddie and Amelia to rebuild or repair the
bridge across Namozeen Creek called Wills's Bridge. Peter
Randolph, Jr. recommended by the Court to the Governor
for lt. col. of the 49th Regiment, 4th Brigade and 1st Division
Virginia Militia. Road leading from Cellar Creek to Leath's
Creek and from Jordon Jackson's to Jennings Ordinary presented. William Old qualified as attorney. Peter Randolph, Jr.,
deputy attorney for the commonwealth, resigned and the Court
appointed Peter Bland in his place.

April 22, 1811. Dabney Carr, judge. William Yates ap-
pointed prosecutor for the commonwealth and qualified. Hodi-
jah S. Meade, who produced license signed by Spencer Roane,
Francis T. Brook, and Peter Johnston, admitted to practice law.
Jos. B. Ingram appointed surveyor of road from Nottoway Meet-
ing House to Rowland's Church, in room John A. Robertson.
James H. Munford, surveyor Richmond Road from Cocke's Road
to the county line, to be worked by the hands of John Morgan,
Susan Hood, William Wills, Edmund Wills, Eliza Osborne, Robert
Tucker, Richard Hawks, Richard Weeks, Emanuel Weeks, Sr.,
Joshua Hawkes, Benjamin Bevill and himself. William Perry
appointed surveyor of the road from Little Nottoway at Ran-

dolph's to the road leading from Henderson's to Morganville. Lewis Featherston surveyor of Irby's Road from Leath's Creek to Cocke's Road. Samuel Dunnivant surveyor of the road from Jennings Ordinary to the branch near Furgusson's old tavern. James Vaughan surveyor of the road from the branch near Furgusson's old tavern to the county line. Dower assigned Mrs. James Cooke, 129 acres, (map recorded in Order Book); plat dated 1805, shows George Smith's corner post oak and Dupuy's pine, etc.

April, 1812. Peter Randolph, judge. William Yates was attorney for the commonwealth. (At the September term, James Semple presided for Judge Randolph). William C. Greenhill nominated to the Governor as lt. col. of 49th Reg. Mil. in place of Peter Randolph resigned. John Epes moved, on part of his children, who are heirs and legatees of Thos. R. Williams, deceased, to file exception to the account of D. G. W. one of the executors,—granted. William Perry licensed to keep ordinary at the Court House. Estate of William Dyson, deceased, divided: 608 acres north side Deep Creek, adjoining Ward, Francis Dyson and Osborne, between the widow and children; sons, Francis and Thomas W.; daughters, Elizabeth (wife Daniel Verser), Mary (wife Major Isaac Winfree); also Martha and Nancy J. Dyson. (Martha married William Smith). Division of the estate of Richard Oliver, deceased, 773 acres on both sides Deep Creek: 250 acres to widow Mary, adjoining Dr. James Jones, metes and bounds; names Namozine Road, Cooper Branch, and tavern on place. [Examined this Order Book up to page 340 (O. B. No. 5, 1809-13).]

In Nottoway Order Book, Nathan Ward is mentioned as jailer, April, 1817.

Superior Court, September 1818. Judge Peter Randolph; Francis Fitzgerald, clerk; William Yates, commonwealth's attorney; Samuel Morgan, sheriff. This was the court which tried Dr. George S. G. Bacon for the murder of Dr. John S. Hardaway. The record shows the resignation of William Yates as prosecuting attorney in the counties of Dinwiddie and Nottoway and the appointment of John W. Jones in his stead at this term. (Nottoway was then in fifth judicial circuit, comprising the counties of Nottoway, Dinwiddie, Lunenburg, Brunswick, Amelia, Powhatan and Chesterfield.)

Nottoway County Court, May 6, 1819. Tyree G. Bacon qualified as colonel of 49th Regiment, Virginia Militia. "Ferguson's Old Tavern" appears in records of 1819.

April 26, 1824. Thomas T. Bouldin, judge. Commonwealth *versus* Reuben Wicks; Jury: William S. Smith, H. R. Anderson, Archer Robertson, John G. Jones, Thomas Clay, Abraham Buford, Brightwell Rather, Thompson Penick, Henry Craddock, John W. Connally, Robert Jones and James M. Taylor. Guilty verdict on April 27, 1824. Took an appeal to Court of Appeals.

Board of Overseers of the Poor.

1832. Asa Crenshaw, president, Dr. William C. Jackson, physician; 1835, Dr. Austin Watkins, physician; 1839-40, William R. Jennings, president.

Land Book Nottoway County, 1862.

Wm. A. Borum, 1008½ acres, Flat Creek, Value $$11,585.00 (Adjoining A. Miller) ; Wm. A. Bragg, 1520 acres, West Creek, Value $17,917.00 (Adjoining W. F. Ward) ; Wm. R. Bland, 1486¼ acres, Cellar Creek, Value $14,163.00; R. H. Beverly, 774 acres, Flat Creek, Value $15,340.00; Grief T. Cralle, 1612¼ (3 tracts), Nottoway River, Value $17,509.00; Thos. H. Campbell, 1536½ acres, Value $21,372.00; Mary & Fanny Fitzgerald, 1477 acres, Little Nottoway, Value $18,270.00; Daniel H. Hardaway, 2779½ acres (1 tract), Little Nottoway, Value $35,355.00; R. A. A. Watson, 937 acres, Deep Creek, Value $9,953.00; R. A. A. Watson, 87 acres, Deep Creek, Value $2,889.00.

Clerks of Nottoway County.

There have been up to date (1890) only five regular clerks of the county. The records begin in 1789 when Isaac Holmes was clerk, which position he held until 1793, when Peter Randolph became clerk. The latter held office some ten years perhaps (the order book in clerk's office will show date) and was succeeded by Francis Fitzgerald. Fitzgerald was succeeded by Richard Epes, and he by Herman Jackson, the present incumbent.

Sheriffs.

1790, William Cryer (Robert Booth, William Booth, deputy sheriffs) ; 1792, Rawleigh Carter; March 1793, William Greenhill qualified as sheriff; October 1793, Rawleigh Carter was sheriff; 1795, Freeman Epes (William Cabaniss, deputy) ; 1799, William Watson; 1809, Richard Dennis; 1810, Captain James Dupuy; 1815, James H. Munford; 1816-17, Edmund Wills (H. R. Anderson, deputy sheriff) ; 1818, Samuel Morgan; 1820-21, Abraham Hatchett; 1822, Tyree G. Bacon; 1824, Richard Epes; 1827, Richard Y. Bland (John A. Hatchett, deputy) ; 1828-29, John D. Royall; 1826, R. Y. Bland; 1832, James H. Munford; 1833, John P. Dupuy; 1835, John H. Knight; 1837, Sam B. Jeter; 1839-40, Nathan Ward; 1843, Dr. A. H. Campbell; 1844, Williamson Dickinson; 1846, William B. Wilson (M. W. Robertson, deputy) ; 1848, William T. Wills; 1850, Ed. T. Jeffress. Also Joseph Dupuy, William Hatchett, Richard Epes.

Justices of Peace, Nottoway County.

Deed Book 2, p. 28, shows that Richard Bland, William Watson and Richard Dennis were justices in 1798. Deed Book 2, p. 67, shows that Robert and Francis Fitzgerald were justices in 1798; p. 75, shows that Freeman Epes was a justice at the same time; Pincham, Williams shown justices in 1799. (Nottoway Deed Book 2, p. 95.)   Daniel Verser and Isaac Winfree, shown justices in 1799.   (Nottoway Deed Book 2, p. 166.) Deed Book 2, p. 175, 179, shows that Richard Bland, Samuel Morgan and Dabney Morris were justices in 1800. 1805, Freeman Epes, John Bass, Edmund Wills, Daniel Verser, gents., justices; also Joseph Dupuy, Abraham Hatchett, Richard Epes.

WILLS AND DEEDS.[74]

ALLEN, JAMES, 1793. Will. Witness, Hannah Watson. A man of intelligence and property. One of his daughters married Francis Smith. Children, Joseph, John, Ben, Charles, Mary, Elizabeth, Sally, Patsy; grandsons, Christopher and Daniel. Prince Edward County Records.

ALLEN, JAMES, SR., 1808. Will. Witnesses, Samuel Watson, Jr. and Allen Watson. Daughters, Martha and Sallie Watson (unmarried), Hannah, Elizabeth Simms, Mary; wife, Margaret; sons, Daniel, John, James. Prince Edward W. B. 4, p. 122.

ANDERSON, CHARLES, of Southam Parish, Goochland, 1745. Deed to William Watson, of same county and parish, conveys land in Goochland. Goochland D. B. 5, p. 343.

ANDERSON, CHARLES, 1789. Deed, September, 1789, conveys land to Thomas Comer, 19 acres with Mill place (Maxey's Mill) on Mallory's Creek, adjoining Henry Anderson and George Bagley. Nottoway D. B. 1, p. 13.

ANDERSON, REYNARD, of Nottoway, 1790. Deed to Uriah Lipscomb, of Nottoway, for land in Nottoway on Winningham Creek. Nottoway D. B. 1, p. 68.

ARCHER, EDWARD, 1789. Will. Executor, Friend George Robertson. Wife, Mary; son, William, given land on Swift Creek and on Appomattox River; son, Field, "land whereon my father lived" on Second Branch Road, also lots in Petersburg held as tenant in common with George Robertson; son, Edward; devised lands in Dinwiddie, Lunenburg, Halifax, on Green River in Kentucky, etc. Chesterfield W. B. 4, p. 244.

ARCHER, ELIZABETH, 1785. Will. Executors, Edward Archer, William Downman and George Robertson. Daughters, Agnes Downman, Martha Field Walthall, Michal, Elizabeth Mosely, Mary Archer; grandson, James Robertson; grand daugh-

---

[74]In the following pages, W. B. refers to Will Book, and D. B., to Deed Book.

ters, Elizabeth Osborne Downman, Elizabeth Osborne Moseley, Martha Moseley, Martha Field Robertson, Martha Field Walthall, Martha Field Downman. Chesterfield W. B. 4, p. 1.

ARCHER, JOHN, 1764. Deed from John Archer and John Hylton to Richard Eppes, of Chesterfield, for lots in Bermuda Hundred. Chesterfield D. B. 4, p. 557.

ARCHER, JOHN, SR., 176- (?). Will. Daughter, Ann Robertson, and other children. Chesterfield W. B. 2, p. 28.

ARCHER, WILLIAM S. (Mr. Archer died March, 1855). Will at Amelia, 185- ; executors, colonel Thomas Tabb and Dr. John B. Harvie. Inventory shows 2500 books in library, 16 mules, 7 horses, 40 head of cattle, 10 oxen, 120 hogs, 107 sheep, 80 bbls. corn, 30,000 pounds of oats, 3000 bushels wheat, 88 negroes; had large property in Mississippi. Amelia W. B.

ATKINSON, ROGER, Olive Hill, Chesterfield County, 1829. Will. Executors, Brother Thomas, and son Dr. Thomas P. Requests executors to make sale of my three tracts of land in County of Chesterfield, purchased of Thomas E. Gary, Thomas B. Manlove and Peter Andrews" . . . etc.; also "all my stock, crops and plantation utensils on my Hyde and Dan River plantations" . . . . to pay his debts. Gave daughter, Sally B. Jones, all lands on south side of Hyde River upon condition her husband, Dr. Joseph Jones, pay for 200 acres of it at not less than $11.00 per acre; also negroes previously put in his possession To son, Thomas Atkinson, "one-sixth of my estate for use and support and education of the children of my son, John Atkinson." (This Thomas Atkinson was Dr. Thomas P. Atkinson, as appears from subsequent clauses.) One-fifth part estate given in trust to Thomas for the benefit of children of daughter, Caroline E. T. Mayo. Residue of estate to children, Jane B. Pryor, Robert Atkinson, Lucy Pryor and Nancy P. H. Atkinson, in equal portion, having already advanced to "other three children equal property." Gives his wife, Sarah, in pursuance of marriage contract, life estate in 22 slaves. Speaks of his wife's sister Robertson. Chesterfield Superior Court Deeds, Wills, etc., since 1809, page 50.

ATTWOOD, JAMES, 1747. Deed. Conveys land on Flatt Creek and Frank's Creek, adjoining Isham Vaughan and others; also near head branches of Buckskin Creek. Amelia D. B. 3, p. 6.

ATWOOD, JAMES, 1762. Deed from James Atwood and Mary, his wife, of Amelia, to William Jennings, of Hanover, for two tracts of lands of 200 acres each; the first tract beginning in Robert Moody's, now James Oliver's, line where it crosses Deep Creek, etc., being the lower part of 600 acres bought by Atwood of William Hudson, 1748; the second two hundred acres spoken of as lying above that two hundred acres which James Atwood gave to his son William Atwood. Amelia D. B. 8, p. 48.

ATWOOD, WILLIAM, 1763. Deed from William Atwood, of Prince Edward, planter, to William Jennings, Sr., planter, of

Amelia, for two hundred acres, it being part of a greater tract patented by William Hudson and conveyed by James Atwood by deed of gift to William Atwood, lying between Cabin Branch and Deep Creek. Amelia D. B. 8, p. 48.

BACON, TYREE G., 1830. Will. Executors, Nathan Ward and brother William Bacon. To son James, "tract he now lives on, called Jennings"; daughters, Mary, Sally and Eliza; Petronella Marshall seems to have been another daughter; grandson, Herbert T. Bacon. Inventory and appraisement show 17,809 dollars. Nottoway W. B. 6, p. 186.

BALDWIN, SAMUEL, 1793. Deed from Samuel Baldwin, of Charlotte County, and Elizabeth Baldwin, of Nottoway, to George Baldwin, of Nottoway, land on West Creek bounded by John Blankenship, William Rogers and John Gilliam, being part of tract late the property of William Baldwin. Nottoway D. B. 1, p. 385.

BARDWELL, Nottoway. Owned whole tract got from Col. Burke's estate. Deed from him to Bradshaw, *et als*, 1891. Bradshaw became purchaser, Feb. 1897. Judge William Hodges Mann, trustee.

BARKSDALE, WILLIAM J., 1859. Will. Inventory appraises personal property at $103,457.00 Amelia W. B., 1859.

BELL, WILLIAM, 1793. Deed. William F. Bell and his wife, Frances, convey water grist mill and land on Flat Creek, known as Bell's Mill, to John Mann. Nottoway D. B. 1, p. 304. William Bell, prior to 1794, sold his mill on Flat Creek to John Mann, and Mann sold to Booker, of Prince Edward, and half to another party, 1794. Nottoway D. B. 1.

BELL, WILLIAM, 1795. Deed from William Bell and wife, and Peter Ellington and wife, to Daniel Jones, of Nottoway, land on Flatt Creek bought by Bell of William Watson and Archibald Yarborough; mill now owned by Owen Smith, of Prince Edward, and others. Speaks of James Dupuy's (Jr) corner and Pulliam's Road, etc. Nottoway D. B. 1.

BIBB, WILLIAM, 1789. Deed from William Bibb and Sarah, his wife, of Prince Edward, to Augustus Watson, of said county, land on Harris's Creek. Prince Edward D. B. 8, p. 158.

BIGGER, WILLIAM, 1752. Deed from William Bigger, of Goochland, to John Watson, his son-in-law, and other children, conveying slaves, etc. Goochland D. B. 6, p. 233.

BLAND, EDWARD, 1831. Will. Wife, Rebecca; son, William Richard; daughters, Ann A., Martha B., Rebecca, Sarah, Frances and Virginia; nephews, Richard E. and Peter B. Jones, who with sons-in-law, Henry C. Worsham and George W. Harrison, were made executors. Inventory and appraisement of estate aggregates 34,000 dollars, and includes "Abbeville," "Springfield" (with grist mill), and "Round Top" plantations. Nottoway W. B. 6, pp. 257, 443.

BLAND, PETER, 1796.   Deed from Peter Bland and Elizabeth, his wife, to Richard Dennis, forty acres "on both sides of Leath's or Middle Cellar Creek." Nottoway D. B. 1, p. 551.

BOGGEFF, HENRY, 1789.   Deed from Henry Boggeff, of Botetourt County, to Samuel Cocke, of Surry, land near Dudley's Bridge and adjoining Christopher Harrison, Richard Bennett, Bryan and Dudley. Nottoway D. B. 1, p. 28.

BOLLING, ROBERT, 1752.   William Watson one of the executors of Robert Bolling, deceased, brought suit against Worsham, administrator. Chesterfield County Court Order Book 1, p. 199.

BRAXTON, CARTER, 1773.   Deed.   Conveyance to Samuel Watson, a negro woman and two children. Prince Edward D. B. 5, p. 183.

BROADDUS, RICHARD, 1800.   Deed to Robert Dickinson for land on Mallory's Creek (Agnew's place called "Inverness"). Nottoway D. B. 2, p. 155.

BROOKING, THOMAS V., 1801.   Deed.   Conveyance from Thomas V. Brooking and wife to Richard K. (?) Cralle, all of Nottoway, of the old Samuel Sherwin estate on Winningham Creek, etc; speaks of Sherwin's Road. Nottoway D. B. 2, p. 250.

BROOKING, VIVIAN, 1789.   Deed to Isaac Holmes and wife (Elizabeth Thacker Holmes, daughter of grantor) 18 negroes. Nottoway D. B. 1, p. 7.

BROWN, LAWRENCE, 1744.   Deed to Seth Ward, of Henrico, to land on West Creek, near Captain Field Jefferson's mill, and patented by Brown, 1737. Amélia D. B. 1.

BURRUS, CHARLES, 1743.   Deed.   Charles Burrus, of King William County, conveys to John Watson, Jr., of Hanover County, land in Goochland, on Tuckahoe Creek, north side James River.   Goochland D. B. 4, p. 318.

BURTON, ABRAHAM, 1736.   Will.   Lived on Appomattox near mouth of Deep Creek. Gives son, Abraham Burton, this tract. Amelia W. B. 1, p. 135. (Son Abraham died, 1758, leaving this land to his son, Peter.)

CHAMBERS, ALLEN, 1798.   Deed to Abner Watson, of Prince Edward, for land beginning at Rutledge Road, etc. Witness, Drury Watson, Jr. Prince Edward D. B. 11, p. 287.

CHAMBERS, JOSIAH, 1785.   Will, dated 1781, probated 1785: executors, John Watson and Charles Allen. Order of court shows that John Watson, Sr. was one of the witnesses examined in court as to execution. Wife, Mary; sons, Josiah, John and Allen; daughters, Elizabeth Allen, Betty Ann, Susannah. Prince Edward W. B. 2, p. 9.

CHAMBERS, MARY, 1800.   Will.   Executors, son-in-law Charles Allen, and brother Jesse Watson; witnesses, John Watson, Jr., Drury Watson, Jr., and Hannah Watson. Son Josiah and four daughters. Prince Edward W. B. 3, p. 182.

COCKE, STEPHEN, and others, 1790 (?).   Deed from Stephen Cocke, John Gooch, Richard Jones, Jr., William Fitz-

gerald, Francis Fitzgerald, Rowland Ward, Jr., and William
Cross Craddock, trustees of Nottoway Parish, by act of assembly,
1788, to James Henderson, land known as "The Glebe," on east
side of Lazaretta Creek and adjoining Robert Fitzgerald, Cocke,
Winn and others. Nottoway D. B. 1, p. 99.

COCKE, WALTER, 1801. Deed from Walter Cocke and wife
(Ann Carter Cocke), of Surry County, to Francis Epes, of
Lunenburg, to 915 acres (Rittenhouse place), bounded by lands
of Nathaniel Robertson, James Henderson, Nottoway Glebe land
and Irby's Courthouse Road; witnesses, Francis Epes, of Prince
George, and others. Nottoway D. B. 2, p. 266. (Tom Epes told
me that Richard, Frank and Peter Epes were brothers and came
from High Rock, in Prince George County. Peter stayed in
Lunenburg; Richard was grandfather to Dick Epes, clerk, according to old Tom Epes.)

COMER, 1800. Deed. Sale of Comer's Mill to Peter Bland
(the dam being then broken). Nottoway D. B. 2, p. 179.

COMER, THOMAS, 1809. Will dated 1809, probated 1811.
Leaves property to wife, Elizabeth. Nottoway W. B. 3, p. 105.

COOK, JAMES, 1802. James Cook shown as owning land on
south side of Namozine Road. Nottoway D. B. 2, p. 343.

CORLEY, 1779. Deed. Witnesses, Drury Watson, Jesse
Watson and Josiah Watson. From Corley, of Cumberland, to
John Watson, Jr., of Prince Edward, 176 acres in Prince Ed-
ward, etc. Prince Edward D. B. 6, p. 211.

CRADDOCK, CATEY BASS, 1816. Will, dated November 15,
1816; to her brother James (or Joseph) Craddock, her undivided
interest in land in Hardin County, Kentucky. Amelia W. B.
8, p. 516.

CRADDOCK, CLAIBORNE, 1855. Will dated October 29, 1855.
Amelia W. B. 17, p. 465.

CRADDOCK, HENRY, 1783. Will. Witnesses, Moses and William Cross Craddock. To brother Robert, 200 acres due him
by military warrant; "balance of money due me from the publick," to brothers Charles, David and Robert; and "all clothing
due me from the publick" to Robert; other brothers, Edward and
Archibald; sisters, Edith, Hannah Craddock and Sarah; friend,
William Cross Craddock. Amelia W. B. 3, p. 204.

CRADDOCK, JAMES, 1868. Will, dated June 28, 1868; William Cross Craddock appointed executor, but Joseph M. Gills
qualified in $700. Leaves daughter, Mary O. Hatch, "one dollar,
and no more"; leaves son, William C. Craddock, remainder of
estate, including a tract called Louis's on Vaughan's Creek, and
all the interest he has to a tract of land in Ohio County, Kentucky, containing 1500 acres (patented by William Cross Craddock). Amelia W. B. 20, p. 58.

CRADDOCK, MARTHA, 1822. Will dated Jan. 21, 1822; devises land and negroes to brothers and sisters. Amelia W. B.
9, p. 410.

CRADDOCK, OBEDIENCE, 1816. ˙Will, dated January 2, 1816; gives her interest in the Kentucky land to her brother Henry, and sisters Marthey and Catherine. Amelia W. B. 8, p. 459.

CRADDOCK, RICHARD, 1785. Will dated Feb. 8, 1785; appoints his brother John and William Cross executors and guardians. Sons, James, Richard, William Cross Craddock, Asa, Claiborne, William Claiborne and Robert; Gives to William Cross Craddock three hundred acres on "Tomerhawk Branch" and "Flatt Creek"; leaves land in "Kaintucke" to son William and three younger sons (not named); mentions Jane and Mary. Amelia W. B. 3, p. 329.

CRADDOCK, THOMAS, 1820. Will dated September 17, 1820. Estate to sisters Marthey and Elizabeth Hamblen. Amelia W. B. 9, p. 198.

CRADDOCK, WILLIAM, 1741. Deed. William Craddock, of Amelia County, to James Powell Cocke, of Henrico County, land on Flatt Creek and Walnut Branch. Amelia D. B. 1, p. 225.

CRADDOCK, WILLIAM, 1748. Deed from William Craddock, of Amelia, to Mary, Judith, Richard and William Cross Craddock, his children, for land in Amelia bought of Atwood and others. Amelia D. B. 4, p. 36.

CRADDOCK, WILLIAM CROSS, 1794. Deed from William Cross Craddock, of Amelia, (attorney for Robert Craddock, of Kentucky), to Thomas Comer, for land on Church Road adjoining Henry Anderson. Nottoway D. B. 1, p. 571.

CRADDOCK, WILLIAM CROSS, 1795. Will dated March 7, 1795, recorded July, 1795. His friends, James Hill, George Baldwin and Charles Craddock, executors and guardians, gave bond for 15,000 dollars, with Matthew Robertson Parham, David Booker and John Townes, Jr., sureties. Sons, John Hill, Samuel, James, Thomas, and Henry; daughters, Marthey, Catey (Bass), Fanny, Obedience, Elizabeth Hamblen, wife of Abell (?) Jackson Hamblen, Mary, wife of Joseph Folkes. Amelia W. B. 5, p. 177.

CRENSHAW, DAVID, 1797. Deed from David Crenshaw to Peter Randolph for 570 acres on southside Little Nottoway (at Iron Bridge). Plat recorded; only one in Deed Book 1. Nottoway D. B. 1, p. 635.

CROSS, 1792. Deed from Cross and wife to Irby shows that Stephen and John Cock had a mill pond on Little Nottoway River near Batt's Bridge. Nottoway D. B. 1, p. 237.

CROW, JOHN, 1748. Deed from John Crow, of Goochland, to John Watson, Jr., of Hanover, conveying land partly in Goochland and partly in Hanover. Goochland D. B. 5, p. 79.

CROW, JOHN, 1745. Deed from John Crow, of Goochland, planter, conveying to John Watson Jr., of same county, land lying in Goochland and Hanover. Goochland D. B. 5, p. 442.

DALBY, WILLIAM, 1796. Deed from William Dalby, of the parish of St. Martin, Hanover County, to John Harper, of

Amelia County, for land on Little Sailor Creek in Nottoway, adjoining John Dalby; the same land devised by his father Nightingale Dalby, deceased. Nottoway D. B. 1.

DAVIS, ASA, 1796. Deed from Asa Davis and wife to Nathaniel Lee, of Petersburg, to one hundred acres of land on which said Davis lived, beginning at the "rode" adjoining the land of Colonel Samuel Sherwin's estate and along Sherwin's line to the creek adjoining Ranard Anderson's line, etc. Nottoway D. B. 1, p. 559.

DAVIS, JAMES, 1789. Deed from James Davis, of Charlotte, to Asa Davis, of Nottoway, 105 acres between the Carolina road and a branch of Winningham's Creek; speaks of Davis's store and Samuel Sherwin's line, as bounds. Nottoway D. B. 1, p. 10.

DENNIS, RICHARD, of Rawleigh Parish, Amelia County, 1772, conveys to her grandson Richard Pryor, son of John Pryor, of Nottoway Parish, a negro girl "Cate" and her increase. Amelia D. B. 11, p. 462.

DENNIS, RICHARD, SR., of Rawleigh Parish, Amelia County, 1772, conveys to John Pryor, of Nottoway County, in consideration of natural love for said Pryor, his son-in-law, land beginning at "Shorts Corner" on Cellar Creek. Amelia D. B. 11, p. 451.

DUPUY, (CAPTAIN) JAMES, 1823. Will. Executors, James P. and James H. Dupuy. Sets apart, along with other lands to pay debts, the tract containing Jennings Ordinary, on Namoseen Road, etc; speaks of adjoining Robert Dickinson's estate and the tract bought of Peter R. Bland; intersecting line of Walton's tract; also of joining T. G. Bacon's field and Mrs. Susan Cook's dower tract. Daughter Elvira, not then of age (afterwards Mrs. Eggleston) 250 acres adjoining the main road above Jennings Ordinary, Lodwick Brown, Mrs. Roberts's dower and along Lumpkin's path to "my line of Basset Watson's tract," striking across to Pulliam's Road, etc.; daughter Nancy L. Jeffress (wife of Elisha Jeffress) already advanced her share in 1804; daughter Polly P. Dickinson already advanced her share; as also sons Asa, John P. and William J. Dupuy; daughter Elizabeth G. Osborne (dead) and grand-daughter Elizabeth C. Osborne; bequest to son Joseph; speaks of Deep Creek and Cabin Branch; son James given 528 acres of the house tract. Nottoway W. B. 5, p. 107. *Note:* Charley Dickinson, of Hollins, Virginia, son of W. R. Dickinson, told me Elisha Jeffress built Purnell Dickinson's (his father) house.

DUPUY, JOHN BARTHOLOMEW, 1790. Will. Wife, Mary; sons, John, James and Peter; daughter, Magdaline Watkins. Bought place he resided upon from John Garrant; gives to Peter land devised him (testator) by his father, also land he (testator) bought of William Watson. Nottoway W. B. 1, p. 37.

DUPUY, MARY (Widow of John B. Dupuy), 1793. Will. Nephews, Milton, Samuel, Waller and Zachary Ford, Thomas,

Robert Geers and Christopher Dejarnette; nieces, Mary Overton, Lucy Morriss, Ann Ford and Betty Ford Crenshaw. Nottoway W. B. 1, p. 83.

DUPUY, PETER, 1773. Will. Witnesses, Bartholomew Dupuy, John Maddox, John Dupuy. To son, John Bartholomew Dupuy, thirty pounds; to son Peter, one negro; to son James, "half the tract of land which I am now possessed with, I desire he may have it at the lower end joining the lands of Abraham Forrest and Josiah Hundley," also a negro. To daughters, Ann and Martha Jackson, and five grandchildren, Elijah, Anthony, Charles, Ann and Elizabeth Hundley, eighty pounds to be divided among them; lends to wife, Judith Dupuy, half the land on which he dwells, for life, and at her death to John Bartholomew Dupuy; also lends her three negroes. Amelia W. B. 2, p. 237.

DUPUY, PETER, 1798. Deed from Peter Dupuy, of the county of Powhatan, to Nicholas Vaughan, conveyance of land on Ellis fork of Nottoway River, adjoining lands of Nicholas Vaughan, William Hundley, John Hurt, Curtis Jackson and Williams Jackson. Nottoway D. B. 2, p. 17.

DYSON, FRANCIS, SR., 1830. Will. Executors, son-in-law John Dyson, and son Francis Dyson. To son Francis (not then 21) tract of land on headwaters Little Creek, called the Hall Front (?), etc.; to son John tract purchased of William Jones, lying on West Creek and attached to tract purchased of Richard Jones, etc.; daughter, Elizabeth Webster; to daughter Amelia G. Jackson, tract purchased of Daniel Verser, Sr.; daughter Mary W. Jeter; daughter Louisa Dyson; left wife considerable estate. Nottoway D. B. 6, p. 187.

DYSON, WILLIAM, 1803. Will dated 1795, probated 1803. Lends wife, Mary, upper half of tract bought of Thomas G. Peachy on Deep Creek; gives son, Francis, tract bought of Stephen Hall (called in my time "Linnwood"; see will of Francis Dyson); to son Thomas, lower half of tract bought of Peachy; daughter, Mary Winfree. Nottoway W. B. 2, p. 3.

DYSON, WILLIAM, 1803. Fiduciary account of William Dyson's executors, 1803, shows that Captain Daniel Verser married Elizabeth Dyson; also that negroes belonging to the estate, about which there was suit in Richmond, were brought from Daniel Dyson's in Chesterfield. Items: paid John Jones for preaching funeral sermon, one pound, 4 shillings; paid Edmund Maynard for application of the stone to negro bit by mad-dog, 2 pounds, 5 shillings, 4 pence. Nottoway W. B. 3.

EGGLESTON, JOSEPH, 1791. Will dated 1791, probated 1793; executor, son, Joseph Eggleston; surety, Daniel Hardaway. Son, Joseph; daughters, Jane Segar Cocke, Ann Hardaway, Mary Meade and Elizabeth Archer, wife of John Archer; granddaughter, Judith Eggleston Cocke, and grandson, Seth Hodijah Meade. Directs that he be buried at "Grub Hill." Wife to live in retirement at Kennon's if she desires. She had an annuity of thirty pounds from Captain William Bentley. Amelia W. B. 4, p. 340 (?).

ELLETT, JOHN, 1736. Deed from John Ellett to John Watson, Jr., conveying land in St. James Parish, Goochland, as per patent of March 17, 1736. Goochland D. B. 3, p. 523.

EPPES, EDWARD, JR., 1754. Deed from Edward Eppes, Jr., of Prince George, to William Kennon, of Chesterfield; land on Old Town Creek, being lands given Lewis Eppes, father of Edward, by will of George Archer, dated 1729. Witness, Francis Epes, Jr. Chesterfield D. B. 2, p. 195.

EPES, ELIZABETH, 1678. Will. Executors, her son-in-law, Richard Kennon and Francis Epes; witnesses, Mary Randolph, Elizabeth Cocke, Anne Isham. Two papers proved at the same court, held at Varina, 1678, dated and executed at different times during that year. She lived at Bermuda Hundred; widow first of William Worsham, and last of Colonel Francis Epes; children by the Epes marriage, William, Littleberry, and Mary Epes; names her daughter, Elizabeth Kennon, daughter Mary Worsham, sons John Worsham and Charles (presumably Worsham). Henrico County Court, Minutes, 1678.

EPES, COLONEL FRANCIS, 1678. Verbal will, proven in court by the testimony of witnesses who were with him in his last illness. Richard Cocke and William Randolph testified that he wished his estate divided between his four children and wife, and that he hoped his brother would settle one of them at "Causons" and another at . . . (a place not made out by me. Randolph said his conversation with the Colonel took place a day or two before his death while he was lying dangerously wounded (at his house, one of the others had said.) Henrico County Court, Minutes, 1678.

EPPES, FRANCIS, of Bermuda Hundred. Will dated 1733, probated 1734. Devised large tracts of land in Henrico, Chesterfield and Goochland ("Longfield," "Winterpock," "Skinquarter," etc.) ; sons, Francis, Richard and William; wife, Sarah. Henrico Deeds and Wills, Vol. 2, p. 459. (His son Francis died shortly after, without marrying; will at Henrico).

EPES, FRANCIS, 1772. Will. Executors, brother Peter Epes, son Freeman, friends Stephen Cocke and Richard Jones, son of Colonel Richard Jones; further administration granted Edmund Wills and William Fitzgerald, 1817, with 40,000 dollars security bond. Lived in Nottoway Parish: mother, Sarah Epes; wife, Mary Epes; children, Freeman, Sarah, Martha, Francis, Mary, Thomas, Lucy and John; devised to son Freeman, among other things, "Causons" in Prince George and land adjoining on Cattail Run, also 900 acres on Joseph's Swamp in same county, also small tract on Cox road in Dinwiddie and lot in Blandford town, (the last two willed to him by Thomas Williams) ; to Francis 993 acres on Whetstone Creek, in Amelia, bought of Jordan Anderson, also 1100 acres on Rough Creek in Charlotte, bought of Thomas Williams, and patented in decedent's name, adjoining lands of Peyton Randolph, Edmund Ruffin, John Seddon, etc.; to son Thomas, 1452 acres on Nottoway River, Amelia, bought of John Bowery; to son John 400 acres whereon testator lived and given him by his father, also 300 acres bought of Henry Hasten, 104 acres bought of William Gamblin, but patented in his own name, 397 acres bought of Thomas Bowery, also 387 on Flatt Creek in Lunenburg, bought of Colonel David and Peter Garland. Amelia W. B. 4, p. 136.

EPPES, FRANCIS, of Chesterfield, 1772. Deed to John Osborne for one lot in Gatesville. Chesterfield D. B. 7, p. 81.

EPPES, FRANCIS, 1775. Deed from Francis Eppes, of Charles City County, to Gibbs, for land in Chesterfield, on road from Courthouse to said Eppes's plantation on Appomattox River. Chesterfield D. B. 8, p. 50.

EPPES, FRANCIS, 1778. Deed from Francis Eppes, of Charles City, and John Hylton, of Chesterfield, executors of John Hylton, of Chesterfield, whose will was probated 1773, conveying land to Nathaniel Friend. Chesterfield D. B. 8, p. 305.

EPES, FRANCIS, 1790. Division of estate of Francis Epes, by commissioners of county court, John Doswell, William Irby, William Crenshaw and Stith Hardaway. To Mrs. Mary Epes, west part of Couzins tract, 200 acres; to William Fitzgerald, in right of his wife, Sarah, east part of same 200 acres; to Freeman Epes, north part of "Nottoway" tract, 413 acres; to Edward Wills, in right of his wife, Lucy, land in Lunenburg on Flat Rock Creek, 520 acres; to Francis Fitzgerald, in right of his wife, Mary, east part of tract in Charlotte on Rough Creek, 548 acres; to John Epes, west part of same, 558 acres; to Thomas Epes, south part of the "Nottoway" tract, 561 acres. Good many slaves divided also. Amelia W. B. 4, p. 274.

EPPES, FRANCIS, 1796-7. Deed from Francis Eppes and Elizabeth, his wife, of Chesterfield, conveying the Bermuda Hundred tract of land (756 acres), lots in Bermuda Hundred Town, and another tract all in Chesterfield, to their son, John Wayles Eppes, in consideration of his marriage with Mary Jefferson, daughter of Thomas Jefferson, reciting that Mr. Jefferson had already conveyed "Pantops," in Albemarle (819 acres) and thirty-one slaves. Chesterfield W. B. 14, p. 32 and 258. [Possibly this should be D. B.]

EPPES, FRANCIS, 1802. Deed from Anderson and wife to Woodlief Eppes, Irby Eppes and Francis Eppes, children and heirs of Francis Eppes, deceased, and Mary Eppes, his widow, and John Royall, administrator of said Francis Eppes, conveying land on Tommy Hitton Creek. Nottoway D. B. 2, p. 330.

EPPES, FRANCIS, 1808 and 1810. Will. Account of sales aggregating 3822 pounds, personal estate of Francis Eppes, at Holcomb's, *alias* Randolph's Tavern, in Amelia (where several race horses were sold), and at "Eppington," in Chesterfield, rendered by John W. Epes and Jarman Baker, executors. (The deceased was son of Richard Eppes of Bermuda Hundred and lived at "Eppington" on the Appomattox, in Chesterfield, later the home of the Thweatts. United States senator John Wayles Eppes was his son and an executor of his will.) This account shows that his widow, Elizabeth Eppes, was also dead at this date, and two daughters were living, Misses Matilda and Sally Eppes. Chesterfield W. B. 9, p. 637.

EPES, FRANCIS, SR., 1833. Will. Executors, Francis and Thomas W. Epes; bond $75,000. Wife, Sarah G.; sons, Francis, Thomas W. and Peter; daughters, Martha, Eliza, Adeline Epes; daughters Mary Stith and Sarah Middleton. To son Francis, 150 acres in woods from upper end of tract called "Cheatham's," and adjoining his own tract purchased of Friend, etc.; to T. W., gives balance of "Cheatham's"; to Peter, land in Lunenburg. Nottoway W. B. 6, p. 413.

EPES, FREEMAN, 1800. Deed. Conveyance from (Colonel) Freeman Epes and Jane, his wife, of land on Cub Creek, in Charlotte County, to Edward Dennis. Nottoway D. B. 2, p. 192.

EPES, COLONEL FREEMAN, 1810. Will. Administrators, P. B. Jones and John Epes, Jr. Inventory and appraisement, 1810. In Nottoway County, 3,836 pounds; in Charlotte County about half of this. Nottoway W. B. 3, pp. 27-31.

EPES, ISHAM, 1745. Deed from Isham Epes and Amy, his wife, of Bath Parish, Prince George, to Thomas Bowery, late of Island of St. Christophers, for 1993 acres in Amelia County, on Sellar Fork of Deep Creek, beginning at Taylor's lower corner, etc., being land patented by Epes in 1734 and 1745. Amelia D. B. 1.

EPES, ISHAM, 1750. As appears from deed to Elbank, Isham Epes lived in Prince George, 1750. Amelia D. B. 4, p. 14.

EPPES, ISHAM, 1754. Bond given by Isham Eppes, of Dinwiddie County, with Thomas Scott and John Dabney sureties, to save from harm Richard Eppes and Augustine Claiborne, who were sureties of Isham Eppes on bond as administrator of William Worsham, deceased, of Chesterfield. Chesterfield D. B. 2, p. 97.

EPPES, JAMES, 1772. Deed from James Eppes, of Charles City County, to McWhann (?) for land in Chesterfield, lately property of Henrietta Maria Eppes. Chesterfield D. B. 7, p. 196.

EPPES, JOHN, 1758. Deed from John Eppes, of Dinwiddie, to John Winn, of Amelia, conveying land on Lazaretta Creek, patented by Eppes, in 1744. Amelia D. B. 6, p. 331.

EPES, JOHN, of Nottoway County. Will dated January 26, 1816, probated November 7, 1816; executors, Dr. John Fitzgerald, Dr. Archibald A. Campbell and son-in-law, William B. Cowan; witnesses, Samuel G. Williams, David Vaughan, John Vaughan. (W. B. Cowan qualified as executor with bond of

$300,000.) After provision for a decent burial and funeral expenses, all just debts to be paid; one-third of all estate, both real and personal, to wife, Frances H. Epes, for life and at her death to be equally divided between children "and the children of such of them as may die leaving children," with the exception of "undutiful daughter," Mary W. Epes, who had run off with Bartlett P. Todd to be married, in Carolina, and so incurred her father's displeasure. She is left "the one-fourth part of the judgment obtained in Lunenburg Court against the estate of William Williams, deceased, and also the one-fourth of the value of negro man Lewis, the woman Jinny and girl Jinny that I got in right of my children by my first marriage from the estate of their grandmother, Mrs. Catherine Williams . . . to which she is entitled as heir of her said grandmother"; remainder of estate equally divided between children, with exception of above mentioned daughter. In lieu of one-third of estate for life, wife may choose a fee simple estate of $10,000. Instructions as to account of property advanced to son-in-law, William B. Cowan.

EPES, JOHN F., Nottoway, 1827. Will dated 1827, probated 1829; executor, father-in-law, Samuel Scott. Owned place called "Jordans," adjoining Cocke's; names wife, Mary A.; children, Thomas R., Ann C., and Samuel. Nottoway W. B. 6, p. 48.

EPES, PETER, 1834. Will. Asa Oliver, guardian for children in 40,000 dollar bond, and executor of will. Wife, Martha C.; children, Mary Helen, Richard, Isaac Oliver and Andrew Jackson Epes; gave a home to his sister Mary Elizabeth Epes. Executor directed to furnish his mother with home on her dower land, called "Beverly Green." Nottoway W. B. 6, p. 437.

EPPES, RICHARD, 1751. Deed from Richard Eppes, of Dale Parish, Chesterfield, to John Royall, of Raleigh Parish, Amelia County, conveying land in Chesterfield, known as "Winterpock," willed to him by his father, Francis Eppes. Chesterfield D. B. 1, p. 272.

EPPES, RICHARD, 1751. Deed from "Richard Eppes, of Chesterfield, Gentleman" conveying to "William Eppes, Gent.," "dividend plantation" in Chesterfield, known as "Skinquarter," being land devised to Richard Eppes by his late brother, Francis Eppes, in 1736. Chesterfield D. B. 1, p. 197.

EPPES, RICHARD, 1755. Deed to Agnes and Robert Kennon, for land on Winterpock Creek, being part of a patent to Captain Francis Eppes, 1703, William Eppes, a witness. Chesterfield D. B. 2, p. 296.

EPPES, RICHARD, of Bermuda Hundred, Chesterfield, 1762. Will, dated May 20, 1762; executors, wife, with friends Peter Randolph, Colonel Archibald Cary, Richard Adams and Thomas Adams. To wife Tabitha (who was a Bolling), considerable estate, among the bequests "my four wheeled chaise," and lots and houses in Bermuda Hundred town, Chesterfield, and money; son, Francis, then under age, given lands at Winterpock and in

Amelia, slaves, etc., silver tankard and eleven silver spoons marked M. B. (some Bolling perhaps) and silver spoons marked F. E. (probably Francis Epes) ; daughters, Martha Bolling, Sarah and Tabitha, all under age; son, Richard Henry, land at Winterpock and in Amelia, and all decedent's lands in Henrico purchased of his brother William Eppes, commonly called "Longfield," and silver purchased by executors and marked with the family Arms. ("Longfield," I notice from Henrico records, was the same or near by "Curles") ; gives nephew Richard Harris tract on Swift Creek called "Grillses." Chesterfield W. B....

EPPES, WILLIAM, 1755. Deed. "Eppes and wife, of Salem, in the Province of Mass. Bay, gentleman," etc., of one part, and Peter Randolph, of Chatsworth, in Henrico Colony, of Virginia, Esq., of the other; conveying land on the Appomattox at a point beginning in William Kennon's line on the river to the mouth of Skin Quarter Creek, and then up to Spring Branch, etc.; recites that this land was patented by Francis Eppes, the father of William Eppes, in 1733. Chesterfield D. B. 2, p. 305.

FITZGERALD, JOHN, 1741. Deed from John Fitzgerald, of Prince George County, to John Gilliam, of same county, conveying 934 acres patented by Fitzgerald in 1741, in Amelia, on heads of West's Creek and Deep Creek. Amelia D. B. 1.

FITZGERALD, JOHN, 1749. Deed from John Fitzgerald, of Prince George, to John Archer, of Chesterfield, conveying land in Chesterfield. (Same date John and Anthony Irby owned land in Chesterfield). Chesterfield D. B. 1, p. 57.

FITZGERALD, THOMAS, 1816. Will. Witness, Francis Fitzgerald, Jr. Wife, Anne R.; son, William; daughter, Sarah Epes; brothers, John, William and Robert. Nottoway W. B. 3, p. 336.

FITZGERALD, WILLIAM, 1793. Deed from William Fitzgerald and Sarah, his wife, to John Epes, land east side Cellar Creek, adjoining Moore and others. Nottoway D. B. 1, p. 322.

FLETCHER, NATHAN. Will, dated 1809, probated 1810. Witnesses, Robert and Nathan Ward. Son, James, given all land; grandson, James N. Fletcher; grand-daughters, Martha Fletcher, Martha Ann Fletcher, Mary C. Fletcher. Nottoway W. B. 3, p. 22.

FORBES, GEORGE, 1754. Will. Merchant at Goode's Bridge, Chesterfield County. Leaves his property to brother William, at Aberdeen in North Britain. Chesterfield W. B. 1, p. 78.

FORREST, ABRAHAM, etc., 1795. Deed from Abraham and Josiah Forrest to Peter Dupuy, conveying land in fork of Flat Creek and Ellis Fork, etc., to mouth of William Hundley's line branch, adjoining William Jones, etc. Nottoway D. B. 1, p. 491.

FORSTER, RICHARD, 1797. Agreement between Richard Forster and John and Augustus Watson, by which said Watsons agree to farm the sheriff's place of said Forster for his two years for 100 pounds. Prince Edward D. B. 11, p. 125.

FOWLKES, ASA. Will dated 1806, probated 1807. Lived on south side of Nottoway River; gives this land to brother, Joseph; wife, Sally, and uncle, William Fowlkes. Nottoway W. B. 2, p. 355.

FOWLKES, AUSTIN. Will dated 1804, probated 1805; cousin, William Fowlkes, one of the executors. Wife, Polly P.; daughter, Nancy. Notoway W. B. 2, p. 158.

FOWLKES, GABRIEL, etc., 1775. Contract between Gabriel, John and Joseph Fowlkes, James Wade and John Clark; give up their interest in estate of Gabriel Fowlkes (their father) to Joseph Fowlkes, on condition he take care of Richard Fowlkes (who seems to have been a brother). Amelia D. B. 13, p. 320.

FOWLKES, GABRIEL, SR., 1790. Deed to Gabriel Fowlkes, Jr., both of Nottoway County, for land on Little Nottoway, beginning at middle of the mill house, adjoining Road Jones and Sheriff Peter Jones, Richardson, John Bass, etc. Nottoway D. B. 1, p. 48.

FOWLKES, GABRIEL, SR., 1800. Conveyance of land in forks of Little Nottoway; signed by himself; wife, Elizabeth. Nottoway D. B. 2, p. 184.

FOWLKES, GABRIEL, 1815. Names large family. Nottoway W. B. 3, p. 306.

FOWLKES, HENRY B., 1808. Will. Executors, brother William and friend Asa Vaughan. Land in Nottoway and Lunenburg. Sons, Theoderick, Liberty B., John B., Elisha, Branch, Charles H. and Henry; daughter, Elizabeth Crenshaw. Nottoway W. B. 2, p. 441.

FOWLKES, JENNINGS, 1774. Deed to John Fowlkes, land on Mallory's Creek, part of land bought by George Walton, of William Yarboro, 1774. Amelia D. B. 13, p. 9.

FOWLKES, JENNINGS. Father of Jennings and grandfather of Cousin Mat. Nottoway W. B. 1.

FOWLKES, JENNINGS, 1802. Estate appraised 1802; shows $10,000. Nottoway W. B. 2, p. 11.

FOWLKES, JOHN B., 1816. Will. Executors, friends Archer Robertson and Captain Joseph I. Fowlkes. Brothers, Henry and Elisha; nephew, Asa, son of Henry. Nottoway W. B. 3, p. 337.

FOWLKES, JOSEPH I., 1796. Deed from James Farley, Jr., to Joseph I. Folkes, for land bounded by James Cooke, William Bell, Henry Cabiness, and Nathaniel Robertson, deceased. Also a deed from Henry Cabiness to J. I. Fowlkes, to land adjoining the above and lying on Lazaretta Creek and bounded by William Bell, widow Baldwin, Thomas Hudson, George, Mary and Casimore Cabiness. Nottoway D. B. I.

FOWLKES, JOSEPH I., 1796. Deed to Gabriel Fowlkes to land on Little Nottoway, adjoining Simeon Walton's, William Fowlkes', Abraham Hatchett's and the Church Road. Nottoway D. B. 1.

GILES, ARTHUR, 1752. Will. Brothers, William and Nicholas; sister, Sarah; godson, Charles Lewis. Amelia W. B. 1, p. 89.

GILES, WILLIAM B., 1830. Will. Left about 7698 acres of land (from casual reading); at "Wigwam" and at the mill a large number of cows, horses, hogs, etc.; personal property other than slaves valued at $7874.56; ninety-three negroes valued at $25,660; whole personal estate entered at $33,534. Amelia W. B. (1830).

GOOCH, JOHN, SR., 1802. Conveyance to Isaac Winfree of land on Deep Creek, adjoining Stephen Johns, Joel Tanner, Daniel Verser, Dicy Bradshaw and Dr. James Jones. Nottoway D. B. 2, p. 277.

GOOCH, JOHN, SR., 1802. Deed from John Gooch, Sr., to John Gooch, both of Nottoway, conveying a water grist mill on Deep Creek, and land adjoining Joseph Jennings, Jr., called Jennings' Mill, and afterward called Bacon's Mill. Nottoway D. B. 2, p. 381.

GOOCH, JOHN, JR., Nottoway, 1803. Deed to Freeman Epes, conveying water Griss mill on Deep Creek and land bounded by lands of T. G. Bacon, P. Dunnivant, Joseph Jennings, Sr., and James Dupuy, Jr. Nottoway D. B. 2, p. 422. This mill became a landmark as Bacon's Mill.

GREEN, — —, 1796. Deed to Allen Watson, of Prince Edward, for land on Bush River; witness, Josiah Watson. Prince Edward D. B. 10, p. 458.

GREEN, MARSTON, 1794. Deed to son, Grief Green, for 400 acres purchased of Archibald Yarboro. Nottoway D. B. 1.

GREEN, MASTON. Will dated 1813, probated 1814; witnesses, R. and Lucy Bolling, etc. Wife, Lucy; son, Grief; grandsons, Maston Green Harper, Joel Brown Harper; grand-daughters, Elizabeth Apperson Tunstall, Martha Tabb Green and Louisa Green. Had mill on place where he resided. Nottoway W. B. 3, p. 247.

GREENHILL, DAVID, 1772. Will. Wife, Catherine; sons, Joseph, William, Samuel, Philip Whitehead; daughters, Sarah, Lucy, Martha. Says he was son of Paschal Greenhill and that his mother was then alive. Gives estate descended to him from his uncle, Joseph Greenhill, in Great Britain and Rhode Island, to his sons-in-law, Nelson Jones and Thomas Williams; to son-in-law, John Leigh, who married daughter Elizabeth, land on Cellar Creek and place called Hinton's. Devises land on Meherrin River in Brunswick County, and large number of slaves. Amelia W. B. 2, p. 59.

GREENHILL, ELIZABETH, 1774. Will. Was mother of David Greenhill and widow of Paschal; says Nelson Jones married her grand-daughter Lettice, and Thomas Williams married her grand-daughter Catherine. Devises much property. Amelia W. B. 2, p. 117.

GREENHILL, WILLIAM C., 1832. Deed, November, 1832, from E. A. Lynch and wife, of Maryland, to William C. Green- hill, of Nottoway, to "all those lands in the county of Chester- field, known as Cobbs and Mount Airy, containing by estimate eight hundred acres," etc., in consideration of $4000. Chester- field D. B. 29, p. 130.

GREENHILL, WILLIAM C., 1834. Will. "I leave my estate after payment of all my just debts, both real and personal" etc. "to be equally divided between my sister Catherine and my friend John E. Meade, of Prince George County"; legacy to "my relation Prudence Jones, the wife of Lew Jones, of Nottoway," etc. Inventory shows 35 negroes valued at $9,500.00, case duel- ling pistols at $20.00, pair pocket pistols at $5.00, fish seines, etc., total value $12,087.55. Chesterfield W. B. 13, p. 79.

GRIGG, MARY, 1813. Will. Brothers, Edward and John Redford; four children, Peter, Agnes J., Edward J. and James H. Grigg. Notoway W. B. 3, p. 195.

HADEN, ANTHONY, 1745. Deed from Anthony Haden, of King William County, conveying to John Watson, of Hanover County, 400 acres in Goochland and Hanover. Goochland D. B. 5, p. 62.

HALL, — —, 1798. Deed to Joseph Watson, of Prince Ed- ward, for 400 acres in Prince Edward and Charlotte Counties. Prince Edward D. B. 11, p. 235.

HARDAWAY, DANIEL, 1807. Inventory and appraisement of Daniel Hardaway's estate, 1807; signed by Daniel Hardaway (probably administrator). Estate valued at upwards of 6000 pounds. Amelia W. B. 7, p. 358.

HARDAWAY, DANIEL, 1833. Will. Wife, Sarah T.; D. S. H. Hardaway and Sally Ann seem to have been children. Amelia W. B. 13, p. 35.

HARDAWAY, DR. JOHN S. Will dated July 3, 1818, probated April 22, 1819; executors, friend, Captain James Fletcher, and brothers Daniel A. and Richard E. Wife, Martha, given all estate except medical library and bank stock, etc.; brother, Daniel Hardaway given bank stock, medical library, etc.; brother, Richard E. Hardaway, given two riding horses and slaves; daughter, Sally Ann. Amelia W. B. 9, p. 87.

HARDAWAY, RICHARD E., 1830. Will; executors, William Old, and wife; witnesses, Hadijah Meade and S. Neblett; names wife, Mary, and children. Nottoway W. B. 6, p. 200.

HARDAWAY, STITH, of Rawleigh Parish, Amelia County. Will dated 1765, probated 1767. Son, Stith Hardaway, given all his land on Little Nottoway and in Lunenburg; son, Daniel Hardaway, named in the order of court probating the will. Amelia W. B. 2, p. 211.

HARDAWAY, THOMAS, of Bath Parish, Prince George County, 1747. Deed to Stith Hardaway, land on West's Creek between lines of Stephen Beasley and Richard Jones. Amelia D. B. 2, p. 237.

HARPER, JOHN, 1808. Will. Sons, Vivaldi and Stephen D.; wife, Frances E. Nottoway W. B. 2, p. 440.

HASTEN, HENRY, 1762. Deed to Francis Epes, of Nottoway Parish, Amelia County, for land on Cellar Creek, bounded by Cousins and Moore and on road known as Irby's road; land bought by Hastens of James Hinton, 1753. Amelia D. B. 7, p. 562.

HENDERSON, JAMES, 1793. Deed. Land conveyed by James Henderson to trustees of Nottoway Parish, being on Lazaretta Creek, adjoining Cocke's, Henderson's, Robert Fitzgerald's and Winn's. Nottoway D. B. 1.

HENRY, DOROTHEA, 1796. Deed. Dorothea, wife of Patrick Henry, relinquishes to Augustus Watson her dower in 936 acres in Prince Edward, already sold by Mr. Henry to same, 1792. Prince Edward D. B. 10, p. 442.

HIGGIN and wife, 1790. Deed from Higgin and wife, of Caroline, to John Robertson, of Nottoway, to land on Little Nottoway and Malerey's Creek; speaks of adjoining lands of Daniel Marshall, Henry Fowlkes, Robert Jennings, Robert Smith, James Chambers. Nottoway D. B. —.

HILL, WILLIAM, 1741. William Hill and John Jennings, of Amelia, to Charles Hudson and Charles Snelson, of Hanover County, executors of Thomas Partridge; land on Vaughan's Creek. Amelia D. B. 1, p. 259.

HILL, WILLIAM, 1752. Shown as selling land to Robert Jennings, Gent., of Hanover, a part of land patented by him in 1748 at Williamsburg. Amelia D. B. 4, p. 249.

HOWSON, JOHN, SR., 1797. Deed. Land on Deep Creek to Asa Davis, including a site whereon said Howson formerly had a mill. Nottoway D. B. 1, p. 615.

HUDSON, WILLIAM, 1737. Deed to John Hull, land on West's Creek, at mouth of Barebone, part of a patent to Jonathan Moal (?), 1733. Amelia D. B. 1, p. 38.

HUDSON, WILLIAM, 1745. Deed to Higden Roberson, both of Amelia, for land on Deep Creek. Amelia D. B. 1.

HUDSON, WILLIAM, 1748. Deed from William Hudson, planter, of Amelia, to James Atwood, planter, of same county, for six hundred acres on Deep Creek, being part of a greater tract patented by Hudson, 1737, beginning at Robert Moody's line, then crossing Cabin Branch, etc. Amelia D. B. 8, p. 90.

HUGHES, ASHFORD, 1740. Deed from Ashford Hughes, of Goochland, to Matthew Watson, of Parish of St. Martins, Hanover County, conveying land on Beaver Dam Fork of Muddy Creek, a south branch of James River in Goochland County. Goochland D. B. 3, p. 306.

HUGHES, ASHFORD, of St. James Parish, Goochland, 1749. Deed to Matthew Watson, of Frederickville Parish, Louisa

County, conveying land on Beaver Dam Fork, Muddy Creek, a south branch of James River, in Goochland. Goochland D. B. 5, p. 539.

HYLTON, JOHN, 1773. Will. Devised large property, making Charles Carter, of "Corotoman," Francis Eppes, of "Wintipock," John Archer and Thomas Jefferson, and some members of his family, executors. Chesterfield W. B. 2, p. 281.

IRBY, CHARLES, 1760. Deed. Charles Irby, Gent., of Nottoway Parish, conveys to John Irby, of same parish, land adjoining John Cock, Maston Green, John Winn and Nottoway glebe; part of tract patented by Irby, 1739. Amelia D. B. 7.

IRBY, EDMUND, 1831. Settlement of account of his executors, Lew Jones and William R. Johnson. Nottoway W. B. 6, pp. 304-309.

IRBY, WILLIAM, 1812. Will. Wife, Elizabeth, daughter of Thomas Roper Williams; to son Edmund gives tract on which he, Edmund, lives, called "Batts," bounded north by Johnny's Branch, bought of Richard Cross; also several small tracts; to son William Blunt (when he reaches twenty-one), gives tract "on which I now live," bounded south by Johnny's Branch, east by Pace and Thomas, north by Thomas Epes, west by the river; also several smaller tracts; to daughter, Elizabeth W. Irby, considerable property. Nottoway W. B. 3, p. 139. Page 170 contains his appraisement (and writes after his name Surry), in Nottoway 2,639 pounds, in Lunenburg, 2,343 pounds.

ISHAM, MRS. KATHERINE, 1686. Will. Executors, son, Joseph Royall and son-in-law, Francis Epes. Mentions daughters Mary Randolph, Ann Epes and Sarah Wilkinson; grandchildren, William, Henry, Elizabeth and Mary Randolph, also Joseph Royall, Richard Dennis, Isham Epes, Francis Epes, Sarah Royall, Richard Perrin, Mary, Sarah and Ann Perrin, Katherine Farrar Perrin. Henrico then, but probably Bermuda in Chesterfield.

JACKSON, JOHN, of St. Andrew's Parish, Brunswick, 1734. Deed to his son-in-law, John Watson, land on Reedy Creek. Clerk's Office, Brunswick County.

JACKSON, JOHN, of Brunswick County. Will dated, 1740, recorded 1746. Mentions his daughter Rebecca and John Watson, Jr. Clerk's Office, Brunswick County.

JEFFRESS, MARY. Will dated 1809, probated 1810; executors, sons James and John. Sons, James, John, Coleman, Thomas, Richard, and Elisha; daughters, Susanna Walker, Edith Fowlkes, Dicey Jordon, Jiney Wooten; son-in-law Gabriel Fowlkes and his children, Polly G., Elizabeth, Jane, and William J.; grand-daughters, Martha C. Hardin, Mary G. Hamlet, Polly G., daughter of James Jeffress; grand-children Griffin, Polly W. and Thomas Filbert Smith. Nottoway W. B. 3, p. 11.

JEFFRESS, THOMAS, SR., 1793. Will probated 1794; witnesses, Richard Bennet, Jr., John Overstreet, Robert B. Munford and Barbee Miller; executors, friends Henry Stokes and Gabriel Fowlkes, Jr., and sons, James and John appointed. Wife, Mary; Sons, James, Thomas, John, Coleman, Elisha and Richard; daughters, Edith, Susanna Walker, Elizabeth Fowlkes, Lucrecy Smith, Diesey, Jane Wooten; son-in-law Joseph Jennings, who married daughter Mary; grand-daughter Patsy Coleman Jennings. Gives considerable quantity of land in Lunenburg County on both sides of Dry Creek to his sons. Nottoway W. B. 1, p. 121.

JENNINGS, JAMES, 1767. Deed from James Jennings and Philadelphia, his wife, and Mary Jennings, all of Nottoway, to George Walton, of Amelia, for land on Cabin Branch and Deep Creek, etc. Amelia D. B. 9, p. 60.

JENNINGS, JOHN, 1771. Deed, March 28, 1771, to William Watson, both of Amelia, for land adjoining Watson, and Jesse Walton, on Cabin Branch, etc. Amelia D. B. 11, p. 240.

JENNINGS, JOHN, 1773. Deed to Jeremiah Walker for sixty acres on Deep Creek, on the Church Road, etc. Amelia D. B. 12, p. 226.

JENNINGS, JOHN, 1775. Deed to John Robertson, land near Mallory's Creek, adjoining Edward Robertson's (deceased) line; same land John Norris sold to Dickerson Jennings. Amelia D. B. 13, p. 277.

JENNINGS, JOHN, 1777. Deed to Jeremiah Walker for land on Church Road, touching Walton's line, to the main road, to the Church road, etc. Amelia D. B. 14, p. 112.

JENNINGS, JOHN, 1777. Deed to Jesse Walton for land beginning at Walker's line, and along main road to corner opposite Brooks' house, etc. Amelia D. B. 14, p. 111.

JENNINGS, JOHN, 1778. Deed to William Jennings, conveying land on the great road, beginning near Jennings Ordinary; mention, as boundaries, Jesse Walton's line and Cabin Branch. Amelia D. B. 14, p. 353.

JENNINGS, JOHN. Will, dated September 11, 1783; witnesses, Joseph Dickerson and James Jennings. Gives to sons William and Joseph his "Griss" mill on Deep Creek just below Cabin Branch. Amelia W. B. 3, p. 362.

JENNINGS, JOSEPH, April, 1770. Deed to William Watson, both of Amelia, to land north side of Cabin Branch, adjoining Vivion (formerly Moore's), William Jennings, Watson's, Walton's, Royall's and John Jennings; being part of a larger tract supposed to be entailed on said William Watson by his father, William Watson. Amelia D. B. 11, p. 101.

JENNINGS, JOSEPH, 1774. Deed from Joseph and Anne Jennings, his wife, to Samuel Thompson, of Amelia, for land on Deep Creek, beginning at Oliver's line and running to Stuart's line, Cabin Branch, etc. Amelia D. B. 13, p. 86.

JENNINGS, JOSEPH, JR., 1794. Deed from Joseph Jennings, Jr., of Nottoway, to Jesse Walton, land on Deep Creek; reserving for Gooch's mill-pond to be raised, etc., and also the privilege of said Jennings of setting fish trap at head of pond. Nottoway D. B. 2, p. 228.

JENNINGS, JOSEPH, SR., 1802. Deed from Joseph Jennings, Sr., and Anne, his wife, and James Camp and Sarah, his wife, to Philip Dunnivant, Jr., of Amelia, conveying land on Namerseen Road, beginning at Richard Oliver's corner, on Deep Creek, etc., near Gooch's mill dam. Nottoway D. B. 2, p. 374. (This was subsequently Dr. Royall's place.)

JENNINGS, JOSEPH, SR., 1805. Will. Devises property to daughter, Mary Oliver, wife of Richard Oliver, and, in event that bad treatment of his daughter by her husband shall force a separation, he requires his executors to obtain a divorce in Nottoway Court in the case of Mary Oliver *vs.* Richard Oliver, by himself, her next friend (a suit which appears already to have been instituted). Names son, Langly B.; daughters Martha Talbot, wife of David G. Talbot, Sarah Camp, Elizabeth Hall, Jiney Jennings, and Armon; wife, Anna. Owned plantation five miles below where he lived, and known as Fergussons. Nottoway W. B. 2, p. 146.

JENNINGS, JOSEPH (index says Joseph C.), 1808. Will. Wife, Anne; children, John W., Langly A., Polly, Nancy L. B., and Martha Coleman Housen. Nottoway W. B. 2, p. 408.

JENNINGS, WILLIAM, 1764. Deed from William Jennings and wife Mary to George Walton, all of Nottoway Parish, land on Deep Creek, touching Watson's line; one acre excepted at the falls for a mill. Amelia D. B. 8, p. 412.

JENNINGS, WILLIAM, SR., of Amelia, 1766. Deed to James Jennings, of Amelia, for land on the branches of Deep Creek, beginning at the mouth of Cabin Branch, up the creek to Geo. Walton's line and thence to Watson's line, etc. Amelia D. B. 9, p. 5.

JENNINGS, WILLIAM, May, 1769. Deed to Joseph Jennings, both of Amelia, for land lying between their home places, and touching Cabin Branch. Amelia D. B. 11, p. 60.

JENNINGS, WILLIAM, July, 1773. Deed of gift to his son, Joseph, of two hundred acres, lying on Cabin Branch, "being the tract wherein I now live," etc. in Amelia County. Amelia D. B. 12, p. 80.

JENNINGS, WILLIAM, SR., 1774. Deed to Jesse Walton, land at the falls of Deep Creek, adjoining lands of Jesse Walton and Thomas Payne, etc. Amelia D. B. 13, p. 84.

JENNINGS, WILLIAM, 1786. Contract between William Jennings and Joseph Jennings, Sr., partners in a griss-mill on Deep Creek, just below mouth of Cabin Branch, in consideration of the damage to some of the land of Joseph Jennings, Sr., agreeing that he and his heirs, whosoever of them should be actually in possession of the plantation on which he lived, should have grinding "hopper free" at the mill. Amelia D. B. 17, p. 395.

JENNINGS, WILLIAM, SR., 1792. Deed from William Jennings, Sr., and Molley, his wife, to Joseph Jennings, Sr., both of Nottoway, conveying land in Nottoway on south side of Cabbin Branch, bounded in part by Jesse Walton's and the main road above Jennings Ordinary. J. S. Anderson, Langley B. and Joseph Jennings, Jr., witnesses. Nottoway D. B. 1, p. 294.

JOHNSON, WILLIAM R. Will, dated at Richmond 1844; all in his own writing, probated 1849; executor, W. R. Johnson. Gives $10,000. to daughter, Virginia Pegram; balance of estate divided among sons W. R. Johnson and Marmaduke, daughter, Frances Jane Johnson, two grandsons, William R. J. Dunn and Thomas H. Dunn. Chesterfield W. B. 18, p. 268. Appraisement of estate in Chesterfield, 1849: real and personal $17,269; "Oakland" only land mentioned, $8000.; appraisement in Roanoke County, Virginia, called "Bellgrove," $25,000., aggregating $40,986.50. Chesterfield W. B. 18, p. 329.

JONES, ABRAHAM, 1738. Deed. Abraham Jones, Jr., of Prince George County, to Charles Jennings, Jr., of Elizabeth City County, land on Nottoway River and Hurricane Swamp. Amelia D. B. 1, p. 229.

JONES, BRANCH, 1794. Receipt from Augustus Watson to Batt Jones, executor of Branch Jones, deceased, in full of fiduciary demand on part of his wife, Sarah Branch Jones, only child of Branch Jones, deceased. Nottoway D. B. 1.

JONES, CAPTAIN DANIEL, 1772. Will. Gives son Daniel estate already delivered, also twenty head cattle, etc.; mentions daughters Sarah, Mary, Martha, Rebekah, Elizabeth, (the last three to have 500 pounds each), and Prudence; to sons Richard and Edward, 1400 acres of land in Mecklenburg County on Finney Wood Creek; also to Richard place on which "I live," containing 500 acres on south side West Creek; to daughters eight or nine slaves each. Mentions brothers Richard and Peter. Amelia D. B. 2, p. 42. He is named in Inventory and appraisement as "Capt. Daniel Jones."

JONES, DANIEL, 1795. Will. Executors, Richard Jones and Francis Fitzgerald, friends, named; the latter qualified with Richard Jones, (son of Daniel probably); John Epes and Edward Bland, sureties; witnesses, Richard Jones, Edward Jones and Benjamin Ward. Wife, Catherine; sons, Littleberry H., Theoderick, George, Patrick and Daniel; daughters, Louisa and Frances, to whom he gave 750 pounds and other personalty. Gave Daniel land on Flat Creek, bought of William Bell, to have possession December 25, 1796. Devised land on Butcher's Creek, Mecklenburg County. Nottoway W. B. 1, p. 198.

JONES, DANIEL. Inventory and appraisement of estate of Daniel Jones. Large list, and among articles, "Obscurity" (stud horse), 250 pounds; corn, 480 barrels, valuation, 480 pounds; "chariott" and harness (new), 150 pounds; chariot and harness (old), 40 pounds; one deer, 1 pound 10 shillings; tobacco, 25,535 pounds, the crop (1795) 382 pounds, 10 shillings. Nottoway W. B. 1, p. 218. NOTE: This Daniel Jones lived at "Mount Airy" and married the widow Ward of "West Creek," who was Catherine Cralle. His son George lived at "Old Homestead," the home of the late Branch Cralle Jones, who was one of his sons. An older son was Francis, of Brunswick, who married a daughter of Thomas Thweatt, of Dinwiddie, and was father to Rev. T. T. Jones, George Jones (who married a Pryor), Freeman Jones and William Jones, of Lawrenceville. Patrick Jones, son of Daniel, lived at "Buckskin" (Dr. J. C. Bragg's), and one of his daughters married William A. Bragg, Sr., of Petersburg; his widow married Dr. Austin Watkins.

JONES, DANIEL. Report of commissioners dividing estate of Daniel Jones, deceased, including "Mt. Airy." Nottoway W. B. 2, p. 241.

JONES, FRANCIS, 1827. Account of Nathaniel H. Jones, as executor of Francis Jones, shows that the children of decedent were Catherine C., Frances A., Edgar, Thaddeus, Dorothy C., and Greenhill Jones. Thaddeus was killed at Lunenburg Court House, by John James Jones, a kinsman, and Edgar was killed at a barbecue in Dinwiddie, near San Marino. Nottoway W. B. 6, p. 40.

JONES, JAMES, 1800. Deed of sale of glebe lands in Nottoway and the boundaries thereof, to James Jones and John Patterson. Nottoway D. B. 2, p. 420.

JONES, JOHN W. Will, dated 1847, probated 1848, all in handwriting of testator; two sons executors; bond of $90,000.00 given by executors, no security. Gives to sons James B. and Alexander Jones "Gravely Hill" and tracts adjoining named "Branches," and considerable personalty; daughter Mary W. Towns, wife of George W. Towns, provided for in trust; wife, Harriet Jones, land adjoining that allotted her in the division of her father's estate in Chesterfield, also life estate in tract on which he resided; "The Neck of Land" to sons, and other provisions to daughters, etc.; legacies to grand-daughters Harriet W. Towns, Margaret Towns, Mary Towns, Anne Towns, and to grandsons, John Towns, John W. Jones, Peter Edwin Jones. Chesterfield W. B. 17, p. 539.

JONES, JOHN W., 1848. Appraisement at "Gravely Hill," March, 1848. Personal property $13,736, includes 550 barrels of corn, 15000 pounds of tobacco, 35,000 pounds of fodder, 15000 pounds of oats; at farm on James River, "The Neck of Land," February, 1848, personal property $4,075., 785 barrels corn; at "Bellwood," late residence of the deceased, November, 1848, good many thousands (not added), probably $17,000.00; library at $100. Chesterfield W. B. 18, p. 111.

JONES, LEWELLING, 1800. Deed from Lewelling Jones and Prudence, his wife, of Lunenburg, conveying property to T. G. Bacon, on Little Creek; shows that the wife of said Jones was

Prudence Ward, orphan of Rowland Ward, Jr., deceased, and that she had brothers Henry and Rowland· Nottoway D. B. 2, p. 138.

JONES, LITTLEBERRY HARDIMAN, 1802. Deed to Benjamin Ward, of land on Flat Creek, it being tract ("Bellefield") conveyed by William Bell and wife and Peter Ellington and wife to Daniel Jones, in 1795, and devised by him to Daniel Jones, Jr., his son, and by him conveyed, 1801, to L. H. Jones, trustee. Nottoway D. B. 2, p. 305.

JONES, MAJOR PETER, 1753. Will, probated 1759; names executors, his friends, Richard Jones, Jr., Peter Jones (son of Major Richard Jones) and Edward Jones; will signed by himself; witnesses, William Poythress, Thomas Williams, Richard Jones, Sr. Gives to wife, Dorothy, the plantation "I now live upon" and slaves; to son John 1000 acres land below Spinners Branch; to sons Thomas, William and Richard, all land on West Creek, purchased of Thomas Jones; to daughter, Ridley Branch, property already in her possession; to daughters Elizabeth and Margaret, 180 pounds each and slaves; speaks of property on West Creek "where John Mayton is overseer," and on Deep Creek "where William Butler is overseer"; mentions daughter Sarah Jones. Amelia W. B. 1, p. 133. Inventory and appraisement shows among other things, 41 negroes, 98 cattle, 120 hogs, 54 sheep, 8 horses, etc.

JONES, PETER, SR., 1791. Deed from Peter Jones, Sr., of Amelia, to Augustus Watson, of Prince Edward, in consideration of marriage between him and Sarah Branch, graddaughter of said Peter Jones, 400 acres of land in Nottoway, called Cannon's (afterwards Kennon's), bound on north by John Royall, west by Batt Jones, south by the Griggs, east by Robert Jones. Nottoway D. B. 1791, p. 183.

JONES, PETER BRANCH, 1802. Deed to Robert Fitzgerald, 800 acres in Hell's Corner. Says it was the same land conveyed to grantor by "will of my grandfather, Peter Jones ('road') deceased, of Amelia," etc. Nottoway D. B. 2, p. 336. There was a "Road" Peter Jones and a "Sweathouse" Peter Jones, who are mentioned in the deeds at Nottoway.

JONES, PETER B., 1813. Will. Executors, friends Major John Epes and Edward Bland. Wife, Martha, and three children, Mary E., Peter B. and Elizabeth B· Owned land bought of Augustus Watson, on eastern side of lower fork of Woody Creek and also Ellett's. Nottoway W. B. 3, p. 229.

This was probably Peter Branch Jones, son of Bartholomew Jones and Margaret, daughter of Rowland Ward, his wife; grandson of Peter Jones and Sarah Tanner; the grandfather died in 1799. (The foregoing I have from Rev. S. O. Southall, but don't know where he got the descendants of Peter and Sarah Tanner Jones.) I think he was the father of Colonel Travis H. Epes's wife, Elizabeth B., and that his other daughter became

Mrs. Col. Isham Lundy. Judge Branch Jones Epes told me he thought his father and mother were first cousins.

JONES, RICHARD, of Saint Andrew's Parish, Brunswick County, 1746. Will recorded 1747. Devised lands on Nottoway River in Brunswick and Stoney Creek, in Prince George, this last to his son Daniel Jones. Mentions sons Lewellyn, Richard, Robert and Daniel, and grandson Phillip, son of Daniel; wife, Rachel. Clerk's Office, Brunswick County.

JONES, COLONEL RICHARD, 1758. Will, probated 1759, names Richard, Peter and Daniel Jones, executors. Devised large estate already delivered for most part; names daughter Amy Watson, wife of William Watson; sons, Richard, Peter and Daniel; gives daughter Prudence Ward 400 acres in fork of West Creek, commonly called "Lesters," and estate already delivered; daughter Rebekah Ward, sundry mulatto slaves "now in possession of my step-mother Mrs. Rachel Jones"; daughter Martha Jones; to son, Lewellyn Jones, "the plantation on which I now live" containing 1006 acres, and personalty. Amelia W. B. 1, p. 150.

JONES, RICHARD, 1778. Will. Executors, brother Peter Jones, Stephen Cocke, Littleberry Royall and son Richard. Wife, Elizabeth; children, Margaret Jones, Elizabeth Royall, Sarah, Rachel, Thomas, William and daughter Amey Cock. Amelia W. B. 2, p. 306.

JONES, RICHARD, 1798. Deed to son, James Jones, of land purchased of James May, the widow and orphans and executor of Richard Willson, Charles Stuart, Samuel Cobbs and Thomas Worsham (deeds from the first four parties recorded in Amelia, and the last one in Nottoway) ; lands bounded by lands of Rowland Ward, Robert Jones' estate, John Howson, Asa Davis, Stephen Johns, John Gooch, the estate of Jeremiah Bradshaw, Bowler Hall and Alexander Bruce; land lying on road known as Irby's Courthouse Road. Nottoway D. B. 2, p. 31.

JONES, MAJOR RICHARD, 1834. Case, Jones's administrator *versus* Comer's executors. Suit brought by administrators of Major Richard Jones *versus* Thomas Comer's executors, and argued at great length and decided for defendant by court, which found Jones guilty of fraud. 5 Leigh 350.

JONES, THOMAS, 1791. Deed from Thomas Jones and wife, Prudence, of Amelia, to Stephen Beasley, of Nottoway, of land in Nottoway; speaks of adjoining lands of Branch Osborne, William Dyson, and William Bass; also bounded by Deep Creek. Land devised to grantor by his father, Richard Jones. (In my day, residence of DeFerney). Nottoway D. B. 1. Stephen Beasley also bought land adjoining on Deep and Little Creeks from Peter Beverly, of Chesterfield, at same time.

KENNON, WILLIAM, 1746. Deed. William Kennon, the elder, to William Kennon, the younger, both of Henrico County, land on Appomattox River, patented by former in 1730. Amelia D. B. 2, p. 231.

LAFORCE, RENE, of Goochland, 1748. Deed to John Watson, of same county, conveying land in Goochland, north side of James River. Goochland D. B. 5, p. 493.

LAMKIN, PETER. Will. Father of Mrs. Bacon. Nottoway W. B. 1.

McRAE, JOHN, 1800. Deed from John McRae, merchant, of Petersburg, to Samuel Morgan, to tract of land in Nottoway, commonly called "Burnt Ordinary," on both sides of Irby's and Cock's roads (formerly known as Edmundson's Old Ordinary; also called Morganville). Nottoway D. B. 2, p. 203.

MANN, JOHN, JR., 1794. Deed to James Mann for land on both sides Barebone Creek, adjoining Robert Vaughan, Daniel Jones, Thomas Cook, Rowland Ward and John Mann, Sr., (including all the tract of land and improvements which Catholick Mann, deceased, devised to said John Mann.) Nottoway D. B. 1, p. 398.

MANN, JOHN, 1794. Deed to Barbee Miller, for 491 acres on west of Flatt Creek; speaks of joining John Motley's and William Hurt's lines, and Pulliam's old road. Nottoway D. B. 1794, p. 363.

MILLER, BARBEE, 1794. Barbee Miller is shown as owning land west of Flatt Creek on "Pulliam's Old Road." About this time William Bell sold his mill on Flat Creek to John Mann. Nottoway D. B. 1.

MOODY, ROBERT, 1750. Deed to Abraham Forrest, of Gloucester, for land on Deep Creek and the Cooper's branch, being part of patent to Moody for 774 acres, 1737. Amelia D. B. 3, p. 223.

MOODY, ROBERT, 1750. Deed to James Oliver, both of Nottoway, for land on both sides Deep Creek, to the Cooper's Branch, to Randle's corner, etc., it being part of a tract Moody lived on, and patented by him, 1737. Amelia D. B. 3, p. 202.

MOORE, GEORGE, 1795. Deed. Land conveyed to Frances Thacker Holmes, Margaret Brooking Holmes, John Ballard Holmes, Vivion Brooking Holmes and Lucy Holmes, infants of Isaac Holmes; near the house lately occupied as clerk's office, etc. Nottoway D. B. 1.

NASH, —, 1801. Deed from Nash and wife to Samuel Watson, Sr., of Prince Edward, for land on Briery River. Witnesses, Joseph and Hannah Watson, etc. Prince Edward D. B. 12, p. 147.

NELSON, —, 1791. Deed to John Watson, Jr., of Prince Edward, land on south of "Roan Oak Road." Witnesses, Joseph and Josiah Watson. Prince Edward D. B. 8, p. 326.

NOBLE, STEPHEN, 1802. Deed to James Dupuy, of land bought of Jesse Walton, on Cabbin Branch, which divides it from land of Joseph Jennings, Sr. Nottoway D. B. 2, p. 304.

NOMAX, 1741. Deed to Francis Epps, of Prince George, to land in Amelia, on branches of Nottoway River and Deep Creek, bought of Matthew Smart, of Martin Brandon Parish, Prince George. Amelia D. B. 1, p. 214.

OLIVER, ISAAC. Will probated 1799; names son Carter and friends Abraham Hatchett, Grief Green, Rawleigh Carter, Sr., executors; witnesses, William Carter, William Boram, Lemuel Bruce. Sons, Carter, Charles, Asa; daughters, Elizabeth and Polly; wife, Judith, to whom he gives land upon which he lived, devised to him by his father's will; younger children, Matilda, Rebecca, Sally, William and Elisha. Nottoway W. B. 1, p. 347.

OLIVER, JAMES, 1743. Deed, James Oliver and Elizabeth, his wife, land on Great Nottoway River and Snales Creek, patented by James Oliver, 1743. Amelia D. B. 2, p. 15.

OLIVER, JAMES. Will, dated and probated, 1787; executors, Simeon Walton, Abraham Hatchett, and son, Isaac; witnesses, John Howson, Sr., John Howson, Jr., David Craddock. Sons, John, Asa, Isaac, James, William, Richard; daughters, Elizabeth Forrest and Sarah Bottom. James had a son Benjamin; Elizabeth had a daughter, Pattie; Sarah had a daughter, Frances. Gives to Richard land on north of Deep Creek and eight slaves. Gives James land in Halifax County. Land on south side of Deep Creek, divided into seven equal shares. Amelia W. B. 4, pp. 44, 45.

OLIVER, JOHN, 1764. Will. Wife, Lucy; brothers, Isaac and James. Clerk's Office, Brunswick County.

OLIVER, LUCY, 1765. Speaks of Isaac, son of James (Oliver). Clerk's Officer, Brunswick County.

OLIVER, RICHARD, 1801. Deed from Richard Oliver, conveying one-third of his estate to Abraham Hatchett and John Robertson, Sr., in trust for the benefit of his wife, Mary, in consideration of her dismissing a suit for alimony in court. Nottoway D. B. 2, p. 226.

OSBORNE, ABNER, 1805. Will. Lived on land lying on Deep and Sellar Creeks; had, besides, two farms on Namozine and West Creeks; also owned "Presque Isle" on James River, which he devised to grandson Abner Osborne Watkins; gave remainder of his estate to wife, Elizabeth, and his son-in-law and daughter, Conrad and Lucy Webb. (large estate). Nottoway W. B. 2, p. 172. In this will there is a place described as "my level plantation" and given to Conrad and Lucy Webb. I think this is the level joining "Westbury," which Clerk Dick Epes told me belonged, when he was a boy, to a Mr. Webb of New Kent [County].

PATTERSON, JOHN, 1796. Deed. Administrator of Henry Anderson, conveys in September, 1796, land on Mallory Creek, adjoining Comer's Mill Pond, to John A. Robertson. Nottoway D. B. 1, p. 577.

PAYNE, THOMAS, Nov. 16, 1778. Contract between Thomas Payne, John Jennings, and Jesse Walton, each of Amelia, for the erection of a mill at the falls of Deep Creek, etc. Amelia D. B. 15, p. 96.

PAYNE, THOMAS, 1780. Deed to Nathaniel Robertson, of Amelia, conveying for 29,975 lbs. tobacco, 250 acres and one-third of water mill on southside Deep Creek, it being a part of a tract bought by Thomas Payne, of James Pressnell, in 1766, on which Payne lived, and was known by the name of Payne's plantation, whereon Rowland's Church stood. Amelia D. B. 16, p. 105.

PENNIL, 1777. Deed. Pennil, of Bedford, to Joseph Watson, of Charlotte, conveys land in Prince Edward. Witnesses, John Watson, Jr., James Allen, Jr., and Samuel Watson. Prince Edward D. B. 5, p. 542.

PORTER, JAMES MAY, 1789. Deed from James May Porter, of Pittsylvania, to Rowland Ward, Jr., to land on a branch of Deep Creek, bounded by Robert Jones, Joel Tanner, Stephen Johns, etc. Nottoway D. B. 1, p. 24.

PORTER, WILLIAM MAY. Deed, April, 1795, to William Robertson, infant son of Molley Robertson, widow (James Dupuy was his guardian), land on Deep Creek bought from Nathaniel Robertson; speaks of adjoining lands of Littleberry Royall, Pleasant Walton, Cabiness and J. Farley, etc. Nottoway D. B. 1, p. 475.

PRYOR, JOHN, 1765. Deed from Muse and wife, of Caroline County, to John Pryor, of Amelia County, conveying land in Amelia on Sellar Creek, and Deep Creek, now called Leath's Creek, being land that said Muse purchased of William Westbrook and which was patented by John West, 1736. Amelia D. B. 8, p. 597.

PRYOR, JOHN, 1785. Will. Executors, son-in-law, John Timberlake, and son, Richard; witnesses, Richard Dennis, Martha Pryor. Gives to sons Richard and Luke tract of land on which he lived, lying on Leath's Creek, bought of Muse, etc.; remainder of this tract to son Phillip, on condition his daughter Ann have use of part of the house for a home; names son Samuel and daughters Elizabeth Timberlake, Mary Boling and Ann Pryor; directs executors to raise two hundred pounds to educate Phillip and Luke; mentions legacy from his deceased brother Luke Pryor. Amelia W. B. 3, p. 385. (This John Pryor may have been the same mentioned in the Revolutionary Rolls in the State Library as a Captain in the Continental Army.)

PRYOR, LUKE, 1802. Deed. Shown that Luke Pryor had left Nottoway, gone to Dinwiddie and sold land to Peterson Old. Nottoway D. B. 2, p. 375.

PRYOR, PHILIP, 1742. Deed from Philip Pryor, of St. Martin's Parish, Hanover County, and Ann, his wife to — — Berry, conveying lands in Amelia. Signed in presence of Major Pryor, Lodwick Tanner, and William Baldwin. Amelia D. B. 1, p. 307.

PRYOR, RICHARD, 1790. Deed to Edward Bland, of Prince George, to land in Cellar Creek Country, adjoining Daniel Sturdivant, Vaun's orphans, Edward Bland, Luke Pryor, orphan of John Pryor, and Phillip Pryor, orphan of John. Nottoway D. B. 1, p. 53.

PRYOR, SAMUEL, 1754. Deed. ———— Munford to Samuel Pryor, of Rawley Parish, Amelia County, land on both sides of Sweat-house Creek, in Amelia. Amelia D. B. 5, p. 53.

PRYOR, SAMUEL, 1756. Deed to ———— Cousins, conveying the above tract. Amelia D. B. 5, p. 252.

PRYOR, SAMUEL. Will dated and probated 1790. Brothers, Philip (not then twenty-one), Richard and Luke Pryor. Amelia W. B. 4, p. 167.

PRYOR, THORNTON, 1758. Deed from ———— Ellis and wife, to Thornton Pryor, of Amelia County, conveying land on Horsepen Creek. Amelia D. B. 6, p. 448.

PRYOR, THORNTON, 1761. Deed to ———— Shelton, conveying land in Nottoway Parish, in the forks of Nottoway, part of land Thornton Pryor purchased of John Ellis and wife. Amelia D. B. 7, p. 527.

PRYOR, THORNTON, 1763. Deed. Thornton Pryor, of Halifax County, N. C., conveys land to Samuel Pryor, of Goochland Co., land formerly part of estate of his father, Samuel Pryor, deceased, and then in hands of Mother Prudence Pryor. John Pryor one of the witnesses who proved this deed in Amelia Court. Amelia D. B. 8, p. 220.

PRYOR, THORNTON, 1772. Deed. Thornton Pryor, of the province of North Carolina, conveys to John Thweat, of Prince George County, land bought of ———— Ellis, except that sold to Shelton. Amelia D. B. 11, p. 365.

PURNALL, WILLIAM, 1757. Deed from William Purnall, of Nottoway Parish, to George Forest, of the same, for land on Deep Creek, part of patent to William Hudson, in 1737, and sold to Purnall by James Presnell. Amelia D. B. 6.

RANDOLPH, ELIZABETH, of Dale Parish, 1775. Will. Executors, son Grief Randolph and grandson John Archer. Daughter Ann Leonard; grandson, Henry Randolph; grand-daughters, Elizabeth Wormley Randolph, Elizabeth Sherwin, Ann Randolph Watson; grandson John Archer given silver spoons marked F. E. A. Chesterfield W. B. 3, p. 209.

RANDOLPH, GRIEF, 1757. Deed to John Archer, Sr., both of Chesterfield, conveying six negroes assigned by the county court of Charles City County to his wife, Mary, as her part of her father's (Edmund Eppes) estate. Chesterfield D. B. 3, p. 216.

RANDOLPH, HENRY, 1769. Will. Sons, John, William, Peter and Thomas; possibly other children; all his lands in

Amelia to be equally divided between his sons Peter and Thomas. Chesterfield W. B. 2, p. 6.

RANDOLPH, HENRY, of Nottoway, 1796. Deed to John Clay, of Amelia, to land on which Randolph lived, adjoining Mrs. Blodgett, Henry Vaden.and Edward Bland's estate. Nottoway D. B. 1, p. 585.

RANDOLPH, PETER, 1790. Deed to John A. Schwartz, of land in Nottoway and, referring to boundaries, speaks of Cock's, Jordan's, Drinkwater's and Cryer's; also of Francis White's Tavern, Cock's and Crenshaw's roads and Green's Church. Sarah Randolph, grantor's wife, privily examined by Abner Osborne and Edmund Wills. Nottoway D. B. 1, p. 73. (Said to be present site of Blackstone.)

RANDOLPH, PETER, 1793. Deed to Edward Bland, of Prince George, for land adjoining Theodorick Bland, Henry Randolph, Joshua Spain and Phillip Jones. (Cellar Creek country). Nottoway D. B. 1, p. 347.

RANDOLPH, PETER, 1793. Deed to William Irby, land beginning at the fork of Jordan's and the Courthouse road, bounded by John Epes's, Bowry's, Theo. Epes's, Cellar Creek, Jordan's Road and Johnny's Branch. Nottoway D. B. 1, p. 360.

RANDOLPH, PETER, 1798. Deed from Peter Randolph and Sarah, his wife, to Henry Dennis, conveying a tract on Celler Creek, bounded by Luke Pryor, Isham Clay and others, it being the same land recovered of the heirs of Lettice Bland, deceased. Nottoway D. B. 2, p. 14.

RANDOLPH, PETER, 1800. Case between Peter Randolph and Dennis, showing that Randolph then lived at or near the Court House. Nottoway D. B. 2, p. 160.

RANDOLPH, PETER, 1800. Deed of lease to John Roberts for land in and around the Court House; states that there was a spring near the Court House called Mrs. Washington's spring; and also that Francis and Robert Fitzgerald and Henderson owned adjacent lands. Nottoway D. B. 2, p. 153.

RANDOLPH, RICHARD, 1745. Deed from Richard Randolph, of Henrico, to John Watson, Jr., of Goochland, 450 acres on upper side Little Buffalo and south side of Wheelin's Spring Branch, part of patent to Randolph, 1745. Amelia D. B. 2, p. 179.

RANDOLPH, RICHARD. September 18, 1746. Deed from Richard Randolph, of Henrico, to John Watson, Jr., of the county of Goochland, five shillings, conveying land in Amelia (now Prince Edward) surveyed for John Mullins and granted to said Randolph by patent dated March 10, 1745, containing 496 acres, 451 acres of said patent lying on upper side of Little Buffaloe and on south side of said Mullin's Spring Branch. Richard Randolph (SEAL). Witnesses, W. Womack, Obadiah Woodson, Charles S. Spradling [?]. Amelia D. B. 2, p. 179.

ROBERSON, CHRISTOPHER, SR., 1740. Deed from Christopher Roberson, Sr., of Amelia, to his son Henry Roberson, of same county, to land on both sides of Woody Creek and on Cits Branch. Amelia D. B. 1, p. 196.

ROBERTSON, ARCHER, (Nottoway) 1830. Will. Wife, Nancy; sons, M. W. and John A. Robertson; son-in-law, H. R. Anderson; and other children, not named. Mentions his mill. (This was "Lame" Archer Robertson, of "Eleven Oaks," Robertson's Tavern.) Chesterfield [?] W. B. 6, p. 197.

ROBERTSON, CHRISTOPHER, of Middlesex, 1796. Will names nephews (children of his brother Benjamin), Elizabeth Carter, Hannah, Alicia Corbin Robertson, Benjamin Needler Robertson, William Robertson, Chesterfield W. B. 4, p. 507.

ROBERTSON, EDWARD, 1750. Deed to Robert Rowland, land on Lazaritta Creek for water mill. Amelia D. B. 4, p. 16.

ROBERTSON, EDWARD, 1769. Will. Appoints his brother Nathaniel Robertson, and son, Christopher, executors. Sons, John, Christopher, Edward, George Cabness; daughters, Pressiller Mays, Anne, Mary Ann, Martha, Elizabeth Moody. Gives sons Edward and George Cabness land on Mallory Creek; gives his mill and 10 acres for use of his family. Amelia W. B. 2, p. 302.

ROBERTSON, EDWARD. Had mill on Mallory Creek; *vide* deed from him to Bagley. Amelia D. B. 13 (1774).

ROBERTSON, FRANCES, 1768. Will. Sons, William and James. Chesterfield W. B. 2, p. 171.

ROBERTSON, REVEREND GEORGE, 1735. Deed. Conveyed to his son George 2,100 acres in Amelia. Henrico D. B.

ROBERTSON, GEORGE, 1775. Will. Son James, land in Skinquarter; sons George, Lodowick; daughters, Phebe Sims, Margaret Coventon, Jane Farrar; son-in-law, George Brown. Chesterfield W. B. 3, p. 394.

ROBERTSON, GEORGE, 1790. Contract between George Robertson, of Chesterfield, and John Brander, of Dinwiddie, by which the former rents certain property in Chesterfield to the latter, all on Swift Creek and on which he then resided, including a mill. Field and John Archer, witnesses. Chesterfield D. B. 12 (1790).

ROBERTSON, GEORGE, 1792. Deed from George Robertson and Betsy, his wife, of Pittsylvania, to John Robertson, of Nottoway, land on north side Mallory's Creek, bounded in part by Henry Anderson and John B. Dawson. Nottoway D. B. 1, p. 328.

ROBERTSON, GEORGE, 1795. Will, not signed nor witnessed. Friends, George Markham and Jesse Cogbill, and sons, James and Archer, executors. Wife, Michal, given plantation on which he lived, except mill, etc.; son, James, plantation on Appomattox, bought of Richard Kennon, also land bought of William Downman, and personalty; son, Archer, plantation on Winterpock Creek, and land on Flat Creek in Amelia County, also lot 28 in

Pocahontas division of Petersburg (conveyed to him by Richard Wilton, Jr.) and personalty; son, George, land on which he lived after wife's death, including land bought of his brother, John Robertson, and William Worsham, also lots and land in Petersburg owned by him as tenant in common with heirs of Edward Archer in Pocahontas (bought of Wilton); daughters, Martha Field Brander and Ann. Mentions slaves in possession of John Archer and Mrs. Elizabeth Moseley, of Halifax; also mentions "profits of my trade with Trents, Scott and Co.," and speaks of his lands, 5000 acres in Kentucky, on Beaver Dam Creek, of Green River, and several tracts in Chesterfield. Probably none of the children twenty-one except James. Chesterfield W. B. 5, (1795).

ROBERTSON, HENRY. Matter concerning Henry Robertson, showing whom he married, etc., together with other historical matter. Amelia D. B. 7, p. 595.

ROBERTSON, HENRY. Will dated 1781, probated 1782. Son, Warning Peter Robertson, given his mill tract on both sides of falls of Little Nottoway by patent 970 acres, also mills, etc.; sons, David, Edward and William Henry given 1400 acres in Charlotte on Buffalo Creek and Blue Stone Creek. Son John given "plantation whereon I now live when he comes of age," also "my Butterwood tract"; son Daniel given land on Middle Fork of Meherrin, "400 acres adjoining my son Christopher Robertson's line"; daughter, Suzannah Shelton; wife, Tralusia Robertson. Amelia W. B. 3, p. 123.

ROBERTSON, JAMES, of Dale Parish, Chesterfield County, 1757. Wills. Executors, wife Mary and brother John Robertson. Wife Mary given plantation on Swift Creek for life, to go to son George after her death; son George, land on Winterpock Creek; land in Amelia to sons James, George and John; daughters, Martha and Mary. Chesterfield W. B. 1, p. 272. Inventory taken at his late dwelling, etc., 1758, shows among other things, 14 slaves; at his quarter on Winterpock, where Day was overseer, 8 slaves; at his plantation in Amelia, where Raffity was overseer, 16 slaves, etc. Chesterfield W. B. 1, p. 482, 483.

ROBERTSON, JAMES. Will dated January 21, 1792; witnesses, Carter Lallard, William Booth; friend, William Cryer, executor. Son, William Robertson, at hospital at Williamsburg; son, Stephen Robertson, at hospital at Williamsburg; daughter, Mary Fannin. Nottoway W. B. 1, p. 63.

ROBERTSON, JAMES, of Amelia. Will dated 1810, probated, 1822. Son George given land on Flat Creek, purchased of brother Archer; son John Alexander given land "I now live on"; son, James, land and plantation on Swift Creek, including 200 acres "adjoining that which I drew at division of land of my brother George, deceased"; also "one-half lot and houses I hold as tenant in common with the representatives of Branch Tanner"; daughters, Anne, Frances and Caroline; brother-in-law, John Archer; cousin, William Archer. Amelia W. B. 8, p. 341.

ROBERTSON, JAMES, SR. Will dated 1811, probated 1828. Sons, John A. Robertson, James Robertson, George Robertson, William H. Robertson and Theoderick Robertson; daughter, Mary E. Robertson; son-in-law John R. Robertson. Amelia W. B. 11, p. 301.

ROBERTSON, JEFFERY, 1784. Will. Wife, Judith; wife's son, Henry Mills; sons, Jeffery, Tyree, Nicholas, Matthew, David, Mills; daughter, Elizabeth Bass. Chesterfield W. B. 3, p. 519.

ROBERTSON, JOHN. Will. Executors, Thomas Burfoot and Walthall Robertson. Wife, Anne, land on Sappone Creek; son, Walthall, land in Madison county; daughters, Elizabeth Turpin, Martha; sons, John, Richard Henry; grandson Francis Cox Robertson, land in Kentucky. Chesterfield W. B. 5, p. 195.

ROBERTSON, JOHN, 1765. Will. Son Francis, land on river; sons William and George, land in Amelia, part of it at mouth of Flat Creek, etc.; daughters, Martha, Mary Walke, Mary Robertson; grandson John (son of John), grandson, John Walke; wife, Sarah. Considerable estate; lots in Pocahontas. Chesterfield W. B. 1, p. 444. Inventory shows 2000 pounds in Amelia and Chesterfield; named therein "Captain" John Robertson, 1766; George, executor. Chesterfield W. B. 2, p. 187.

ROBERTSON, JOHN, 1768. Daughter, Elizabeth; sons, Isaac and John; land in Chesterfield and Mecklenburg. Chesterfield W. B. 2, p. 170.

ROBERTSON, JOHN, 1791. Deed to Henry Jennings, land between Mallory's Creek and Cold Water branch and Little Nottoway River. Nottoway D. B. 1, p. 138.

ROBERTSON, JOHN, 1791. John Robertson and Sarah, his wife, to James Jennings, land on north side Little Nottoway, at mouth of Mallory's Creek; mentions Cold Water branch, and Fowlkes's corner as marking lines. Nottoway D. B. 1, p. 137.

ROBERTSON, JOHN A., 1798. Deed from John A. Robertson and Elizabeth, his wife, to Peter Bland, for a tract near Comer's Mill. Nottoway D. B. 2, p. 95.

ROBERTSON, JOHN, of Nottoway County. Will signed July 11, 1826, probated November 2, 1826; John H. Knight, Joseph M. Fowlkes, Forster Hudson, witnesses; Archer Robertson and William Robertson appointed executors, and qualify with Henry R. Anderson, Joseph C. Fowlkes and Tyree G. Bacon as sureties. All just debts to be paid; to son James D. Robertson one bedstead and furniture and one cow and calf to him and his heirs forever; after the payment of debts and the above specified legacy to son, James D. Robertson, the balance of estate, both real and personal, to be equally divided amongst following named children and grandchildren: one portion to Archer Robertson, one other portion to William Robertson, one other portion to James D. Robertson, one other portion to Henry I. Robertson, one other portion to the children of Jennings Robertson, one other portion to the children of John Robertson, one other portion to Nancy Jennings and one other portion in the hands of son, Archer Robertson, as trustee for the benefit of Edward Robertson, wife and children. The negro man Booker, for which a bill of sale was lately executed to Henry I. Robertson, to be thrown into the estimate of estate, or said Henry I. Robertson to account for his full value; also the negro girl in possession of daughter, Nancy Jennings, to be taken into estimate of estate and to be accounted for by her in like manner. Property heretofore given daughter Elizabeth May to be considered as her full part of estate, conferred on her and her heirs forever; she is, therefore, intentionally left out of this instrument. Nottoway W. B. 5, p. 421.

ROBERTSON, JOHN A. Will dated 1858, probated 1859. Son, John A.; daughters, Margaret H. Winfree and Martha A. Gregory; granddaughter, Harriet F. Robertson; wife, Mary B., given plantation called "Goose Island," etc. Amelia W. B. 18, p. 230.

ROBERTSON, MARGARET. Will dated April 15, 1812, probated November 5, 1812. Three children, Gervis Broadnax, Emily Harriet Broadnax, Frances Holmes Broadnax; Richard Cocke, guardian for son Gervis. Appoints brother, Ballard Holmes, guardian. Test., Peter R. Bland, A. Robertson, John S. Hardaway. Nottoway W. B. 3, p. 180.

ROBERTSON, MARY (alias Wilkinson). Deed to Major Richard Jones, et als. Nottoway D. B. 1.

ROBERTSON, MARY, 1790. Deed of gift from Mary Robertson (commonly called Wilkinson), to her children and grandchildren, conveying her estate after death; sons, James Robertson and John Robertson; grandsons, John Royall (son of John), James Jones (son of Richard, Jr.); daughter, Elizabeth Comer; grand-daughters, Mary Epes Jones, Elizabeth Royall, Mary Robertson (daughter of James), Mary Robertson (daughter of John), Martha Ann Jones, Caroline Jones, the two latter being daughters of Richard, Jr. Nottoway D. B. 1, p. 166.

ROBERTSON, MARY (alias Wilkinson), 1803. Deed. Release to her sons Littleberry and John Royall, of all her interest in the estate of Joseph Royall, deceased, of Chesterfield County, at the time of his death, which afterwards belonged to his son, John Epes Royall, in right of his father, etc. Nottoway D. B. 2, p. 420.

ROBERTSON, MARY, (alias Wilkinson), 1805. Will dated May 11, 1798, probated November 7, 1805. Executors, son Littleberry Royall and grandson, John A. Robertson; witnesses, Freeman Epes and Presley Jeter. Sons, Littleberry Royall, John Royall, James Robertson, John Robertson; daughter, Elizabeth Comer; grandsons, John Archer Robertson, James Jones, James Robertson (son of James); granddaughters, Sarah R. Robertson, Mary E.

Robertson (daughter of James), Mary E. Robertson (daughter of John); gave to sons, John Royall and James Robertson their bonds, executed to Thomas Wilkinson for 5000 and 7000 pounds of tobacco respectively, and recovered by testatrix in a suit in the high court of Chancery, "now in the hands of Major Richard Jones, my agent." Nottoway W: B. 2, p. 217.

ROBERTSON, MICHAL, 1808. Will. Sons, James, Archer and George; daughter, Martha Field Brander, wife of John Brander; grand-daughter, Harriet McCraw, daughter of William McCraw. Chesterfield W. B. 7, p. 73.

ROBERTSON, NATHANIEL. Deed dated October 1, 1774, to Thomas Spain, upper part of land Robertson bought of Neil Buchanan. Amelia D. B. 13, p. 88.

ROBERTSON, NATHANIEL, Dec. 20, 1790. Deed to William May Porter, of Nottoway, of land on south side of Deep Creek, beginning just above Jesse Walton's mill dam, and extending to Joseph Jennings' line; lower part of land purchased by Robertson of Thomas Spain (or Pain), except part sold Jesse Walton adjoining mill, etc. Nottoway D. B. 1, p. 122.

ROBERTSON, NATHANIEL, 1790. Deed from Nathaniel Robertson and wife to James Farley, land beginning at James Farley's line where it crosses Roland's Church Spring Branch, and also bounded by Deep Creek. Nottoway D. B. 1, p. 156.

ROBERTSON, NATHANIEL, 1791. Deed from Nathaniel Robertson and Anne, to Littleberry Royall and Presley Jeter, for four acres of land for thirty pounds, on both sides Lazaritta Creek, it being the place where said Robertson had a mill for many years, which he purchased of Robt, Rowland. Nottoway D. B. 1, p. 182.

ROBERTSON, NATHANIEL, July, 1791. Deed. Nathaniel Robertson and William May Porter convey land on southside Deep Creek, next to Jesse Walton's mill pond, to Pleasant Walton. Nottoway D. B. 1, p. 168.

ROBERTSON, NATHANIEL, 1793. Deed of privilege from Nathaniel Robertson to Jesse Walton, to raise his mill dam and saving him harmless for all the land drowned of the tract he (Robertson) bought of Thomas Pain. Nottoway D. B. 1, p. 337.

ROBERTSON, NATHANIEL, July 4, 1793. Deed to William May Porter, land formerly accupied by Robert Robertson, deceased, and adjoining lands of James Farley, Robert Winfree, Pleasant Walton and Charles Cabiness. Nottoway D. B. 1, p. 376.

ROBERTSON, NATHANIEL. Will dated Jan. 10, 1794, probated February 6, 1794. Son, William Robertson, executor; witnesses, Abraham Hatchett, L. Royall, Elizabeth Morris; test., Benjamin Pollard . . . Speaks of children, Richard Robertson, Elizabeth Fowlkes, Sarah Spain, James Robertson, Mary May Porter, Robert Robertson and Martha Walton; also sons Paschal Robertson and William Robertson; wife, Anne Robertson; then speaks of four younger children, Nathaniel Thompson, Peter, Christopher and Nancy Robertson. Nottoway W. B. 1, p. 104.

ROBERTSON, TRALUSIA. Will, dated August 12, 1790. Executors, sons, David and Daniel Robertson; witnesses, Nathaniel Fletcher, Jr., James Fletcher, Larkin Anderson, W. Robertson. Son, John Robertson; father, Hans Henrick Stegar; brother, William Stegar. Land to son John when he reaches 21; mentions daughter Dolly Pollard. Nottoway W. B. 1, p. 27.

ROBERTSON, WARNING PETER, 1791. Deed to Freeman Epes, for land in fork of Little Nottoway River and Lazaretta Creek, touching Winn's corner and Mill road to corner store near Winn's Church Road. Nottoway D. B. 1, p. 162.

ROBERTSON, WILLIAM, of Dale Parish, Chesterfield, 1757. Will. Wife, Frances; son, James, land on Hatchers Branch, etc.; son, William, land on Winterpock Creek; grandson, John (son of William), land on Sappone Creek, etc.; daughters, Margaret Rudd, Frances Baugh, Mary Owen, Jennett; grand-daughter, Isebell Robertson; son-in-law, John Claiborne. Chesterfield W. B. 1, p. 275.

ROBERTSON, WILLIAM, of Dale Parish, Chesterfield, 1764. Will. Sons, William and Bridgwater; daughters, Elizabeth Clyborne, Martha Blanchet, Minigh Robertson, Lois Robertson; brother, George Robertson. Chesterfield W. B. 1, p. 437.

ROBERTSON, WILLIAM, of Manchester Parish, 1774. Will. Wife, Sarah; sons, John, William, James, Archerbald; sons-in-law, William Beasley, Matthew and Miles Robertson; daughters, Martha and Ann. Chesterfield W. B. 2, p. 340.

ROBERTSON, WILLIAM. Will dated Nov. 27, 1784. Witnesses, James Robertson, John Walke, George Robertson and Henry Talley. Wife, Betty Branch Robertson; sons, John, William and Henry Worsham Robertson. Amelia W. B. 3, p. 310.

ROBERTSON, WILLIAM, 1797. Will. Sons, John, William; daughters, Lucy Cheatham, Mary, Tabitha Eliot, Ann, Margaret, Frances. Chesterfield W. B. 5, p. 133.

ROBINSON, PETER, 1814. Will. Executors, friends Samuel Morgan and Stith Thompson; witnesses, John Robertson, Isham Perdue, Wood Jones. Gives to Nancy Gholson and her two children, William Yates and Cary Ann, "one-half of slaves I got by my wife," etc., also to Nancy Gholson, the silver plate that was the property of her mother; Sally Taylor Cary, sister of Nancy; gives to L. T., George B. and Charlotte L. Cary "one-half the slaves I got of their mother"; gives legacy to Winifred Terry; late wife Elizabeth; daughters, Elizabeth A. Jones, wife of Richard K. Jones, Martha, Caroline, Mary Stith. Nottoway W. B. 3, p. 249.

ROWLAND, ROBERT, 1747. Deed to John Smith, of Goochland County, land on Lazaritta Creek, part of patent to Rowland, 1745. Amelia D. B. 2, p. 242.

ROWLAND, ROBERT, 1760. Deed to Nathaniel Robertson, both of Nattoway Parish, for four acres with water griss mill on Lazaritta Creek, part of a patent to Rowland, 1746. Amelia D. B. 7, p. 229.

ROYALL, JOHN, of Amelia County. Will dated 1786; probated 1791. Executors, Peter F. Archer and son John; witnesses, William B. Giles, Richard Ogilby, R. Archer, Chastaine Cocke. Gives wife plantation and eleven negroes; sons, John and Joseph; grand-daughters, Elizabeth Royall and Mary Eppes Robertson; grandsons, James Robertson and John Royall Robertson. Amelia W. B. 4, p. 200.

ROYALL, JOHN, 1793. Deed from John Royall and Sarah, his wife, to Samuel Pincham; land bounded by a branch of Cellar Creek and opposite Abner Osborne's land, and adjoining Richard Dennis; speaks of line crossing the "Namozine" Road to Parham's line. Nottoway D. B. 1. (Query: What Namozine Road?)

ROYALL, JOHN, 1796. Deed to James Davis to land "beginning where Jackson's road makes into Cock's road," (on fork of two roads). Nottoway D. B. 1.

ROYALL, JOHN, 1827. Will dated 1824. Executor, son, John D. Royall; grand-children, John R., Sarah Ann, and Henry C. Robertson. Nottoway W. B. 6, p. 33.

ROYALL, JOSEPH, 1783. Will. Executors, brother Littleberry and cousin William, of Amelia. Wife, Lucy; son, John, a minor; mentions brothers Littleberry and John. Chesterfield W. B.

ROYALL, LITTLEBURY, of Dale Parish, 1749. Will. Witnesses, Richard Eppes and others. Wife, Mary; brothers, Richard, John; sons, Joseph (given land on Appomattox), Littleberry, John. Chesterfield W. B. 1, p. 5.

ROYALL, LITTLEBERRY, 1827. Will. Executors, friends James and Lew. Jones. Wife, Jane; children all minors; son, Edward Littleberry, given tract of land on Lazaretta, and that part of his land bought of Rowland Ward and Isaac Oliver (described in part as "thence down the Lazaretta to the north of a branch running from the Meeting House spring into Robertson's mill pond," etc.); son John Eppes, "all my land on N. W. side the road leading from Robertson's Tavern to Joseph I. Fowlkes"; son Joseph Thornton Royall. Nottoway W. B. 6, p. 44. NOTE: The testator lived at "Heath Court," one mile northwest of the present town of Crewe, on the southwest side of the old road to Burkeville (northside of present road) on the hillock south of the spring in the ravine which is one of the head springs of the creek flowing into Deep Creek at the upper end of "Mountain Hall" lowgrounds.

ROYALL, RICHARD, 1753. Bond of indemnity signed by Honorable Peter Randolph and Richard Eppes to save Richard Royall from the claim of the heirs of Littlebury Royall, deceased, to 580 acres in Chesterfield county, known as "Martin's Swamp," patented by Captain William Randolph, Francis Eppes and Joseph Royall in 1680. Chesterfield D. B. 1, p. 532.

RUTHERFORD, WILLIAM, 1755. Deed to Phillip Watson, of Richmond, merchant, mortgaging slaves, etc. Goochland D. B. 6, p. 450.

SHERWIN, 1801. Deed from Matthew Cheatham and Martha, his wife, of Chesterfield County, to Francis Epes, of Lunenburg County, conveying land on Winningham, etc., the share of Martha (Sherwin) Cheatham in her father's (Samuel Sherwin) estate in Nottoway. Tells who the daughters of Sherwin were: Elizabeth, Mary Ann Massey Sherwin, Martha Sherwin, Tabitha Randolph Sherwin and Amelia Taylor Sherwin. One married Brooking. Samuel Sherwin left will 1786. Nottoway D. B. 2, p. 257.

SHORE, DR. JOHN, late of Blandford. Will. Executors, wife, son Thomas, friends Edmund Wills (Nottoway), Thomas Atkinson (Dinwiddie), Joseph G. Wilder (Petersburg). Devised houses and lots in Blandford. Sons, John, Thomas, Robert, William, Henry Edwin; wife, Anne; daughters, Mary Boyd, Anne Elizabeth Batte, Rebecca Marshall. Wife, Anne, was daughter of Robert and Mary Bolling (the former was then deceased). Enjoined his executors to make personal application to Mrs. B. in behalf of his wife and children in regard to property and "should she deny that justice so long with-held from them," suit is directed to be brought. Nottoway W. B. 3.

SHORE, THOMAS, of Violet Bank farm, Chesterfield County, 1800. Will. Wife, Jane Gray; daughters, Jane Grayson, Elizabeth Smith and Maria Louisa. Devised large property in Chesterfield, Dinwiddie and land in Bourbon County, Ky., where John Breckenridge was his attorney in part. Late of the firm of Shore and McConnico; and Shore, McConnico and Bitson. Wife, Jane Gray, brother John Shore, friends John Grayson, John Wickham, Thomas Bennet, Needler Robertson and nephew Conrade Webb, executors and guardians. Chesterfield W. B. 5, p. 315.

SIMKINS, JOHN, 1734. Deed from "John Simkins of the Parish of Phirino and county of Henrico, to John Watson, Jr., of same parish and county," conveying land in Goochland County on north side of Appomattox River. Goochland D. B. 2, p. 5.

SMITH, BURRELL, 1828. Will dated 1827. Wife, Mary; son, Kennon; daughter, Polly Burrell Roan. Nottoway W. B. 6, p. 465.

SMITH, JOHN BLAIR, 1791. Deed from John Blair Smith, attorney for Samuel Stanhope Smith, late of Prince Edward, now of Princeton, N. J., to Samuel Watson, of Prince Edward, land on both sides of Briery River, adjoining Colonel Scott, extending to Little Briery, etc.; also conveyance 1793 by Ann Smith, wife of Samuel Stanhope Smith, of her interest, etc. Prince Edward D. B. 9, p. 161, 325.

STEWART, CHARLES, 1802. Deed from Charles, Alexander,

and Rachel Stewart, widow of Charles Stewart, deceased, conveying land in Nottoway to Joseph Jennings (Caffe), adjoining P. Dunnivant, Joseph Jennings, Sr., L. B. J [ones?] and B. Ward. Nottoway D. B. 2, p. 391.

STEWART, 1802. Deed. Conveyance of land on Barebone Creek, (known now as Hamm's), by Stewarts, to Benjamin Ward; names the Stewarts, Alexander, Charles, and Rachel; speaks of the father as Charles Stewart, deceased. Nottoway D. B. 2, p. 354.

STILL and wife, 1789. Deed to Isaac Holmes to land on little Cellar Creek, or Leath's Creek; land devised to Jeremiah Still, by his father, George Still, and adjoining Featherstone, Moore, etc. Nottoway D. B. 1, p. 107.

TABB, JOHN, 1798. Appraisement of John Tabb's estate. Silver plate, 137 pounds; at Mansion House, 9584 pounds; Dowdies, 1830 pounds; Clark's 1305 pounds; Grub Hill, 1531 pounds; Haw Branch, 2040 pounds; Mouslen's, 1414 pounds; Cox's, 1930 pounds; Lester's, 2070 pounds; Lorton's, 1775 pounds; Doolittle, 1301 pounds; Wintercomack, 1100 pounds; Monksneck (Dinwiddie), 1322 pounds; mill, 66 pounds; some articles omitted, at other places; cash in house 122 pounds; total, 31,879 pounds (equal to $154,613.). Frances Tabb, administratrix, and William B. Giles, administrator. Amelia W. B. 6, p. 189.

TABB, COLONEL THOMAS. Will dated and probated 1769. Large estate. Amelia W. B. 2, p. 309.

TANNER, JOEL, SR., 1750. Deed, showing he patented land on Deep Creek in 1750, June 1st. Nottoway D. B. 1, p. 548.

THOMAS, WOODLIEF, 1795. Deed from Woodlief Thomas and wife to James Williams, land on north side of Jordan's Road, between Cellar Creek and Hurricane Swamp, and bounded as by patent to Hugh Martin, February, 1763. Nottoway D. B. 1, p. 494.

THOMPSON, 1779. Deed from Thompson and wife to John Watson, of Prince Edward, land in Prince Edward. Prince Edward D. B. 6, p. 143.

TYREE, BENJAMIN, 1770. Land conveyed to Drury Watson, of Prince Edward, adjoining Captain John Morton, etc. Samuel and John Watson, Jr., witnesses. Prince Edward D. B. 6, p. 75.

VAUGHAN, ABRAHAM AND DAVID. Appraisement of estates, 1764 and 1769 respectively. Amelia W. B. 2, p. 80, and 261.

VAUGHAN, GEORGE. Will, dated 1766, probated 1771. Wife, Mary; sons, George, Benjamin, William and David; daughters, Susannah Norris, Elizabeth Thacker, Mary Haines, and Sarah Padgett. Owned land in Hanover County. Amelia W. B. 2, p. 14.

VAUGHAN, HENRY. Will dated 1755, probated, 1756. Wife, Hannah; daughter, Sally, wife of George Smith. Amelia W. B. 1, p. 119.

VAUGHAN, JAMES. Will dated 1799, probated 1800. Daughters, Frances, Ann and Lucy; son-in-law, James Shields; land in Kanawah County. Amelia W. B. 6, p. 189.

VAUGHAN, JAMES, 1833. Will. Executors, two nephews, James A. and Albert G. Vaughan (James A. qualified with bond of $100,000.) Witnesses, John and Thomas W. Webster and John H. Jackson. Wife, Jane H., land on "west end of my tract" so as to include mansion house for life; remainder to four daughters, Frances J., Sarah E. L. R., Julia Ann T., and Amelia E.; daughter Martha A. E. Mills already provided for; son, Joseph N. M. given land adjoining dower tract. Nottoway W. B. 6, p. 408.

VAUGHAN, NICHOLAS. Will dated 1811, probated 1816. Witnesses, Willis Piller, Josiah Noble,. John Rudd, Williamson Jackson. Land equally to three sons, Richard, John and Thomas, already granted by deed, charging them with 100 pounds each to his two daughters, Elizabeth Hudson and Judith Vaughan. Nottoway W. B. 3, p. 323.

VAUGHAN, ROBERT. Will dated 1777, probated 1779. Wife, Martha; sons, Willis and James; daughters, Phebe Mays and Ann Johnson. Gave James land on Flatt Creek. Amelia W. B. 2, p. 341.

VAUGHAN, ROBERT, SR. Will dated 1800, probated 1805. Owned land in the fork of West and Barebone Creeks, left to wife for life; remainder to sons James and Asa (describes metes and bounds); gives son John land in Charlotte, where he resides; son Robert land in Henrico; son Joseph, proceeds of Kentucky land sold to Richard I. Munford for 1000 pounds; daughters, Elizabeth Hundley, Martha Cook, Ann Wright, and Mary; considerable slaves. Nottoway W. B. 2, p. 226.

VAUGHAN, SAMUEL. Will dated 1781. Son, Samuel, land on Tucker's Run, in Prince George County; daughters, Amy Clay, Silvania Westbrook, and Sarah Vaughan; grand-daughter, Mary Everet Vaughan. Amelia W. B. 3, p. 56.

VAUGHAN, THOMAS. Will probated 1751; wife, and friend Joseph Motley, executors; Robert and Lewis Vaughan, witnesses. Wife, Elizabeth; sons, Thomas, Nicholas, Bartholomew, John; daughter, Elizabeth. Amelia W. B. 1, p. 74.

WALKER, JEREMIAH, 1783. Deed to Robert Winfree for land on Deep Creek, at the Church road to the Great road, to pointers, along Walton's line, etc. Amelia D. B. 16, p. 253.

WALTON, GEORGE, 1770. Deed to Jeremiah Walker, both of Amelia, for land on Deep Creek, touching Jennings's line, etc. Amelia D. B. 11, p. 90.

WALTON, GEORGE, 1770. Deed to Jesse Walton, both of Amelia, for land marked by Deep Creek, John Jennings's line, Walker's corner, etc. Amelia D. B. 11, p. 92.

WALTON, JESSE, 1800. Deed to Stephen Noble, of Amelia, for tract of land ("Woodland"), in Nottoway, on Deep Creek and Cabbin Branch; speaks of lands adjoining belonging to Pleasant Walton, Joseph Jennings, Jr. and Sr., and James Cook; Speaks of Jesse Walton's mill pond and grist mill, etc. Nottoway D. B. 2, p. 170.

WARD, ALBERY B., 1801. Deed from Albery B. Ward and wife, to John Robertson, to land on Lazaretta Creek, bounded by Littleberry Royall, Uriah Lipscombe, Leonard Ward and Daniel Marshall. Nottoway D. B. 2, p. 189.

WARD, BENJAMIN, 1783. Appraisement of estate by order of County Court. Amelia W. B. 4, p. 234, 275.

WARD, BENJAMIN, 1784. Appraisement of estate of Benjamin Ward, deceased, by order of county court; shows: slaves, 4,010 pounds; horses and colts (28 in number) 423 pounds; land on Ward's Fork, 1200 acres, 1800 pounds; land on Tunstall's, 880 acres, 1320 pounds; land on West Creek, 667 acres, 1354 pounds; total 4474 pounds. Land on West Creek allotted to Daniel Jones, who married the widow. David Crowley was executor. Peter Randolph, Joseph Eggleston, Jr. and James Cook, commissioners. Amelia W. B. 4.

WARD, BENJAMIN, of Raleigh Parish, Amelia, 1785. Will. Witnesses, Philip W. Greenhill, William Tagg, and William Panton. Disinherits son Benjamin for unheard of behavior and undutiful conduct with a servant; gives grand-daughters Elizabeth Ward Greenhill and Ann Greenhill a slave a piece; to daughter, Elizabeth, wife of William Greenhill the land on which he resided, "980 acres patent." Amelia W. B. 4, p. 60.

WARD, HENRY. Will dated and probated, 1765. Wife living. Sons, Benjamin and Henry; brothers, Benjamin Ward, Sr. and Rowland Ward. Gave daughters 500 pounds apiece. Owned Ward's Fork in Charlotte County, and land on Butcher's Creek, in Mecklenburg County (?); bought land of Colonel Ruffin. Amelia W. B. 2, p. 94.

WARD, ROBERT. Will dated 1809, probated 1810. Witnesses, Daniel Hardaway, James Fletcher. Brother Nathan; daughter Elizabeth C. Ward; daughter-in-law, Martha D. Ward. Gives friend William C. Greenhill, "my Buzzard colt." Nottoway W. B. 3, p. 13.

WARD, SETH, 1746. Deed. Seth Ward, of Henrico, to Henry Ward, of Amelia, land in Amelia, south side of West's Creek, part of patent to Lawrence Brown and land which Seth Ward bought of Samuel Jones on West's Creek. Amelia D. B. 2, p. 176.

WATSON, ABNER. Will dated and probated 1835. Sons, Benjamin B. and Joseph D. Watson, executors, with bond of $40,000.; Drury Watson and Joseph A. Watson, witnesses. Wife Mary, loaned land in North Carolina and five negroes, etc.; directs land in Prince Edward to be sold to pay debts, etc.; son, Benjamin B. given four negroes; son, Joseph D., negroes; son, Frederick W., negroes; son, Abner Y., negroes; daughter, Susan

Elizabeth, negroes; daughter, Mary, to have right to live on tract called Perkinson's in North Carolina. Prince Edward W. B. 7, p. 402.

WATSON, ALICE, a widow,[75] 1709. Conveys to her son Joseph property in Henrico, including the Indian Peter, in consideration of her maintenance. Henrico Deed and Will Book.

WATSON, ALICE, 1711-12. Deed to sons John and Benjamin, conveying one Indian wench and one Indian girl.

WATSON, ALLEN, 1858. Inventory and appraisement of his estate at three places, ———, $14,000; Briery, $8,896; Bush River, $7,520; totalling $30,416. Prince Edward W. B. 10, p. 481.

WATSON, ANN, 1751. Ordered that Ann Watson, widow and relict of Joseph Watson, deceased, be summoned to appear at next court, etc. Chesterfield County Court Order Book 1, p. 117.

WATSON, ANNE, 1756. Last will and testament of Anne Watson, deceased, presented by John Watson, executor, named therein, and probated 1756. Henrico County Court Order Book.

WATSON, ANN. Inventory and appraisement of estate of Ann Watson, deceased. John Watson and Joseph Dillon administrators, 1818. Prince Edward County Will Book 5.

WATSON, AUGUSTUS, of Nottoway, 1792. Deed to Batt Jones, of same county, tract of land called Cannon's, deeded by Peter Jones, Sr., of Amelia. Nottoway D. B. 1, p. 271.

WATSON, AUGUSTUS, 1794. Receipt from Augustus Watson to Batt Jones for all legacies and demands of his wife, Sarah Branch Jones, only child of Branch Jones, deceased, for whom Batt was executor. Nottoway D. B. 1, p. 395.

WATSON, AUGUSTUS, 1800. Deed. Augustus Watson and Sarah Branch Watson, his wife, to Martin Pierce, 299 acres. Prince Edward D. B. 12, p. 1.

WATSON, AUGUSTUS, 1806. Deed of gift of personal property to his cousin, Ann T. Thornton. Prince Edward D. B. 13, p. 536.

WATSON, AUGUSTUS, 1806. Shows Augustus Watson lived in 1806 on Appomattox River. Sandy Ford Road was on this tract. (Clerk tells .me Sandy Ford is on the Appomattox not far from Farmville.) Prince Edward D. B. 14.

WATSON, AUGUSTUS, 1815. Inventory and appraisement of estate of Colonel Augustus Watson, deceased, taken at his late residence in this county, 1815. Prince Edward W. B. 5, p. 225.

WATSON, BENJAMIN, 1715. Will. Witnesses, John Watson and others. Will gives son John plantation Lewis Orange lives upon and other land on head of Gilly's Creek and personalty; to daughter Judith "plantation I first lived at joyning upon Peg Slash and the plantation my mother Watson now lives on with

---

[75] Widow of John Watson of Henrico, 1702; see p.

240 acres belonging to them both," and personal property; to his brother John some personalty; to brother-in-law William Allen some personalty; to wife, Aggie, "plantation I now live upon for life" and made her executor of will. Henrico Deed and Will Book, p. 15, 17.

WATSON, BENJAMIN, 1758. Deed from Benjamin Watson, of Lunenburg, to William Watson, of Prince Edward, conveying personal property. Witness, Douglas Watson. Prince Edward D. B. 1, p. 149.

WATSON, BRANCH J., 1815. Inventory and appraisement of estate taken at his late residence in Prince Edward County, 1815. Signed by Elizabeth W. Watson and others. Prince Edward W. B. 5, p. 11.

WATSON, BURWELL, 1792. Inventory and appraisement of his estate. Mecklenburg W. B. 3, p. 125.

WATSON, DRURY, 1780. Deed. Conveys to John McCargo land in Prince Edward, bought of Benjamin Tyree. Witnesses, Jesse Watson, John Watson and others. Sally, wife of Drury Watson, was privily examined, etc. Prince Edward D. B. 6, p. 332.

WATSON, ELIZABETH, 1762. Came into court and chose John Ware for her guardian. Henrico County Court Minutes, 1762.

WATSON, FRANCES (FANNY), 1861. Gives all estate to Sims Allen. Prince Edward W. B. 11, p. 144.

WATSON, HENRY, 1795. Inventory and appraisement of estate. Mecklenburg W. B. 3, p. 264.

WATSON, ISAAC. Will dated 1782, probated 1783. Appoints Anthony and Joseph Bennett, Jr., executors. Leaves realty and personalty. Names wife, Brambley; sons, Bennett and Isaac Watson, and five daughters, Mary, Rebeccah, Fanny, Tabitha and Martha Watson. Mecklenburg W. B. 2, p. 37.

WATSON, JAMES, 1690. James Watson, who married Margaret, the widow of Thomas Dupray, summoned to court in connection with some orphans. Henrico County Court Minutes.

WATSON, JAMES. Will dated and probated in 1772. Mentions mother Rebecca, and brothers, Burrell, Henry and Jacob. Left a plantation and some personalty. Mecklenburg W. B. 1, p. 125.

WATSON, JAMES. Will dated and probated 1824. Polley, wife of James Dillon, brothers John and Littleberry, executors; Benjamin A. Watson, James Bondurant, John C. Allen, Allen Watson and Chappell Love, sureties, $20,000. Directs his land to be sold and divided into eleven equal parts, one to "child of my brother Samuel Watson," one to "children of my sister Sarah Bondurant," and one part to "each of my brothers John, Benjamin, Allen, Littleberry and my sisters, Polley Dillon, Hannah Watson, Elizabeth Ker, Martha Love and Nancy Allen." Prince Edward W. B. 6, p. 76.

WATSON, JESSE. Will dated August 11, 1812, probated with Joseph A. Watson as executor, February 11, 1813. Testator names wife, Mary, brother Joseph, sons Joseph A. and Jesse, executrix and executors; signed by himself, August 14 [1812]; witnesses, N. Watson, L. Watson, Robert Smith, Josiah Watson, David Flournoy and William Womack, Sr. All estate to be kept together till some one of his children reach twenty-one years or get married, then such child to have so much of the estate as his brother Joseph, his wife Mary, and his friends Thomas Green, John Booker, Cousin John Watson, Drury Watson, Samuel Watson, son of John, or any three of them shall think can be spared from supporting his wife and family, raising and schooling his children, and raising sum of money hereafter mentioned. As soon as practicable 200 pounds each be given his sons Joseph A. and Jesse Watson . . . and likewise 100 pounds each to his daughters Hannah A. and Mary Ann Elizabeth; the tract of land on which he lives to be equally divided upon his wife's death, or when they shall reach twenty-one years, between John William M. Watson, Elisha N. and Robert Allen Alexander Watson. Lunenburg W. B. 1810-1818.

WATSON, JOHN, 1678. Deposition of John Watson recorded. Henrico County Court Minutes.

WATSON, JOHN, 1685. Ordered by court to take charge of his son John's horses and convert them into cash, etc. Henrico Court Records.

WATSON, JOHN, 1686. Guardian for the orphans of Henry Rowen. Accounts settled in county court. Henrico Court Records.

WATSON, JOHN, JR., 1686. An account furnished court of the sale of horses belonging to John Watson, Jr., by his father, John Watson. Henrico Court Records.

WATSON, JOHN, 1687, one of a jury at this term; and at court at Varina, 1688; appointed one of the appraisers of an estate; again on jury 1690. Henrico County Court Minutes.

WATSON, JOHN, 1689. Deed from Thomas Cocke, gent. to John Watson, planter, both of Henrico County and Parish, conveying land in said county on Chickahominy Swamp, being part of 1600 acres patented by Cocke, and "crossing ye Indian Cabbin Branch." Henrico D. & W. B. (1688-97), p. 52.

WATSON, JOHN, allowed 200 acres of land for importing four persons into the colony, "legally proved in Court," viz: Francis Hayes, John Cole, Ralph Denby, and Thomas Ascroft. Henrico County Court Minute Book, court at Varina, August, 1689.

WATSON, JOHN, 1726. To Robert Mosby land in Henrico, patented by grantor, 1724, on Long and Hungry Branch, adjoining Pleasants. Henrico D. & W. B. 1, p. 28.

WATSON, JOHN, 1726. Land to Thomas Pleasants, "part of my patent on north side of Long and Hungry Branch." Henrico D. & W. B. 1, p. 47.

WATSON, JOHN, 1746. Deed from John Watson, Jr., to
Anthony Cole, conveying land in Goochland as per patent, dated
Mar. 17, 1736. Goochland D. B. 5, p. 198.

WATSON, JOHN, JR., of Goochland, 1748. Deed to John
Crow, of same county, for land in Goochland, purchased by said
John Watson, of Rene Laforce. Goochland D. B. 5, p. 486.

WATSON, JOHN, of Henrico County and Parish, 1749. Deed
of gift to Mary Watson Hynds, daughter of his wife, Martha
Watson, to twenty negroes, 500 pounds in money, and other
personalty, and 395 acres of land in said county on Chickahominy
Swamp and Allen's Branch, to be delivered to her at her marriage or when she becomes twenty-one. If she have no issue,
this property is to go to his children. Henrico D. & W. B. —,
p. 121.

WATSON, JOHN, of Henrico, 1749-50. Will. Land in Henrico County given William Putnam; land in Henrico County
given Watson Putnam; land in Goochland County adjoining
Joseph Pease and Ben Woodson given Moses Bramfield; to
daughter, Elizabeth Watson, land in Henrico County upon the
brook, etc.; to daughter Susannah Watson, land called Samson's,
etc.; to wife, Martha, home plantation, etc. Wife, Martha, William Putnam and Nathaniel Bacon, executors; witnesses, Nathaniel Bacon and others. Henrico D. & W. B. (1749-50). D.
& W. B., Vol 2, p. 40, in an inventory and appraisement calls
him "captain."

WATSON, JOHN, 1751. Deed to William Gray proved, in
Court, and ordered to record. Amelia County Court Order Book
3, p. 8.

WATSON, JOHN, 1758. Nathaniel Bacon settled his accounts
as guardian for John Watson's orphans and the estate of Mary
Watson Hynes. Henrico County Court Minutes, 1758.

WATSON, JOHN, of Prince Edward, 1759. Deed to Morton,
land on Great Buffalo. Witness, John Watson, Jr. Prince Edward D. B. 1, p. 168.

WATSON, JOHN, SR., of Prince Edward, 1761. Deed to
George Smith, of Amelia, for tract on Little Buffalo, being part
of a larger tract on which he, Watson, then lived, and patented
by him March 10, 1745. Witnesses, John Watson, Jr., Josiah
Chambers and Richard Morton. Prince Edward D. B. 2, p. 52.

WATSON, JOHN. Will dated and probated 1763. Sons, William, John, Burwell, Henry, Isaac and Jacob; son-in-law, William Poole; wife survived. Lunenburg W. B. 2, p. 176.

WATSON, JOHN, SR. Will. Executors, sons Drury and
Samuel,—$10,000.; witnesses, Abner Watson, John A. Watson,
William P. Watson. Wife, Mary; daughter, Betty Ann; sons,
Drury and Samuel given land "whereon I now live on Little
Buffalo"; daughters, Nancy, Mary, Susannah Thorn. Prince
Edward W. B. 6, p. 479.

WATSON, JOHN, Gent., 1787. Conveyance to William Bibb, Gent., of land on Harris's Creek; no wife mentioned. Prince Edward D. B. 8, p. 2.

WATSON, JOHN, JR., 1793. Deed of gift to land on Falling Creek, to sons Thomas and Augustus, by John Watson, Jr., of Prince Edward, tract of land on which grantor lived and where grantees had lately erected a merchant mill. Prince Edward D. B. 9, p. 317.

WATSON, JOHN. Will dated 1794, mentions wife Lucretia and son James (not then twenty-one). Brunswick County Clerk's Office.

WATSON, JOHN, 1795. Deed from John Watson, sheriff, of Prince Edward, to Bigger, for land sold at tax sale. Prince Edward D. B. 10, p. 229.

WATSON, JOHN, etc., 1796. Deed to Venable from John and Thomas Watson, of Prince Edward, to land in Prince Edward; Nancy, wife of John, and Sally, wife of Thomas, privily examined. Augustus, John Watson, Jr., Lucy Watson and others witnesses. Prince Edward D. B. 11, p. 1.

WATSON, JOHN, 1796. Power of attorney from John Watson, Sr., of Prince Edward, to his trusty friend, Allen Watson, of same, to demand or compel from the widow of Benjamin Watson, of Franklin County, Georgia, a negro man, Gilbert, loaned the said Benjamin Watson for his life. Witnesses, Allen Chambers and Drury Watson. Prince Edward D. B. 10, p. 434.

WATSON, JOHN, JR., 1797. Power of attorney from John Watson to John Watson, Jr., to sell land in Kentucky. Prince Edward D. B. 11, p. 124.

WATSON, JOHN, SR. Will dated 1702, probated at Verina, 1706. John Watson, planter, of Henrico County, devises several tracts of land in the county of Henrico, principally on the Chickahominy Swamp, some of which he patented in 1690. Leaves to his wife, Alice, plantation on which he lived, called "Cowtale (or Cattale) Quarter," with personalty; her land to go to his son Benjamin at her death; to son John, land on Upnam Brook, etc.; to son Joseph, land on Chickahominy Swamp bought of Thomas Cocke; to son Benjamin, in addition to the home tract, land on Chickahominy Swamp bought of Maxfield, etc.; to daughter Sarah, wife of Michael Johnson, one shilling and no more. Indian boy Peter to be set free at thirty years of age. Wife sole executor. Benjamin Hatcher, Sr., Benjamin Hatcher, Jr., James Young and C. Evans, witnesses. Henrico D. and W. B. (1706), p. 15.

WATSON, JOHN. Will signed February 3, 1797; probated June 17, 1805. Gives to son John one acre of land, more or less, joining the land he lives on, and likewise one negro by name Dick, and one negro girl named Aggie and her increase, which he has in possession, and likewise one negro man named Nick; gives to son Drury a negro woman named Aggie and her increase, which he has had in his possession for years past, and of late has placed said Aggie into possession of his daughter Susanna; gives negro boy, Phil, Fannie's son, to Hannah Watson, his son Drury's daughter; gives negro boy named John to Elizabeth Watson, his son Drury's daughter, and one feather bed and furniture; lends to daughter, Mary Chambers, 200 acres of land, more or less, agreeable to the lines as they stand at present, being the land whereon she lives, for her use during life, and after her death the said 200 acres of land to her son, Josiah Chambers; gives one negro woman named Jane, and her increase, which was lent to Josiah Chambers and by him willed to his children, as they·are mentioned in his will; gives daughter Susanna one negro named Peyton, which she has in possession, and one negro girl; gives to son Samuel one negro woman and her increase and one boy; gives to daughter Judith one negro boy and one woman and her increase and one woman named Fanny and her increase and one negro girl and her increase; gives to son Joseph one negro boy and one girl and her increase and one other boy; gives to son Jesse Watson one negro woman named Lucy and her increase from this date, and likewise John, Tom, Nancy and her increase, likewise Lewis and Lydia and her increase, and one boy named Nott, which he has in possession; gives to son Josiah two negroes, Peter and Hannah and her increase, which he has in possession, and one negro man named Isham; gives to son Abner two negroes, and likewise old Dick and likewise Pepesley and her increase and her daughter and her increase; likewise the plantation he now lives on, 300 acres, and a cart and yoke of oxen, which he now has; lends to granddaughter, Judith Nelson, one negro girl named Cate, during her (Judith's) life, and after her death to be divided with increase, among her children. His old negro woman, Aggie, to have liberty to live with which of his children she pleases, but if she should live to get so infirm as not to be able to maintain herself, to be maintained at the equal expense of his children. All the residue of personal estate not here devised to be equally subdivided between his children. Estate not to be appraised, nor executors to be held to give security. Appoints three sons, John, Joseph, and Jesse Watson, the sole executors of will. Attesting witnesses, Drury Watson, Jr., Allen Chambers, Charles Allen. Upon the oaths of Drury Watson, Jr., and Charles Allen, Jesse and Joseph Watson qualified as executors. Prince Edward W. B. 3, p. 403. NOTE: In the appraisement, one book, "Confession of Faith"; four and three-quarter gallons of rum; eight old books. Inventory of cash, 11 pounds, 11 shillings, 9 pence.

WATSON, JOHN, SR., 1801. Deed. John Watson, Sr., and Anne, his wife, to John Watson, Jr., conveys land bought of John Thompson. Prince Edward D. B. 12, p. 75.

WATSON, JOHN, 1803. Deed. John and Ann Watson, his wife, and Augustus and Sarah B. Watson, his wife, to Robert

Venable, land on Sandy Foard Road and Falling Creek. Prince Edward D. B. 13, p. 29.

WATSON, JOHN, SR., 1813. Deed to Joseph Watson, 176 acres in Prince Edward (sold). Witnesses, Abner Drury and John A. Watson. Prince Edward D. B. 15, p. 115.

WATSON, JOHN. Will dated 1854, probated 1856. Gave to John Bondurant, John Watson, son of Littleberry, and John Watson, son of Allen, household furniture, etc.; sister, Martha Love, wife of Chappell Love, legacy; sister, Sally Bondurant, legacy. Frees slaves and sends them to Liberia. Divides lands in Charlotte County and Prince Edward County into six equal parts; one part given to brother, Littleberry Watson, one part each to brother Allen, sister Sally Bondurant, sister Nancy Allen, sister Martha Love, and one part to four of brother Benjamin Watson's children,—Louisiana, Samuel, Elizabeth and James,— "subject to removal of slaves on the above lands." Provides money for slaves in Liberia. Friends, Robert J. Smith and Joseph Dupuy, executors, and by codicil, William F. Scott added. At Circuit Court, 1856, will contested by Littleberry Watson, Sally J. Bondurant, Martha Love, Nancy Allen, Davis Lee and Elizabeth, his wife, Louisiana Watson, Robert Shackleton and Mary Ann, his wife. Jury impaneled and found for the will. Smith and Dupuy qualified as executors; gave bond, $80,000. Inventory and appraisement in Charlotte County, slaves valued at $17,200.; in Prince Edward County, slaves values at $18,175.; total personal estate in Prince Edward County $37,859.16; total personal estate in Charlotte County, $18,672. Inventory and appraisement made by commissioners appointed by Circuit Court, $61,791.90. Executors' account shows sixty-six negroes sent to Liberia. Prince Edward Superior Court W. B., p. 67.

WATSON, JOHN A. Will dated 1821, probated 1823. Josiah Watson, a witness. Wife, Nancy; children not named. Prince Edward W. B. 6, p. 21.

WATSON, JOSEPH, 1742. Deed. Joseph Watson, of Henrico County, and Anne, his wife, John Watson, Jr. (son of said Joseph Watson), of Goochland County, planter, and Mary, his wife, convey to Anthony Haden, land lying part in Goochland and part in Hanover Counties (formerly said to be in Henrico, as is expressed in patent for same to said Joseph Watson and John Watson, his brother, dated at Williamsburg, Sept. 5, 1723, which county was since divided, therefore said now to be in the counties of Goochland and Hanover); half of this tract was purchased of his uncle John Watson by John Watson, Jr., by deed dated 1740, remaining of the records of Hanover. Goochland D. B. 4, p. 91.

WATSON, JOSEPH, 1751. (Lived in Henrico). Will. Executors, son-in-law Thomas Jones and son John. Names son John; daughters, Martha Bell, land in Amelia, etc., Lucy

Jones, land in Brunswick, etc.; grandson, William Watson; wife, Anne. Henrico D. and W. B. 2, p. 170.

WATSON, JOSEPH. Will dated 1827, probated 1828. Wife, Fanny; Sims Allen given "land I live on," etc.; James Allen, brother of Sims, land on south side of road leading from Briery Meeting House to Moore's old ordinary; Allen Watson, three negroes; Littleberry Watson, son of Samuel, one negro; Joseph Watson, son of Jesse, "the land and plantation on Buffalo I bought of De Graffenreidt and a part of the tract I bought of Charles Price's trustees"; Joseph Watson, son of Abner, four negroes; Drury Calhoun, son of Hannah, the daughter of brother Drury, given legacy; Susan Wade, sister of his wife, Fanny Wade. Nominated Drury Watson, Samuel Watson (son of John), and Sims Allen, executors. Sims Allen qualified with bond of $25,000. Prince Edward W. B. 6, p. 426.

WATSON, JOSEPH A. Will dated June 23, 1864; codicil, 1868; probated July 1868. Wife, Jane C.; children, Alexander J., Joseph W., Frances J. Scott, Martha S. Watson, Armistead E., Branch A., Rochette B. and Joanna B. Watson; recites that son Joseph P. Watson died in Galveston, Texas, August 25, 1867. Prince Edward W. B. 12, p. 152.

WATSON, JOSIAH. Will dated 1827, probated 1828. Lends wife, Polly, 19 negroes, etc.; son, Matthew Edward Andrew Hercules Nelson Watson, given legacy; daughter, Polly N. Thackston; grand-daughters, Mary Ann Rebecca Watson, Louisa N. Watson, Mary E. Watson, Emilia Ann Watson, given negroes; grand-daughters, America Jane Geers and Elizabeth Frances Geers. "John Geers run off to North and South Carolina." Son-in-law, James Thackston. John Watson, Samuel Watson and other, witnesses. James Thackston qualified as executor, bond $40,000. Prince Edward W. B. 6, p. 477.

WATSON, MARTHA. Deceased 1802; inventory and appraisement of estate. Mecklenburg W. B. 5, p. 81.

WATSON, MARY. Will dated and probated 1836. Gives her property to grand-daughters Mary A. R. Fuqua, Eliza Frances Geers and Mary Elizabeth Watson, and great-grand-daughter Virginia Nelson Fuqua, and daughter Polly Nelson Cox. Prince Edward W. B. 7, p. 466.

WATSON, MATTHEW EDWARD ANDREW HERCULES NELSON (signed simply Nelson Watson). Will dated 1831, probated, 1832. Sister Polly V. Thackston given property and after her death said property to go to Mary Ann Rebecca Fuqua and Louisa Nelson Watson. To Eliza Frances and America Jane Geers, Mary Elizabeth Watson and Emaline Ann Watson, one-half of estate after certain things, etc. Prince Edward W. B. 7, p. 272.

WATSON, SAMUEL. Deed from Ker and wife in trust to Samuel Watson and Fred Argyle for the benefit of James Watson, Jr., conveying two lots in the town of Scottsville, in Powhatan County. Powhatan D. B. 2, p. 111.

WATSON, SAMUEL, SR., 1801. Deed. Nash and wife to Samuel Watson, Sr., of Prince Edward County, 350 acres on Briery River. Joseph and Hannah Watson, etc., witnesses. Prince Edward D. B. 12, p. 147.

WATSON, SAMUEL, 1809. Shows division of estate of Samuel Watson, deceased. Lands on head branches of Bush River and on Briery. Recites it is agreed among the children who are of age that Benjamin A. Watson, John Watson, Samuel Watson, son of John, and Hannah, his wife, and John Ker and Elizabeth, his wife, shall have on a division the lands on Bush. It is agreed that James Watson, Polly Watson, John Watson, Samuel Watson, Littleberry Watson, Samuel Watson, son of John and Hannah, his wife, and John Ker and Elizabeth, his wife, shall sell unto Benjamin A. Watson 339 acres, beginning at Josiah Watson's corner, etc. Agreement shows that Ben. Watson was married and his wife was named Dicey. Prince Edward D. B. 14, p. 330.

WATSON, SAMUEL, SR. Prince Edward County Deed Book 13, p. 316, shows that Samuel Watson, Sr., was alive in 1805.

WATSON, SAMUEL. Will dated April 6, 1814, probated 1814. Devises to wife, Rebekah A. Watson; daughter Mary Ann R. Watson, Allen Watson to be her guardian; brothers Allen and John Watson named executors. D. Flournoy, Thomas T. Scott, James Allen, witnesses. Executors qualified June 20, 1814, with Benjamin A. Watson, James Allen, Drury Watson, Abner Watson and James Watson, securities. Prince Edward W. B. 4, p. 485.

WATSON, SAMUEL, JR. Executor's account, 1814-1816, of John Watson for estate of Samuel Watson, son of Samuel. Prince Edward W. B. 5, p. 92.

WATSON, SAMUEL. Deceased 1861. Inventory and appraisement of estate, $36,000. Permelia P. Watson, administratrix. (She was a Booker). Prince Edward W. B. 11, p. 187.

WATSON, THOMAS, 1796. Deed from Thomas Watson and Wife to John Watson, to undivided half interest in land and mill, etc., devised to Thomas and Augustus Watson by aforesaid John Watson. (Clerk's certificate calls him John Watson, Sr.; also commission as justice calls him senior.) Prince Edward D. B. 11, p. 17. Sheriff John Watson executed writ, permitting Thomas and Augustus to erect mill dam there. Ibid., p. 25.

WATSON, THORNTON, 1794. Inventory and appraisement of estate of Thornton Watson, deceased. Prince Edward W. B. 2, p. 216.

WATSON, WILLIAM. Will dated 1751, probated 1752. Executors, Richard, Edward, Daniel Jones. Mentions wife Amy; son William and daughters. Amelia W. B.

WATSON, WILLIAM, 1755. Conveyance of land from William Watson of St. Patrick's Parish, Prince Edward County, to Mary Graham, of same parish and county; land lying on both sides Spring Creek in same county. Margaret, wife of William Watson, privily examined. Prince Edward D. B. 1, p. 55.

WATSON, WILLIAM, 1762. Deed to Julius Allen conveying 800 acres in Henrico, given him by his grandfather, Joseph, and patented by him 1741, in consideration of 400 pounds. Signed own name. Henrico D. and W. B. 2, p. 738.

WATSON, WILLIAM, 1769. Deed from William Watson, son and heir of William Watson, late of the county of Amelia, deceased, to Richard Jones, gent., of same county, conveying land in Prince Edward on Buffalo. Prince Edward D. B. 4, p. 102. ("Glenmore" Watsons.)

WATSON, WILLIAM, 1773. Deed to John Jennings, Sr., both of Amelia, for land on Cabbin Branch, near Jennings Ordinary, where Nicholas Quesenburey "now liveth and keeps ordinary," touching the Church road, Deep Creek, Musterfield Spring. Amelia D. B. 12, p. 109.

WATSON, WILLIAM, 1773. Deed to Joseph Jennings for land on Cabbin Branch "beginning near a small pond of water by the road side at Jennings Ordinary, where Nicholas Quesenburey now lives and keeps Ordinary, and running a straight line through the middle of said Ordinary House to the Spring commonly called the Musterfield Spring," etc. Speaks of Charles Steward's line, Royall's line as two of the boundaries. Amelia D. B. 12, p. 108.

WATSON, WILLIAM, 1774. Deed from William Watson and Nancy (Anne Randolph), his wife, to John Baldwin, of Amelia, for land on the head of Deep Creek; citing Pain's line, Watson's Church road, the church, and Cabiness' line as boundaries, in part. Amelia D. B. 13, p. 50.

WATSON, WILLIAM, 1777. Deed to Jennings, conveying a tract near Jenning's Ordinary, beginning at Charles Stuart's corner, thence along Williamson Piles' line to a road commonly called Pulliam's, etc. Amelia D. B. 14, p. 27.

WATSON, WILLIAM, 1799. Will. Wife, Elizabeth; son Benjamin and two daughters. Powhatan W. B. 2, p. 573.

WATSON, WILLIAM, 1806. Will. Executors, sons Robert and John Watson. Mentions sons Robert and John; grandsons William Mason, William (son of Robert); daughters, Elizabeth Mason, Sarah Collier, Martha Malory, Nancy and Mary. Brunswick County Clerk's Office.

WELLS, JOSEPH, of Nottoway, 1796. Deed to Richard F. Burke, of the county of Norfolk, land in Prince Edward and Nottoway, on both sides of the county line. Nottoway D. B. 1, p. 551.

WEST, ABRAHAM, 1762. Deed from Abraham West, of Prince Edward, to John Pryor, of Amelia, one hundred acres in

Amelia, in the immediate forks of the main Celler and Leath's Creeks, bounded by Westbrook, etc.; patented by John West in a tract of 400 acres. Amelia D. B. 7, p. 535.

WESTRBOOK, ———, 1771. Deed. Westbrook and wife to John Pryor, of Nottoway Parish, Amelia County, land on Cellar and Leath's Creeks. Amelia D. B. 11, p. 218.

WHITE, FRANCIS, 1792. Deed from Francis White and wife to Woodlief Thomas, land on Jordan's road between Cellar Creek and Hurricane Swamp, being part of a patent granted Hugh Martin in 1763. Nottoway D. B. 1, p. 319.

WHITLOCK, ———, 1783. Conveyance to Jesse Watson, of Prince Edward, of land on Bush River, etc. Witnesses, Samuel Watson, etc. Prince Edward D. B. 7, p. 96.

WILKINSON, THOMAS. Will dated March 19, 1782; executors, Thomas G. Peachy, James Henderson and William Fitzgerald. Leaves wife Mary, of Nottoway Parish, his estate for life, then to be remitted by bills of exchange to his brother Abraham. Mary, the wife, renounces her claim under the will and claims her dower. The will witnessed by Peter Lamkin, W. M. Cralle, Thomas Payne, Stith Hardaway; the renunciation of Mrs. Wilkinson witnessed by Richard Jones, and Daniel Verser. Will refers to land as in Little Nottoway, adjoining Robertson's line. Amelia W. B. 3, p. 298. Thomas Wilkinson's appraisement contains 15 gallons of brandy, 13 gallons of rum, 1 case and bottles, 5 wine glasses, 1 decanter.

WILLIAMS, THOMAS R., 1798. Will. Witnesses, Edward Bland, Edmund Irby, Alexander Wilson, John Woodward. Wife, Catherine; sons, William, David G., John F., Joseph G., Samuel G.; daughters, Catherine and Rachel Epes, Elizabeth Irby (wife of William Irby), Sarah G., Martha G. and Ann R. Williams; sons-in-law, William Irby, Thomas and John Epes; grandsons, Thomas R. and John Epes. Names executors: sons-in-law, and son David G. Williams, friends William Greenhill, William, Francis and Robert Fitzgerald to divide his estate in accord with directions of his will. Nottoway W. B. 1, p. 326.

WILLIAMS, THOMAS R., 1812. D. G. Williams, one of the executors of Major Thomas R. Williams, deceased, settles his account, 1812, involving 2,119 pounds. Mentions Major Richard Jones, Captain Francis Fitzgerald, Colonel Freeman Epes. Attorneys, Edmund Bland, George Hay, George K. Taylor. Nottoway W. B. 3, p. 161. On page 199 is settlement of John Epes, one of the executors of same. Among the items are:

1798, To John Marshall, his fee, two pounds, eight shillings
1798, To Edmund Randolph, his fee, two pounds, eight shillings
1799, To John Wickham, his fee, five pounds, two shillings
1799, To Dr. James Jones, his fee, four pounds, four shillings

1799, Cash,—Miss Williams, wedding shoes, 1 pound, 8 shillings, 6 pence

1800, To Z. Ramsey (dancing master), one pound, 16 sh.

1800, To cash paid, midwife's fee, twelve shillings

1800, To Grief Green (attorney), his fee, one pound, 10 shillings

1801, To Edmund Randolph, his fee, five pounds.

WILLINGHAM, JOHN, 1739. Deed. John Willingham, of Brunswick, to Samuel Sherwin, of Glouschester, land on Winingham's Creek, of Deep Creek. (Name spelled with 1 & n). Amelia D. B. 1, p. 129.

WINFREE, ROBERT, 1793. Deed. Land below said Winfree's house and on Deep Creek, conveyed to Jesse Walton. Nottoway D. B. 1.

WINFREE, ROBERT, 1794. Deed from Robert Winfree and wife to James Cook, land on Deep Creek, bounded by Jesse Walton, William Watson, William Bell, Joseph Jennings, Sr., and James Farley. Nottoway D. B. 1, p. 381. (Place known now as "Cook's".)

WINFREY, CHARLES, 1789. Deed to Shadrack Holt, conveying land on Ellis Fork of Flat Creek. Nottoway D. B. 1, p. 57.

WINGO, JOHN. Will dated and probated, 1755. Sons, Thomas, William and James Wingo; daughters, Elizabeth Hill, Mary Hurt and Susannah Harris. Amelia W. B. 1, p. 114.

WINN, JOHN, 1794. Deed from John Winn, of Mason County, Kentucky, and John Tabb, of Amelia County, Virginia. to Freeman Epes, to land on Lazaretta Creek, adjoining lands of Peter Randolph and Robert Fitzgerald. Nottoway D. B. 1.

WINN, RICHARD, 1788. Deed from Richard Winn, of Prince Edward County, to Freeman Epes, of Amelia, in consideration of 1500 pounds loaned by Epes, conveying fifteen slaves. Nottoway D. B. 1, p. 55.

WOODSON, CHARLES, JR., 1775. Deed from Charles Woodson, Jr., and Anne, his wife, of Cumberland, to John Watson, of Prince Edward, land in Prince Edward on Falling Creek, adjoining Venable and others. Prince Edward D. B. 5, p. 389.

WORSHAM, JOHN. Deed from Booker and Royall, 1756, to Kennon, recites that John Worsham, by deed at Henrico, 1722, conveyed certain land to his son Daniel in Chesterfield; that Daniel died intestate and left three daughters, Phebe, wife of John Booker; Elizabeth, wife of John Royall; and Martha, wife of Stith Hardaway, who left issue, two sons, Daniel and Stith Hardaway. Chesterfield W. B. 3, p. 36.

WORSHAM, THOMAS, etc., 1791. Deed between Thomas Worsham, of Nottoway, and William Worsham, of Prince Edward, conveying land north side of Deep Creek, adjoining Richard Jones, Rowland Ward and John Howson, devised to them by will of their father, John Worsham, of Chesterfield, 1769. Nottoway D. B. 1.

WORSHAM, WILLIAM, 1752. Will. Executors, Isham Eppes and Captain John Archer. Lands in Amelia. Father-in-law Isham Eppes, wife Annie, daughter Elizabeth Eppes (not yet twenty-one). Chesterfield W. B. 1, p. 84.

WYNINGHAM, JOHN, of Amelia, 1738. Deed to Samuel Sherwin, of Gloucester, land on southside of Wyningham Creek, and bounded in part by James Anderson, and Captain Starke's, formerly Richard Fletcher's. Amelia D. B. 1.

LAND PATENTS.[76]

BLAND, JOHN, 1820. 240 acres "between Deep and West's Creeks, Amelia, on both sides Namozine Road." P. B. 69, p. 194.

BOLLING, FRANCES, (daughter of Drury Bolling), 1727. 697 acres in Prince George "on lower side Seller Fork of Deep Creek." P. B. 13, p. 122.

BOLLING, FRANCES, 1735. 3251 acres in Amelia, "on both sides Little Seller Fork, Deep Creek." P. B. 16, p. 268.

BOLLING, JOHN, 1725. 2353 acres in Prince George, "on upper side Flatt Creek between upper and lower Horsepen Branches." P. B. 12, p. 343.

BOLLING, ROBERT, 1732. 3831 acres in Prince George, "in the fork between the Little Creek and the Main Deep Creek"; also 9272 acres on both sides of Nummisseen Creek and upper side of Tucker's Branch. P. B. 15, pp. 6 and 7.

BOTTOM, THOMAS, 1728. 400 acres, "on main fork of West's Creek of Deep Creek," in Prince George County. P. B. 13, p. 450.

COCKE, ABRAHAM, 1738. 2698 acres in Amelia, on north side Great Nottoway River, and on both sides Little Nottoway River. P. B. 18, p. 125.

COCKE, JAMES POWELL, 1727. 1581 acres in Prince George County, in the main fork of Knibb's Creek. P. B. 13, p. 315.

COCKE, JAMES POWELL, 1732. 1050 acres in Prince George, "on main fork of Knibb's Creek," adjoining Henry Anderson. P. B. 14, p. 490.

CRADDOCK, WILLIAM, 1737. 236 acres, Amelia, "both sides of Flatt Creek adjoining his own line." P. B. 17, p. 312.

CRADDOCK, WILLIAM, 1740. 999 acres, Amelia, "on both sides of Flatt Creek." P. B. 19, p. 742.

CRAWLEY, WILLIAM, 1733. 2985 acres on both sides of Deep Creek, in Prince George. P. B. 15, p. 98.

CRAWLEY, WILLIAM, 1737. 3714 acres in Amelia, on both sides Deep Creek and both sides Rocky Run. P. B. 17, p. 458.

CRYER, WILLIAM, 1737. 700 acres in Prince George and Amelia, on both sides Tommahitton Swamp. P. B. 17, p. 431.

---

[76]From Land Patent Books in the office of the Register of the Land Office, Richmond; referred to as P. B.

DUPUY, JOHN JAMES, 1745. 800 acres, Amelia, "on both sides the north or Ellis' Fork, of Flatt Creek." P. B. 22, p. 563.

ELLIS, JOHN, 1743. 1066 acres, Amelia, "both sides Flatt Creek." P. B. 21, p. 406.

ELLIS, JOHN, JR., 1735. 218 acres "on upper side Flatt Creek," in Amelia County. P. B. 16, p. 218.

EPES, CAPTAIN FRANCIS, 1638. 1700 acres in Charles City county, on south side of James River, in consideration of "his own adventure into this colony" and the transportation of sundry other persons named (including his sons John, Francis and Thomas), all of them having come over in a Spanish frigate, 1629. P. B. 1, Vol. 2, p. 537.

EPPS, COLONEL FRANCIS, 1653. "Colonel Francis Epps, Esq., one of the Council of State for this Colony," 280 acres in Charles City County, south side James River and south side Appomattox, adjoining his own land, due for transporting six persons into the colony. P. B. 3, p. 219.

EPPS, CAPT. FRANCIS, 1668. 1980 acres southside of James and Appomattox Rivers in Charles City, adjoining his own land, etc. P. B. 6, p. 203.

EPS, CAPT. FRANCIS, 1697. 68 acres in Henrico, north of James River "on ye heads of Long Feald Land," etc. P. B. 9, p. 105.

EPES, FRANCIS, 1698. Francis Epes, of Henrico County, 60 acres in that county. P. B. 9, p. 161.

EPPS, CAPTAIN FRANCES and others, 1701. Captain Francis Epp's, Mr. William Epp's and Captain Littleberry Epp's, 1000 acres in Charles City County, south side Warwick Swamp and north side of Joseph's Swamp, due for transportation of twenty persons. P. B. 9, p. 380.

EPES, CAPTAIN FRANCIS, and others, 1703. Captain Francis Epes, Mr. Isham Epes, Mr. Francis Epes, Jr., Mr. George Robinson, minister, Mrs. Elizabeth Kennon, Mr. Philip Jones, Mrs. Martha Stratton, Mr. George Archer and Mr. James Hill, 4000 acres in Henrico (now Chesterfield), north side Appomattox River, at mouth Winterpock Creek, due for importing eighty persons (named, including one Francis Epes). P. B. 9, p. 540.

EPES, FRANCIS, 1716. 311 acres in Henrico. P. B. 10, p. 302.

EPES, FRANCIS, JR., 1716. Francis Epes, Jr., of Henrico, 690 acres in Henrico, on the Appomattox near Winterpock, adjoining Colonel Francis Epes. P. B. 10, p. 301.

EPES, FRANCIS, 1717. 1790 acres in Henrico, south side Swift Creek, adjoining Colonel Francis Epes, for importing nine persons, etc. P. B. 9, p. 346.

EPES, COLONEL FRANCIS, 1717. 1000 acres in Henrico, north side Appomattox and about mouth of Nooneing Creek. P. B. 10, p. 345.

EPES, FRANCIS, JR., 1717. 280 acres in Henrico, north side Swift Creek. P. B. 10, p. 346.

EPES, COL. FRANCIS, 1725. 750 acres in Prince George, south side Appomattox River on Winticommick Creek. P. B. 12, p. 347.

EPES, FRANCIS, SR., 1725. 200 acres in Prince George, north side Chamberlain's Bed above mouth of Burnt Quarter Branch. P. B. 12, p. 274.

EPES, FRANCIS, JR., 1726. 200 acres in Prince George, south side Gravelly Run. P. B. 12, p. 472.

EPES, COL. FRANCIS, 1727. 2350 acres in Henrico, north side Appomattox River, east Skin Quarter Creek. P. B. 13, p. 193.

EPES, FRANCIS, 1728. 400 acres in Prince George, on both sides Cattail run. P. B. 13, p. 481.

EPES, COL. FRANCIS, 1730. 6500 acres in Goochland County, etc. P. B. 13, p. 485.

EPES, FRANCIS, 1733. 375 acres Prince George, "on upper side the Seller Fork of Deep Creek, adjoining Matthew Smart." P. B. 15, p. 142.

EPPES, FRANCES, Gent., of Prince George, 1733. 375 acres in Prince George, upper side Seller fork of Deep Creek, adjoining Smart. P. B. 15, p. 142.

EPPES, FRANCIS, 1740. 400 acres in Amelia, "Beginning in his brother Isham Eppes's where it crosses Seller Creek, thence . . . down Williams's branch," etc. P. B. 19, p. 882.

EPPES, FRANCIS AND ISHAM, 1740. 694 acres in Prince George, south side Gravelly Run, etc. P. B. 19, p. 880.

EPPES, FRANCIS, 1756. 51 acres in Prince George, both sides Little Cattail. P. B. 33, p. 262.

EPPES, FRANCIS, JR., 1756. 104 acres in Amelia, lower side Seller Creek. P. B. 33, p. 262.

EPPES, FRANCIS, 1770. 41 acres in Prince George, adjoining Colton and others. P. B. 39, p. 177.

EPPES, FRANCIS, 1770. 76 acres in Prince George, south side Joseph's Swamp. P. B. 38, p. 872.

EPPES, FRANCIS, 1773 and 1774. Seven acres on Hatchers Run, in Dinwiddie, and 400 acres in same county on Chamberlayn's Bed. P. B. 41, p. 333, and P. B. 42, p. 747.

EPPES, ISHAM, 1734. 150 acres, Prince George, "on the Seller Fork Deep Creek"; 400 acres "on ridge between branches of Little Nottoway River and branches of Deep Creek." P. B. 15, p. 364.

EPPES, ISHAM, 1743. 1560 acres in Prince George, between Hatcher's and Gravelly Runs. P. B..23, p. 645.

EPPES, ISHAM, 1745. 1993 acres, Amelia, "on north side Little Nottoway.

EPPES, ISHAM, 1745. 365 acres in Prince George, on Picture Branch and both sides Upper Nottoway River Road. P. B. 25, p. 77.

EPES, ISHAM, 1748. 353 acres in Prince George, south side Hatcher's Run. P. B. 26, p. 591.

EPPES, ISHAM, 1755. 200 acres in Dinwiddie. P. B. 32, p. 614.

EPPES, ISHAM, 1773. Two acres in Dinwiddie. P. B. 41, p. 332.

EPES, JOHN, 1720. 400 acres in Prince George county, both sides of Reedy Branch of Butterwood Swamp or Creek. P. B. 11, p. 36.

EPES, JOHN, 1728. 367 acres in Prince George, on forks Georges branch of Nummisseen Creek. P. B. 13, p. 404.

EPPES, JOHN, 1739. 1167 acres in Prince George, in fork of Georges Branch and Nummisseen Creek. P. B. 19, p. 641.

EPPES, JOHN, 1750. 149 acres in Prince George, north side White Oak Swamp. P. B. 30, p. 435.

EPPES, JOHN, JR., 1744. 260 acres in Amelia, north side Little Nottoway River and on both sides Lazaritta Creek. P. B. 23, p. 679.

EPES, JOHN AND ISHAM, 1721. John and Isham Epes, of Prince George, 538 acres south side Gravelly Run in Prince George. P. B. 11, p. 65.

EPES, THOMAS AND WILLIAM, 1725. 385 acres in Prince George, lower side Butterwood Swamp. P. B. 12, p. 413.

EPES, WILLIAM, SR., 1722. 137 acres on Gravelly Run in Prince George. P. B. 11, p. 181.

EPES, WILLIAM, JR., 1733. 100 acres in Prince George, north side Joseph's Swamp, adjoining his residence. P. B. 15, p. 30.

EPPES, WILLIAM, 1746. 400 acres in Prince George, both sides the road, lower side Nummisseen Creek, adjoining Bolling. P. B. 25, p. 362.

EPES, WILLIAM, 1748. 1013 acres in Prince George, south side Josephs Swamp. P. B. 26, p. 595.

EPES, WILLIAM; BOLLING, ROBERT; and others, 1721 and 1722. 5000 acres on both sides Nummisseen Creek in Prince George. P. B. 11, p. 83.

FITZGERALD, JOHN, 1724. 853 acres in Prince George, "on south side Nummisseen Creek," etc. P. B. 12, p. 227.

FITZ GERRALD, JOHN, 1740. 934 acres in Amelia, "on the head of West's Creek of Deep Creek," etc. P. B. 19, p. 988.

FITZGERALD, JOHN, 1741. 2836 acres in Prince George and Amelia, both sides Nammisseen Creek, adjoining Robert Bolling. P. B. 19, p. 959.

FITZGARRALD, WILLIAM, 1742. 1053 acres in Amelia, on lower side Main Deep Creek, etc.; 1817 acres in Amelia, on north side Little Nottoway River. P. B. 21, pp. 120 and 134.

FLETCHER, RICHARD, 1734. 300 acres in Prince George, "on the north or upper side of the Woody Creek of Deep Creek." P. B. 15, p. 397.

GILLIAM, JOHN, SR., 1732. 183 acres, Prince George, in the main fork Deep Creek, known by the name of the Island. P. B. 14, p. 417.

HARDAWAY, STITH, 1740. 388 acres in Amelia, "on the fork between Little Nottoway River and the Lazaritta Creek, adjoining John Epes' Line." P. B. 19, p. 790.

HARDAWAY, THOMAS, 1735 (or 1736). 576 acres in Amelia, "on upper side West's Creek, between lines Stephen Beasley, Richard Jones and William Mote." P. B. 17, p. 82.

HARRIS, WILLIAM, 1736. 575 acres in Amelia, "on the main fork of Deep Creek and Winningham's Creek." P. B. 17, ·p. 287.

HAYS, RICHARD, 1749. 300 acres, Amelia, on upper side Main Deep Creek and both sides of Mole's Path. P. B. 28, p. 551.

HINTON, CHRISTOPHER, 1730. 321 acres "on lower side of Kitt's Horsepen Branch, of the lower Seller Fork of Deep Creek." P. B. 13, p. 521.

HUDSON, WARD AND JAMES, 1772. 344 acres, Amelia, "on north side Deep Creek." P. B. 40, p. 678.

HUDSON, WILLIAM, 1737. George II, in consideration of £5, grants to William Hudson 1000 acres in Amelia, on Deep Creek. Mentions Robert Moody's line and crossing Cabin Branch, and a corner near Lazaritta in giving boundaries. Jan'y 2nd, 1737, 11th year George II. Signed: William Gooch, Lt. Gov. and Com.-in-Chf. of the Colony. P. B. 17, p. 455.

HURT, WILLIAM, of Caroline, 1738. 400 acres "on both sides of Ellis Fork of Flatt Creek," Amelia County. P. B. 17, p. 528.

IRBY, CHARLES, 1739. 760 acres "on north side Little Nottoway, adjoining John Eppes and others." P. B. 18, p. 407.

IRBY, EDMUND, 1726. 400 acres in Prince George, "on the ridge between head branches of Deep Creek and the branches of Little Nottoway River." P. B. 13, p. 40.

JEFFERSON, FIELD, 1740. 390 acres in Amelia, on Barebone Branch of West's Creek. P. B. 19, p. 665.

JONES, PETER, JR., 1722. 233 acres in Prince George County, "on the east side of Deep Creek, beginning against John West's Island," etc. P. B. 11, p. 112.

JONES, PETER, 1728. 587 acres in Prince George County, "on lower side Deep Creek, etc." P. B. 13, p. 374.

JONES, PETER, 1735. 2021 acres in Amelia, "lower side Deep Creek, adjoining Richard Jones, Jr., John Clay and others," etc. P. B. 16, p. 142.

JONES, RICHARD, 1737. 400 acres in Amelia County, "on lower side of Main Fork of West's Creek, and on both sides of the Hunting Path." P. B. 17, p. 495.

JONES, RICHARD, Gent., 1735. 1287 acres "on lower side of Deep Creek, running to Seller Creek, adjoining William Short," in Amelia County. P. B. 16, p. 137.

JONES, RICHARD, Gent., 1735. 1623 acres, Amelia, on upper side West Creek. P. B. 16, p. 91.

JONES, RICHARD, JR., 1738. 400 acres in Amelia "on upper side of Little Creek of Deep Creek, adjoining land of his father and others," etc. P. B. 18, p. 133.

JONES, RICHARD, 1742. 300 acres in Amelia, on South side Buckskin Creek. P. B. 20, p. 389.

KENNON, RICHARD, JR., 1736. 387 acres, Prince George County, "on upper side Flatt Creek and upper side Haw Branch." P. B. 17, p. 238.

KENNON, ROBERT, 1734. 400 acres in Prince George, "on the ridge between the Seller and Wooddy Forks of Deep Creek," adjoining William Short, George Smith and George Bagley's line. P. B. 15, p. 228.

LEATH, ARTHUR, 1746. 303 acres, Amelia, "on both sides Middle Seller Fork Deep Creek." P. B. 24, p. 229.

LEATH, PETER, 1731. 400 acres in Prince George, "on lower side of the middle Seller Fork of Deep Creek. P. B. 14, p. 310.

MAYES, JOHN, 1732. 845 acres in Prince George, "on the south or lower side of Deep Creek." P. B. 14, p. 493.

MOODY, ROBERT, 1737. In consideration of 4 pounds grant of 774 acres on both sides Deep Creek in Amelia. Mentions William Hudson's line. P. B. 17, p. 498.

MOTLEY, JOSEPH, 1745. 390 acres, Amelia, "north side Ellis Fork of Flatt Creek and both sides the road." P. B. 24, p. 204.

MOTLEY, JOSEPH, 1745. 1083 acres, Amelia, "on both sides of Flatt and Little Creeks." P. B. 22, p. 275.

OLIVER, JAMES, 1748 (or 1749). Amelia County; 25 acres both sides Deep Creek, adjoining land Samuel Jones, Higden Robertson (or Robinson), Booker and Bruce. P. B. 28, p. 627.

ORNSBY, JOHN, (Clerk), 1743. 4054 acres in Amelia, on both sides of Nottoway Road, between the branches of Deep Creek and the branches of Tommohitton Swamp, beginning in Francis Rany's line where it crosses the middle Seller Creek, etc. P. B. 23, p. 574.

PERKINSON, WILLIAM, 1736. 200 acres "on heads of the main Buckskin Creek," in Amelia County. P. B. 17, p. 258.

PRYOR, PHILIP, 1741. 386 acres on ridge between the branches of Great and Little Nottoway Rivers, adjoining Bolling and others. P. B. 20, p. 15.

RANDOLPH, HENRY, 1725. 1053 acres in Prince George County, on lower side of the Beaver Pond branch of Deep Creek. P. B. 12, p. 199.

RANDOLPH, RICHARD, 1736. 5430 acres on both sides the Appomattox in Goochland and Amelia. P. B. 17, p. 161.

RANDOLPH, WILLIAM, 1733. 3800 acres in Prince George, Goochland, and Brunswick on both sides the Appomattox, including part of Sandy River and Green Creek, etc. P. B. 15, p. 149.

ROBERSON, EDWARD, 1743. 383 acres, Amelia, "North side of Lazeritta Creek of Little Nottoway River." P. B. 21, p. 374.

ROBERTSON, HENRY, son of Christopher Robertson, of Amelia County, 1739. 970 acres both sides Nottoway River, in Amelia, adjoining Yarboroughs, etc. P. B. 18, p. 404.

ROBERTSON, CHRISTOPHER, 1733 400 acres, Prince George, and 150 acres adjoining, "on both sides of Woody Creek of Deep Creek." P. B. 15, p. 180.

ROBERTSON, GEORGE, 1727. 599 acres on "upper side Flatt Creek," in Prince George County. P. B. 13, p. 116.

ROBERTSON, GEORGE, 1732. 3638 acres in Prince George, on upper side Flatt Creek and on Appomattox River, adjoining William Bass, Bolling and others. P. B. 14, p. 469.

ROBERTSON, HENRY, 1740. 150 acres, Amelia, "on upper side Deep Creek, adjoining line of Robert Bolling." P. B. 19, p. 828.

ROBERTSON, JOHN, 1727. 250 acres in Prince George, "on heads of the Horsepen branch of Nottoway River, on north side thereof." P. B. 13, p. 122.

ROWLAND, ROBERT, 1745. 400 acres, Amelia, on both sides Lazaritta Creek. P. B. 23, p. 864.

ROWLAND, ROBERT, 1746. 284 acres, Amelia, on both sides Lazaritta Creek, and 200 acres on south side of said Creek. P. B. 24, p. 453 & 592.

ROYALL, RICHARD, 1742. 322 acres, Amelia, both sides of Barebones Branch, of West's Creek. P. B. 20, p. 443.

SHANNON, WILLIAM, 1735. 435 acres in Amelia, on south side of Appomattox River between Smark's [?] and Little Creeks. P. B. 16, p. 238.

SMART, MATTHEW, 1733. 300 acres "on the ridge between the branches of Deep Creek and Little Nottoway River." P. B. 15, p. 187.

STARK, WILLIAM, 1736. 1719 acres in Amelia, on head branches Deep Creek; also 195 acres in Amelia, on the Rocky Branch of Deep Creek and both sides the main Deep Creek Road. P. B. 17, p. 175 and 176.

TABB, THOMAS, 1737. 2400 acres, Amelia, "between Buckskin and West's Creeks, adjoining Henry Lester, et als, lines." P. B. 17, p. 324.

TANNER, JOEL, 1741. 200 acres in Amelia county, on north side Winningham's Creek, of Deep Creek. P. B. 20, p. 363.

TAYLOR, JOHN, 1735. 303 acres, Prince George, "on lower

side of Deep Creek, beginning above the Sappone Indians' Cabbins." P. B. 16, p. 158.

TOWNS, WILLIAM, 1742. 1595 acres, Amelia, "on forks of Buckskin Creek." P. B. 21, p. 136.

WARD, BENJAMIN, 1728. 780 acres in Prince George, between the head branches of Knib's Creek and the head branches of Beaver Pond branch of Deep Creek. P. B. 13, p. 423.

WATSON, JOHN, 1635. 150 acres "situate at the New Poynisson and bounded south upon the river," etc., "for the adventure of himself into this colony," 50 for himself, 50 for his wife, Elizabeth, and 50 for his servant Richard. P. B. 1, Vol. 1, p. 225.

WATSON, JOHN, 1644. 1 acre on the River in James Citty County, near the Brewere Poynt, adjoining Isaac Watson, etc. P. B. 2, p. 10.

WATSON, JOHN, 1655. 300 acres in Lancaster County, for transporting six persons into the colony (naming them). P. B. 3, p. 356.

WATSON, JOHN, 1677. 478 acres in Henrico, north of James River "at a place called White Oak Branch, or Swamp, that falleth into Chickahominy." P. B. 6, p. 632.

WATSON, JOHN, 1689. Allowed 200 acres of land for importing four persons into the colony (legally proved in court), viz: Francis Hayes, John Cole, Ralph Denby and Thomas Ascroft. Henrico County Court Minute Book, Court at Varina, Aug., 1689.

WATSON, JOHN, 1716. 541 acres in Henrico on Northern branches Upnam Brook, formerly granted John Pleasants, deceased, 1713. P. B. 10, p. 254.

WATSON, JOHN, 1724. 400 acres in Henrico, "on branch of Chickahominy Swamp, called Long and Hungry." P. B. 12, p. 135.

WATSON, JOHN, 1731. 400 acres in Henrico, adjoining his own land and standing on head Rockey Branch; also 400 acres adjoining this, and 400 acres on Upperam Brook, a branch of Chickahominy; also 400 acres on northern branch of Upnam Brook. P. B. 14, p. 186, 190, 336, 339.

WATSON, JOHN, 1733. 400 acres in Henrico, crossing the main northern branch of the Chickahominy. P. B. 15, p. 28.

WATSON, JOHN, 1735. 395 acres in Henrico, north of James River, adjoining Holland and Boatright. P. B. 16, p. 117.

WATSON, JOHN, 1740. Granted 400 acres on south side Appomattox River in Amelia, adjoining John Franklyn's line. P. B. 19, p. 689.

WATSON, JOHN, 1742. 121 acres in Henrico, north of James River, adjoining Mosby. P. B. 21, p. 47.

WATSON, JOHN, September 20, 1745. 425 acres in Goochland, among the branches of Little Guinea Creek. P. B. 24, p.

132. This land adjoins John Watson's land, and in consideration of 45 shillings.

WATSON, JOHN, 1746. 4623 acres in Amelia County. P. B. 25, p. 47.

WATSON, JOHN, 1751. 725 acres in Goochland, on branches of Little Guinea Creek. P. B. 29, p. 422. 425 acres of this tract already included in other patent.

WATSON, JOHN, 1748. 330 and 404 acres "on lower side Little Buffalo River, Amelia (now Prince Edward), adjoining Randolph and Morton," etc. P. B. 26, p. 311, 466.

WATSON, JOHN, 1780. 165 acres on the branches of Rough Creek, Prince Edward County. P. B. "E," p. 196.

WATSON, JOSEPH, 1736. 121 acres in Amelia, southside and on Appomattox River, adjoining Mays, Morton, Lisle, etc. P. B. 17, p. 294.

WATSON, JOSEPH, 1741. 800 acres in Henrico, north side James River. P. B. 20, p. 38 & 40.

WATSON, JOSEPH and JOHN, 1723. 400 acres in Henrico, north side James River, adjoining Thomas Farrar, and others. P. B. 11, p. 243.

WATSON, WILLIAM, 1672. 750 acres in New Kent, on the branches of Mattadegun Creek, etc., for importing fifteen persons into the colony, naming them. P. B. 6, p. 411.

WATSON, WILLIAM, 1738. 3952 acres in Amelia, (2000 acres having been granted of this in 1737), beginning on Flatt Creek, lower side and zig-zagging southward to Little Creek; lines cross Cabin Branch, Deep Creek; etc. P. B. 18, p. 131.

WATSON, WILLIAM, 1743. 1500 acres both sides Mallory's Creek, in Amelia County. P. B. 21, p. 628.

WATSON, WILLIAM, 1744. 3385 acres, both sides Sweathouse Creek, in Amelia County. P. B. 22, p. 169.

WATSON, WILLIAM, 1745. 577 acres on Wintercomack Creek, in Amelia. P. B. 22, p. 257.

WATSON, WILLIAM, 1749. Patent to William Watson, of 5077 acres, Amelia, on both sides of Flatt Creek and head branches of Deep Creek, shows that he runs up Little Creek across to Hudson's line, and followed his line across Deep Creek, etc. (Watson had three or four patents to this land at different dates) and this included some smaller tracts patented by John Dyer, Barnaby Wells, and Daniel Coleman. P. B. 28, p. 615.

WATSON, WILLIAM, 1750. Amelia. 2650 acres "on head branches Bush and Briery Rivers." (The above name settled, lived and died at "Glenmore," in what is now Nottoway County. He married Amy, daughter of Col. Richard Jones, of Amelia, and his son, William, was one of the early justices in Nottoway. He died in 1751 or 1752, and his will is at Amelia Court House.)

WEBSTER, THOMAS, 1726. 800 acres in Prince George County, in the fork between Smacks Creek and the Appomattox River. P. B. 13, p. 35.

WHOOD, THOMAS, 1723. 151 acres in Prince George, "in the Seller Fork of Deep Creek." P. B. 11, p. 211.

WILLIAMS, THOMAS, 1736. 3043 acres in Prince George County, on north side Hatcher's Run, etc. P. B. 17, p. 496.

WILLIAMS, THOMAS, 1748. 1510 acres in Prince George, on head of Rocky Run, etc. P. B. 26, p. 618.

WILLIAMS, THOMAS, 1748. 3815 acres in Prince George County, on both sides Hatcher's Run, etc. P. B. 26, p. 620.

WINNINGHAM, JOHN, 1738. 536 acres in Amelia, "on lower side Winningham's Creek of Deep Creek." P. B. 18, p. 78.

WORSHAM, JOHN, JR., 1741. 345 acres, Amelia, on both sides of Barebone Branch of West's Creek, adjoining William Worsham, et als. P. B. 20, p. 41.

WYNNE, PETER, 1754. 275 acres, Amelia, "on head main Seller Creek." P. B. 32, p. 384.

WYNNE, CAPTAIN PETER, 1723. 342 acres in Prince George, "on both sides Nummisseen Road," between Nicholas Overby's and Captain Ballard Herbert's. P. B. 11, p. 336.

YARBROUGH, SAMUEL, etc., 1746. Samuel, William, Hezekiah and Moses Yarbrough, 1372 acres, Amelia, "on both sides Little Nottoway River and Mallory's Creek." P. B. 25, p. 54.

MARRIAGES, EPITAPHS AND OBITUARIES.

MARRIAGE RECORDS.[77]

CHESTERFIELD COUNTY.

Henry A. Tatum to Amelia Sherwin Brooking, Jan. 11, 1827.

George Fitzgerald to Susan F. Thweatt, May 19, 1831.

Edward Cox to Tabitha R. Sherwin, September 20, 1797.

Archibald G. McIlwaine to Martha Dunn, February 16th, 1826.

Theodorick Pryor to Lucy E. Atkinson, October 11, 1827.

MISCELLANEOUS MARRIAGES.

Married in Baltimore at Grace Church, the 9th of May, 1854, Dr. Augustus Hopkins, of Henrico, to Mrs. Mary K. Wortham, of Nottoway.

On Tuesday, 30th ultimo, by Rev. John Jones, Captain William H. Cousins of Dinwiddie to Miss Martha Robinson, daughter of the late Rev. Peter Robinson, of Nottoway.—*Richmond Enquqirer, April 23, 1819.*

---

[77]A great many marriage bonds of Amelia County had been copied by Mr. Watson from *William and Mary College Quarterly Historical Magazine*, vols. 15, 16, 17; they are not reprinted here.

On Wednesday, the 7th, by Rev. Richard Jones, Peter Epes, Esq., to the amiable and very interesting Miss Martha C., daughter of Isaac Oliver, Esq., of Nottoway County.—Petersburg *Republican,* April 6, 1821.

EPITAPHS.

AMELIA COUNTY.

From an upright shaft at Grub Hill Church in Amelia, on May 28, 1900, I copied:

Here lie the remains of Richard E. Hardaway, who was born on the 3 of January, 1796, and died on the 22nd of September, 1830. This stone is erected to his memory by the direction of his bereaved widow, Mary Hardaway.

1. The remains of John Archer and Elizabeth, his wife, here repose. They lived to a mature age in unbroken conjugal affection and happiness, estimable and esteemed in every relation of life. He died March, 1812. She died March, 1826. Their children placed this tablet over their graves, the memorial of enduring affection and reverence for their best of parents.

2. This monument is erected to the memory of William S. Archer by his affectionate sisters to whom he stood almost throughout their lives in the double relation of father and brother. He was born March 5th, 1789, died March 28th, 1855.

To mark their devoted affection, veneration and love, this humble inscription and inadequate tribute to his worth is from the hand of one who knew and loved him from his cradle to his grave. The kindliness of his disposition, the generosity of his character and his high and refined sense of moral right endeared him to his friends. His highly cultivated literary taste, his mind well stored with ornamental and useful knowledge, his calm and profound judgment, and his noble chivalry of character placed him in the councils of the nation in the proud rank of the distinguished men of his time. He lived and died without fear and without reproach.

3. Francis Key Gwynn, infant son of Thos. P. and Mildred A. Gwynn, died the 8th of May, 1841, aged two years and seventy eight days.

4. Sacred to the Memory of Joseph E. Archer, son of John and Elizabeth Archer, who died March, 1812, aged 18 years.

5. Richard Archer, son of Col. William Archer. *Ob.* 16th August, 1796. *Ae.* 57.

6. Martha J. Archer, born July 10th, 1803, died March 4th, 1882.

7. Anne Archer, born March 24th, 1805, died September 12th, 1880.

8. Sacred to the memory of Elizabeth J. Archer, daughter of John and Elizabeth Archer, who died October 14th, 1856.

DINWIDDIE COUNTY.

About one mile northwest of Burgess (the intersection of the White Oak and Boydton Plank roads in Dinwiddie) is "Sweden," the home of Col. Peterson Goodwyn, long a member of Congress, who died about 1818. The house, a long, rambling, large, old-fashioned building, is now untenanted and on its last legs. The graveyard, enclosed by a thick stone wall, is 150 yards north of the dwelling and contains many graves and a large stone vault. With Cutler Galusha, I visited the place and copied the following epitaphs on October 1, 1909:

1. Erected to the memory of Albert Thweatt Goodwyn, who died 13th April, 1847, and in the 47th year of his age.

2. Beneath this slab are laid the earthly remains of Martha T. Goodwyn, wife of Albert T. Goodwyn, and daughter of Major Elisha and Judith King, who died July 12th, 1831, (or 1851) aged 24 years.

3. Sacred to the memory of Peterson Goodwyn, son of Col. Peterson Goodwyn, late of Greenesville County, Virginia, who died on October 15th, 1836, aged 36 years, leaving an affectionate wife, six children, and a large circle of relatives and friends to deplore their untimely loss.

4. Alberta M. Goodwyn, only daughter of Albert T. and Martha T. Goodwyn, who died October 12th, 1832, aged three years.

At "Sweden" in Dinwiddie in the vault, in which are six coffins:

1. Thomas Whitworth, born June 4th, 1794, died June 24, 1874.

2. Elisha H. Whitworth, wife of Thomas Whitworth, and daughter of Col. Peterson Goodwyn. Died Dec. 29th, 1847.

3. Mary A. Willson, infant grand-daughter, died July 1, 1876.

4. Thomas Willson, infant grandson, died July 18th, 1861.

At "Sweden," on Hatcher's Run in Dinwiddie:

1. Erected by Fletcher H. Archer to the memory of his beloved wife, Eliza Ann Eppes Archer, who died in Petersburg, April 22nd, 1851, aged 24 years, 11 days, leaving an infant daughter.

(Inscription follows)

(NOTE: She was the daughter of Daniel E. Allen, who married a daughter of Col. Peterson Goodwyn of "Sweden.")

2. Beneath this stone lie the remains of Daniel E. Allen, who died at Mayfield near Petersburg in this county October 24th, 1847, aged 62 yrs.
To commemorate the virtues of a beloved and most affectionate father, his daughter Eliza Ann Eppes Allen has caused this tablet to be erected.

3. Inscribed to the memory of Anny (possibly Amey) Eppes Allen, wife of Daniel Allen and daughter of Col. Peterson and Elizabeth Goodwyn, who departed this life November 1st, 1829, leaving a disconsolate husband and infant daughter to deplore the loss of an affectionate wife and tender mother.

About three quarters of a mile northwest from Dinwiddie Courthouse on the face of a hill sloping toward the south, is "Pea Ridge" (as some call it), the home of the late Dr. E. Harvie Smith, who came to Dinwiddie from Gloucester,—having a large practice before the war and large land estates and married a second time an Anderson of Brunswick (kin to S. G. Gilliam). The doctor was a hospital surgeon at Richmond during the war and did not return to Dinwiddie for some years. He was consul at Naples and member of the House of Delegates from Dinwiddie after the war, having gone over to the Republicans. He was the father of John Ambler Smith, M. C., from Richmond. Northeast and a hundred yards from the house site (burnt some years ago) is a large burial ground enclosed by the doctor with a stone wall. In December, 1907, I copied the following from the only tombstone there:
Mary Cary, daughter of Col. John Ambler, and wife of Hon. John Hill Smith, died September 24, 1843.

LUNENBURG COUNTY.

Henry H. Chambers, M. D. Born in the County of Lunenburg on the first of October, 1790. He removed to Alabama in 1812, was elected one of her representatives to the Senate of the United States, and died in his native county on his way to the city of Washington on the 24th day of January, 1826, in the 37th year of his age. He discharged his duties in life and died with Christian faith in a happy immortality. Erected to his memory by his son Henry C. Chambers, of Mississippi, A. D. 1859.

Copied by me from the tombstone in Lunenburg County about two miles southwest of Kenbridge on the 8th of October, 1911.

(signed)   A. B. Dickinson.

NOTTOWAY COUNTY.

The Dupuy family lived for many generations on or near Flat Creek, from a time long antedating the formation of Nottoway County. In the burial ground of Captain James Dupuy— the plantation now owned and occupied by James D. Fowlkes— I copied the following epitaphs from tombs in good state of preservation on April 5, 1895:

1. In memory of James Dupuy, descendant of the French Huguenots, and officer in the American Revolution, born May 5, 1758, died June 30th, 1823.

2. In memory of Mary, wife of James Dupuy, and daughter of William and Ann Purnell, born Mar. 13th, 1763, died Feb. 15th, 1828.

3. In memory of John Purnell Dupuy, born Feb. 22nd, 1790, died Dec. 27th, 1851.

4. Sacred to the memory of William J. Dupuy, born May 17, 1792, died December 13, 1853.

5. To the memory of William P. Dupuy, born Feb. 6th, A. D. 1819; died September 26th, 1829. (Also a verse)

6. To the memory of Alexander Dupuy, born June 7th, A. D. 1825, died October 18th, 1829.

7. In memory of Robert Dickinson, born November 25th, 1767, died December 25th, 1818.

Here are also the graves and slabs of three infant children of R. E. and M. J. Shore. Mrs. Shore was an Eggleston, granddaughter of Captain James Dupuy.

Inscription on old tombstone on place near Blackstone: Sacred to the memory of William B. Smith, born Jan. 18, 1817, died April 18, 1846.

At "Glenmore," the old seat of the Watson family in Nottoway (I don't know what name it bore in old times), there is this burying ground north of the house uninclosed and perhaps one hundred yards or more distant was a horizontal stone, imported from England, my great-grandma Robertson used to say, with the following inscription copied by me, April 5th, 1897:

Here lie the remains of Amy Watson, daughter of William and Amy Watson, who departed this life the 20th September, 1769 in the 18th year of her age. All the virtues, graces and shining accomplishments which adorn the sex were united in this amiable, young lady, to make her death sincerely regretted and her memory ever dear to her acquaintance.

At Hendersonville, one mile northwest of Nottoway C. H. in small wooden enclosure between the county road and railroad I copied the following inscription on May 4, 1906:

Sacred to the memory of James Henderson, a native of Scotland and, for upwards of sixty years, an inhabitant of this country, who departed this life the 8th day of November, 1817, aged eighty years.

May 7, 1889, I copied the following from the burial ground at "Mountain Hall," Nottoway, which is at the back of the garden west of the house and enclosed with a substantial stone wall (the work of Charles Hingston, an English stone-mason, who lived and did much work in Nottoway before the war).

1. Sacred to the memory of James Jones, M. D., graduate of the University of Edinburgh, born 11 December, 1772, died 25 April, 1848.

A man whose character none can contemplate without admiration or admire without profit. A statesman honored for his talents, erudition and patriotism. A christian deeply imbued with the spirit of the gospel. In the closing scene of life he exhibited the humble tranquil submission which religion inspires. His devoted wife erects this frail memorial to his virtues.

2. Maria Ann Jones, born Dec. 24th, 1798, died Nov. 24th, 1810.

3. Mary Frances Jones, born July 4th, died October 31st, 1799.

(Some verses below)

NOTE: The dates are not very distinct in the latter two. Flat slab over these graves.

There is also an upright tomb marking the grave of Mrs. Catherine Jones, widow of Dr. Jones, who died 1860, which I neglected to copy.

Major Richard Jones, of "The Poplars," left about a mile and a half north of Nottoway Courthouse on the southern slope of a hill overlooking the Jones's old mill-pond on Woody Creek a family burial ground, now enclosed with an iron railing. I am informed that the house stood a few yards north of the graveyard, a site now marked by a walnut tree, some ten inches in diameter. Across the old mill-road toward the southeast is a very large negro burying-ground. I copied, May 10, 1906, the following from the tombstones in the first-mentioned burial ground:

1. In memory of Sarah Campbell, daughter of Col. Freeman Epes, and wife of Dr. A. A. Campbell, of Nottoway County. Born March 23, 1793, and died Nov. 26, 1833. She was twenty years a member of the Methodist church, during which time her life was in strict conformity to the faith she professed.

Davidson *fecit*, Petersburg.

2. Mary J., wife of B. C. Jones, born April 2nd, 1814, and died August 6th, 1861. (This was copied for me and may not be entirely accurate.)

3. Catherine Frances Fitzgerald, wife of George Fitzgerald, and daughter of Archibald A. Campbell, born July 22nd, 1817, and died Sept. 24, 1838.

4. Dr. John Patterson, born November 24th, 1800, and died August 31st, 1836.

5. Archibald Campbell, eldest son of Dr. John and Martha E. Patterson, born Dec. 15th, 1835, and died September 29, 1845, age 11 yrs. and nine months.

6. Hamlin E. Patterson, second son of Dr. John and Martha E. Patterson, born August 4th, 1835, and died March 5th, 1837.

7. Martha E. Patterson, wife of Dr. Jno. Patterson, mother of Archibald C. and Hamblin E., infants deceased, and daughter of Archibald A. and Sarah Campbell, was born September 3rd. 1812, died Sept. 27th, 1849.

8. In memory of Richard Tyree Bacon, born March 8th, 1821, and died September 27th, 1825.

9. Also an infant of Dr. A. A. Campbell, the date sunk below the surface.

NOTE: I am informed that Dr. George S. C. Bacon, and his wife, who was a Jones, are buried here. Also Dr. Campbell and his son, Dr. Algie Campbell. The remains and tombstone of Hon. Thomas H. Campbell were taken from here and re-interred in the cemetery at Blackstone about 1903.

IN SHOCKOE CEMETERY, RICHMOND, VA.
Sacred to the Memory
of
Sam'l. Taylor
born in Cumberland Co., Va.
Sept. 15th, 1781
died in this city
Feb. 23rd, 1853.

In Memory of George E. Ward, M. D.
Son of William F. and Rebecca E. Ward
of Nottoway County, Virginia.
Born January 4th, 18—
Died March 25th, 1851.

Amelia Sherwin, wife of Dr. Henry A. Tatum
and daughter of Thomas Vivion Brooking,
born July 15th, 1804;
Died, May 11th, 1865.

Henry Augustus Tatum, M. D.
1798-1862.

Benjamin Watkins Leigh, born June 18th, A. D. 1781;
died Feb. 2nd, A. D. 1849. This monument is erected
to his beloved and honored memory by his wife, Julia
Leigh.

Julia Leigh, wife of Banjamin Watkins Leigh,
born January 2nd, 1801, Died April 15th, 1883
(other side)   Daughter of John Wickham

In memory of Major Benjamin Watkins Leigh, Jr.
Born January 18th, 1831.
Died on the field of Gettysburg
July 3rd, 1863.

In memory of Elizabeth Wickham Fry
wife of Chas. Meriwether Fry
born May 5, 1824
Died Jan. 13, 1895.
Also three infant children of Mr. Leigh.

OBITUARIES.

Death of Mrs. Martha Bibb, wife of Hon. George M. Bibb, and daughter of the late Gov. Charles Scott.—*Richmond Enquirer*, May 8, 1829.

Robert Dickinson, about fifty years of age, died in Nottoway County on December 25, 1818, and was buried at James Fowlkes's. He was the father of Judge Asa Dickinson.

Mrs. Jane Anthony Miller, consort of Giles A. Miller, died February 23, 1854.—*Richmond Enquirer*, March 14, 1854.

Mr. Buck Newman's family Bible says William Doswell was born 1799.

GENEALOGICAL NOTES.

ARCHER.

Vide Richmond *Critic*, May 19, 1889.

Richmond Enquirer, May 25, 1814, for obituary of Major Peter F. Archer who died at his seat near Scottsville, Powhatan County, April 25, in the fifty-eighth year of his age. He was the son of Colonel William Archer of Amelia—colonel of the Minute Men of that county—and began to serve under his father in 1776. Afterward he was in the Virginia corps of cadets at Philadelphia, 1776, under General Hugh Nelson. At Brandywine, his brother, Lieutenant Joseph Archer, was killed by a musket ball. His brother John, aide-de-camp to General Robert Lawson, while securing the public stores at Charlottesville, was run through the body several times and left for dead by Tarleton's cavalry. Subsequently his father was made prisoner in Amelia, carried to Portsmouth and died of smallpox. Peter F. Archer served as lieutenant in the Virginia Line under General Greene in the Southern Campaign.

He married Frances Tanner, daughter of Branch Tanner, Esq., of Chesterfield County. This lady brought him four sons and three daughters and died in 1797. Some years afterward he married Judith Cock, daughter of Stephen Cock, of Amelia, who with four children survived.

William S. Archer lived at "The Lodge" in Amelia; had two old maid sisters (one of them, Miss Betsy Archer). He was, I think, a son of the Revolutionary officer who died in a British prison.[78] His aunt married Major Joseph Eggleston of the Continental army. He himself did not marry; in his will left his property in trust so as to fall eventually to his natural son, William S. Archer Work.[79]

BLAND.

Vide "The Bland Papers," Ed. by Charles Campbell (Petersburg, 1840).[80]

The first Bland in Virginia was Theodorick Bland, who bought and established the estate of "Westover," afterward the home of Colonel William Byrd (1645). He built a church and gave to his county a courthouse, a prison and ten acres of land. He is buried at "Westover," where a tombstone bears the date of his birth, death, etc. He married a daughter of Richard Bennett, governor of the colony. His grandson, Richard Bland, Mr. Jefferson pronounced the "wisest man south of the James River."

Richard Bland died in 1776. He was called the "Virginia Antiquary," and was a political writer of the first rank. He was the author of "Letter to the Clergy"[81] and "An Enquiry into the Rights of the Colonies."[82] He was a member of the first Continental Congress in Philadelphia and is described by Cooke as "a blind old man with a bandage over his eyes." (Cooke, "Virginia," p. 406, 420, 435).[83]

The Bland manuscripts were purchased by Mr. Jefferson of the executor of Colonel Richard Bland.

Reverend William Bland, of the Episcopal Church, married Elizabeth Yates, the daughter of the president of William and Mary College. Their daughter, Nancy Bland, married Richard Pryor, and was the mother of Dr. Theodorick Pryor.

Mrs. Captain Robertson remembers that her father, Captain Fowlkes, was intimate with old Ned Bland, a lawyer and wealthy man.

---

[78]Grandson of Colonel William Archer who died on a British prison ship; son of Major John Archer.

[79]cf his will, p.

[80]Bland, Theodorick, Jr., "The Bland Papers" . . . Ed by Charles Campbell. Petersburg, 1840-1843. 2 Vols.

[81]"A Letter to the Clergy of Virginia . . ." Williamsburg, 1760.

[82]"An Enquiry into the Rights of the British Colonies" . . . Williamsburg [1766?].

[83]Cooke, John Esten, "Virginia; A History of the People." Boston and New York, 1883. (American Commonwealths.)

In my great-grandmother's (Mrs. Eliza Robertson) young days a Peter Bland lived between "Woodland" and the Ordinary[84] (at Akin's place). They called him Peter Rodney Bland. He had married a Miss Bacon (kin to Colonel T. G. Bacon) and had lost his property. His wife was much esteemed and was a sister to Mrs. Isaac Oliver. Isaac Oliver was a man of wealth; he was a brother of Asa Oliver, of Hendersonville. Peter Bland lived in a four room house, two rooms downstairs and two above, and the young people of the neighborhood gathered there frequently to dance, when "Old Fred Cooke played the fiddle."

A lawyer of the name of Peter R. Bland lived years ago near Maxey's Mill, at "Malvern," a place subsequently owned by Mrs. Dr. Sam Royall. He was a man of means. While there he lost his wife, and some weeks after her death her shroud was found in a spring on the plantation. It was known from this that the grave had been violated, and Mr. Bland was so disturbed that he asked Captain Fowlkes, Colonel Bacon and Robert Dickinson to meet upon a day to examine and reshroud the remains. They assembled, but the daughters were so distressed at the thought of disinterring their mother that it was concluded best not to undertake the task. It was subsequently learned that one of Mr. Bland's negroes had robbed the grave to get the clothes.

The Blands, Munfords and Morgans lived in the lower end of Nottoway County.

Booker.

Edmund Booker, of Amelia County, served in the Virginia Convention of 1788. The Bookers have frequently been prominent in politics since that time.

Richard Booker, of Amelia County, was at William and Mary College with William B. Giles.

William L. Booker was commonwealth's attorney of Amelia County and a prominent lawyer. He attended Hampden-Sidney College and was a member of the Phip. Society. His son, Thomas H. Booker, lives at Daniel Worsham's (1894). William L. Booker had a brother, Dr. John (?) Booker, who was a man of parts.

Bouldin.

Originally from Pennsylvania, I think, and settled in Charlotte County.

Louis C. Bouldin came to Nottoway from Charlotte and began the practice of law. He married Catherine Crawley Ward, of "Bellfield," daughter of Benjamin Ward, of "West Creek." He lived at "Bellfield" some three years and then purchased "Heathcourt," where he lived until his death about the year

---

[84]Jennings Ordinary.

1862. He was a brother of Honorable Thomas Tyler Bouldin, M. C. (who died in his seat as successor to John Randolph)[85] and of James Wood Bouldin, also a member of Congress. Judge Wood Bouldin, of the Virginia Court of Appeals, of Halifax, was a son of T. T. Bouldin and the present Wood Bouldin is his son. Louis Bouldin was many years prosecuting attorney for several counties and represented the Nottoway and Charlotte District in the Virginia Senate. He resigned. After the Constitution of '51 he was a candidate for circuit judge against Thomas L. Gholson, but was defeated.

BROOKING, BRODNAX AND HOLMES.[86]

Colonel Vivian Brooking married Elizabeth Brodnax and had daughter, Elizabeth Thacker Brooking, who married Lieutenant Isaac Holmes. Their children were: John Ballard, Vivian B., (Dr.) Isaac, Lucy, and Margaret B. Lucy married Edward C. Smith. Margaret B. married Samuel Brodnax.

Mary Brodnax Smith, daughter of Lucy and Edward C. Smith, married John Alexander Robertson, and their children were: George Edward, John C., Francis Brodnax, Fred. Smith, Robt. Stanley. The children of Margaret B. Holmes and Samuel Brodnax were: Jervis, Anne, Louisa, William, Frances, Emily H. Frances married John Alexander Robertson.[87] Emily H. married Thomas Maclin Lundie. The children of Frances and John Alexander Robertson were: (Dr.) John Alexander, Martha Archer and Margaret Holmes.

Henry Brodnax married Ann Holmes, only sister of Colonel John Holmes, of Bowling Green, Va. Their children were: William, (Judge) Henry, Elizabeth Power.[88]

William married Mary Walker and had children: (General) William H. and Meriwether Bathurst. William H. married Ann Withers. Meriwether Bathurst married Ann Walker, and had son, (Dr.) Robert Walker Brodnax, who married Cornelia Batte and had son (Dr.) John Wilkins Brodnax.

Elizabeth Power, daughter of Henry Brodnax and Ann Holmes, married John Woolfolk, and they had daughter, Ann Holmes, who married William Grymes Maury.

Mention of petition of Vivian Brooking, administrator of Isaac Holmes, deceased; names widow, Eliza T. Holmes, and

---

[85]Died while addressing the House of Representatives, Feb. 11, 1834.

[86]The data in regard to these three families, in rough tables in an unknown handwriting, were preserved among Judge Watson's notes.

[87]John Alexander Robertson was married three times. His first wife was Fanny Archer, daughter of James William Archer, of Chesterfield; his second wife, Frances Brodnax; and his third wife, Mary Brodnax Smith.

[88]There was another son of Henry Brodnax and Ann Holmes, Freeman, who died young.

children of deceased, Francis T. Holmes, Margaret B. Holmes, Lucy Holmes and Vivian B. Holmes; applying for certain land, account of Revolutionary service.—Journal, House of Delegates, 1795, p. 12.

CARTER.

Old Mr. Charles and Frank Carter were sons of Rawleigh Carter, Esq. The latter lived at Mrs. Cochran's place on the road to Jeffress' store.

There was an old Billy Carter who lived where Asa Carter now lives (1891). His place was known in old times as "Puff Hollow," and John B. Oliver's place as "Fritter Grove" from the customary desserts dispensed upon these tables. These names sprang up (or the latter at least) about the time Mrs. Dr. Tuggle came upon the carpet.

Frank Carter became bound in debt to, and was sold out by, John B. Oliver, his cousin. Old John B. attended the sale and would weep every time a darkey was sold and say he was "mighty sorry for Cousin Frank," but he "sold another nigger every time." (Related by Colonel Jeffress).

CRADDOCK.

Colonel William Craddock lived in the vicinity of Perkinson's, Amelia County, in sight of old Captain William Perkinson's. He was a Revolutionary officer and made a hairbreadth escape from the British on the public road near his house during the Revolution.

He married Obedience Hill, of Amelia. His daughter, Polly Craddock, married Captain Joseph Fowlkes.[89] He lived in easy circumstances, and my great grandmother, Mrs. Eliza Robertson, was wont to visit his home in her childhood.

The family burying-ground was upon his plantation.

Henry Craddock allowed 200 acres for services as sergeant in Virginia Continental Line for three years. "Military Certificates," Book 1, p. 33.[90]

Robert Craddock got certificate for 2666⅔ acres of land for military service as lieutenant in Virginia Continental Line from January 1, 1777, to March 20, 1783. "Military Certificates," Book 1, p. 32.

DYSON.

Frank Dyson (Captain Jones's father-in-law) was a son of Frank Dyson, who sometime represented Nottoway in the Legislature.

---

[89]See p. 164.
[90]"Military Certificates," three ms. volumes in the Virginia Land Office; sometimes referred to as "Military Land Warrant Books."

The elder Frank Dyson and Tom were brothers, I think. John Dyson was a brother of Frank Dyson, Jr. Frank Dyson, Jr., married a sister of Joseph N. Vaughan.

EGGLESTON.

Dr. Edward Eggleston is a native of Amelia and a brother of Dr. Joseph Eggleston, the dentist. His father was Joseph Cary Eggleston, a lawyer and native of Amelia, who removed to Indianapolis and died there. This, Dr. Richard F. Taylor thinks, was the Eggleston whom William Giles carried to Hampden-Sidney in the foot of his sulky, though Dr. Pryor thought his name was Everard Eggleston. These Egglestons were relatives of Major Joseph Eggleston of the Revolution.

EPES.

Memorandum of Epes family from notes collected by Judge B. J. Epes, of Dinwiddie, and furnished me by him.

See Hening's "Statutes," Vol. 1, p. 154, 299 and 372; *Virginia Magazine of History and Biography*, Vol. 3, p. 393-401; *Scribner's Magazine* (1904), Vol. 36, p. 573-586.

Sallie Epes, sister of Capt. Jack Epes (father of old Mr. Freeman Epes) married William Fitzgerald, of "Leinster," of which union there were ten children.

Mary Epes, sister of Sallie Epes, married Francis Fitzgerald, of "The Castle," brother of William, of "Leinster."

John Wayles Eppes was son of Francis Eppes, of "Eppington," in Chesterfield; he was also son-in-law of Thos. Jefferson. He moved from "Eppington" to "Saratoga" near Willis Mountain in Buckingham. The Hubards of Buckingham are his descendants.

William Pope Dabney, in a letter dated December 22, 1892, states:

"John Wayles Eppes lived at his plantation, "Eppington," on Appomattox in Chesterfield. He had a summer home near Willis Mountain on the edge of Buckingham. He was member of Congress from the Chesterfield district and was moved up to Buckingham as the last resort to beat John Randolph, and would not have done it but for the great influence of his father-in-law Thomas Jefferson, who exerted it to the utmost; and it is said that the sage, philosopher and ex-president, under pretense of seeing his old friends, went electioneering in his carriage from county to county."

Mr. Francis Epes qualified as one of the justices of Henrico, 1682. (Minutes of County Court, Henrico, 1682).

Mr. Francis Epes qualified as high sheriff under appointment from the Colonial Governor; date of commission, April 19, 1686. (Minutes of County Court, Henrico, 1686.)

Richard Eppes appointed guardian to his daughter Sarah Eppes, 1752. (Chesterfield County Court Order Book, No. 1, p. 166).

August 1775, the Virginia Convention in session at Richmond, proceeded to elect officers of the forces being raised for the war, and of the first regiment (Patrick Henry, colonel) Francis Eppes was elected major.

Francis Eppes was sergeant-at-arms of the House of Delegates, 1776, at Williamsburg, and was, I suppose, in same position to the Convention which preceded the House; his son, Freeman Eppes, was by resolution temporarily in his place at this session. Peter Eppes was sheriff of Prince George Co. that year. (See Journal House of Delegates 1776, p. 69 and Acts of that session, p. 39).

EPES of Essex County, Massachusetts:[91]

Captain Daniel Epes died 1692, intestate. Honorable Symonds Epes, Esq., (Ipswich), died (with will) 1741; brother of Daniel; owned "Castle Hill," a fine estate. Captain Daniel Epes's widow was Elizabeth Epes. Daniel Epes and Symonds Epes must be his sons, as they qualified as administrators. Symonds Epes's estate appraised at 2,133 pounds. His wife was Mary Epes and son Samuel, which last, I think, left a will.

William Epes died October 7, 1765, intestate. Records Essex County, Mass. Probate docket.

He considered it likely that this family was related to the Epes family of Southside Virginia.

FITZGERALD.

There were three old Fitzgerald seats in Nottoway: "The Castle," "Belfast" and "Leinster."

The first remembered of "Leinster" was as the residence of Captain William Fitzgerald, an officer at Guilford in the old war [Revolutionary War].

His first wife was Sallie or Sarah, Epes, sister of Captain Jack Epes (who was father of old Mr. Freeman Epes) and of this marriage there were ten children.

His second wife was the widow of Daniel Jones, who had married the widow of Benjamin Ward, of West Creek, whose maiden name was Catherine Cralle, of Amelia County, and who was known as the "Queen."

The marriage of Captain Fitzgerald and the widow Jones took place at "Leinster" and at the same time and place Sarah Fitzgerald, a daughter of Captain William Fitzgerald by his first wife, was married to Mrs. Jones's son, Benjamin Ward, Jr.

Nottoway Deed Book 2, p. 50: Marriage contract between William Fitzgerald and Catherine Cralle Jones (widow of Ben-

---

[91]Data obtained by Mr. Watson during a trip through Massachusetts.

jamin Ward and Daniel Jones) dated 1797; "in view of the marriage about to be had."

Miss Lizzie Ward told me her grandmother in her old age hated the fact that she had gone to "Leinster" to marry her husband. There were no children of this second marriage. Mrs. Fitzgerald died and was buried at "Leinster."

Francis Fitzgerald, of "The Castle," was brother of William, of "Leinster." He married, first, Mary Epes, sister of Captain Jack Epes and sister of the first Mrs. William Fitzgerald. Of this union there was one daughter, Betsy, who married George Jones, son of Mrs. William Fitzgerald (formerly the widow Jones).

Francis Fitzgerald's second wife was Kate Ward, and their children were: Catherine, who married a Williams; Louisa, married Dr. Robert Shore; Fanny, married Rev. Dr. Theodorick Pryor (of sacred memory); Mary, never married and lived to a good old age at "The Castle,"[92] and two sons, Benjamin (of "Aspen Circle") and Robert. Benjamin married Miss Elizabeth Ward; Robert died single (I think) in early manhood.

Among the children of Captain William Fitzgerald, of "Leinster," were Dr. John, who graduated at Edinburgh in 1800 and who married Louisa Jones; Francis (clerk), who married Fanny Jones, and Sarah married Benjamin Ward. He had also a daughter who married Littleberry Jones, son of Daniel Jones, of "Mount Airy," by his first wife, who was a Miss Baker; another who married a Booth; and another, Pattie, who married Hamlin Epes of Botetourt [? illegible].

[Another note says] Kate Ward married Frank Fitzgerald of "The Castle" whose first wife was Mary Epes; the only child of this marriage being, I think, Dr. Robert Shore's first wife, who left an only child Louisa, who married Robert F. Ward.

Nottoway Deed Book 2, p. 67, shows that Robert and Francis Fitzgerald were justices in 1798.

Dr. John Fitzgerald, son of Captain William Fitzgerald, was father of William ("Pony"), of "Leinster," and John, of "Walnut Hill."

Francis, clerk, was father of Dr. George ("Glebe"); Captain Charles, of "Belfast," Amelia; Rev. James Henderson Fitzgerald, of Buckingham County.

There was also a James H.—probably Henderson—Fitzgerald, member of the House of Delegates from Amelia, who married a lady in Fredericksburg, got old James Henderson's estate, was very rich and died in Paris.

Richmond Enquirer, Nov. 18, 1817: James Henderson, of Nottoway County, a native of Scotland and a man of many virtues, who died Nov. 8, 1817. He was a merchant.

---

[92]Destroyed by fire in 1922.

State Library, Revolutionary Officers Continental and State Line, War. Vol. 1: List of persons of the State line in Continetal establishment: John Fitzgerald, captain of infantry, Continental.

Fitzgerald, John, 1782.

Lieutenant John Fitzgerald paid for military services, 1783, (See Revolutionary Soldiers, War 4, (State Library) p. 37.

FLETCHER AND HARDAWAY.

Richmond Enquirer, July 19, 1845.—Notice of the death of Captain James Fletcher on June 27, in the 74th year of his age. Left an aged widow, an only daughter and several grandchildren.

Dr. Mat. Harrison, of Brunswick County, was a descendant of Mrs. Captain Fletcher.

Martha Ann Fletcher, daughter of Captain James Fletcher, of "Somerset," married Dr. John S. Hardaway, of Amelia, one of whose two daughters, Jacqueline, by this marriage, married T. Freeman Epes and became the mother of all his children. Another daughter of John S. Hardaway, Sally Ann, married Horace Hardaway, her first cousin, a son of Dr. Daniel Hardaway, brother to Dr. John S. Hardaway. She became the mother of Dr. Daniel, Jack Hardaway, etc. Dr. John S. Hardaway died July 4, 1818, and is buried at "Somerset," his tomb being of marble.[93] Martha Ann Hardaway, widow of Dr. John S. Hardaway, married Dr. Robert Shore and became the mother of R. E. Shore, Mrs. Robert Ward, Mrs. Dr. W. H. Robertson, etc. Dr. Daniel Hardaway lived and died at "Hardaway's" on West Creek.

Richard Eggleston Hardaway (died 1832, buried at "Grub Hill") was father of John S. Hardaway, of "Glenmore," Amelia. Dr. Daniel Hardaway, Dr. Jack Segar Hardaway and Martha, called Patty, Hardaway (who spent her early life at "The Hermitage," in Amelia, with the Meades and was the mother of Lewis E. Harvie, Dr. John B. Harvie, William Old and Major Charles Old) were brothers and sister. Martha Hardaway married Edwin Harvie, by whom there were two sons, Lewis E. Harvie of "Dykeland," Amelia County, and John B. Harvie, of "Fighting Creek," Powhatan County. After Edwin Harvie's death she married William Old, by whom there were two sons, William Old and Major Charles Old.

There were six Hardaway brothers, namely, James, William, Daniel, Thomas, John and Joel. The Amelia Hardaways are directly descended from Daniel as shown by the following record which was prepared by John S. Hardaway of "Glenmore," Amelia County:[94]

---

[93]Died as result of affray; see p. 58.
[94]This table was contributed by Mr. Horace Hardaway, of Amelia County, now of Bristol, Va.; son of John S. Hardaway.

Daniel Hardaway, of Nottoway County, married Miss Worsham; issue, three children.

1. Daniel, married Anne Eggleston.
2. Stith, died unmarried.
3. Judith Archer, married Lewis; one son, Stith Lewis, and three daughters, who intermarried with the Cockes and Randolphs of Virginia.

Daniel, second, and Anne Eggleston left six children.

1. Dr. Daniel, married Sally Jones; two children, Horace and Anne Maria Fitz Gerald. Horace married his cousin Sally Anne; left six children, Daniel, Jack Segar, Richard E., Margaret, Harvie and Sally. All lived in Nottoway County, Virginia.
2. Dr. Jack Segar, married Miss Fletcher, left two daughters, Sally Anne, who married her cousin Horace, and Jacqueline, who married Freeman Epes, of Nottoway County, Virginia.
3. Martha, married Edwin Harvie, of Richmond. After his death in 1811, she married William Old, of Powhatan. Her sons are Lewis E. and John B. Harvie, and William and Charles Old.
4. Maria, married Seth W. Jones. They removed to Yallabusha County, Mississippi.
5. Eliza, who married Benjamin L. Meade, of Richmond, where she is living (1894), aged 73, with her son, Richard E. Meade.
6. Richard Eggleston, married Mary Rutherfoord, of Richmond, Va., and died young, leaving two daughters, who died in their youth, and one son, John S. Hardaway, of Chula Depot, Amelia County, Virginia, who has five sons and six daughters, namely, Richard Eggleston Hardaway, John Stegar Hardaway, Jennie G. Hardaway, William Old Hardaway, Mary Rutherfoord Hardaway, Thomas Rutherfoord Hardaway, Sallie Gaines Hardaway, Kate Harrison Hardaway, Horace Hardaway, Nannie Winston Hardaway, and Lucy Stanley Hardaway.

John S. Hardaway's home estate was near Chula Depot and is known as "Glenmore."

FOWLKES.

The first Fowlkes came to Nottoway (then Amelia) at the time of, or prior to, the Revolution. Two brothers of that name came from Wales, and a sister: John, Joseph and Polly Fowlkes.

John and Joseph settled in the neighborhood at Maxey's Mill, and married, respectively, Sarah and Mollie Jennings, daughters of William Jennings of the same vicinage (and granddaughters of old Jennings of Hanover.)

Polly Fowlkes married a wealthy gentleman of Prince Edward County named Wade.

The Joseph Fowlkes who married Mollie Jennings was the father of Captain Joseph ("Church Jr.") Fowlkes, of Fowlkes

Tavern, Nottoway, who was my great-great-grandfather. Captain Fowlkes married Polly Craddock, a daughter of Colonel William Craddock, of Amelia. From the union of John Fowlkes and Sarah Jennings sprang Colonel Jeffress's ancestors and those of Paschal Fowlkes, Esq. Captain "Church Jr." Fowlkes was so called from the circumstance of the old Colonial church of Nottoway Parish being located on his plantation above Leneave's Hill. The church was an immense structure; larger than any country church my great-grandmother could recall; a very long building, nicely finished; plastered within and provided with a large gallery for the darkies. It had high pews with closing doors, and what my great-grandmother called three pulpits, one above the other. The pews were not rented she supposed. There was one marked "the Gentlemen's Pew" and another, opposite, called the "Ladies' Pew."

At the time Captain Fowlkes purchased the surrounding lands the church was not reserved and passed with the soil. However, the public road separated his dwelling from the church. He, subsequently, got a decree of court to move the road beyond the church and so, having it situated upon his lot, used it as a granary. The panels of the pew doors he used as wainscoting in his parlor. (Now remaining in the house).

Bishop Meade in his notice of Nottoway Parish in his "Old Churches and Families" animadverts very severely upon this alleged profanation. The old Colonial church was finally destroyed in the great hurricane of 1837.

A graveyard, since demolished, was in the vicinity and many were the ghost stories told by the darkies in that locality.

Captain Fowlkes some years afterwards built, at his own expense, the "Republican Church" near the site of the old Colonial and employed old Asa Cabiness (Doctor Cabiness's father) to do the carpentry. He designed the church for the use of all denominations and hence named it "republican." The Presbyterians, later, sought to buy and remove it a short distance. He refused to sell, but gave it to them, whereupon it was taken down and transplanted accordingly.

Of the union of Captain Joseph Fowlkes and Polly Craddock there were several children, among them Eliza (my great-grandmother), who married Captain Henry S. Robertson, of Nottoway, and Fanny, who married Archer Robertson, of Chesterfield.

HASKINS.

Nottoway Deed Book 2, p. 194: Contract recorded showing the genealogy of the Haskins family; the descendants of Benjamin Haskins who died 1798; in Brunswick, Nottoway and Prince Edward Counties; includes some of the Ligons in Prince Edward.

JEFFRESS.

The following I had from Colonel W [illiam] C. J [effress]: The original seat of the Jeffresses is near Knight and Oliver's Mill in Lunenburg County.

John Jeffress there was the father qf numerous sons; one, Elisha Jeffress, settled in Mecklenburg; another married a daughter of Captain James Dupuy, of Nottoway; Colonel Edward T. Jeffress, another son, built up "Oakland" (Jeffress Store) and was for years a merchant at that place. He married, first, a Fowlkes, sister of Paschal Fowlkes, of "Hyde Park," and during the war married again, a Miss Gravatt, of Port Royal, Caroline County. Was a large slaveholder.

Colonel William C. Jeffress is a son by the first marriage. He settled first at "Woodville," about 1847; bought of Walter Middleton who was a druggist in Farmville.

Thomas H. Jeffress married to Christiana Blackwell, June 12, 1816.—Lunenburg Will Book, 18, p. 249.

Same book records the marriage of Griffin Smith, and Sally G. Jeffress, 1814; and Edmund T. Jeffress and Dicy Fowlkes, September 15, 1814.—Lunenburg Will Book 18, p. 227, 249.

JENNINGS.

William Jennings (William, I think) was a very wealthy widower and the first of the name in Nottoway. He was the missing link in Mrs. Hardesty's fortune schemes, being the son of the rich old Jennings of Hanover who was heir to the Jennings fortune in America.

He had moved from Hanover just before his death and settled on what is now Dr. Royall's plantation, and is supposed to be buried in Dr. Royall's pines in the old burial ground.[95]

He had several sons to settle in Nottoway, too. Joseph Jennings, one son, lived at Jennings Ordinary and the place derived its name from him.

Much excavating has been done in Nottoway seeking to find the Jennings fortune, or proof of inheritance.

Deed Book 4, Amelia, p. 249, speaks of William Hill selling land to "Robert Jennings, Gent., of Hanover"; a part of land patented by him in 1748 at Williamsburg. Date of deed to Jennings, 1752.

JONES.

Taken from letter written by Mrs. Kitty Jones, Blackstone, Va., October 26, 1888: "My Aunt, Mrs. James Jones, gave me all the information I have as regards Dr. Jones himself or his family; therefore I think it must be authentic. Mrs. Jones

---

[95]Referred to elsewhere in Mr. Watson's notes as "Jennings' burial ground."

stated that three brothers, named, respectively, Peter, William and Richard Jones, came from Wales to this country.

"Peter settled in Dinwiddie County near or on the spot where Petersburg now stands. The place was called Peter's house, afterwards Peter's town and then Petersburg. I think there is a statement something like this in Howe's History of Virginia.[96]

[96]cf Howe, Henry, "Historical Collections of Virginia," 1845, p. 243.

"I have often heard my father say his family came from Wales.

"William Jones took up the land on what was then called the Indian Trail, afterwards the Namozine Road, from near Mr. J. N. Vaughan's farm to Dennisville. William Jones died unmarried and his property was diverted from the Jones family.

"Richard Jones, the grandfather of Dr. James Jones, settled in Nottoway Co. about a mile east of the Court House, where still may be seen the family burial ground with a number of tombstones.

"Major Richard Jones, his son, was thrice married; first, to Mary Robertson, of Amelia County, a near relative of old Dr. William H. Robertson, of Amelia. Dr. James Jones was the only son of this marriage who lived to years of maturity; one other died in infancy and there were a number of daughters, most of whom married and moved to Tennessee or Alabama.

"Major Jones then married a widow, Nicholson, who was Elizabeth Fletcher, a sister of old Captain James Fletcher of this county [Nottoway]. There were two sons of this marriage, Richard and Nathan.

"Richard (our father) married Elizabeth Epes. Nathan died when about ten years old.

"Neither Dr. Jones's grandfather, father nor himself had any middle name.

"Major Richard Jones married the third time a widow, Mrs. Elizabeth Campbell, widow of Dr. Archibald Campbell, and mother of Dr. Archibald Campbell of "Blendon," Nottoway Court House."

I copied the following from Mrs. Catherine Jones's Bible some years ago at "Homestead," Nottoway; it was probably Dr. Jones's Bible:

James Jones and Catherine Harris were married 10th Sept., 1797.

Note: The following styles itself to be "an exact copy of a register kept by my father Richard Jones on one of the blank leaves of the New Testament by Burkett":

Richard Jones was married to Mary Robertson December 14th, 1769.

Elizabeth Jones, daughter of these, was born Dec. 7th, 1770.
James Jones, son, was born Dec. 11th, 1772.
Mary Epes Jones, daughter, was born Aug. 16th, 1777.
Richard Jones, son, was born Aug. 8th, 1780, died Oct. 8th, 1781.
Martha Ann Jones, daughter, was born Dec. 26th, 1784, died 179—.
Caroline Jones, daughter, born 1787, died 1794.
Mary Jones, wife of Richard Jones, died 1784.
James Jones entered Hampden Sidney College June 8, 1788; began medicine with Jo. Mettaur,[97] Prince Edward Co., May 1793; then eight weeks with Dr. George Brown in Baltimore; Philadelphia 1793 (Dec.) Read medicine with Jno. Patterson, Nottoway, 1794; Scotland, 1795, in ship "Bowman"; graduated Edinburgh, June, 1796, and returned November, 1796.
Dr. Jones died 25 of Apr. 1848—nine o'clock Tuesday A. M.[98]

Frances Harris died 1776, age 41.
William Harris died 1797, age 73.
Mary Harris, died 1798, aged 18.
Ann Osborn died 1799, age 30.
Hamlin Harris died 1801, age 31.
Susan Ruffin, 1825, age 61.
Elizabeth Jones, died 1831, age 72.
Sarah S. Fletcher, died 1855, age 86.
Mrs. Catherine Jones, died 1860, age 88.
Died at his late residence in Nottoway on August 30th, Dr. John Patterson in the flower of his age.

[Signed]   Walter A. Watson

March 8th, 1896.

The following is taken from a letter written to Judge Watson Feb. 25th, 1897, by Mr. Flournoy Rivers, Pulaski, Tenn.:

"In 1805 Richard Jones died in Robertson County, Tenn., testate, leaving wife, Martha, and children. His wife Martha was the daughter of Rowland Ward (died in 1800 in Amelia County) and Rebecca his wife (died in Davidson County, Tenn., 1805.).

"Richard Jones and Martha Ward married in Amelia county in November, 1774.

"Richard Jones with a brother, Peter, came to Tennessee from Amelia County as did the Ward mother and children. Peter Jones died in Wilson county, Tenn., 1811.

"Among other children of this Richard and Martha Jones, a daughter, Dorothy Chamberlain Jones, became the wife of

---

[97] John Peter Mettaur; cf Johnston, George Ben, "A Sketch of Dr. John Peter Mettauer of Virginia."
[98] See account of Dr. James Jones, p.

John H. Camp, June, 1808; and in October 1808 the widow Martha married John H. Camp's father, Captain John Camp. "Dr. John H. Camp and wife were my great grand-parents."

Francis Jones, of Brunswick, who married a daughter of Mr. Thomas Thweatt, of Dinwiddie, was elder brother of Mr. B. C. and G. W. Jones. He was father to Rev. T. T. Jones, George Jones, who married Dr. Pryor's daughter, and William Jones, the Republican politician of Brunswick.

Richmond Enquirer, February 1, 1848, contains notice of the death of John Winston Jones at his home in Chesterfield. Towns,[99] the then Governor of Georgia, was a son-in-law, and the *Macon Journal* notices his having been called to Virginia to attend Jones's bedside.

Richmond Enquirer, March 31, 1848.—John W. Jones: Resolutions offered at county court at Chesterfield by Holden Rhodes, Esq.

Richmond Enquirer, Feb. 4, 1848: Resolutions in legislature on death of John W. Jones, offered in Senate by Judge Cox[100] and in the House of Delegates by Lewis E. Harvie.

Washington, Sept. 12, 1917.   Had lunch with Congressman Wm. A. Jones, of Richmond County, and E. E. Holland, of Nansemond County, today and talked with Jones about his kinsfolk on his father's side. He said Gen'l. Jos. Jones of "Cedar Grove," Prince George County, in the suburbs of Petersburg, was his great-grandfather and married an Atkinson. He established his grandfather at "Bellevue" on the Appomattox River in Chesterfield. His grandfather married a Lee of Westmoreland. His father, Judge Thos. Jones, of Richmond County, was born at "Bellevue," went to school at the "Wigwam" in Amelia and at Chapel Hill, N. C.; waited upon Dr. Theodorick Pryor when he married an Atkinson at "Olive Hill" in Chesterfield. Jones said, as a youngster during the last year of the war, he was at "Bellevue," then the residence of his cousins, when General Lee dined there. One purpose Gen'l Lee had in going was to see an oil painting of his father Gen'l Henry Lee, which Jones says is still there in possession of some maiden cousins of his, and is believed to be the only portrait extant of "Light Horse Harry."[101]   W. A. W. [Walter A. Watson]

---

[99]George Washington Bonaparte Towns.

[100]James H. Cox.

[101]At this time (1925) there is still an old portrait at "Bellevue" in the possession of a member of the family, Miss Margaret Jones, thought by some to be a pastel, by others perhaps the work of St. Memin. This, however, is not the only portrait extant of General Henry Lee; there is also in existence an oil painting by Stuart; a copy by W. L. Sheppard is in the Virginia State Library.

Peter Jones, died in 1799; married Sarah Tanner, and had issue:

I. Elizabeth Jones, married May 25, 1780, Littleberry Royall.

II. Peter Jones; owned land in Dinwiddie; he settled in Lunenburg County.

III. Archer Jones. His father left him "My Homestead," 2500 acres, also 2200 acres near "Butterwood." He married, Nov. 28, 1793, his cousin Frances Branch. Scott, daughter of James Scott, and had issue:

1. Archer Jones, married Sarah Scott, daughter of his uncle, Samuel Scott.
2. Frances Scott Jones, married (1) Dandridge Epes (2) ―――― Shore and had issue by both.
3. Sally Tanner Jones, married Edwin G. Booth, Sr., and had issue.
4. Branch Osborne Jones.

IV. Robert Jones, died in 1804. His father gave him 650 acres near the mill. He married, Jan. 5, 1783, Ann, daughter of Rowland Ward and had issue:

1. Rebecca Jones, married, May 1840, David C. Jones. (David Jones married, I think, the second time).
2. Mary Ann Jones.
3. Sarah Tanner Jones, married, Aug. 1811, Daniel Hardaway, and they were parents of Horace Hardaway and Mrs. Maria J. Fitzgerald.
4. Elizabeth Royall Jones, married, Nov. 1815, Thos. Goode.
5. Maria W. Jones, married, July 1820, Thos. Wylie.
6. Edward Henry Jones. His father gave him 100 acres in Dinwiddie.
7. Seth Jones, married, Feb. 1816, Maria Hardaway.
8. Robert B. Jones.
9. Richard Sam'l. Jones, of "Horsepen Plantation."
10. William W. Jones, married, Jan. 1828, Prudence Mann.

V. Batte Jones, married Feb. 11, 1777, Margaret, daughter of Rowland Ward, and had issue:

1. Peter Branch Jones (800 acres on Little Nottoway).
2. Martha Jones.
3. Sarah Jones.
4. Rebecca Jones.
5. Margaret Jones.[102]

―――――――

[102]The above was sent to Judge Watson by some one, name unknown, but seems to have been worked out in careful detail.

The following Jones genealogy was taken from a letter written by Mr. William Clayton Torrence:

Daniel Jones (son of Col. Richard Jones, of Amelia) died in Amelia County in 1772. He married (probably a Miss Sturdevant) and had issue: 1. Richard Jones. 2. Edward Jones. 3. Daniel Jones. 4. Sarah Jones. 5. Mary Jones. 6. Martha Jones. 7. Rebecca Jones. 8. Elizabeth Jones. 9. Prudence Jones.

Daniel Jones, Jr., of "Mount Airy," son of Daniel Jones, married Catherine Crawley Ward. He died in Nottoway County (date unknown at present). Daniel and Catherine Jones had issue: first, Patrick Jones, of "Braggs"; second, Geo. Jones, of "Mount Airy," who married Betsy Fitzgerald, only daughter of Francis Fitzgerald, of "The Castle," by his marriage with Mary Epes, sister of Captain Jack Epes and sister of Mrs. William Fitzgerald, of "Leinster"; Daniel and probably others.

The names of these children are proved: Geo., by Nottoway County tax books in Auditor's office, Richmond; Daniel, by deed quoted in Jones letter as of record in Nottoway; Patrick, by deed in Amelia 1812 or 15 from Catherine Fitzgerald, Sr., to her son Patrick Jones. The land conveyed by Catherine Fitzgerald was part of the tract formerly conveyed by Daniel Jones the elder to his son Daniel Jones the younger.

The Nottoway tax books show also that the widow of Daniel Jones married Fitzgerald.

There is a tradition that Patrick had two children, Ann and Catherine, and that Ann was the Ann Jones who married William Bragg.

The Lewelyn Jones who married Prudence Ward was son of Peter Jones, of Lunenburg Co., and Jane Stokes.

Prudence Ward was the daughter of Roland Ward, Jr., who was son of Roland Ward and his wife, Rebecca, daughter of Col. Richard Jones, of Amelia.

Daniel Jones first married a Miss Baker and had children of that marriage, among them Littleberry Jones. He then married Catherine Crawley Ward, widow of Colonel Benjamin Ward, of "West Creek." There were several children of this marriage, among them George and Patrick Jones. He lived at "West Creek" after his marriage with Mrs. Ward.

Daniel Jones, of "Mount Airy," was the owner of the old mill and ditch site and was the father of Dr. George Jones (father of B. Cralle Jones, William and Mrs. Ward) who lived at Wm. Cralle Jones's place; Patrick Jones, who lived at Dr. J. C. Bragg's place; Fanny, who married Francis Fitzgerald, the clerk; Louisa, who married another son of Captain William Fitzgerald, of "Leinster," Dr. John Fitzgerald. Dr. Bragg's father married a daughter of Patrick Jones; Dr. Austin Watkins married his widow.

E. G. Booth, Sr., married a sister of Archer Jones, as also did Dandridge Epes.

Samuel Jones, of Powhatan County, was a nephew of William B. Giles.

OLIVER.

Isaac Oliver and Asa Oliver, both of whom, I think, lived at Hendersonville, had a brother, Charles, who lived in Roanoke County. His son, Yelverton, was a devotee of race horses, and Clerk Dick Epes says was the founder of the Louisville and New Orleans race tracks. Grandma Eliza says Isaac Oliver married a Bacon (daughter of T. G. B.).[103] A daughter of Isaac Oliver married Peter Epes, of "Walnut Hill," and they were the father and mother of Isaac, Dick Epes, etc.

The Olivers in Nottoway as given me by Mr. R. W. Oliver, the 23rd of July, 1915:

"My grandfather was Richard, who was born at Culliton's, this side of Kies. His father's name was James, who was born in Hanover. I think my grandfather's mother was Green (a relative of a General Green). My grandfather Richard married a Jennings. He was the youngest son of his father and died comparatively young. He had brothers whose names I don't remember. Asa, Isaac and Charles were nephews of my grandfather, I think. Charles went to Roanoke and became wealthy. Raised and ran horses. His son, Yelverton, followed this business to New Orleans. This was his only son. He had two grandsons, Charles and Dick. One of his daughters married Dr. Kent.

"My great-grandfather got large land holdings in Mecklenburg and Halifax, and the Olivers in those counties are his descendants. My grandfather's children were:

1. Robert, went south to Florida, married in Virginia, and was grandfather to Thomas B. and Robert Oliver. His son James came back to Virginia, married his cousin Barrett, settled in Amelia, and lost his life falling from an oat stack near Mannboro.

2. Richard, moved to Halifax. Married here in Nottoway; left children in Halifax.

3. John Billups Oliver, married Miss Carter, sister of Sharpe [Carter] and Mrs. Colonel John H. Knight and Dr. Josephus Carter, who went to Mississippi. He lived near Jeff-ress' Store, and his children were: Lucy Jane, who married Dr. R. B. Tuggle, Charles H. Oliver, who married Miss Ingram, from Missouri, and whose only child was J. Collier Oliver. The latter married Jane Robertson, who, I think, was the daughter of Booker Epes's overseer.

4. George W. Oliver, married Hannah Ann Jennings,

---

[103]Tyree G. Bacon.

daughter of Micajah, who lived on Little Nottoway River, where Henry Archer Jennings lived in my time. His children were: (1) R. W. Oliver, (2) M. J. Oliver, deceased, who married first Craddock, and second Robertson, daughter of Major Daniel Robertson (at head of Fitzgerald's Mill Pond). (3) Joseph Thomas Oliver, deceased, married Mary Jennings, daughter of Joseph Jennings, of Lunenburg, and left children. (4) George W. Oliver, married—[illegible] Gallagher, of Prince Edward, and had family in Lynchburg. (5) Mary J. Oliver, married W. J. Burton, of Halifax, and left descendants. (6) Pattie B., married William G. Overton, of Chesterfield, and left children. (7) Susan J., married Robert B. Oliver, now living at my father's place near St. Marks. (8) Nancy B., married Baker Townsend, of Lunenburg, and has descendants.

"Daughters of my grandfather, Richard Oliver:

1. Mary, married Bass and moved to Halifax.
2. Ermine, married Barrett of Amelia (grandmother of T. B. and R. B. Oliver).
3. The youngest sister married Hale Gallion, of Lunenburg; she had son named Richard, who had son named Emmet, now of Washington."

PLEASANTS.

Governor and Senator James Pleasants lived at "Contention" in Goochland County. He was born at a place called "Cold Comfort" in Powhatan (Judge Dabney I think states this). He practiced law in early life at the Amelia bar; he declined high judicial position from a distrust of his abilities, the chief judgeship, it is said. No picture of Governor Pleasants is extant, so far as I know.[104] He was the father of John Hampden and Hugh R. Pleasants. The latter never married; he was the founder of the *Richmond Dispatch,* a literateur and a hard drinker. Hampden married a Miss Massie and was the father of two children, Mrs. Douglas Gordon, of Fredericksburg, and James Pleasants, of the Richmond bar. Mrs. Gordon was the mother of Hon. Basil B. Gordon of Rappahannock.

Hampden Pleasants was killed about 1846 in a duel with Thomas Ritchie, Jr., at Mayo's Bridge or Belle Isle.[105]

---

[104]Since this was written, a portrait of Governor James Pleasants has been located. It is by Chester Harding and is now in possession of Governor Pleasants's great-grand-daughter, Mrs. J. Q. Lovell, of Baltimore, Md., sister of the late Hon. Basil Gordon.

[105]The statement as to the exact spot on which the duel occurred seems to be left by Mr. Watson open to inquiry. I have learned through a daughter of Mr. Thomas Vaden, Mrs. C. C. McRae, who lived near, that her father had stated the exact spot was at a point several blocks west of Mayo's Bridge, under a large elm tree which stood close to the bank of the old canal, and near what was known as the "Round House" of the Southern (then Danville) Railroad, a building used during the Civil War as a hospital for Confederate soldiers.—Mrs. Walter A. Watson.

Richmond Enquirer, October 5, 1814, records death of Samuel Pleasants, editor of the *Virginia Argus*. He was public printer of Virginia at the time.

PRIDE.

John Pride served in the Virginia Convention of 1788 and the Virginia Legislature and was speaker of the Virginia Senate in 1789.[106]

Thomas Pride, a fox hunter, now lives in Amelia, some four miles of the Court House.

There was an old Colonial church called "Pride's Church" near what is now called New London in Amelia County. Dr. Pryor preached there in his early ministry.

PRYOR.

On the paternal side the Pryors (see "Pryor, a Biographical Sketch" by Thomas Supplee)[107] were of ancient lineage even in England. They originally came to Britain from Normandy with the Conqueror in 1066. The first of the name in Virginia was John Pryor, who settled in Hanover County. He was contemporary with William B. Giles and Patrick Henry and a friend of both. He never held public position, but was an extensive farmer and gave his name to a celebrated brand of Virginia tobacco, the "Blue and Medley Pryor," as well as to a fine apple. He and Governor Giles left Hanover and settled in Amelia County (now Nottoway), Giles at the "Wigwam" and Pryor on Seller's Creek.

Richard Pryor was a son of John Pryor. He married Nancy Bland and settled in Dinwiddie County, where he bought some three thousand acres of land and where he died, when his oldest son, Theodorick Pryor, was about ten or fifteen years of age.

Dr. Theodorick Pryor's ancestors were of distinguished connection in the Colonial history of Virginia. No household of the Colony combined greater social and intellectual excellence than the Blands of Prince George County. Dr. Theodorick Pryor's maternal great-grandfather was Reverend Theodorick Bland of the established church. His maternal grandfather, Reverend William Bland (also Episcopalian) married Elizabeth Yates, the daughter of the president of William and Mary College. Of this marriage was Nancy Bland, Dr. Pryor's mother, a near relation of John Randolph's mother.

Dr. Theodorick Pryor was born on the old Pryor place at Annsville, near San Marino, Dinwiddie County, Va., January 9, 1805. His early education was prosecuted at an academy in Dinwiddie County and at Lawrenceville in Brunswick County. He

---

[106]Also the sessions 1790-1793.

[107]Suplee, Thomas D., "The Life of Theodorick Bland Pryor." The subject of this biography was the grandson of Dr. Theodorick Pryor.

entered Hampden-Sidney College in June, 1823, and graduated in September, 1826, with the highest distinction. He was a member· of the Union Society. There were at college with him William Daniel, Thomas Tabb Giles, James C. Bruce and William Ballard Preston. Giles and Bruce were "Phips." Giles was regarded as a young man of great promise; Bruce not noteworthy at that time. He left college before graduation and went to Harvard and then to the University of Virginia. After graduating at Hampden Sidney, Dr. Pryor studied law one year at the University of Virginia, where he became the friend of R. M. T. Hunter and Lewis E. Harvie. He, together with most of the Hampden Sidney men, joined the Patrick Henry Society, now defunct. James C. Bruce, Hunter and the Prestons were members also. Dr. Pryor had a contest for public orator with Bruce on Henry's birthday while at the University. Hunter was his friend and champion and Bruce was badly beaten. In carrying this election, Hunter scored his first victory as a political manager. Hunter told Roger Pryor, the son of Dr. Theodorick Pryor, years afterwards in Congress that that was one of the most exciting political contests in which he had ever engaged.

Hunter's means at the University were competent, though not liberal. He was a diligent, hard working student and a man of unconquerable energy.

After leaving the University Dr. Pryor married Lucy Atkinson, daughter of Roger Atkinson, of "Olive Hill," Chesterfield County, and spent two years in the practice of law. Of his marriage with Lucy Atkinson two children survive, Roger A. Pryor and Mrs. Robert D. (Lucy) McIlwaine, of Petersburg, Va. His brother, Sam Pryor, married, I think, Mrs. William F. Brodnax, of Dinwiddie County.

The Atkinsons were an old and aristocratic English family which has given many names to the ministry, both Presbyterian and Episcopal, in Virginia and North Carolina. (See Slaughter's "History of Bristol Parish").[108]

His wife having died, Dr. Pryor entered Union Theological Seminary at Hampden Sidney, Va., January 9, 1831, as a student of theology under Dr. John Holt Rice. Owing to the illness of Dr. Rice, the president of the institution, he left in July and went to Princeton Seminary, but returned to Union Seminary in the fall of 1831 to continue the study of theology under Dr. Baxter, who had succeeded to the chair. He was licensed by East Hanover Presbytery in April 1832 at Portsmouth. He came to Nottoway as a licentiate and filled Dr. White's pulpit until the fall. In September of this year he was called to the charge and was ordained and installed by East Hanover Presbytery at Shiloh Church, in Nottoway, and was married to his

---

[108]Slaughter, Philip, "A History of Bristol Parish."

second wife, Miss Frances Epes, December 2, 1832. Drs. Plummer and White assisted in the ceremony, I think.[109] In 1853 he accepted a call to the Third Presbyterian Church of Baltimore, Md., where he remained only one year and returned in 1854 to the Second Presbyterian Church in Petersburg, Va., and did effective work there both in influencing the building of the church and in enlarging the congregation. He continued in that charge until 1863, when, at the request of East Hanover Presbytery, he became a chaplain in Army of Northern Virginia, Longstreet's Corps. (*Vide*, "Christ in Camp," by J. William Jones).

After the war he ministered for nearly two years at a small church in Brunswick County, and in 1867 he accepted a call from his first and tenderly loved people in Nottoway County. He has frequently been called to larger and in some respects more desirable fields—such as the College Church at Hampden-Sidney, Tinkling Springs in Augusta County, Charlotte Courthouse, Hopkinsville, Ky. and Galveston, Texas. He has for more than half a century proclaimed with unfaltering fidelity the Calvanism of the Cross, and with Dr Payson may say: "I sometimes weary in, but never *of,* the service of the Lord." Whether as priest of his people in Nottoway, in Baltimore, in Petersburg or in Brunswick, or as father or neighbor, to those around him he was always the same devout Christian man, whose character was beyond reproach and above suspicion. I have heard him say, "In early life I sometimes preached doctrinal sermons, but in late years I try to preach plain gospel." I have also heard him say, "I always tell my wife and friends that I cannot keep a secret, and if they don't want anything told not to tell it to me."

Dr. Pryor is[110] a man of sturdy common sense, strong mind and rugged eloquence; single and honest in his processes of thought; a man who possesses the cordial respect of the people of all sections. Of him Colonel William C. Jeffress says: "Dr. Pryor fulfills my idea of a model pastor. He is blessed with an uncommon share of good, practical sense not usually possessed by men devoted to theology and sermonizing. He is not too sanctified to take a just and proper interest in public affairs. He is

---

[109] A letter of Hon. Lewis S. Epes, December 14, 1923, states: "Dr. Theodorick Pryor was married three times. His first wife was Miss Lucy Atkinson. She was the mother of Roger A. Pryor. His second wife was Frances Epes, sister of my grandfather, Thomas Freeman Epes. His third wife was Frances Fitzgerald, of "The Castle." There were three children of the second marriage,—Frances, who married Thomas Campbell, of "The Oaks"; Nannie, who married George Jones; and Campbell, who died a few days ago in Washington."

[110] Evidently written before 1890, when Dr. Pryor died. According to A. J. Morrison's "College of Hampden-Sidney, Dictionary of Biography," p. 275, Dr. Pryor was buried under the pulpit of the Brick Church, of Nottoway Court House.

punctual to inform himself on questions agitating the public mind."

Dr. Pryor heard the joint debate between General Dromgoole and George E. Bolling, of Petersburg, in the forties at Nottoway Courthouse. Dromgoole had been much the worse for drink, when Major Anderson rallied him by asking him about John Tyler. He replied: "John Tyler deceived the Whig Party, the Whig Party deceived John Tyler and both deceived the country." In personal conversation Dr. Pryor related to me the Dromgoole-Duger duel.

Dr. Pryor quotes William S. Archer as saying that Dromgoole was the ablest man in the Democratic party. Dr. Pryor also related to me Jefferson's opinion of Dr. John Holt Rice. Some distinguished lawyer of South Carolina, son-in-law of Dr. Priestly, of England, and editor of his works, had applied for Judge Lomax's place at the University of Virginia, and Dr. Rice, the then editor of the *Virginia Evangelical Magazine*,[111] attacked his name in a production of such great force that Mr. Jefferson said that had the author of the article turned his attention to politics he would have been President of the United States.

While a student at Lawrenceville, Dr. Pryor heard the maiden speech of John Y. Mason before a jury at Brunswick Courthouse. He describes him as a spare, handsome young man, elegantly dressed. He never heard him speak afterwards.

Roger A. Pryor visited Mason in Paris en route to Athens, where he created great amusement with a toy mouse. Dr. Pryor attended the convention of 1829 and heard Governor Giles's reply to General Taylor.

Dr. Pryor had a kinsman, Captain Pryor, at Hampton who distinguished himself in the War of 1812. General Pryor, the collector of the port of Norfolk, long ago, was also a kinsman; as was Luke Pryor of Alabama, United States Senator.

Dr. Pryor said that the disposition of his son, Roger A. Pryor, to engage in dueling had given him great trouble. His first duel was with Charles Irving. No shots were exchanged. He met Robert Ridgway at Blair's Mill near Washington; General Rusk of Arkansas, his second; fired in the ground intentionally; second shot averted by the arrival of Preston S. Brooks. Roger Pryor met a son of John Minor Botts also, whom he declined to shoot at because of his infirmity.

Dr. Pryor gave me an account of his visit to Governor Wise when Roger went off to fight Ridgway. Roger also challenged Colonel Thomas F. Goode at Boydton; and President W. A. Smith of Randolph-Macon College gave Dr. Pryor an account of it.

Dr. Pryor said he called upon President Jefferson Davis once or twice when Roger Pryor got into difficulties with the Confed-

---

[111]*The Virginia Evangelical & Literary Magazine.*

erate government. President Davis opposed the disbanding of Roger Pryor's brigade and sent a note, written in the presence of Dr. Pryor, to Secretary Seddon saying: "Please assign General Pryor a brigade as soon as practicable; he is entitled to it." President Davis finally yielded to Secretary Mallory's importunities and Roger Pryor always thought that the President had mistreated him, but Dr. Pryor thought he did not.[112]   Dr. Pryor also called upon President Davis after the Gettysburg campaign, by invitation, as Mr. Davis wanted to learn some of his views as to that battle.

Roger A. Pryor was a man of striking and graceful presence, of most fascinating manner and irresistibly charming speech. He was orator, editor, soldier, politician, leader of popular assemblages, tribune of the people. The death of William O. Goode, of Mecklenburg, the representative of the district, occasioned a new Congressional election in the fourth Virginia district in November, 1859. The candidates were Roger A. Pryor and Thomas F. Goode. Pryor was nominated by the convention of the Democratic party, which met at Farmville, September 21, 1859. Lewis E. Harvie was chosen chairman. The convention contained 225 delegates and Pryor was nominated by acclamation. Colonel Hopkins, of Powhatan, was proposed, but his name was withdrawn. Pryor made a speech. Of Roger Pryor and of that campaign William Pope Dabney in a letter dated December 22, 1892, states: "Roger A. Pryor and myself graduated in the same class of Hampden-Sidney. I know every step in his life. His appearance as candidate for Congress from this district against Thomas F. Goode, of Mecklenburg, Hopkins, of Powhatan, Tom Campbell, of Nottoway, and Lewis E. Harvie, was magnificent. With long hair, classic face, dressed in the finest style; with gestures which he practiced as a boy before a glass; with the fire of genius in his eye and his clear, well-tuned and penetrating voice; and with a speech carefully prepared and, it is said, committed to memory and the same nearly all over the district, he came from the editorial chair in Washington, entered the lists and beat all the old political leaders. He certainly produced the greatest effect before the people ever produced here by any man except Randolph."

Roger Pryor told Colonel William C. Jeffress after the great Breckinridge speech at Nottoway Courthouse in 1860 that he always aimed to go steadily up in his speeches to the climax at the end. To a crowd that came to pay him tribute in Charleston, S. C., he said that only one thing was necessary to force Virginia out of the Union, "a blow struck"; that done and he promised that "Virginia would go out in one hour by Shrewsbury clock." He spoke in the African Church, that old temple

---

[112]*i. e.*, Dr. Pryor thought that President Davis had done all that he reasonably could for Roger A. Pryor.

of politics ("Old Sweat House") Richmond, on the night of March 18, 1861, building crowded to its utmost capacity; about 300 citizens from Petersburg came, headed by a band. Mr. Pryor thanked God that the Union was destroyed; that the Southern States had gone never to come back. He urged Virginia to do her part and said if she stood firm against the Union there would be no war. He called Mr. Lincoln "a feculent excresence of Northwestern vulgarity" (speech quoted in *Richmond Examiner* of March 19). He spoke at Amelia Courthouse March 28, 1861.

Pryor, Richard, shown justice of Dinwiddie in 1800.—Nottoway Deed Book 2, p. 185.

RANDOLPH.

The following is taken from a letter written at Powhatan Courthouse, July 18, 1889, by William Pope Dabney:

"The Randolph family in this county was a very extensive one and owned large bodies of land in the southern part of the county. Colonel William Randolph, a vestryman of Peterville Church, St. James Parish, resided near this place about 150 years ago, where Dr. John B. Harvie lived and died. His daughter married John Taylor, of "Horn Quarter," King William County, father of Mrs. Carter Lee, Mrs. Decatur Whittle, and Mrs. John Gilliam, who lived in this county. If sons, they lived in Caroline.

"There were other Randolphs—Dr. Jack Randolph, known as "Possum Jack," an eccentric man who horse-whipped John Randolph of Roanoke at Genito in this county on account of his telling Gouverneur Morris of the early indiscretions of his wife, Nancy Randolph, with his brother, Richard Randolph, at "Bizarre" in Cumberland. They were all related, but how I do not know.

"John Randolph's only love was Maria Ward, who declined to cherish the platonic attachment to him he desired, and she married Peyton Randolph, author of the Reports,[113] whose only descendant is Mrs. John Williams of Richmond, daughter of Dr. J. G. Skelton.

"I have examined the Page book[114] and find that Peter Randolph, born at "Turkey Island," was son of William Randolph, known as "Counsellor Randolph," by his wife Elizabeth, daughter of Peter Beverley, William Randolph being the son of William Randolph of "Turkey Island," the progenitor from Yorkshire, England, and his wife, Mary Isham of Bermuda Hundred. Peter Randolph was born in 1708, removed to "Chatsworth" in Henrico just below Richmond and married about 1733 Lucy, daughter of William Bolling.

---

[113]"Reports of the Court of Appeals of Virginia."
[114]Page, Richard Channing Moore, "Genealogy of the Page Family in Virginia."

"I see no other Peter mentioned, but a better genealogy of the Randolphs is found in Rev. Philip Slaughter's "History of Bristol Parish, Dinwiddie Co.," to which I refer you. From the traditions of the past, the Randolphs of this county (with the exception of Colonel William) were not remarkable for talent or sobriety.

"It is a very numerous family with ramifications. There is a family of the name in Goochland County.

"Brett Randolph, of "Capua," one of the executors of Richard Randolph's will, was born in England and came over to this country and married a Miss Randolph by whom he obtained "Capua." I have heard of the name of Peter Randolph, but I do not know that he ever lived in this county. Probably the most extended sketch of the family you will find in the Page genealogy, published by Dr. R. Channing Page of New York."[115]

The same writer says in a later letter, Dec. 22, 1892:

"My grandfather, at whose house John Randolph stayed the night after our court when he made a speech to our people, told me that was his first appearance before the people and that he was wholly unknown in the county and district. I have the account of his appearance, how his speech was received, etc., as described by my grandfather in a most vivid manner."

The will of John Randolph is recorded in Chesterfield County and he refers to himself as of Cumberland County. Probably he was at "Bizarre" at the time of the writing, as he stated he was about to set out by water for Norfolk. "Bizarre" was in Cumberland County about one mile above Farmville on the Appomattox River; now owned by one Jackson.[116]

Judge Randolph delivered a charge to the Grand Jury of the Amelia Circuit Court in 1814 which was of such ability as to merit publication in the *Richmond Enquirer* of July 20, 1814.

ROBERTSON.

George E. Robertson, of Chester, says (September 28, 1905): The first Robertson in Virginia was Reverend George Robertson, rector at Blandford, and that among his sons were George, of Chesterfield, who lived and died on Swift Creek, near Petersburg, on the old stage road (known as Jordan's Road and later as the Boydton Plank Road) where the Swift Creek Mills now stand. The house was of brick and now remains in part. He is buried there, grave unmarked. George E. Robertson has a commission for this George Robertson of Chesterfield signed by Patrick Henry, Governor, in 1778, appointing him lieutenant colonel of militia for Chesterfield County; also another com-

---

[115]Page, Richard Channing Moore, "Genealogy of the Page Family in Virginia."

[116]This note appears in Judge Watson's handwriting on a page of his copy of Garland's, "The Life of John Randolph of Roanoke."

mission dated 1780 from Governor Edmund Randolph appointing him to office in the militia.

The will of this George Robertson is recorded in Chesterfield, dated 1795 (Book 5, I think) and names his sons, James, Archer and George, and daughter Anne. James Married Martha Field Archer, of Chesterfield, ("Archer's Hall," James River) and lived at "Goose Island," Amelia County. He was grandfather of George E., John C., etc., of Chesterfield County. Archer was my own great-grandfather (Walter A. Watson). Reverend George Robertson conveyed to his son George 2100 acres of land in Amelia County. Of this family were Colonel James Robertson, Sr., of Amelia, who died August 19, 1828, aged 77; James Robertson, Jr., of Amelia, State senator, 1816-22, who removed to Louisville, Ky.; John Robertson, Sr., of Amelia, who died 1826, aged 71; Dr. William H. Robertson, of Amelia, and General Beverley H. Robertson, C. S. A. (See Deed Books, Henrico County, Va., 1735).

Archer Robertson, of Chesterfield, married Fanny Fowlkes, of Nottoway County, and the children of this marriage were Joseph Samuel, James Craddock and Fanny Bet.

Joseph Samuel Robertson married Mary Ann Robertson in Nottoway County, Dec. 23 (or 31) 1841, ceremony performed by Rev. Nelsen Head of the M. E. Church. Children: Henrietta H. Robertson, born Aug. 14, 1843, married Rev. James S. Crostick, (M. E. Church), Nov. 2, 1859, died June 22, 1862; James A. Robertson, born Aug. 27, 1845, killed at Williamsburg, May 5, 1862; Josephine Leonora Robertson, born Aug. 10, 1847, married Meredith Watson at Powhatan Court House, Va., Sept. 5, 1866, died at "Woodland," Nottoway Co., Dec. 2, 1913, of pneumonia. Joseph S. Robertson died at "The Vineyard," Nottoway Co., Jan. 16, 1847, from injuries inflicted by a slave. Mary Ann Robertson married, 2d, George D. Horner, Jan. 31, 1849. The latter was born Dec. 24, 1827. Children: Marion L. W. Horner, born Feb. 22, 1850; Henry T. Horner, born Aug. 17, 1853.

James Craddock married ——— Downs; Fanny Bet, married ——— Sanderson.

Eliza Fowlkes, sister of Fanny Fowlkes, married Captain Henry I. Robertson, of Nottoway; their children were: Joseph, Mary Ann, Patrick Henry, Caswell F., Rebekah, Laura and Helen. Joseph married ——— Ingram and ——— Newman (no descendants living) ; Mary Ann married Joseph S. Robertson; Patrick Henry married Virginia Dyson; Caswell F. married ——— Vaughan, ——— Quesenbury, ——— Tucker, ——— Shearer; Rebekah married James Nicholas; Laura married Captain L. Justis; Helen married ——— Enochs, of Tennessee.

Captain Henry Robertson was a brother of Archer ("Lame" Archer) Robertson of "Eleven Oaks," who was, I think, high sheriff of Nottoway about 1825. I think "Lame" Archer was kin to the Archers of Amelia. His son, Mallory W. Robertson, was sheriff of Nottoway in the fities. One of his daughters married Major H. R. Anderson, of Nottoway, who was the father of W. Henry Anderson, of Nottoway, and Honorable Clifford Anderson, of Georgia; also of Mrs. Lanier, who was mother to Sidney Lanier, the poet.

Major Anderson was born in the neighborhood of Harry Dyson's present residence. He lived at Dr. Royall's once and died while there. (These notes I had from my great-grandmother Robertson, Eliza Robertson, *née* Fowlkes). Patrick Henry Robertson and Caswell Fowlkes Robertson, brothers, and sons of Captain Henry I. Robertson, of Nottoway County, removed to Dyer County, Tennessee, about 1865 in the vicinity of Dyersburg. James Robertson, born in Brunswick County, June 28, 1742, moved to Wake County, North Carolina, with his father about 1750; was one of the "Regulators" of 1771; Captain at battle of Point Pleasant, Va., 1774; settled at Nashville, Tenn.; made Brigadier General by Washington, 1792; died at Chickasaw Bluff (Memphis) September 1, 1814. (These facts are given by Granville Goodloe, of Arkadelphia, Ark., in *William and Mary College Quarterly*, July 1894. Vol. 3).

Court Records of Lunenburg County, Va., show marriage bond December 25, 1772, William De Graffenreidt and Elizabeth Robertson. Letter of consent from Thomas Robertson; witness, Tscharner de Graffenreidt. David Robertson, attorney for the Commonwealth about 1809 (clerk's books will show). He was perhaps a son of an old Scotch lawyer who lived where Archer Bevill now resides. (Data from Mr. Freeman Epes).

John Archer Robertson, who married a sister of John D. Royall, was the connecting link between Dr. William Robertson's family and old Archer ("Deaf" Archer) Robertson. They were both related to this John Archer Robertson.

There was an Archer Robertson who was a defaulter in Petersburg years back, but who he was I don't know.

Journal, House of Delegates, December 22, 1813: Petition of Elizabeth Robertson, of Nottoway County, praying a divorce from John A. Robertson, her husband; or at least that a law may pass empowering her to hold property which she may hereafter acquire independent of him.

John A. Robertson, petition against the terms of the divorce of his wife Elizabeth Robertson to the Virginia legislature.— *Richmond Enquirer*, December 19, 1818.

ROYALL.

Old Littleberry Royall, a very wealthy old planter who lived at "Heathcourt," was thrice married; the first two wives were both named Betsy Jones, but no children survived. In late life he married a poor and uncultivated girl named Jane Thornton, by whom he had three children, Edward, John Epes, and Joseph.[117]

They went to the school in Dr. Dupuy's woods taught by old Converse[118] the father of the editor of the *Christian Observer*.[119] Old Converse pulled John Epes's ears so that he injured the child, and Mr. Royall withdrew him from school. He died young.

Edward Royall was an extraordinarily handsome man and spent his fortune travelling and frolicking in England and on the Continent. He was presented to Queen Victoria, who complimented his personal appearance. He returned to Virginia with no fortune save his wardrobe. Went to live at "Mountain Hall" with Dr. Jones awhile and studied some law; then went to Petersburg and attempted to practice, but was not successful and (I think) killed himself.

He and Joe were both students of Hampden-Sidney, I think (and Edward a member of Philanthropic Society). Joe was a great athlete, but extremely eccentric. He went to live in Dinwiddie on a farm.

Mrs. Littleberry Royall afterwards married a Mr. Oliver from below Petersburg, who proved to be a polished adventurer and unprincipled brute. He was in debt, and Mrs. Royall's forty-odd negroes, which included her dower, went to his creditors.

Littleberry Royall had a brother, John Royall, who lived near Blacks and White (now Blackstone), who was the father of John D. Royall, sometime a legislator of Nottoway.[120] His daughter (J. D. Royall's sister) married John Archer Robertson, from whom she afterwards obtained a divorce.

The maternal grandmother (Marianne Pleasants) of the esteemed tutor in our family in my youth, Thomas E. Royall, was a sister of Hampden Pleasants; his mother was a Smith; his paternal grandmother was a Hobson of Powhatan County; his grandfather was William Royall, of Charles City, who was a friend of John Tyler and lived near "Sherwood Forest."[121]

---

[117]cf. his will, p.

[118]Amasa Converse.

[119]Rev. Francis Bartlett Converse. He was associated with his father, Amasa Converse, as editor of the *Christian Observer* until the death of the latter in 1872. For account of the vicissitudes of fortune of these men and their journal see the *Christian Observer*, vol. 101, p. 870, Sep. 3, 1913; "Encyclopaedia of the Presbyterian Church in the United States of America." Philadelphia, 1884.

[120]Virginia House of Delegates, 1812-1814.

[121]In a letter, dated March 1925, the Thomas E. Royall mentioned above has furnished the following information: "My maternal grandmother, Marianne Pleasants, sister of John Hampden Pleasants, married Granville Smith, of Goochland. They were the parents of Adelaide Preston Smith, my mother, who married Dr. Samuel Hobson Royall, of Chesterfield Co., Va. My grandfather, William Royall, was a native of Charles City Co., Va. He married Susan Hobson, of Powhatan. After his marriage, he removed to Powhatan Co., Va."

SMITH.
William Smith, a son of Kennon and grandson of old Burwell Smith, read law under Mr. Bouldin[122] as at the same time did William C. Knight.
Old Burwell Smith was a particularly parsimonious and illiterate man, but he accumulated much property.

TABB.
The original ancestor came here and established a country trading post and by close transaction, without antecedent influence, accumulated the great possessions so well known. Two other men in Virginia did the same thing, W. H. McFarland's father in Lunenburg and James C. Bruce's father in Halifax or Charlotte, all men who commenced life in poverty.
Governor Giles married a Tabb, his first wife and mother of Thomas Tabb Giles.
"Mill Quarter," a noted estate of about 6000 acres, on the line of Dinwiddie and Amelia, now owned by Mr. Mason, an Englishman, and which once held a mill pond covering 1,100 acres, was a part of the Tabb estate.

TAYLOR.
The head of this family in 1890 is Dr. Richard Field Taylor (M. D.) of Amelia County, Va. His homestead was "Farm Hill" on Deep Creek, which was burned some seventeen years since, and he now resides upon an adjoining estate. His father was Richard F. Taylor, of Dinwiddie (or Prince George), and his grandfather Richard F. Taylor also. The Harrisons and Byrds of "Brandon" and "Westover" are his near relations. His father had an only brother, the celebrated George Keith Taylor, of Prince George County, near Petersburg, who married a sister of Chief Justice John Marshall and whose only descendant, so far as I know, was the mother of the present William L. Royall, Esq., of Richmond. His grandmother was a daughter of Bishop Keith and hence the introduction of this name. George Keith Taylor was said by some to have been the most eloquent man in Virginia after Patrick Henry.
Dr. Taylor married Miss Rosalie Martha Green, daughter of Colonel Armstead Green, of "Farm Hill," Amelia County. His mother's residence was at "Spring Garden" on the suburbs of Petersburg and burned in 1865 with all the library of George Keith Taylor. At "Farm Hill" all his own and father's library was burned.
Miss Eveline H. Taylor, the authoress, was a sister of his and an invalid during her life. She died young (1808-43). Her unpublished manuscripts are still in Dr. Taylor's possession;

---

[122]From its position in Mr. Watson's notes, this reference appears to be to Louis C. Bouldin.

also birds in water colors from Wilson's ornithology and from nature. She was a friend of Miss Epes Ward, afterwards Mrs. Dr. Robert E. Shore, of Nottoway.

Dr. Taylor attended Harrison's Academy at the "Wigwam" in 1826 and went to Winchester to read medicine under Dr. William Holliday (father of Frederick W. M. Holliday) about 1829. Subsequently studied medicine in Philadelphia in the thirties. Was a member of the State Legislature from '62 to '65. Beat Lewis E. Harvie once or twice. Especially influential in making Allen T. Caperton Confederate Senator over Rives and others. Taken prisoner with Judge William W. Crump at Williamsburg in 1862. Important information imparted by them and a chaplain named McVeigh to Governor Smith,[123] with bearing upon Jackson's flank movement, prevented Burnside's march from Roanoke Island upon lines south of the James, etc.

On the retreat, spent the night at Dr. Phil Southall's house ("Woodstock," Amelia County) with General Mahone; could get nothing out of Mahone except abuse of the Confederate authorities and that in the presence of subordinates.

Governor Holliday's mother was a Taylor.

Colonel Thomas Taylor was born in Amelia County, September 10, 1743. He was the son of John Taylor, civil engineer and surveyor, who moved to South Carolina in 1754 and settled near what is now the city of Columbia, where he died. Colonel Thomas Taylor married Anne Wyche, daughter of Peter and Alice (Scott) Wyche, of Brunswick County, Va., January 2, 1767. She was the sister of Drury Wyche. Colonel Thomas Taylor was elected to the Provincial Congress of South Carolina in 1775, was a member of the South Carolina Convention of 1788 and was opposed to the Federal Constitution. He was an officer in the American Revolution under General Sumter. He was colonel of militia and commanded the troops which invested Granby and gained this victory. He died November 1833. His wife survived him after 67 years of married life.[124]

(This information was given me by George W. Taylor, of Demopolis, Ala., member of Congress from that state, from the papers of the South Carolina Historical Society: "History of John Taylor and his Descendants," by B. F. Taylor, of Columbia, S. C. Also data taken from Columbia, S. C., *Telescope*, November and December, 1833, in Library of Congress).

Gen. Robert B. Taylor, of Norfolk Borough. The recognized rival at the bar of Leigh, Johnson, and Stanard. He was remarkable for his graceful manner, the fineness of person and

---

[123]John Letcher was Governor in 1862; William Smith was a colonel in the Confederate army; was Governor, 1846-49; 1864-65.

[124]A distinguished family; his son, John Taylor, was Governor of South Carolina; related to the families of President James Madison and President Zachary Taylor.

finished style of his public speeches. He was a supporter of the old Federal Party and with them much opposed to the War of 1812, but when war began enlisted in his country's service and commanded the troops at Norfolk. Ran against Wilson Cary Nicholas of Albemarle and Gen'l. [John P.] Hungerford in the legislature for Governor in 1814. Nicholas was elected, Taylor getting a large minority. In the Convention of 1829-30, he represented his district but soon resigned in consequence of instructions from his constituents he could not conscientiously discharge. Was the advocate of what was called the "white basis" in the Convention.

Thweatt.

A daughter of Thomas Thweatt, of Dinwiddie County, married Francis Jones, of Brunswick County.

Thomas Thweatt had a brother, Dick Thweatt, who lived at "Eppington" in Chesterfield County. He (Dick Thweatt) kept a female school which Mrs. Chambliss attended. One of his daughters, Mary Epes Thweatt, was Reverend Mrs. Berkeley[125] of Amelia County; another married Reverend Augustus B. Tizzard; another married Dr. Richard Haskins and was the mother of Meade Haskins.

Vaughan.

Joseph N. Vaughan was a son of James Vaughan, who lived at Jenkins. His mother, who afterwards married a Jenkins, was a Craddock, I think.

"Old Truly" Vaughan was Joseph Vaughan's uncle.

Verser.

Daniel Verser, a soldier of the Revolution, lived at Patrick Allen's place, and was much respected in the community. On jury which tried Dr. Bacon, 1818. He married twice, once a Winfree and once a Dyson (sister of Tom Dyson). William Verser (Colonel "Buck") was a son by the Winfree wife, I think. Francis and Daniel were other sons. A daughter by the Dyson marriage married Jesse Vaughan and was the mother of T. H. Vaughan.

Colonel "Buck" Verser was once attorney for the commonwealth in Nottoway. He married twice: a Thweatt of Prince Edward and a Winfree. John Verser and Nathan Verser were his sons. Colonel Verser was probably a soldier of 1812. He had no legal ability, and taught school in his latter years. (This information comes from Clerk Dick Epes.)

---

[125]Parke Henry Farley Berkeley, who was rector of Grub Hill Church, Amelia County.

WARD.

Notes taken from letters written by Mr. John H. Ward, of Louisville, Ky., July 20, and 29, 1893:

"The tradition in our family is that there were three brothers in the army of Cromwell when he occupied Ireland and that they after their term of service ended went into business in Dublin, were not successful and emigrated to America and settled first in Virginia. Afterward some of them went to North Carolina, and the Wards in the State of New York are probably of the same family. The horse racing and horse loving trait in Colonel Benjamin Ward makes me feel a kinship, and I believe there is one. My father was General W. T. Ward.

"My grandfather, William Ward, came from Amelia County, Va., to Green County, Ky., about 1812. His father died in Amelia County, Va., about that time, leaving in his will certain property to my father, William T. Ward, and his brothers John and Edward."

The following was mostly related to me by Miss Lizzie Ward in 1899:

Colonel Benjamin Ward of Revolutionary times, who lived at "West Creek" in Nottoway (then Amelia), married a Miss Katherine Cralle, or Crawley (the "Queen"). He was supposed to have been killed by his horse, returning from his mill one night; by some thought to have been murdered. She continued to reside at "West Creek" after his death and then married Daniel Jones, of "Mount Airy," who had addressed her before her first marriage, and who was himself a widower of family. Upon his death she married William Fitzgerald, another widower, who had also been a beau in her younger days. Thus she married all the beaux of her younger life in turn. Colonel Benjamin Ward is probably buried at "Old Homestead"; he had an unmarried brother, Henry (Hal) Ward, who, Miss Lizzie Ward thinks, owned the Burke place, "Old Homestead," which she thinks was perhaps the old settlement where her great-grandfather and the old Wards were buried. Hal Ward was buried there within her recollection. She says there was no white burial ground at "West Creek" and that there was one at "Old Homestead."

Benjamin Ward, son of Colonel Benjamin Ward, married Sarah Fitzgerald, daughter of William Fitzgerald, of "Leinster." He lived with his mother at "West Creek," where he was married,—the place being his after her dower. He continued there awhile, where his mother always reserved and kept the best room in the house, and then bought "Bellfield." He had the Alexander house and the overseer's house at "Ingleside," near "West Creek," built for his two sons, Davey and Tom, who died in early life.

Kate, daughter of Colonel Benjamin Ward, married Frank (Francis?) Fitzgerald, of "The Castle," and became the mother of Mrs. Pryor, Mary, and Robert Fitzgerald. Nancy, daughter of Colonel Benjamin Ward, went crazy.

Robert F. Ward married Louisa Shore, daughter of Dr. Robert Shore and grand-daughter of Francis Fitzgerald, of "The Castle." He (Robert F. Ward) went to "Ingleside" to live in 1870.

William Ward, of "West Creek," married once, Miss Lawson, daughter of Fabius Lawson, clerk of Amelia County, who lived at Dennisville. There was a son, Fabius, who held some state or city office in Richmond and another son, professor in Cincinnati Medical College, where George Edward Ward was educated.

In Nottoway Order Book, Nathan Ward is mentioned as jailer, April 1817.

Rowland (or Roland) Ward married Rebecca, daughter of Colonel Richard Jones, of Amelia County; died in 1800 in Amelia County. His widow Rebecca and children moved from Amelia County to Tennessee; she died in Davidson County, Tennessee, in 1805. Daughter, Martha, married Richard Jones in Amelia County, in November 1774.

Roland Ward, Jr., had a daughter, Prudence Ward.

WATKINS.

Reverend Abner Watkins was a Baptist clergyman of Lunenburg County who preached at old "Chestnut Hill" Church, which is now Dr. R. B. Tuggle's granary. His son, Dr. Austin Watkins, whom Dr. Jones pronounced an excellent physician, came to Nottoway County and married the widow of Patrick Jones, who lived at Dr. Bragg's place. He was a man of fine social qualities and popular manners; a member of the House of Delegates between 1818 and 1830.[126] The Bragg place reverted to the wife's first children upon her death and Dr. Watkins removed and married the widow of Peter Batte Jones.

The Watkinses of Dinwiddie supposed to be of Welsh origin. James Watkins came to Virginia in 1608.

WATSON.[127]

1. John Watson, the elder, lived in Prince Edward County near Hampden-Sidney College. Married —— Allen (probably). Children:
2. Joseph
3. Drury
4. Jesse
5. Josiah

2. Joseph Watson, of Prince Edward County, lived on

---

[126]Sessions, 1822-23, 1823-24, 1829-30.
[127]Owing to the fragmentary and unarranged character of the Watson family notes, it was found necessary to adapt them to some scheme of arrangement which would be clear.

Buffalo near George Bruce's. He married, first, Fanny Allen, by whom there were no children; second, a Miss Wade, his housekeeper. At his death he left his property to Joseph Watson, his nephew, and Simms Allen, his first wife's nephew.

3. Drury Watson, of Prince Edward County, had a daughter who married Drury Calhoun. Their son, Drury Calhoun, was a member of Briary Church. Drury Watson was a great fiddler and dancer. He lived to be nearly 100 years old, and lived about among his relatives, generally with Drury Calhoun near Briary.

4. Colonel Jesse Watson, of Prince Edward County, married Mary Meredith, of King and Queen County. He died in Lunenburg County and is buried at "the old place" (my grandfather's) in Lunenburg County. My grandmother, a granddaughter of of Colonel Jesse Watson, says his wife Mary (Meredith) Watson, with whom she lived in her early married life at "the old place" in Lunenburg, used to tell her that she and two of her sisters were brought to Prince Edward County in their childhood and lived with old Mrs. Smith near Hampden-Sidney. She married early, and one of her sisters married a Walker near Jamestown. She had a brother, Elisha Meredith, in Prince Edward County who married a Michaux, probably, and who was a merchant at the courthouse. Mary Meredith's father was Pleasant Meredith, of King and Queen County, where she was born and where he was supposed to have died. She died when about seventy-seven years old. She was pretty; had black hair and eyes. Her father was married four times; he used to say he had "shod his horse all around, now he wanted to get on and hold the bridle."

The following declaration was found with papers:

Know all men by these presents that we Jesse Watson and Francis Watkins are held and firmly bound, unto Beverly Randolph, Esq., Governor of the Commonwealth of Virginia, in the sum of 50 pounds.

The condition of the above obligation is such that whereas there is a marriage shortly intended to be solemnized between the above bound Jesse Watson and Polly Meredith, daughter of Pleasant Meredith, of Henrico County, if therefore there be lawful cause to obstruct the same, then this obligation to be void, else to remain of force and virtue—

                                    J. Watson,   Seal.
                                    Francis Watkins,
Dated 10th Dec. 1790.
Witness Richard Watkins.

I, Branch I. Worsham, Clerk of Co. Court of Prince Edward, do certify that the foregoing is a true copy of the files of my office. 7th March, 1839.

                         (Signed)   B. I. Worsham, Clk.

Among the papers making application for pension for the wife of Jesse Watson the following memoranda were found:

To Jesse Watson, Gentleman Greeting,
Know you that our Governor, on recommendation from the County Court of Prince Edward, hath constituted and appointed you 1st. Lieut. in a Company of Militia in the said County. In testimony, whereof, these our letters are sealed with the seal of the Commonwealth and made patent.
Witness, Thos. Jefferson, Esq., our said Gov. at Richmond, the 19th, June, 1780.
(Signed)   Thos. Jefferson.

He served in Captain Lorton's company.
A similar commission, appointing Jesse Watson, Capt. of Militia, in same County, signed Benjamin Harrison, 19th August, 1782.

Another appointing Jesse Watson, Lieut. Col. of the 63rd Reg., 11th. Brigade, 1st Div.
(Signed)   Jno. Page, said Governor, 16th March, 1803.

This application seems to have been made through W. J. B. Bedford, of Charlotte C. H., and only $120.00 per annum was allowed. There were several affidavits from his wife that he served at the battles of Camden and Guilford C. H. These affidavits substantiated by letters from this man Bedford and others, and one R. A. Watson. It seems to have been established to the satisfaction of the pension office that he served under one Captain Charles Allen in active service for a period of 3 or 4 months, and was discharged from the First Regiment of Virginia Militia, Dec. 5, 1780; in 1781 he served as a lieutenant under Captains Charles Allen and Peter Michaux: at the seige of Yorktown. The claim is based upon a nine months' service as lieutenant of Virginia militia. She was allowed pension on her application executed Feb. 22, 1839, while living in Lunenburg County, Va., aged 70 years.
He was married in 1790 and died October 22, 1812.

The above information was secured through inquiry at the Pension Office in Washington on March 23, 1906.

Children of Colonel Jesse Watson and Mary Meredith Watson:
   6.   Josiah Allen
   7.   Jesse
   8.   William Meredith

9. Elisha
10. Robert Alexander Allen
11. Hannah; married William Towler, of Charlotte County. Children: Watkins
                                        Saunders
12. Mary; married ——— Keeling, of Nottoway or Prince Edward County.

6. Josiah Allen Watson, of Prince Edward County, married Jane Bruce, of Lunenburg County. He served in the War of 1812 at Norfolk, Va. Children:

13. Alexander; Married ——— Fowlkes, of Lunenburg County.
14. Joseph William
15. Jacob; died in Galveston, Texas, of yellow fever.
16. Branch W.; married in Texas; a member of the Texas Senate.
17. Armistead C.; married Martin Fox.
18. Bruce. Killed in the Confederate Army.
19. Rosby (or Roshy) B.
20. Martha S.; married George Bruce, of Lunenburg County.
21. Joanna; married Tom Watson, of Texas.

7. Jesse Watson, of Lunenburg County, married Sally Thompson, of Lunenburg County. He served in the War of 1812 at Norfolk. Children:

22. Thomas
23. Joseph
24. Jack
25. Robert
26. Minerva

8. William Meredith Watson, of Charlotte County, married Jane Watkins, daughter of Tom Watkins, of Charlotte County. Children:

27. Louisa A.
28. Minnie
29. Sarah
30. Bettie
31. Polly.

9. Elisha Watson married, first, ——— Nott; second, ——— Crafton; third, ——— Cole. Children:

32. Jesse
33. John
34. Sallie.

10. Robert Alexander Allen Watson, of Lunenburg and Nottoway counties, was born near Meherrin, Va., July 31, 1807; died of pneumonia at "Woodland," Nottoway County, December 31, 1883. He married Mary Elizabeth Watson [no. 56], of Prince Edward County, October 5, 1836. They removed from Lunenburg County to Nottoway County in 1852.

    35. Francis (Frank) Marion, b. Mar. 1838, married Lou A. Watson.
    36. Meredith, b. Sep. 5, 1841; d. Aug. 22, 1893.
    37. Mary Guthry, b. Aug. 21, 1851; d. Oct. 4, 1852.

36. Meredith Watson, of Nottoway County, born Sep. 5, 1841; died at "Woodland," Aug. 22, 1893; married Josephine Leonora Robertson, of Powhatan County, Sep. 5, 1866. Married by Rev. S. A. Lambeth, of the M. E. Church, South. He was an elder in the Presbyterian Church. Volunteer, Company E, Third Virginia Cavalry, Confederate States Army, 1861-65. Children:

    38. Walter Allen, b. Nov. 25, 1867; d. Dec. 24, 1919.
    39. Meredith Leon, b. Jan. 1, 1869.
    40. Mary Campbell, b. Apr. 13, 1871; d. May 1, 1889.
    41. Josephine Nelson, b. Mar. 21, 1874; d. Sep. 1, 1889.
    42. Henry Hunter, b. Sep. 14, 1875.
    43. Robert Daniel, b. Mar. 27, 1877; d. July 22, 1877.
    44. Fannie Archer, b. May 16, 1878.
    45. Lois Willson, b. May 8, 1880.
    46. Helen Christian, b. July 21, 1881; d. June 10, 1889.
    47. Robert Archibald Alexander, b. June 1, 1883; d. Apr. 26, 1884.
    48. Rebekah Shore, b. Nov. 26, 1884.
    49. Calva Hamlett, b. Sep. 24, 1886.
    50. Theodorick Pryor, b. Jan. 10, 1888; d. Aug. 1, 1889.

5. Josiah Watson married Mary (Polly) Nelson, of Cumberland County. She discarded him once but he went back and sang a song he composed (supposedly) and she accepted him. At least the song captivated the mother, who was the main objector. He lived in Prince Edward County about a mile from "the old place" and in sight of the public road. He died in the 1820's and was buried at his place in Prince Edward County near Moore's Ordinary. His wife survived him a few years. Children:

    51. Nelson; born September 2, 1789; served in the War of 1812 at Norfolk, where he was killed.
    52. John Allen.
    53. Mary; married first, ———— Crawley Fowlkes, son of Billy Fowlkes. Lived at Hiram Fowlkes's place in Nottoway County; married, second, James Thackston,

uncle of Dr. W. W. H. Thackston, of Farmville; married, third, Captain Ben Cox.
54.   Rebekah, or Rebecca; married Sam Wilson. Their daughter, Mary Ann, married Ben Fuqua, of Cumberland County. The daughter of the latter married a Colonel Meriwether of Arkansas (probably) and left a daughter who was a nurse in St. Luke's Home some years ago.

52.   John Allen Watson, born September 2, 1789, died November 17, 1822. He was said to have been the handsomest of the Watsons. He was in the War of 1812; served at Norfolk, where he was taken ill of fever and was relieved by his brother, Nelson Watson. He was in the cavalry (Prince Edward, probably). He married Nancy Hamlett, born October 12, 1797, a Methodist, daughter of Jesse Hamlett, who lived near Briery in Prince Edward County, and who married Elizabeth Clark. Nancy Hamlett's grandmother, Elizabeth Clark, lived near Sandy River Church; was a niece to Berry [Littleberry (?)] Clark, father of Colonel Jeffress's first wife. She was a member of Briery Church, as was also her daughter, Elizabeth, who married Cary Anderson, an elder in Briery Church. John C. Hamlett, her son (Mary Elizabeth Watson's uncle) was a Campbellite. He was alive in my time; resided in Prince Edward County. Children:
55.   Louisa Nelson; born October 24, 1817.
56.   Mary Elizabeth, my grandmother; born at her father's home in Prince Edward County, September 21, 1819; married Robert Alexander Allen Watson [no. 10] in Lunenburg County, October 5, 1836. The ceremony was performed by the Rev. Matthew Dance, of the Methodist Episcopal Church. She died of old age at "Woodland," Nottoway County, March 14, 1906.
Grandma Watson attended Hampden-Sidney Commencement, May 4th, 1833, 34, or 5, when she was about 14 or 15 years of age; went with her uncle John Hamlett; Ben Watson's carriage horses ran away on the way; exercises held in the brick building and were of a dramatic character,—one man shot another on the stage; she wore a silk dress; great crowd in attendance; confections, refreshments sold on the grounds; a great frost that morning bit the leaves of the trees which were far developed and the forest was black.
On the way that morning along the Courthouse (Sheltersburg) Road they passed a crowd at or near Bell's Tavern, assembled where some graves were being dug and were informed that two negro traders (Kirbys, father and son) from the South on their return South with their drove had been murdered by the slaves the past night; the axe and club used by them were exhibited in the tavern porch. On the return that evening they were told the negroes had been captured, two of them on the

bridge at Farmville, and that seven had been hanged at Prince Edward Courthouse. My grandmother often attended Briery Church with her grandmother Hamlet (*née* Elizabeth Clark) in her childhood and said that great crowds gathered when Dr. Hoge was to preach, and that in those days, when the services closed, the old men of the congregation (like Dr. Lacy et als) would come around in the church to pay their respects and shake hands with the old ladies present, who commonly sat in the wing of the building. Her grandmother would, on such occasions, present her and her sisters as her granddaughters, "the Miss Watsons." Colonel Tom Spencer was the leading influence in the congregation at that time; the tradition is that no preacher was able to suit him and that he always had his way. Old Drury Calhoun, whose mother was a daughter of Drury Watson, was a member of Briery and shouted there once, the only person grandma ever heard of having done such a thing there. Grandma heard Dr. Plummer[128] preach at Briery when she was a child.

Littleberry, Ben and Sam Short Watson were kinsmen. Littleberry was the fox hunter in Mecklenburg. (I got this from my grandmother September 21, 1896).

Grandma visited once Ben Fuqua at Trent's Mill in Cumberland County, who married her first cousin. [See No. 54.]

57. Emily Ann; born October 1, 1821; married February 3, 1841, James S. Johnson, son of Benjamin Johnson and Elizabeth, his wife (born September 22, 1819). There appears to have been a daughter, Elizabeth, born 1842.[129]

Miscellaneous Watson Notes.

Watson, David. Certificate for 200 acres issued to his representatives for services as private in Continental Line for the war. Warrant No. 5790, issued to Obediah, Letitia and Jesse Watson, heirs and legal representatives of David Watson, deceased, and delivered to Littleton Upshur, Jr., (attorney in part) January 1810. Military Certificates, Book 2, p. 670.

William Watson allowed 400 acres for services as corporal State line for over three years and discharged by government orders.

LIST OF EMIGRANTS

Hotten's Emigrants[130] (State Library)

1634 Jo: Watson (Indexed John) in Mcht. ship Bonaventure from port of London to Virginia, age 28 years.

---

[128]William Swan Plummer.

[129]From a family Bible much torn and defaced at this place. In this Bible was found a letter from Martha F. Morgan, Hopkinsville, Ky., March 2, 1851, to Mrs. Mary E. Watson, "Marble Hill," Prince Edward County, Va., addressing the latter as "Dear Sister"; refers to John unmarried and Sam married; also to six months' old child, Robert Samuel.

[130]Hotten, John Camden, "The Original Lists of Persons of Quality . . ." London [etc.] Chatto and Windus, 1874.

1635   Jo: Watson (Index John) in the "Speedwell" from London to Virginia, age 22 years.
1635   Margaret Watson: age 18, from Port of London to Virginia.
1635   Alice Watson: age 30, from port of London to Virginia.

List of Living in Virginia (Hotten)

1623   Thomas and James Wattson "at Sherlow Hundred Island."
1623   John Wattson "at ye College Land."

Muster Roll (Hotten)

1624   John Watson at ye College Land, came in "William and Thomas" ship.
1624   John Watson, servant in Mr. Stockton's Muster; came in 1624 in the Swan, and age, 24 years.

Watson, James, 1814.

Captain James Watson's Company under Colonel Woodford's squadron in United States service, August 30th to October 23, 1814. Captain, James Watson; fourth lieutenant, Drury Watson; privates, John Watson, Nelson Watson, Littleberry Watson, Samuel Watson, John Watson, Branch J. Watson, Richard P. Watson.[131]

Virginia Militia Pay Rolls,[132] p. 264 (Va. State Lib.)

Prince Edward County Order Book, p. 94 (1793).

John Watson, sworn sheriff of county, with Jacob Woodson, Augustus Watson and others as sureties, 1000 pounds. John Wat-

---

[131]From the War Dept., Adjutant General's Office, Sep. 18, 1923:

The records show that one James Watson served in the War of 1812 as a Capt. of Capt. James Watson's troop of cavalry, 63d Regiment Virginia Militia, attached to squadron commanded by Major John Woodford, organization also designated Major Woodford's squadron cavalry, Virginia Militia. His services commenced Aug. 30, 1814, and the company muster roll, dated Norfolk, Feb. 22, 1815, shows that he was cashiered and dismissed the service Jany. 26, 1815.

The records also show service in the same organization as follows: Branch I. or J. Watson, private. His service commenced Aug. 31, 1814, and he was discharged Nov. 24, 1814, by furnishing a substitute.

Drury Watson, 4th Sergeant. His service commenced Aug. 30, 1814, and he was discharged Dec. 7, 1814, by furnishing a substitute.

John Watson, private. His service commenced Aug. 30, 1814, and he was discharged Nov. 6, 1814, by furnishing a substitute.

John Watson (son of Josiah) private. His service commenced Aug. 30, 1814, and ended Feby. 22, 1815.

Littleberry Watson, private. His service commenced Aug. 30, 1814, and he was discharged Nov. 6, 1814, by furnishing a substitute.

son, Jr., Lee Bird and Augustus Watson, deputies; p. 306 shows he was sheriff, 1795; p. 425 shows Thornton Watson was dead, 1796; John Watson, justice, 1796; p. 492 shows Jesse Watson sworn as major of 1st Bat., 63rd Regt., Augustus Watson, Lt.; Book H, p. 284, shows John Watson deputy sheriff for Clark, sheriff, 1791.[133]
John Watson, Justice 1778 [?].

The 1st Order Book is without index and I made no examination of it and only glanced at index of some of the others. I understand there is a book containing list of marriage licenses in office. I did not see this and could find no very old bonds— none prior to about 1780, I think.

Prince Edward County Deed Book 10, p. 165, shows John Watson justice in 1794.

The poll books at Powhatan show that William Watson was a voter in 1786 and 1796.

WATSON MARRIAGES.

Watson, William, 1767, Goochland County: Marriage bond recorded, of William Watson to Martha Pleasants.

Marriage bonds, 1786. George Watson and ——— Wilkerson.

Watson, Joseph A., 1817: Marriage of Joseph A. Watson to Jane C. Bruce by James Shelburne (or Shelbourne) April 3, 1817. Lunenburg County License Book, p. 313; also Lunenburg Will Book 2, p. 313.

Certificate to obtain a marriage license.

Having applied to the Clerk of the County Court of Powhatan County for a Marriage license and being requested, I make the following certificate as required by act of the Gen. Assembly passed April 7, 1858.

Nelson Watson, private. His service commenced Aug. 30, 1814 and ended Feby. 22, 1815.

Richard P. Watson, private. His service commenced Aug. 30, 1814, and he was discharged Dec. 17, 1814, by furnishing a substitute.

Samuel Watson, private. His service commenced Aug. 30, 1814 and ended Feby. 22, 1815.

These men were from Prince Edward County.

(Signed)   Robert C. Davis,

The Adjutant General.

[132]Virginia, Auditor's Office, "Payrolls of Militia Entitled to Land Bounty. Copied from Rolls in the Auditor's Office at Richmond," Richmond, Va. W. F. Ritchie, Printer, 1851.

[133]In seeking to identify these records the following additional information was secured from the clerk of Prince Edward County, Mr. Horace Adams: that the record book for the period 1771 to 1781 contains notes of the oaths taken before the court by Jesse Watson, ensign (1777), Jesse Watson, 1st lieutenant (1779), and Drury Watson, 2nd lieutenant (1779).

Date of Marriage: Sept. 5, 1866.
Place of Marriage: At Geo. D. Horner's in Powhatan Co.
Full name of parties married: Meredith Watson and Josephine L. Robertson.
Age of husband: 22 years.
Age of wife: 18 years.
Condition of husband: Single.
Condition of wife: Single.
Place of husband's birth: Lunenburg Co.
Place of wife's birth: Nottoway Co.
Place of husband's residence: Nottoway Co.
Place of wife's residence: Powhatan Co.
Names of husband's parents: Robert A. and Mary E. Watson.
Names of wife's parents: Joseph S. and Mary A. Robertson.
Occupation of husband: Farmer.

Given under my hand this 5th Sept. 1866.

M. Watson.

This is to authorize the Clerk of Powhatan Co., Va., to issue marriage license to Mr. Meredith Watson of Nottoway to marry Miss Josephine L. Robertson of Powhatan Co., Va.
Aug. 29th, 1866.

James C. Robertson,
Guard. for Jos. L. Robertson.

Witness, T. G. Leath.
Proved in due form before me by the witness.

R. F. Graves, C[lerk]
Sept. 5th, 1866.

Copy of Marriage certificate in Powhatan Clerk's Office made by me May 30, 1912.—Walter A. Watson.

Prince Edward County Marriage Bonds.

1790. Dec. 10	Jesse Watson and Polly Meredith, dau. of Pleasant Meredith of Henrico. Witness Richard Watkins. Surety on bond 50 pounds, Francis Watkins. Authority in writing from Pleasant Meredith, dated Henrico Dec. 2, 1790, to issue license.

Test. Elisha Meredith and Joseph Michaux.

1799.	Samuel Watson, Jr., and Hannah Watson, dau. of Saml. Watson, Sr.
1803. Oct. 5.	Benjamin Watson and Dicey DeJernatt, dau. of Boller De Jernatt, Decd. Bond signed by Ben. Watson and Francis Jackson and witnessed by Thos. C. Scott.
1808.	John C. Allen and Nancy Watson, dau. of Samuel Watson, Sr., decd. James Watson Womack signed bond. Witness Henry E. Watkins.

1809.	Enoch Watson and Susannah Hill, dau. of John Hill, Sr.
1812.	Samuel Watson and Rebecca A. Watson, dau. of Josiah Watson. Nelson Watson security on bond. Josiah Watson wrote authority to clerk for issuing license. This paper witnessed by Nelson and John A. Watson.
1813.	Littleberry Watson and Polly Thackston, dau. of Benjamin Thackston.
1816.	Joseph Watson and Frances Wade; Sims Allen surety on bond.
1816.	John A. Watson and Sallie H., dau. of John Bigger, Sr.
1817.	Joseph Wilson and D. Watson, dau. of Augustus Watson.
1817.	Allen Watson and Sarah W. Allen, dau. of James Allen. Witness to bond, B. J. Worsham.
1820.	Wilkinson Watson and Mary Gilliam. Witness Wm. Powell. Surety Wm. Gilliam.
1829.	Joseph G. Williams and Jane E. Watson, daughter of Drury Watson; witness Sterling Price; John W. Ritchie, surety.
1836. Sep. 27	Robert A. Watson and Mary E. Watson, dau. of John Watson, dec., late of Prince Edward. $150 bond, with Josiah B. Cox as surety. Witness B. J. Worsham. Authority to issue license signed by John C. Hamlett, September 26, 1836.
1837.	Daniel P. Watson and Lucy A. Wilkerson.
1839.	Archer Womack and F. A. Watson.
1842.	George W. Watson and Caroline Nash.
1848.	Samuel Watson and Pamela P. Booker, Edward F. Booker signed bond.

WOMACK.

Lived in Amelia, Prince Edward and adjoining counties; compiled from family tradition, letters from descendants and public records, April 1913, by Jean Stephenson, Ithaca, New York.

I. William Womack, born January 26th, 1736, died February 17, 1819; married, 1762, Mary Allen, born June 15, 1746, died June 8, 1816. In Halifax County is the marriage bond of William Womack to Mary Allen, daughter of James Allen, dated October 18, 1762. His surety on this bond was William Wright. He moved to Prince Edward County at an early date and is said to have been steward of John Randolph's affairs. Was ruling elder in the Presbyterian Church, 1795.

Children of William and Mary (Allen) Womack:

II. 1. John Womack, moved to North Carolina, married ———— Pryor. Member from Caswell County of Constitutional Convention 1788-9. Had sons: 1. Green, died 1856, married Ann McBryde, 1825, and had son John Archibald Womack, who lived in Chatham County, elder of Presbyterian Church, Commissioner to General Assembly of Church. Member of Legislature 1870-72, etc. 2. David, married ————, had at least one son P. H., who had son Thomas J. Womack. 3. Henry, moved to Tennessee, had children by 1st marriage: Bedford and a daughter who married ———— Connolly. Children by second marriage not known at present.

II. 2. Tignal Womack, married Nancy Rudder July 7, 1795. Moved to Kentucky 1818. Died 1827.

II. 3. Allen Womack, born March 21, 1766, married Sallie Womack 1793. (She was his first cousin, daughter of Charles Womack, brother of William Womack). Moved to Pittsylvania County. Had several children, among them: 1. John, who married ———— Morley, and 2. Allen Watson, born November 27, 1801, married, 1st, Catherine W. Stone, born 1816; married, 2nd, in 1856, Arabella W. Carter, born 1818. Among children were Emma and Charles A., who was born 1843 and married Mary Younger in 1865.

II. 4. Masseniello, or Massennetta, married Elizabeth Venable, daughter of Charles Venable, lived in Cumberland County, moved to Kentucky.

II. 5. Archer Womack, married Anne Faris Flournoy November 21, 1795.

II. 6. Benjamin Womack ————.

II. 7. James Watson Womack, born ————, died 1844, married ————, joined the Briery Church 1823, ordained elder March 29, 1828, elected trustee 1818, was in the Legislature from Prince Edward County. Had at least two sons: 1. Egbert, born 1817, and 2. Benjamin Watson, who married Oct. 12, 1836, Elizabeth Daniel, and had children, Elizabeth D., Violet J., James W., William D., Benjamin A. and Nathan B. Womack.

II. 8. Elizabeth Womack, married Baker Davidson July 3rd, 1795. Said to have married, 2nd, Charles Anderson Raine.

II. 9. Lillius D. Womack, married Sally, daughter of Adam Calhoun, Dec. 12, 1823; was elder at University Va. in 1839.

II. 10. Mary Womack, married Samuel Baldwin Sept. 16, 1799 (?).

II. 11. Nancy, married William Elliott. Briery records show that Ann, daughter of William Womack, married W. Raine.

II. 12. William Womack, settled in Botetourt County. Married there Mrs. Jane Kyle Poague. Their children were: 1. James Watson, died unmarried. 2. Joseph Kyle, died unmarried. 3. Marietta married Dr. Wm. Walkeef. 4. Sarah Ann, married Dr. ―――― Payne, of Alleghany Co.

Womack Family (Direct Line of Descent).

Compiled by Jean Stephenson, 1913.

I. William Womack of E. Dereham, Norfolk, married ―――――.

II. Arthur Womack, A. M., Rector of Lopham, Norfolk, 1578. Married at Hargham, Norfolk, May 12, 1579, to Alice Rowse (buried at Hargham May 8, 1602), buried at Lopham, June 18, 1607.

III. Lawrence Womack, B. D., Rector of Lopham, Norfolk, 1607, and of Fersfield, same county, 1642. Married ――――――. Died July, 1642.

IV. Lawrence Womack, D. D., born in Norfolk, May 12, 1612. Married, 1st ――――――; married, 2nd, at Westley Bradfor, Nov. 18, 1668, Anne, daughter of John Hill and widow of Edward Aylmer; married, 3rd, at St. Bartholomew-the-Less, London, April 25, 1670, Katherine Corbett, of Norwich. He entered Corpus Christi College, Cambridge 1629, graduated B. A. 1632, ordained deacon 1634, commencing M. A. 1639. Was chaplain to Lord Paget and later had benefice in the west of England. In 1660 was prebend in Herfordshire cathedral. In December 1660 archdeacon of Suffolk. In 1661 degree of D. D. conferred. In 1662 rector of Horningsheath, Suffolk, and also of Boxford in 1663. In the same year installed in prebendal stall in Ely cathedral. In 1683 consecrated Bishop of St. David's. Was a great controversial writer.

Died Nov. 7, 1685, buried in St. Margaret's, Westminster.
By first marriage:

V. Edward Womack, born March 12, 1653, died in Suffolk,
England, September 8, 1723. Married ———— ————.

VI. Ashby or Abraham Womack, born August 15, 1683.
Died in Virginia, February 4, 1756. Came from England to Virginia 1716. Married ———— ————.

VII. Richard Womack, born in England, December 7,
1710. Lived in Prince Edward County, Virginia;
moved to Hancock County, Georgia, 1765. Died
there July 23, 1785. Married ———— ————.

VIII. Jesse Womack, born in Virginia 1739, died in
Madison County, Georgia, 1815. Lived in Burke,
Hancock and Madison counties. Married, 1st,
Dorothy Prior, and, 2nd, in Georgia about 1778,
Phebe ————. Was a Lieutenant in the Revolution. By 1st marriage:

IX. John Womack, born in Georgia, December 25,
1776. Married in Georgia about 1797, Frances
Coleman. Moved to Alabama 1800. Lived in
Washington County, Alabama. Died at his home
there "Womack Hill" July 29, 1848. His widow
died in Texas 1852.

X. Aurelia Womack, born February 19, 1804, in Washington Co., Ala. Married Sept. 23, 1827, Isaac
Baker. Moved to Texas 1843. Lived in Grimes
County at "The Cedars" near Plantersville. Died
in Galveston, Texas, February 7, 1881.

XI. Jack Baker, born January 9, 1834, in Washington Co., Ala. Married in Grimes Co., Texas,
January 25, 1859, Cordelia Henrietta Albert Forrester. Lived at "The Cedars," Grimes Co.
Died there, January 4, 1887.

XII. Searcy Baker, born November 11, 1861. Married in Grimes Co., November 21, 1883, Lida
Jane Gibbs. Lives in Houston, Texas.

XII. Mattie, married Edwin Napier Stephenson.

XIII. Jean Stephenson.

APPENDIX I.

EXTRACTS FROM DIARIES.

1888

May 5. My uncle James Robertson killed at battle of Williamsburg, 1862.

June 29. Attended singing class at Ward's Chapel. Spent the night with Haney Tunstall.

June 30. Wrote to C. E. Redd in the interest of Ward's Chapel Musical Club, offering $25.00 and expenses for his services.

July 1. Attended Ward's Chapel Sunday School and gave a talk on the Bible.

Aug. 6. Edgar Williams and I at "Old Homestead" (Mrs. Burk's) for supper.

Sept. 3. Dined with Dr. "Red" and Beverley at Mr. Shore's ("Cedar Grove").

Sep. 30. Ward's Chapel to hear Dr. [Theodorick] Pryor.

Oct. 4. Left Richmond at 11:05 for Charlottesville; called upon Prof. Thornton about four o'clock, P. M. and matriculated a little later. Call from my Beta Theta Pi friends in the evening.

Oct. 5. Attended Mr. Minor's[134] class for the first time, spent a short time with him at the office. With the Beta's at no. 7 Carr's Hill at 5 o'clock, P. M. Adjourned over till 8:30 P. M. Saturday. Cold enough to freeze the horns off a billygoat.

Nov. 6. Presidential election. No disturbance. Carried a man named Ribble down from the University in a carriage at full speed and got to the polls a few minutes too late. Sat up at the Court House until something past midnight figuring the returns. When I left everybody seemed satisfied with the reports from N. Y. I felt very apprehensive lest Cleveland be defeated. Mr. Barbour telegraphed Maj. Mason from Richmond about 12 o'clock, "Virginia is safe."

Nov. 7. All the N. Y. papers concede Harrison's election except *The Times,* published this morning about one thirty.

---

[134]John B. Minor.

Richmond Dispatch concedes Republican victory. Telegram Wednesday night from W. W. Scott that Cleveland carried N. Y. by 1000 majority.

Nov. 8. Not till 12:45 today did I give up all hope of Democracy. Left Charlottesville for Richmond tonight at eight o'clock.

Nov. 12. Returned to Charlottesville.

Nov. 25. My twenty-first birthday; spent the forenoon with Roy revising the Beta Theta Pi catalogue at East Lawn, University of Virginia.

1894

July 9. Lunenburg Court. Judge Perry and I cleared Betty Forrest, charged with poisoning spring.

July 31. At Joe Leath's. Attended the Republican Convention at Burkeville, which nominated R. T. Thorpe for Congress. Visited Mr. Williams on business at "Ingleside" after supper.

Aug. 4. Drove to "Scotland" to see Willie Scott on business. Haney Tunstall drove me to "Bellefield" to see Mrs. [C. C.] Chambliss.

Aug. 18. Woodland. Pretty sick; temperature 103°. Start for Richmond. Go to Old Dominion Hospital and engage Dr. Geo. Ben Johnston's services.

Sep. 11. Taken sick four weeks ago today with typhoid fever at Judge Perry's in Lunenburg. Put on my clothes and walked about the room to-day for the first time.

Sep. 25. Nottoway. Went to "Mountain Hall" and spent the night: Colonel Jeffress talked Tennyson before supper and all the literati after.

Oct. 1. Rose at five, joined the dogs in Dr. Royall's pines, Leon, Hunter, Edgar Williams and I; jumped fox in Willie Scott's, ran him through Childress's and after tough ride caught in pines on left of road leading to Jetersville.

Nov. 6. At Crewe (general election); voted for W. R. McKenney (for Congress). Crewe gave him 161 majority out of 273 votes.

Nov. 12. Leon and Hunter killed deer at Dr. Southall's. Ran by Harper's Hill (Byney's Hill).

Dec. 18. Dinner at "Scotland"; went to Dr. Smithey's and Thos. H. Booker's that evening. Got tangled in J. C. Bragg's and Henry Verser's pines at dark. Cold and windy.

1895

April 10. Spent the night at "Mountain Hall." Col. Jeffress very ill.

April 20. Mass meetings in Nottoway to elect delegates to the convention to nominate county officers. I attend at Court House.

April 27. Democratic Convention at Court House. I received nomination for Commonwealth's Attorney, getting 15 out of 19 delegates, T. H. Vaughan, R. M. Hurt. E. McDaniel and Benj. Irby declining to make my nomination unanimous. Dr. J. W. Bryant presided over the convention and Saml. N. Williams nominated me.

May 12. Pass day at Mr. J. F. Epes's. Call on Mr. Freeman Epes, Sr., in the evening at his old place. He looks every inch the patriarch, the last of his race.

May 19. Represent Anna R. Graves before the coroner's jury at Crewe—tried for infanticide. One of the most horrible days, if not the very most, I ever passed in my life. Go to Blackstone and pass the night with Capt. A. B. Jones.

May 23. At crewe; election day. Sit up till 2:30 for the returns. Satisfied of my election.

May 24. Returns give me every precinct in the county.

May 25. Go to Court House. Attend Canvassing Board. My official majority 369.

June 1. Start to De Ferney's with Fanny and Lois horseback. Spend night with Dr. Southall at "Selma."

June 3. At "New London," Jim Motley's; picnic Farmer's Pond evening.

June 6. Nottoway Court. Qualified as Attorney for the Commonwealth. Rode back with Sam Burke and Peter Leneave.

July 1. Drove with Dick Miller to "Grape Lawn" in Prince Edward; first time I had been on that road since my father carried me to Prince Edward Court House to school (Prince Edward Academy) in 1881.

July 4. Nottoway Court. Prosecuted first criminal as Commonwealth's Attorney—Edwards Scruggs, a negro. Send him to penitentiary 5 years for burglary.

Aug. 1. Nottoway Court. Thornton Jeffress and I drive from "Mountain Hall" to Court House. I sold "Mountain Hall," the home of Dr. James Jones, 373 acres, for $1800, house and tenements.

Aug. 10. A telegram summoning me to Col. Jeffress at Chase City. Found him much changed for the worse and I about despair of his recovery.

Aug. 21. Col. Jeffress died 10:20 tonight. I was alone with him when he began to sink.

Aug. 22. Col. Jeffress buried at "Mountain Hall," Rev. Messrs. Theodore Epes and Gale officiating. T. H. Vaughan,

G. W. Leath, J. R. Leath, Samuel Burke, Leon and myself, pall-bearers. The service began at 10:30 A. M.

Aug. 27. W. H. Verser and I attend School Board at Burkeville. I get Board to build darkey school below the Ordinary, at Henry Forster's (colored).

Sep. 7. Forty dollars my fees this court as Com. Attorney.

Sep. 18. Got up at four to go after fox in Kies. Jumped at Toby Robertson's and lost at Kies' (Hamm's) stable.

Sep. 19. Went to Amelia to see Judge Hundley. Played marbles at Jennings Ordinary with Buck Ellett, Haney Tunstall and Ned Harper.

Oct. 1. Nottoway Circuit Court. Meade Haskins and I lost case, Clay *versus* Matthews. He made a good speech. I did not.

Oct. 5. General Hundley and I argued Nottoway County *versus* Crewe, Judge Mann on other side. I did only tolerably well, I thought. Judge Hundley said I did "handsomely."

Oct. 27. Drury Calhoun buried at Ward's Chapel; services by Rev. Geo. Abbitt[135] of the Episcopal church.

Dec. 24. All of us and Thornton Jeffress go to "Glenmore" to "egg-nog." Mr. Horner's 68th anniversary.

1896

April 14. Attend Confederate Memorial meeting at Court House, the Camp of Confederate Veterans.

May 9. At Burkeville and Crewe. Dr. J. W. Bryant and I elected delegates to the State Democratic Convention at Staunton. I for free silver and Dr. Bryant for gold.

June 4. At Staunton. Democratic Convention. Jas. F. and Sidney P. Epes, James Mann and C. E. Downs and I attend from Nottoway—all for free silver at sixteen to one. John W. Daniel was the great leader of the Convention. His word was simply law; monarchy affords no higher examples of despotism than the power possessed by this man in a free assembly of 2000 Virginians. I was elected alternate from the 4th District to Chicago Convention.

June 17. At home. Dr. Sydnor and Sterling Boisseau here in the evening.

June 20. Mrs. C. C. Chambliss dies today at Valley Shore's in lower end of Nottoway.

June 21. Fanny, Leon and I go to Mrs. Chambliss's burial today at "Bellefield"—the tomb of her ancestors. Rev. T. P. Epes held the burial services. Hot as Mexico.

June 27. I brought the Confederate battle flag for the Reunion in Richmond to "Woodland" this afternoon—the flag of

---

[135]George C. Abbitt, Rector, St. Mark's Church, Richmond, Va.

my father, of my country—and placed it over the yard gate. None but loyalists here.

July 1. Polk Hamlin, of Tennessee, here. First time since the war.

July 2. Leon and I take part in the parade at Richmond, Confederate Reunion. Greatest crowd I ever saw. Wade Hampton finest looking man in the procession. Heard all of Stephen D. Lee's speech.

Oct. 24. Col. Fitzgerald, Jas. Mann and I go to Amelia Springs to speak. Fine day and fine dinner. Spoke in the old Ball Room. Spend the night with Judge Farrar.

Oct. 26. Start for Lunenburg. Night with Colin Bagley.

Oct. 28. Wm. McIlwaine and I speak at Brown's Store.

Oct. 29. Spoke at Pleasant Grove at night.

Nov. 3. Presidential election. Hunter's first vote. He, Leon and I vote the Democratic ticket. Peaceable election. Satisfied by two o'clock that night that Bryan was defeated. Night at Boisseau's.

Nov. 5. Drove to Lunenburg Court House to attend canvassing vote. Spend night there talking to Judge Alexander of Mecklenburg.

Dec. 4. At home sick: had hard time keeping warm this weather: the cook mad, and the wood too long for the fireplace at both ends.

Dec. 12. The boys go after a red in Gully Tavern. Jumped north Burfoot Hunt's old house.

1897

March 1. Take eleven hounds to Judge Farrar's to hunt with Shelton and John Haskins. Shod my horse at Jim Motley's. Run by Truly Vaughan's.

March 8. Shot young buck at Byney's Hill. First deer I ever killed.

March 13. Joe Vaughan, Henry Hillsman and I jump a grey south of Bethel Church and after hard chase by Farley's and Burfoot Hurt's and Bob Holt's, of some one and a half hours, catch on battlefield of Sailor's Creek under a big chestnut oak, said to be the corner tree between Amelia, Prince Edward, and Nottoway, a short distance from, and n. w. of, Swep. Marshall's.

June 29. Connie and I drove from Pamplin in Prince Edward to "Cork" to visit Miss Jennie Michaux; find her very feeble and declining.

June 30. At "Cork." Miss Jennie Michaux starts for home (Bob Dickinson's near Worsham). Never expect to see her again. We spend forenoon at the spring. A sad, sweet, melancholy day.

1898

March 13. Leon and I pass the night with Shelton at "Mohican" to hunt next day.

March 19. Dr. J. W. Southall, T. P. Shelton, J. N. Vaughan, Leon and I fox it to Amelia. Jump deer at "Tip Top."

Sep. 17. Elected Chairman of Democratic Party in Nottoway—unanimously and by rising vote.

Sep. 30. At Circuit Court. Lost case. Bob Southall beat me. Thos. M. Miller, A. D. Watkins, W. H. Mann, Jas. Mann, Meade Haskins, Freeman Epes, H. E. Lee, Frank Saunders, J. S. Parish, Sidney Kirkpatrick and S. L. Farrar in attendance, attys.

Oct. 7. Attend funeral of Dr. P. F. Southall at Amelia Court House. He died on the 6th, aged 76.

1899

Jan. 22. Went to Ward's Chapel to hear F. B. Price, an old school-mate and now missionary from China.

Jan. 23. Fox hunt with Dick Crannis, Tom Sowers, Claiborne Wilson, Buck Morgan, Leon, and Joe Vaughan. Jump at Wooton's; run to old Burkeville and lose.

Jan. 24. Dine with Joe Leath, his 58th anniversary. Present: J. E., J. R., and B. O., and G. W. Leath, T. H. Vaughan, Dr. W. T. Warriner, J. W. Overton (Red Eye), Peter Leneave and myself. The invitation mentioned that he had "killed a stud turkey and two possums."

Jan. 30. At home sick. Hilary Royall here just after his graduation from Annapolis.

Feb. 11. Great snow. A thin coat of snow and sleet had covered the ground since last Monday night, hard frozen. Saturday evening about three-thirty the snow began to fall and continued perhaps the greater part of the night. There was a slight lull Sunday morning and at one time no snow for a short while. The sun was slightly visible about 11 o'clock. It snowed all day Sunday, Sunday night and Monday and stopped Monday night about nine o'clock. The temperature hovered about zero all the week and the ice was still on the trees Tuesday night, eight days. The snow first came from the N. E.—then N. W. The wind a great part of the time, especially Monday evening and Sunday night, was hard and shaving. Snow about knee deep on average; drifts much deeper. Monday night after nine o'clock the stars came out and Tuesday was a clear cold day. Sunset Tuesday was very pretty. I don't think any more snow on ground than I saw in Jan'y or Feb'y, 1895. I remember also one day in that spell more uncomfortable than any in this; it was Friday following Nottoway Court.

Feb. 16. After two clear days and slightly warmer, rain and hail today and a renewed sleet. Sleet on trees now since last Monday night.

1900

July 7. Go to Jeffress' Store to see Horace and Mrs. Jeffress. Write Mrs. Jeffress's will. She will not live long.

July 9. Go to see John Williams and take dinner with L. M. and Thornton Jeffress at "The Hermitage."

July 10. Went to old Tom Williamson's in Prince Edward to take depositions in case "Williamson *versus* Williamson." Met A. D. Watkins. Refreshed by sight of the Blue Ridge at Flippin's on way back after sunset.

July 11. At home. Leon threshed wheat—sowed eleven bushels, made 168 bushels. Mr. Poole here from Lunenburg on business.

July 12. Sat up all night at Henry Verser's with Ernest, who has typhoid fever. Home to breakfast.

Sep. 18. Grandpa Horner buried at Ward's Chapel.

Oct. 12. I set out for "Woodstock," the home of Dr. P. F. Southall in Amelia on the Appomattox, with seven dogs—my other two being sick—to join G. K. Taylor and run the noble red supposed to live in Moore's pines. Bradley Johnson, Ben Grigg and Bob Southall join me at Amelia Court House.

Oct. 15. Fine morning sun as ever lighted Appomattox. Thelius Phaup, G. K. Taylor, Sr. and Jr., Dr. R. F. Taylor, Joe and Richard Grigg and I take up river for the red by way of Moore's into Hardaway's, where we run one grey down with some thirty-five dogs. Poor chase.

Oct. 16. We take Appomattox from Goode's Bridge to "Coverley" (Dr. Meaux's) while Phaup and Grigg take the Chesterfield side to same point or above. We strike no red, fail to ford Appomattox on Meaux's (Wesley Williams) line on Chesterfield bank.

Oct. 17. Jump grey in "Woodlawn" S. E. of "Sunken Castle." Windy, and wire fences all over Chesterfield. Dogs lost me at Goode's Store and went out by Tom Eanes's almost to The Pits [Midlothian coal-pits] at Mr. Tizzard's and the fox bade them good-bye at Dr. Cox's on the Stage Road (Sappony).

Oct. 18. Break camp at "Woodstock." Jump nothing but deer today. Spend night with Mr. Geo. K. Taylor in Terrapin Neck.

1902[136]

Jan. 1. Left New York last night at 8:30 p. m. Rose at sunrise about Bowling Green. Saw boats rowed in Main street, Richmond. James River very high.

---

[136]No diary for 1901 has been found.

Jan. 6. Returned to the convention[137] in Richmond.

Jan. 9. Began my argument in Democratic caucus of Constitutional Convention on suffrage, but stopt at 10 o'clock, after something over an hour, on motion to adjourn. I had prepared myself by careful thought and reflection, but had not written anything and used only a sheet of notes-skeleton.

Jan. 10. Richmond. Resumed speech on suffrage before Democratic caucus of Convention tonight. Spoke something over one and a half hours.· I was generously applauded and the papers were kind in their accounts of me. I was not entirely satisfied myself; my voice was not controlled as well as I could have wished. Judge Green[138] and Alf. Thom[139] were greatly pleased.

Jimmie Epes, schoolmate, college mate and friend of my youth, died at New York one year ago today.

Jan. 24. Attended meeting of Board of Visitors of Eastern Hospital at Williamsburg to consider the rebuilding of the houses recently destroyed by fire.

Jan. 31. Spoke briefly in the Convention on the report of Agricultural Committee. What I knew about the subject was very little. However, I got up a good deal of earnestness on the floor.

Feb. 1. Liquor question up for debate today. Turnbull[140] and Garnett[141] spoke for Barbour resolution. Hill Carter, with more power than either, against it. I drew and got the Committee to accept amendment to submit the whole question to people in separate article and at separate election for ratification or rejection and with this alternation think I shall vote for the thing, thought it ought never to have been brought into the Convention.

Judge Green and Henry Ingram dine with me today. Since Christmas Judge Green and I have dined regularly at the Commercial.[142]

Feb. 2. Amelia. Snow and sleet, beautiful morning, but cold and windy. Walked down railroad to 105 mile post. Met Bob Mason walking in from "Osmore." Read part of a sermon on "the sin of unbelief" and the Bible (15 and 16 John) to Mrs. Southall.

Feb. 3. Reached Richmond 8:40 a. m. Westcott[143] delivered strong speech in Convention today against anti-liquor article being put in Constitution. Judge Green and I dine to-

---

[137] Virginia Constitutional Convention, 1901-1902; Mr. Watson was the delegate from the district of Nottoway and Amelia counties.

[138] Berryman Green.

[139] Alfred P. Thom.

[140] Robert Turnbull.

[141] G. T. Garnett.

[142] Commercial Hotel, formerly between Ninth and Tenth Streets on Main.

[143] N. B. Westcott.

gether. He is advocate of philosophy of "indifference," but like Cousin James Elia in "My Relations," ("Essays of Elia") generally preaches one way and acts another.

Spent part of the evening questioning Edmund Hubard and Cliff Woolridge about the old people of Buckingham and Appomattox. Hubard said of Captain McKinney[144] that the secret of his popularity was that he always had a kind, pleasant word for everybody, and never spoke evil of another; that William M. Cabell was the ablest man of Buckingham for years, great in the power of sarcasm and ridicule. Thomas S. Bocock was very strong before court and jury. Woolridge said Bocock was a man of great simplicity and cordiality of manner. At the church meetings would always go around among the "levellers," invite them to his table, while his wife entertained the "quality."

I went to call on Mr. Goode[145] at 2nd and Franklin after supper. Talked with him about old times and public men. He thought of the debaters he heard in the Senate, winter of '60 and '61, Mr. Davis[146] was the best. Said Davis looked every inch game and a thoroughbred. He thought Roger Pryor— whom he observed only in the Confederate Congress—a rhetorician rather than an orator. Said A. H. H. Stuart told him he thought B. B. Douglas, of New Kent, the equal of Stephen A. Douglas in every particular. Mr. Goode thought him a man of great power. He was with Douglas when he died in Washington, and it was a mistake—he was not killed or injured by G. C. Walker.[147] Mr. Goode thought it improbable that Yancey[148] had died from injury inflicted by Hill[149] in secret session of the Confederate Senate. Hill did strike him with ink bottle. The debate was upon the creation of a Court of Appeals for the Confederate States, Yancey taking the ground of extreme States' rights, that there was no need for a Supreme Court to decide between the States and Hill taking the Hamiltonian side that there was.

Letter from Jos. M. Hurt of Nottoway asking me to come out for Congress in the 4th District.

Feb. 4. Got up with headache. Heard Braxton[150] for three and a half hours on the "Corporate Commission"—strong, logical statement of his case—no attempt at oratory; only fault, prolixity.

---

[144]Philip W. McKinney, captain of cavalry in the Confederate States Army, afterwards Governor of Virginia.

[145]John Goode.

[146]Jefferson Davis.

[147]Beverley Brown Douglas died December 22, 1878. Many thought he died from injuries received at the hands of Gilbert C. Walker, Governor of Virginia, 1869-1874.

[148]William L. Yancey of Alabama.

[149]Benjamin Harvey Hill of Georgia.

[150]A. C. Braxton.

Judge Green and Henry Ingram[151] to dinner with me and Judge Green spent evening in my room talking book talk and about folks in Danville, especially Ola Fowlkes's marriage to old John Holland. Advised me to get and preserve Rosetti's "Blessed Damosel." Attended uninteresting session of caucus on Suffrage tonight. Hal Flood[152] just in from Washington, kept me up until eleven, when, tired and sick, I went to bed.

Feb. 5. Heard Hunton[153] for three hours on Corporate Commission. He was clear, logical, strong and occasionally almost eloquent. Very civil, graceful, but somewhat sarcastic. Altogether, I thought stronger than Braxton. Henry Ingram took the floor at 1:30 and for half an hour. Went to my quarters and to collapse.

Feb. 6. My old friend malaria has come to me again and I may have to call in the Sangrados. Did not go to Convention. Attended Democratic caucus at four in order to vote on Suffrage —for that I was unable to forego; only one vote taken, that between a Grandfather clause (offered by Barbour[154]) and our Report (the Understanding Clause), with result that the latter succeeded by vote of thirty-one to thirty. The vote is not greatly significant and does not clear the situation. Glass[155] got the floor and had it when adjournment came. Judge Green[156] led a humorous and snappy running debate in behalf of the Com's Report, in which he maintained that the negro did not belong to the same genus as the whites; and said he was old-fashioned enough to believe that the Bible proved that we were not of the same blood, and that subordination was the natural state for the sons of Ham. That he was as firm in his convictions as the Rev. man from Prince Edward (Dr. McIlwaine[157]) could be, and as cantankerous in supporting them as the gentleman from Richmond (Charles V. Meredith) had seemed, on the other side. A wiry old man—armed with a rapier—is this dreamy, poetic ex-judge.

George Saunders, Esq., died at Burkeville this week, I see from the papers. An old Buckingham lawyer, who married a sister of Col. R. E. Withers.

Feb. 7. Did not attend Convention today but went to Caucus from four to six p. m. Glass resumed his talk in favour of his plan of suffrage, earnestly contending that a poll tax of $1.50 and reading and writing test would disfranchise eighty per cent of the negroes for the future. R. L. Gordon, of Louisa,

---

[151]John Henry Ingram.
[152]Henry D. Flood.
[153]Eppa Hunton, Jr.
[154]John S. Barbour.
[155]Carter Glass.
[156]Berryman Green.
[157]Richard McIlwaine.

who is nearer to my own opinion on suffrage than anybody else in the Convention—i. e., will give up anything and everything to disfranchise all the negroes—replied to him briefly, but earnestly, strongly, strenuously—urging that the negro could and would pay the poll tax and that under the free school system the negro in the near future would be able to read and write to a man.

Feb. 13. I am still sick and take but little interest in my surroundings. The debate on the Corporation Commission they say has been able. Thom today made an able and impressive appeal against any Constitutional enactment on the subject. His central idea was, the spirit of the future was commercial, we would have to acquiesce and ought to do nothing to deter or cripple the industrial future of Virginia, whose present condition had driven thirty-eight per cent of its population to find homes elsewhere. He delivered the dollar logic effectively.

Feb. 19. The Legislature reconvened today pursuant to adjournment in December. The Convention had gone bag and baggage into Mechanics Hall on Broad Street. I have been abed all day except to sit up once or twice. Dr. Southall and Bob Southall, James Mann, Henry Ingram and others here to see me. Dr. told me about old times in Amelia. Said Amelia Springs was founded by Frank Willson, who was bought out by his brother Thomas Claiborne Willson, who died right upon the bank of Flat Creek below the sulphur spring, where there was another spring (sulphur) which was stronger than the one some yards away, but whose waters mingled with those of the bed of the creek and had to be separated by some pump and other arrangement. Tom C. Willson, who was an enormous man, was engaged at this with one negro who happened to be beyond sight at the time, when an attack of apoplexy, or other cause, precipitated him into the creek, where he drowned before the negro could get him out.

Feb. 20. Sat up most of the day and am gradually pulling myself together. Read larger part of E. A. Pollard's "Life of Jefferson Davis." The author's judgment not comprehensive nor sound, but he is a critic of edge and in language an artist. The book won't do for history, but there is a great deal of history in it and much that others have not published. As I grow older, I am beginning to think that the Confederacy ought to have succeeded, but I am not ready to agree with the author that Jefferson Davis was the cause of defeat. His estimate of Genl. Lee accords more nearly with my own than any I have ever seen in print.

Judge Green, Lindsay Gordon and Henry Ingram came to see me today. They all complain of the bad weather and the new hall of the Convention (Cor. 11th & Broad). The question of incorporating a "prohibition" feature on liquor in Constitution up for debate, but went over till tomorrow.

Feb. 22. Put on my clothes today, first time since yesterday a week. Mr. James F. Epes came to see me today—remaining until after midnight. I was mighty glad to see him. Take him all in all, I know no better nor truer man than this old comrade and friend of my father. Were all the people in Virginia like him, we could do without any Constitution.

Feb. 23. Dr. McIlwaine, just recovered from a spell of sickness, came in this evening. His talk was principally of Dr. Moses D. Hoge. Says Peyton Hoge's Life did not do his uncle justice. I had never read the book. He said Dr. Hoge had a most exalted opinion of Dr. Murkland's[158] power and eloquence. Said Dr. Hoge was wont in his latter years, at Hampden-Sidney commencements, to stay at his house, and on such occasions his reminiscences were the most charming, elegant and interesting he ever heard from any one. He once gave him a most speaking account of a speech Dr. Murkland made at Cambridge, England, on the visit of the Pan Presbyterian Alliance, when he so completely performed the duty that he (Dr. Hoge), who was late on the program, did not speak a word—the subject was finished.

Feb. 25. General Bradley T. Johnson came in to see me this morning. He looks young and well. The snow has run him in town from Amelia. He told me I knew nothing about women, that a woman never gave her real reason for any act, but a superficial one; that she was as sure to conceal her real motives as she would be to hide her ankles.

Feb. 27. Attended Convention today in new hall. Acoustics very bad. U. S. flags in great display. Ate dinner at Westmoreland Club. Voted against and for liquor today.

Mar. 3. Amelia. Not well. Missed meeting of [Democratic] State Executive Committee at Richmond tonight.

Mar. 7. Have been here lounging around the house since Saturday night, trying to recover enough strength to go back to Richmond and be able to discharge my public duty in the Convention on the Suffrage question—so vital an interest to Southside Virginia. I have been trying in vain to entertain myself with Dean Swift, Macaulay's History and the *American Turf Register*. In the *American Turf Register and Sporting Magazine* (John R. Skinner, Balto., Editor) Vol. 4, p. 650, Aug. 1833, I find account of the races at Bellfonte, Va.: "Spring meeting commenced on Wednesday May 29, 1833."[159]

---

[158]Sidney Smith Murkland.

[159]Mr. Watson had copied many of the entries, names of owners, etc., including names of John C. Goode, Captain J. J. Harrison, W. R. Johnson, Col. William Wynn and T. D. Watson, and had written the following note:

Memo.—Goode lived in Mecklenburg and was the father of Wm. O. Goode, of Chesterfield. His father was Thomas Goode, of Chesterfield, also a horse-racer. Harrison lived at "Diamond Grove," Brunswick County. William R. Johnson was horse man of N. C. (Warren County). His son Marmaduke Johnson, born in Chesterfield County, Va. Col. Wm. Wynn and his son William, of Petersburg, were great horse men at this date. Edmund Irby, Esq., of Nottoway, from some references in this volume must have owned some first class horses.

Mar. 10. Return to Richmond. Maj. Daniel[160] again—looking well. I am sorry he returned to the Convention; he is willing to do no effective thing on Suffrage, and his sympathy seems not to extend to the people of the Black Counties. He discussed the race question with me and thinks the negro race will never be mixed with the white. Wish I felt as sure.

Mar. 12, 13, 14, 15. All the week wrangling on suffrage. I have been exceedingly unwell and feeble. Spoke but indifferently on Friday in reply to Daniel. We carried a property qualification--with soldier, etc., exemptions,—by a vote of thirty-four to thirty-two.[161]

Mar. 16. On Saturday on a motion to reconsider we again held the property qualification by a vote of thirty to twenty-nine (several pairs). There may not be backbone enough to hold this advantage, but we have the satisfaction of making the "whitewashers" and "do nothings" spend one uneasy Sunday, whatever comes afterwards.

Mar. 17. Another scuffle with the "whitewashers" on Suffrage today. We struck out the educational provision (the written application for registration) from the Glass plan, but we were slain later in the house of our friends by a measure which killed our property clause.

Mar. 22. Some time during this week 2 Com's of Conference representing the two factions of the caucus—the "disfranchisers" and the "whitewashers"—consisting of Thom, Carter,[162] Hamilton, Barbour, Pollard[163] and Watson for the one; and Daniel, Glass, Westcott, Ayers[164] and Stuart[165] for the other. These again appointed a sub-com. of Watson and Barbour for one, Glass and Stuart for the other. By the next day we reached a conclusion and agreement: six year understanding clause, submission of question then to people as to whether it should continue, at the discretion of the Legislature of 1908. This, known as the Compromise Plan, was beaten in the Convention by the two Halifax delegates changing their vote to other side. It was on Wysor's[166] amendment to make Understanding Clause run only one year. This was the beginning of the end and really the last fight we made for negro disfranchisement.

Mar. 23. At Amelia. Walked over to "The Woodlands" to see General Bradley T. Johnson.

---

[160]John W. Daniel.
[161]From March 8-28, the Convention adjourned each day after roll-call and the Democratic members who, with the exception of eleven members, constituted the body, went into conference upon the suffrage question.
[162]Hill Carter.
[163]John Garland Pollard.
[164]R. A. Ayres.
[165]Henry C. Stuart.
[166]J. C. Wysor.

April 1. Thom spoke in Convention today. My throat very sore. I am trying to get it well enough to speak day after tomorrow against Suffrage article.

April 3. Got floor today soon after four o'clock. Spoke about three quarters of an hour—not entirely to my satisfaction.

April 4. We adjourned today about five o'clock until May twenty-second. In my judgment the Convention has been a public calamity; the political phase of the negro question, soon or late, must be settled, and we have only whitewashed and coddled it. Our children and grand-children will be confronted with the same troubles in the future. The responsibility belonged to this generation, and it should have had the courage to assume it. The Democrats who voted against this cowardice were on last roll: Barbour, Gordon,[167] Thom, Hamilton, Brooke,[168] Flood, Green, Moncure,[169], Robertson,[170] McIlwaine, Marshall,[171] Crismond,[172] Gwyn,[173] Pollard, Waddill,[174] Watson and Campbell.[175] Of these those who really opposed it on grounds of inefficiency as to negro vote were: Gordon, Barbour, Thom, Hamilton, Flood, Green and Watson; on grounds doubtful or not fully known to me, Moncure and Waddill; on grounds religious and of casuistry, McIlwaine and Pollard—could not go the "unmorality" of the "Understanding Clause" for one year. Gordon Robertson did not desire to disfranchise negroes any more than whites—thought the worthless of both races ought to go by same rule. Campbell and Crismond probably preferred doing nothing. Gwyn and Marshall perhaps could not stand a poll tax and the education put upon the white people of their sections. The Black Belt could, I think, have gotten a satisfactory settlement if it had stood together; it became distracted and behaved with great folly.[176-177]

---

[167]R. L. Gordon.
[168]D. Tucker Brooke.
[169]Thomas J. Moncure.
[170]William Gordon Robertson.
[171]James W. Marshall.
[172]Horace F. Crismond.
[173]T. L. Gwyn.
[174]Samuel P. Waddill.
[175]Clarence J. Campbell.
[176-177]A few sentences of comment on several of the representatives of the Black Belt are here omitted. Those who knew Judge Watson best know that they were written in good feeling and good temper and, in fact, in more or less humorous vein, but the determination to omit them has arisen from the fear that the majority of readers might misunderstand their spirit.

In the same way a few other comments upon persons have been omitted here and there throughout.

Their inclusion would in no case have added anything to positive knowledge.

April 9. Spent most of the day walking about Farmville. Walter Richardson, Judge J. M. Crute, Judge A. D. Watkins and others gave me many kind words as to my services in the Convention. The latter urged me to stand for Congress, saying all his people would give me cordial support. I had to decline; my personal relations to Frank Lassiter are such I am not at liberty, I think, to take the field against him.

April 12. "West Creek" the old residence of the Wards, and perhaps the oldest house in Nottoway, was burned this evening. George Verser occupied it; the fire was accidental.

April 13. Edgar Williams and I walked over to "Cedar Grove" this morning. Everything about the place is tumbling to ruin. The old school house where Mrs. Georgiana Epes taught is still standing.

April 14. Take early train for Richmond to meet the Revision Committee of the Convention. Met at Court of Appeals Room at twelve o'clock. Present: Anderson,[178] Chairman, Green, Brooke, Moore,[179] Braxton, Wysor, Meredith, Bouldin, Gregory,[180] Cameron, Jones,[181] and Watson. Daniel, Boaz[182] and Davis[183] (Republican) absent. We worked all the week and got only through with Bill of Rights and most of Suffrage. First I was appointed Committee of one to recast first three sections, and afterward Braxton and Moore were added, and we did so. The plan and arrangement was my own down to and including section 5, (fo the Excluded Classes) and most of the phraseology. Much time was taken up in discussing punctuation. Meredith was death on introducing a comma wherever there was space, and Wysor was crazy about semicolons, Braxton about sticking in a "Provided" everywhere. At the close of our session on Saturday I offered the following resolution: "Resolved: That the turbulent impetuosity of Wm. A. Anderson, the hair-splitting quibbles of Wood Bouldin, the interminable commas of C. V. Meredith and J. C. Wysor are tolerable, but the endless prolixity of A. C. Braxton is grievous unto death." All these were present except Bouldin.

I went one evening this week to Oakwood Cemetery, the first time at the soldiers' graves I could not withhold a tear. Home again Saturday night.

Hodijah Meade died yesterday at Williamsburg, where he was on a visit; a good and true man gone to his rest. He was grandson of General ˙Everard Meade of "The Hermitage,"

---

[178]William A. Anderson.
[179]R. Walton Moore.
[180]Roger Gregory.
[181]Claggett B. Jones.
[182]W. H. Boaz.
[183]Beverley A. Davis.

Amelia. The Meades came to Amelia from Nansemond County. Same stock as the Bishop.[184]

Last Sunday (13th), died at Blackstone, Richard Epes, Esq. He was born 1825 at "Walnut Hill." His father was Peter Epes, who married the daughter of Isaac Oliver, of Hendersonville, who was Richard Epes's mother. His grandfather was Richard Epes. Mr. Epes used to come sometimes to "Woodland" in my childhood and was always attached to my family. He was a fine-looking man, intelligent and distinguished in personal appearance. A year ago I saw him and his brother both mounted upon horses and riding, at the burial of Captain A. B. Jones. Mr. Epes was for a time during the war upon the staff of General Pryor with the rank of captain, I think. He was a man of lasting prejudice, but taken all in all I think he was intellectually the best of his name I have known.

April 22. Revision Committee at work today upon Education Report. I recast 2nd Section at Committee's request.

April 23. Went to Amelia today to act as usher at the marriage of Miss Mary Southall and Thomas R. Hardaway. S. L. Farrar, and Robert Mason, of "Osmore," Buck Gregory, of Norfolk, and I were ushers. The marriage was at the Episcopal Church.

April 24. I passed last night at "Dykeland," home of the late Lewis E. Harvie—with Dr. Taylor. Sat up till 12, and then Dr. Taylor talked to me constantly and gave me no chance to talk with the girls. Rose at 5 and went down to walk in the grove of oak, elm, ash, etc., all of which I was told was planted by Mrs. Lewis E. Harvie. Everything here is hastening to decay. An odd volume of "The Speeches of Calhoun," hanging on a shelf by my bed this morning swept me back 40 years in a moment and was the only distinctive relic of Mr. Harvie I met with. Has God designed that the great War should ruin the very soil upon which we live? "Dykeland," "Osmore," "Coverly," "The Lodge," "Clay Hill"—what desolation!

April 28. Return to Richmond. Perhaps most beautiful day of the Spring—too much so to take sight of a town. Frank Lassiter came to see me to get me to talk with and advise Bob Southall not to run against him. I do not want Bob to run— think he will be beat, and, besides, the position is wholly out of line with his talents and tastes.

May 7 and 8. At Amelia Court House these two days writing the Ordinance of the Convention under which registration is to be held until 1904.

May 10. Alexander Hamilton and I went to Norfolk to spend Sunday with Alf Thom. People in Norfolk have great energy and business enterprise. but they live too high—fine

---

[184]Bishop William Meade, 1789-1862.

clothes, terrapin and duck, make the young men have red faces and soon look old.

May 12. Went to Richmond, where we concluded work of the Committee on Final Revision. Present: Anderson, Brooke, Boaz, Jones, Gregory and Watson (don't recall any one else). Most of the work I did was on the Suffrage and Educational articles and on the Ordinance of Registration.

May 15. At Williamsburg attending meeting of Board of Eastern State Hospital.

May 17. At Blackstone. J. M. Harris and friends propose to me to have Southall and Harris withdraw from the contest and unite on me as a candidate for Congress against Lassiter. I am not willing to accept and do not; and when Southall came at night, he decided to remain in the field and Harris withdrew. I much doubt if Harris ever intended to stand against Lassiter. It is possible to beat Lassiter, but they united too late to put me in the field and take up the fight of Southall and Harris, and I really think it is beyond Southall's power to make the fight. The conference broke up at 12 o'clock. Present: J. M. Harris, Jos. M. Hurt, George and Wilson Cralle, Maj. Harris, T. F. Epes, Cobbs and myself.

May 25. Spent the day with the Taylors at Terrapin Neck. Went over to see Mr. Jo. Willson in the evening.

June 3. Return to Convention.

June 7. Convention adjourned today 1:30 to the 25th. I submitted a few words today on the subject of Registration Ordinance which I prepared to keep a specific date from being fixed on which registration is to be begun in all sections at the same time—preferring to leave the initial date to local boards so that it may be adapted to the convenience of each locality.

June 16. Rain all day—glorious rain—an end of one of the most protracted droughts at this season of the year within the living memory.

June 18. Letter from Dr. O. M. Knight renewing the past friendly relations with that estimable old country squire. He is one of the few survivors, if not the sole, of the first class to graduate from the Va. Military Institute in 1839. Serene be the evening of his days, and hopeful.

June 26. Spoke briefly in Convention today and only fairly. I was too worn out and nervous, but helped defeat the Meredith resolution to adjourn twelve months with power in presiding officer to reassemble the body. We adjourned *sine die* about 4:30 p. m. without especial ceremony. I left hurriedly to avoid taking formal leave of many who have become near and dear to me. I came from the Capitol with Henry Ingram, Judge Green and George D. Wise, and it was impossible not to be impressed with the solemn and melancholy reflections at the thought that some of us had parted for the last time. I did not remain to the banquet tendered us by citizens of Richmond tonight, but left on the six o'clock train for the pines and broom-straw of the dear old Southside. May God protect her if the new Constitution fail.

July 23. At 10:15 today [my sister] Fanny is severed from the home of her fathers and joined to another life[185]; peace and happiness go with the child. The ceremony was performed by Rev. Mr. Scott, of the Presbyterian Church. I led her to the altar. After all was over and the evening come, I went to my oaks where years ago early one rainy summer morning—the morning of the night in which my little brother died (the first time I had ever seen death)—I shed the first tear of grief I remember in this world. The trees are the same; I am the same—all else is changed. To be sure the three principal events in one's life are—birth, marriage, death; and of these the second is the greatest.

Aug. 6. Return home from Amelia today. Attend burial of Abner Robertson at Ward's Chapel. He was the son of Paschal Robertson, who lived on Lazaretto Creek and his mother was a Bradshaw. He was a good soldier of the Confederacy, was wounded and captured at Gettysburg and a prisoner at Point Lookout from July '63 to '65 (22 Mos.) His brother, Robert Robertson, was killed at Gettysburg.

Aug. 8. At Blackstone. District Committee declare Southall nominee for Congress.

Aug. 9. Meet the Board of Registrars from Amelia at the Court House and talk to them earnestly to agree to disfranchise the negro under the new Constitution. They agree and I believe they will do it.

Aug. 30. Got up early and went to Amelia Court House. In the afternoon went to Jetersville and then to Amelia Springs and remained till late. The spirit of the past came back to me again and "hants" patted me on the back when I lay down to drink from the old Sulphur Spring. The old oak tree is gone which stood near the spring, but the place recalls happy recollections even in my own memory. It was here that good old Judge Farrar crowned my maiden political efforts back in 1889, naming me "the boy orator" in a letter to the *Richmond Dispatch*. It was here that I heard Col. Fitzgerald deliver in 1896 what I think was the most effective political speech I ever heard from man. Here, in my younger days, I spent the night once with good old John Haskins—my horse in the stable and dogs in the barn—and at dawn we went out in the autumn morning after "old Mrs. Gus Vaughan" with about 27 steady and true.

September 1. Go to Prince Edward Circuit Court and spend two days. The lawyers there were: Judge William Hodges Mann, Nottoway; Judge A. D. Watkins, Prince Edward; Thomas E. Watkins, Charlotte; W. C. Franklin, Appomattox; Wm.

---

[185]She married Prof. J. H. C. Winston, of Hampden-Sidney College.

Smith, Cumberland; Hon. A. B. Armstrong, Cumberland; _____ McRae, Cumberland; Capt. Richard H. Watkins, Prince Edward; William A. Lancaster, Cumberland; J. S. McIlwaine, Farmville; S. P. Vanderslys, Farmville; J. M. Crute, Farmville. I pass the night with Col. W. W. Forbes at Asa Watkins's, who lives in the fork of Briery and Bush. Colonel Forbes is the son of a Revolutionary soldier,—member of the Secession Convention from Buckingham, went to school at old John T. Bocock's between Appomattox Court House and Bent Creek where Willis P. Bocock taught a sort of academy and educated most of his brothers before he began to practice law. Old John T. married a Flood. Colonel Forbes thought William, a younger son dying in early life, the first of the Bococks. Thought them people of extraordinarily strong minds but somewhat lacking in polish. Thought Thomas Stephens the smoothest one, especially in cultivating the rabble from the hustings. Colonel Forbes is nearing eighty-six, hale, active, and with undimmed eye. Looked again at "Longwood," in returning to town this morning, the home of the Johnstons, etc.

Sept. 4. Nottoway Court. Fewer people at court than I remember to have seen before. The people themselves have really abolished the county courts by non-attendance before the new Constitution brought the axe to the root of the dying tree. Spent the night at Judge Mann's and tried to play ping pong.

Sep. 17. Thursday two years ago today my step grandfather, Mr. George D. Horner, was killed by train in the cut this side of Thompson's Crossing on the Danville Road opposite rock quarry at Tom Wingo's. He was very deaf and did not hear the train, but left home apparently for Paineville—his old home—and not in good spirits. J. R. Jeter came late in the evening with the tidings. He was buried the next day at Ward's Chapel.

Sep. 18. Samuel Burke, son of Col. Samuel D. Burke, died today two years ago at 8 p. m. at his home, Mr. B. C. Jones's. He was buried at Ward's Chapel Sept. 19.

Just before sundown I registered at Jennings Ordinary under the "Understanding Clause" of the new Constitution. C. E. Downs, E. M. Williams and D. P. McCormick, Registrars. I could have registered under property or as the son of a soldier, but thought our people ought to set an example to the more illiterate whites who might be indisposed to submit to an examination.

Sept. 19. Rose at four and joined "Joe Red" (Vaughan) at Mrs. Bouldin's to hunt Flat Creek. We went through Beverley Gills's by New London out to Sailor's Creek—the battlefield portion—and got there by sun rise, then we turned through Overton's (J. M. Hillsman's), Foster's old field, Farley's, crossing Sandy Creek at road leading from Deatonsville to Jamestown, thence through W. B. Chapman's (Meadow's), Rucker's,

Orange's, and about twelve o'clock raised a grey in the low grounds at Nat Carter's immediately on the creek bank (Sandy Creek) below where the road crosses leading from Shepherd's Shop to Providence Church. He made but small run, something like twenty minutes and was put to his end on the road leading from John Robertson's to Stony Point at Mrs. Orange's. I thought I discovered the possible origin of the name of Chinquepin Church at Paineville in the immense quantity of chinquepins I found in the white sandy country above Rodophil; the size and quality also were excellent. Nat Carter lives on the north east side of Sandy Creek, the place that Capt. Giles A. Miller lived at during and since the War. The largest country burial ground is there I ever saw—walled in with rock. It is said to be the tomb of the Woods. Dr. Dick Wood was buried there. Only one tombstone did I notice, that of Nancy Foster— who she was I do not know. North-west of the wall on the same ridge is also a large darkey burial place.

Sept. 29. Rode horseback to Nottoway Court House, where Judge Hancock, from Chesterfield, presided. Judge W. H. Mann, Nottoway; Col. James Mann; Col. Meade Haskins; Hon. R. G. Southall, Amelia; Hon. A. D. Watkins, Prince Edward; Hon. S. L. Farrar, Amelia; Gen'l. John A. Gills, Amelia; H. E. Lee, Nottoway; T. F. Epes, Nottoway; G. S. Wing, Prince Edward; Hon. Jas. F. Epes, Nottoway; and Walter A. Watson were the attorneys in attendance.

Oct. 1. I ride out this evening by "The Poplars"—the old place of the Joneses and Campbells. The remains of Hon. Thos. H. Campbell were taken from the burial ground here and carried to Blackstone this Spring. Went by "Cheatham's" (Dr. Epes's old place) and went to "Belfast" where Charles Fitzgerald, Esq., lived until after the War, when the house was burned. Mr. Fitzgerald was brother of Dr. George Fitzgerald, son of Frank Fitzgerald, the old clerk. Charles Fitzgerald shot himself accidentally, or designedly, it is not known, but generally thought the latter, at a place on West Creek in Amelia near old Hardaway place. At Cheatham's came across an old slave darkey who believed great harm of the new Constitution and told me the negroes held me accountable for what they considered a serious attempt upon their liberty.

Oct. 12. Go to the school house below the church to hear Rev. Mr. James Cook, of Richmond, preach. Good many of old Doctor Pryor's congregation on hand—Wingos, Agnews, Wards, Warriners, Watsons. Sun set clear, and we arranged to give our horse-tails to the wind on the "Chair" road tomorrow at dawn.

Oct. 16. Start at dawn for Williamsburg and reach there at ten to attend meeting of Eastern Asylum Directors. Present: T. McCracken, Fredericksburg; Judge Taylor Garnett, Matthews; D. Coles, Williamsburg; Cowherd, Goochland; Eugene Ould, Campbell; E. H. Clowes, Richmond, and I.

Oct. 25. We go to Chesterfield in search of "Mrs. Tatum"[186] and the reds. Cross the bridge following the big road by "Woodlawn" to Henry Miller's, thence north and left by "Seven Oaks" the seat of the Woods—to Thelius Phaup's; thence through "Longwood" (Tatum's), finally raising deer near Tatum's old bridge site. Located an old graveyard on Goode's Creek, midway between Henry Miller's and Tatum's near "Seven Oaks" with some tombs said to be those of Goodes and Tatums, but I did not have the chance to examine them. Rode to Rowlett's Mill this evening.

Oct. 27. Hunter, Dick Grigg, Tim Taylor and I start for Chesterfield and raise the "varmint" near Dr. Simms's on the Richmond Road and catch in Hudson's on the right not far from Skinquarter Church.

Oct. 28. We rode through Southall's old place "Locust Dale" (Norfleet's) and then along the Bevill's Bridge Road to "The Old Tavern" (Holcombe's also "Mansfield"), where we took the Richmond Road, crossing Deep Creek at the Lower Bridge and taking Green's Road on top of the hill. In the afternoon I walked to see Mr. Joseph Wilson, now in the eighties, and a typical relic of the old time Virginia fox-hunter. He told me he caught two reds and seven greys in a single week in October. The old gentleman rides horseback yet.

Oct. 30. We decided to rest man and beast today. Dr. Richard F. Taylor and I go turkey hunting about Bevill's Bridge. I drive buggy around by Old Tavern to bridge, while he takes dogs through the "mill field," the tract of land on the upper side of Deep Creek in the fork of the Appomattox and so called from Holcombe's old mill site. A stone dam across Deep Creek gave the water power a short distance from the river.

Oct. 31. We rise before day to go to Chesterfield, across Bevill's after a red suspected of lying at "Gravelly Hill." *En route* to Blankenship's a messenger came from Mrs. Taylor to say that young Frank Coleman, a son of the sheriff of Amelia, would be buried that evening at two o'clock; so we broke up at "Gravelly Hill" at 12 and returned to Terrapin Neck.

Nov. 4. Robert G. Southall elected to Congress today; the vote was light, there being practically no opposition to the Democrats. I take Buck Ellett, a cripple, Dr. Southall's old overseer at Goode's, out to vote for Bob.

Nov. 11. Sunday I went to Burkeville to hear Rev. Mr. Virginius Wrenn, of the Episcopal Church, and brought him home with me to spend the night. Monday we walked together

[186]There was a custom among fox-hunters of naming old and wary foxes which had survived many chases. Elsewhere reference is made to "old Mrs. Gus Vaughan."

to Royall's pines, where I gave the "Passen" some account of the Jenningses, Roger Pryor, the Laniers. He knew Sidney Lanier during the war when stationed near his house in Isle of Wight. He was in love with Miss Jenny Hankins, daughter of Gen'l John Hankins, of "Bacon's Castle," Surry Co.

Nov. 14. Hunter, Leon and I go to "Barebones" to pot hunt. First time I have seen the old place since the fire. Nine chimneys like lonely sentinels keept watch over the Revolutionary ruins.

Nov. 17. Explore Penick's Mountain and the head waters of Sandy River, going as far as Green Bay after the fox today.

Nov. 20. Go into the Little Creek country, where the day is passed amid the gloom and relics of "Somerset." Visited the grave of Dr. John S. Hardaway, killed by Bacon, and dying, July 4, 1818. O! I cannot look upon these memorials of a civilization that is past: it is all gone—in the future, the future everything lies.

1907[187]

Oct. 26. Amelia Court. Connie and I drive down to "Oak Grove" in Terrapin Neck to see the Taylors. Go by way of Bridgeforth's Mill. All the family there but George Keith [Taylor], Courtney [Taylor] and Courtney Keith Meade.

Oct. 30. Got up at day and went with the General[188] after the "varmint." From the crest of the hill west of Joe Wilson's old place had beautiful view of the Appomattox just before sunrise. The fog was spread out over the valley for six or seven miles in view and the spot commands a view of as large an area as any, if not more than any other, on that river. Found the fox on his heels north of Green's Road in front of Daniel Robertson's old place (formerly place of Gov. Giles, for whom he was overseer) but got run in Mr. Willson's low grounds. He ran hard and straight down the river and up Wintercomack Creek to bridge (Green's Road), thence across through Hiram Scott's to Namozine Road, where Hays killed the negro, then up and in the road, across the creek again to Cousins's and went in hollow tree in that place at head of Giles's old mill pond. George Keith Taylor and I took her, and carried her home.

Oct. 31. After a visit to Mr. George K. Taylor of several days Mr. Taylor took Constance and me to Wilson's Depot, where we took train for Forest Hill. I am grateful for the opportunity of introducing Connie to my old and true friend, whose kindness and hospitality have in years gone helped me over many heavy days.

---

[187]No diaries, 1903-1906, have been found.
[188]Probably General Bradley T. Johnson.

Nov. 5. Went to Nottoway to vote at Crewe. Voted for H. E. Lee for Commonwealth's Attorney; DeWitt Maxey, Sheriff; G. P. Adams, Treasurer; and J. A. Sydnor of Amelia, House of Delegates (all Democratic nominees) and Judge Mann for Senate. No opposition to any.

Nov. 6. Powhatan Court. W. R. Davis, Democratic incumbent for Sheriff, defeated by eighteen votes by Baugh (Republican). No nominations. Willis B. Smith, Jos. P. Sadler, Haskins Hobson, W. M. Justis, Milton P. Bonifant, attorneys in attendance—also W. V. Thraves, the last three residents of the county and the former ex-residents.

Nov. 7. Another criminal case and chancery cases today. Among the jurors was Robert Lee, son of Charles Carter and nephew of the General; a man of ordinary parts but with some resemblance to his uncle. Spent the night at "Erin Hill" formerly Col. Wm. C. Scott's, where my mother lived about 1858.

Nov. 9. Up at day and with Willie Thraves hunting. A nondescript pack of some fifteen dogs, old and young and crippled. Raised the fox at sunrise at Sampson Jennings's north of and perhaps on "Mill Quarter" where Hilary Harris used to live—now the property of Edmondson of Pittsburg. Had close run but the pack could not keep together and the fox would have gotten away if he had left the neighborhood, but he doubled and doubled in the woods between Fighting Creek and the Court House until after an hour and a half he was wound up in the scrub-oak bushes near young Nicholl's house on Fighting Creek.

Nov. 11. Chesterfield Court. Grand Jury Docket called and a Chancery Suit from Nottoway disposed of (Wing, Eby and Gravatt, Attorneys). E. R. Williams, E. P. Cox, Isaac Digges, F. T. Sutton, of Richmond; Judge J. M. Gregory, of Chesterfield; E. H. Wells and D. L. Pulliam of Manchester; George Mason, Carl Davis, and R. H. Mann, of Petersburg; Hunsdon Cary, of Richmond—Attorneys in attendance.

Nov. 21. Southall Farrar, of Notoway, took dinner with me; travelling for the State Board of Agriculture—experimental farming.

Nov. 25. Richmond. Forty years ago today, as Grandma Watson told me, I was ushered into this world in time for supper. Since then I have seen many changes in my individual, family and public fortunes, but time has given me beyond my deserts and I have no reason for discontent. I and mine are without want, spared great bodily affliction, respectable in station and have the kindly regard of many friends and neighbors. Wrote my mother.

Dec. 3. Drive with Constance to dear old "Walnut Lane" in Hanover. First time we have been there together in years.

Dec. 4. Go to Nottoway Court House and spend the night with Judge Mann. Passed through snow about old Mrs. Sutherland's tavern.

Dec. 5. Nottoway Court. Many of the county officers qualify, among them Peter Leneave for Overseer of the Poor for his district, T. P. Robertson relieved from payment of the poll tax—a Confederate soldier disabled by years and disease. Wm. H. Mann, G. S. Wing of Prince Edward, Henry E. Lee, W. M. Gravatt, T. F. and Allen Epes, A. C. Eby, Meade Haskins, attorneys in attendance.

Dec. 13. Frank White, living on Little Nottoway, a native of Lunenburg, good Confederate soldier and citizen, died yesterday.

Dec. 16. To Dinwiddie Court *via* Seaboard Air Line Ry. Attorneys present: George S. Bernard, George Mason, Chas. T. Lassiter, C. E. Plummer, R. H. Mann, Paul Pettit, Carl Davis, P. H. Drewry, of Petersburg; G. S. Wing, of Prince Edward; T. Freeman Epes, Nottoway; B. J. Epes, of Dinwiddie; E. R. Williams, Richmond.

Dec. 17. Dinwiddie Court. Easy day. Home with Judge Epes, "Gatewood," one and a half miles S. W. of Court House, once the home of Thos. Thweatt, whose daughter old Frank Jones of Nottoway married. It has an oak grove and is a very pretty place for a level piney country. The Judge has been lately paralyzed and is impaired in speech. Told me he was reluctant to qualify as Commonwealth's Attorney lately elected for 1908-1912.

Dec. 18. But little business at Court. Night at J. Y. Harris's—where Maj. Roney used to live. Judge Mann and Henry Lee argue a case from Nottoway in vacation. Spend night with A. M. Orgain, one and a half miles east of Court House—place he built. Mr. Orgain was member of Dinwiddie Cavalry and my father's regiment.

Dec. 20. Dinwiddie. Walked to Chamberlayne's Bed—two miles northwest of Courthouse, where the fight of March 30, 1865, took place. Mrs. Harris told me she visited the field after the battle. On the slope of the hill by the road and southwest of Nott's house, she remembered seeing a good many dead horses and one Yankee, partly buried. On the other side of the creek she found some fifteen or twenty Confederates in the house at Dance's and the Blue House. Said several Confederates were killed in the creek at the ford.

Dec. 22. Left Richmond at 12:30 for Dinwiddie. Rode out to Five Forks horseback to see the battle field of April 1st, 1865. The Confederate earthwork is extant all the way from the Forks on the north side of and immediately beside the White Oak Road to a point one-half mile or more east, where it bends off in a northeast course a hundred yards or more. At some points no embankment is visible. West of the Forks, after going some distance up White Oak Road, you again find it—now on south of road three quarters of a mile perhaps, on "Burnt Quarter"—S. Y. Gilliam's—ending in the vicinity of a large white oak which was undoubtedly there in '65. There is a cannon ball hole in the house at "Burnt Quarter," fired by a Confederate gun. The chimney of the house was knocked down. Night at G. W. Galusha's.

1908

Jan. 2. At Nottoway Court. I appointed E. M. Jones sheriff in place of DeWitt Maxey who tried to commit suicide. I appointed Jones upon condition that he file his resignation with the clerk to be accepted by me, unless he henceforth continued to be absolutely sober. W. H. Mann, Meade Haskins, C. F. Goodwyn, H. E. Lee, T. Freeman Epes, Allen Epes, A. C. Eby, and W. M. Gravatt, of Nottoway; G. S. Wing, Prince Edward; J. T. Thompson, of Farmville; R. G. Southall, of Amelia; Sidney Kirkpatrick, Lynchburg; J. Tinsley Coleman, Lynchburg; and R. B. Davis, Petersburg, in attendance as attorneys.

Jan. 3. No criminal cases this term. Jury and civil cases today. Spend the night with E. M. Jones on Whetstone Creek. Valley Shore told me today of the death at Clayton, N. C., of my old school teacher Mrs. Lelia H. Shore. She was a native of Norfolk (her maiden name being Hendron, I think), the widow of John Shore, of Nottoway, and came to "Woodland" to teach the neighborhood school about 1880. She was a modest, gentle, Christian woman—pretty in appearance and attractive in manner. I learned nothing from her but what was right. Her only child, Kate Epes Shore, is the present Mrs. Thomas, of Clayton. Mrs. Shore died of consumption and had reached, perhaps, her sixty-fourth year.

Jan. 10. Wrote Mrs. J. F. Epes today, the anniversary of Jimmie's[189] death.

Jan. 11. A. D. Watkins, of Prince Edward, and Robert Turnbull, of Brunswick, are feeling the political situation toward making a stand for Congress against Lassiter this fall.

Jan. 15. Frank W. Christian, a lawyer considered at the head of the Virginia bar, was buried today. He was a native of Richmond, but spent his boyhood in Petersburg.

Jan. 16. Today I was re-elected judge of the Fourth Circuit for the term of eight years, beginning February 1st, 1908. The vote was unanimous, I hear, in the General Assembly. I have seriously strained my health in work on the circuit, but there is great compensation in the respect and cordial support of bar and people, so kindly manifested.

Jan. 18. The third anniversary of the most important event in my life.

Jan. 22. William V. Thraves, of Powhatan, left tonight for Oklahoma to try his fortune in the Southwest. He was a toler-

---

[189]James F. Epes.

ably good fox-hunter, but came to the bar too late, I fear, to master the black letter.

Jan. 23. Amelia Court. R. G. Southall, Thos. R. Hardaway, J. M. Turner, G. K. Taylor, Jr., Meade Haskins, Wm. M. Smith (Cumberland), attorneys in attendance.

Jan. 28. Special grand jury summoned to investigate the illegal sale of whiskey in Amelia, there having been no license to sell in that county since 1903. Y. E. Booker, foreman.

Jan. 30. Trial of felony case [in Amelia Court], finished this evening. George K. Taylor, Jr., for defense, made his first speech at the bar. Was more than averagely self-possessed, very good voice, some marks of original thought—and altogether made a better speech than the beginner can claim. He is modest, honest, kind—I hope he may do well.

Feb. 4. Forest Hill. Walk at nightfall down to the hill overlooking the park (Forest Hill Park), and take shelter from the falling snow under the cedars where old Holden Rhodes is said to be buried.

Feb. 5. Writing letters to Powhatan asking to get that county out of my circuit, which is too large.

Feb. 6. Warm as spring. Go to Moseley's Junction to meet E. A. Baugh, Sheriff of Powhatan County and qualify Sampson Jennings and Paul Michaux as his deputies.

Feb. 10. At Chesterfield Court. Take Petersburg Electric Ry. at foot of Perry street (South Richmond) and go to Centralia, thence by "ambulance" (bus—Ward and Lyne competing lines) three miles to Court House. About one half road has been gravelled and the trip is not as bad as it used to be. Set cases up to the twenty-second.

Feb. 12. Forest Hill. Attended meeting at the schoolhouse at Forest Hill, where the neighbors decided to organize an Episcopal Church, to be known as the Church of the Good Shepherd. There is no church here at present, but the schoolhouse is used as a place of union service between the different denominations. Bishop Randolph[190] was present and approved. There are about twenty-three Episcopal families on the Hill.

Feb. 16. Every evening before sunset may be seen long lines of crows flying up the river over Forest Hill, always going west, in the same direction, as far as eye can reach. This has continued a week or more.

Feb. 17. Went to Capitol this morning to see Judge Mann, Mr. [John B.] Watkins, etc., and had bill introduced transferring Powhatan to Fifth Circuit.

Feb. 18. Wrote Ned Jones today accepting his resignation (which he was required to file on his appointment in January) as Sheriff. It was painful to me and hurtful to himself, I know. All the influences have been exhausted on him.

---

[190] Bishop Alfred Magill Randolph.

Feb. 20. Appointed today John B. Tuggle Sheriff of Nottoway.

Feb. 24. Met parties interested in the Church of the Good Shepherd at the house of R. H. Smith, Forest Hill.

Feb. 25. John B. Tuggle qualified today as Sheriff of Nottoway in place of E. M. Jones. He was a valuable and patriotic Democratic election judge in the "dark days," and his appointment is largely in recognition of this.

Feb. 28. Meade Haskins died in Blackstone last night after a brief illness. He was the son of Dr. Richard E. Haskins, and his mother was a Thweatt. He was born at his father's place in Brunswick Co. His mother was a daughter of Mr. Archibald (I think) Thweatt, of "Eppington," on the Appomattox in Chesterfield.

March 7. The Senate passed the bill taking Powhatan into the Fifth Circuit this evening.

March 9. The House of Delegates passed the Powhatan bill today.

March 11. Came to Memorial Hospital at four-thirty, P. M. to be operated on by Dr. George Ben Johnston for appendicitis. Assigned to room no. 1, 1st floor, s. w. corner, window opening on inner court yard. Room memorial to Anne Johnston. Had for nurse assigned me Rebecca Bland, granddaughter of Dr. George C. Bland of "River View" and "Greenhill"—a kind and efficient girl.

March 20. *The Times-Dispatch* contains account of the death of Capt. Wm. E. Royall, of Powhatan, at near ninety. He was buried at "Spring Hill," the paper says, the old Royall place. He was the surviving brother of our old family physician in Nottoway, Dr. Benj. N. Royall. This family went from Charles City County to Powhatan. Mr. Tyler while President offered to send one of the family to S. America as Minister or Consul, but he declined in favor of one of the Crumps—this was either Capt. Royall's father or uncle, the former I think.

March 25. The Doctor bade me goodby this morning and told me I could move this evening. John B. Watkins and J. A. Sydnor (Senator and Delegate in Legislature), Dr. R. S. Powell, E. B. Lewis, B. A. Lewis, H. H. Valentine and his son, the Supt. of Schools of Brunswick, came to see me. Valentine once gave me two hounds (Rena and Roxy)—feather tails. About four I made Forest Hill without mishap. I am grateful to the kind Providence that has returned me home again in some measure of health and strength.

April 4. About one or two o'clock in the evening of Tuesday, April 4th, 1865, Sheridan's cavalry reached "Woodland," my grandfather's home in Nottoway, traveling the Namozine Road. My grandmother said two horsemen in Confederate uniform and representing themselves as of Fitz Lee's cavalry were the first to come, asking for dinner, which being supplied, on leaving they informed her that they were Yankees and that the army would soon follow. In a short time, she said, the woods and fields were literally filled with them. My father, who was in hospital in Farmville, started home, walking. He told me that late in the evening he found the Namozine Road at the woods so packed with Yankees passing (I think towards Burkeville) that he had to wait till towards dark before he could cross the road to get home, where he found the Yanks in the house and he went to the kitchen to get something to eat.

April 19. Forest Hill. Went walking with Gus Royall and William [Thornton] Gilliam. Mr. Gilliam says his grandfather was Colonel William Thornton, of "Oak Hill," on Willis River in Cumberland, who was a very large land owner and a very wealthy man. He was married three times—first Anderson, second Burton, and third Scott (as well as Mr. Gilliam remembered): The first wife was the mother of Colonel John T. Thornton. There were his mother, Mrs. Gilliam, and several sons, one of whom lived in New York at the time of the war and sided with the North. The brother in New York left descendants. Colonel Thornton is buried at family place in Cumberland.

Dec. 3. Nottoway Court. Long docket—cases set up to fifteenth. W. H. Mann, G. S. Wing, H. E. Lee, F. L., Allen and Louis Epes, W. M. Gravatt, F. S. Kirkpatrick, and H. H. Watson (qualified this term), attorneys present.

Dec. 5. Go to "Woodland" with Jim Wooton, one of the jurors. He has bought and is repairing the old tavern at Jennings Ordinary.

Dec. 21. At Dinwiddie Court. Night at Judge Epes's. Big white oak fire. The Judge says sometime in the 50's Mr. Harrison Hobbs, then about 80, and who lived to be 90 years old, told him that General Scott[191] was born at a place west of the railroad depot and a little northeast of the Methodist Parsonage, some hundred yards or more away, and moved with the family to their later home on Laurel Branch. The former place was called Walthall's. Also Mr. H. said Scott practiced law at Dinwiddie a few years, but did not succeed. He was too pompous in manner for the public.

Judge Charles F. Goodwyn died this night at Nottoway Court House, a native of Greensville [County] or Dinwiddie [County].

Dec. 23. Spent last night with Mr. A. M. Orgain, clerk. He woke me in the morning, bringing to my room a bottle of whisky, sugar and water. This custom is fast passing away, surviving with only about half a dozen or so people of my acquaintance in the limits of my circuit.

Dec. 25. Forest Hill. Every body sick. First time in my life that I have not been at "Woodland" on this day.

---

[191] Winfield Scott.

1909

March 26. Powhatan Court. Attorneys present yesterday: T. R. Hardaway, J. M. Turner, George K. Taylor, Jr., Amelia; H. H. Watson, Nottoway; J. T. Thompson, Prince Edward. The new clerk's office in Court House square now occupied, the records having been moved in since last court. The old office still stands on the side of the railroad near the side of the old Court House which, they say, occupied the site of the present railway track. Powhatan Court closed a very remarkable term today, having in one week tried and sentenced five negroes to death for the murder of Mrs. Mary Skipwith and Walter Johnson at "Northeast" in the Genito neighborhood. Their bodies were burnt up in the house.

March 31. W. F. Jackson, of Amelia, died at his home last night. He was the son of Francis Jackson and his mother was a Wills. He had been a lawyer and once member of the Legislature and more recently prominent in Farmer's Alliance politics. He was a member of Amelia Cavalry, C. S. A., very good man; hospitable and lived well.

Spent the night with John Vaughan, who lives at Joe Leath's old place. Patrick Allen was there and sat late telling me of my father's army career forty-four years ago. "Old Rack" talks well.

April 7. Court in Petersburg. Went with Willie McIlwaine to Blandford to burial of Matt. Bland—a son of Dr. George C. Bland, of Nottoway. It was his aunt Miss Nannie Bland that Willie McIlwaine said his uncle Roger Pryor told him was the prettiest and most brilliant woman he ever saw.

Dec. 13. First rain of consequence for several months, breaking a drought almost unprecedented in Virginia. Wells in many places have failed and the streams very low.

Dec. 20. Open Dinwiddie Court. Night at J. Y. Harris's. R. H. Manson, of Lunenburg, there. Confederate Monument erected in public square since my last term. The face and head of figure not good. Governor Swanson delivered the address.

Dec. 23. Open Amelia Court. No crowd and few lawyers. Judge Farrar's picture put on wall of Court House since my last term. Adjourn Court this evening until January third.

Dec. 25. Forest Hill. Attend services at the Church of the Good Shepherd, Rev. Mills Colgate Daughtry [first pastor of the Church of the Good Shepherd] to dinner with us.

Dec. 30. John S. Taylor and Thos. E. Woodfin, two old Confederate soldiers of Chesterfield, to dinner with us. "Col." Southall[192] here to spend the night.

---

[192] R. G. Southall.

1910

Jan. 3. Went to Amelia on early train. Found Robert Turnbull, of Brunswick, one of the candidates for Congress, on train. He is a little uneasy about his nomination. R. G. Southall, T. R. Hardaway, J. M. Turner, George K. Taylor, Jr., and J. G. Jefferson, Jr., of local Bar, in attendance upon Court, and H. H. Watson, of Nottoway, and Henry Riely, of Richmond. Only 238 poll taxes paid in Amelia to qualify for the Congressional Primary, January 25th. There are some sixty or seventy Confederate soldiers left in the county.

Jan. 4. Hunter told me today that Mrs. S. A. Thursfield ("Aunt Sally," as every body called her) died last Friday, the last day of the year. She had lived at the Ordinary so long she was part of it. She was Sally Ann Crafton, born some seventy-five years ago on Ledbetter Creek in Lunenburg. She had some eccentricities and was a landmark in our little neghborhood.

Jan. 6. Appointed H. F. Green Land Assessor for Amelia with the hope that land may be raised in its assessment. It is for the most part now assessed much below its market value.

Jan. 15. Read in the paper of the death yesterday or Friday of B. F. Williams near Jennings Ordinary. He was a native of Pennsylvania, but of New England stock, the family tradition was. He bought some years after the war "Ingleside," the home of Robert F. Ward, and lived on a part of the place since subdivided. He was one of the carpet bag regime elected to [State] Senate 1879, but revolted against Mahone and became one of the "Big Four" who rendered Virginia valuable service. He was a lay preacher in the Methodist Church and a good man but the climate of the South never softened his nasal twang.

Jan. 23. Read "Mississippi As a Province, Territory and State with Biographical Notices," etc., by J. F. H. Claiborne—a somewhat scathing but very interesting book. The sketches of George Poindexter, Robert J. Walker, Wm. M. Gwin and Jacob Thompson are especially good. I note from his book that Peter Randolph was appointed judge by Mr. Monroe in 1823 for the U. S. Court, Mississippi. General Jackson recommended Poindexter. Randolph then lived in Wilkinson County.

Jan. 25. Went to Crewe to vote. Roads in bad state. Vote of Nottoway rather small. Watkins carried all the precincts—got 322; Turnbull, 34; Lassiter, 33; Cocke, 84.

Jan. 31. Calva and I go out with Joe Vaughan hunting down Namozine Road. Jump deer in "Barebones," upper end near "Ingleside," ran down the country through Cardwell's and Joe Vaughan's; crossed the road at Buck Jones's and thence through Bob Bland's (Billy Hastings's and Jack Welch's) and down Little Creek. Got some of the dogs back at "Somerset," where we raised a fox but lost him. Some years since I was at "Somerset." The stumps of the locust avenue on both sides leading to the house still standing and one large oak (perhaps the largest in Nottoway). The tomb-stones and house in state of dilapidation.

Feb. 2. The Congressional District Committee met today and announced canvas of the Primary Return as follows: Turnbull, 1906; Lassiter, 1732; Watkins, 1632; Cocke, 866;—6136.

Feb. 4. Leave Nottoway for Forest Hill. Spend day at Crewe. Qualify W. H. Verser and James A. Walker Land Assessors for Nottoway.

Feb. 6. Forest Hill. Went to see John C. Robertson, who is in bad health. Called at Mrs. T. W. Wood's to see Mrs. Neblett from Nottoway.[193]

Feb. 13. Have accepted an invitation to deliver an address before the Teachers' Conference of the Fourth District at Petersburg, Feb'y 24th, which gives me great anxiety. I have been so long bound to the practical I don't know how to talk about nothing. Hugh A. White, an old schoolmate of Hampden-Sidney, now of Lexington, here to supper.

Feb. 14. Chesterfield Court. The gravel road between Centralia and the Court House has in some places played out under the saw mill wagons and winter rains. Judge J. M. Gregory, Commonwealth's Attorney, being sick, the criminal cases were continued. Civil cases set up to Feb. 28th. George Mason, J. M. Quicke, Hamilton Wilcox, of Petersburg; D [avid] L. and W [illis] C. Pulliam, of Manchester; Haskins Hobson, J. P. Sadler and Judge Gregory, of Chesterfield, and some Richmond attorneys present.

Feb. 16. Chesterfield Court. Turnbull's account of expenses in the Primary published shows he spent $1300.00.

Feb. 24. Connie and I go to Petersburg to spend the night with the McIlwaines on Washington St. My speech to Fourth District teachers in my judgment a failure. For the first time I tried to read from manuscript. The paper was published in full in the *Index-Appeal* the following Sunday.

Feb. 28. At Amelia Court House to qualify members of the Electoral Board. Grigg has broken up tavern keeping to go to live in Norfolk. The Palmores have taken charge of the old tavern.

March 2. Forest Hill. Start today for Nottoway Court tomorrow. Ride with Alexander Hamilton from Richmond to Petersburg. He said I should go to Congress from this district; that he had told Lassiter he would have supported me against him in the late contest. Walk with Charley Deane up to Tilman Dyson's on the railway.

---

[193]Should be Lunenburg County.

March 21. Got up soon to start for Dinwiddie Court. Large crowd at Court—500 people or more. March Court used to be the turning out day for Virginia people but it is not so generally, these years. George Mason, Chas. E. Plummer, R. H. Mann, C. T. Lassiter, P. H. Drewry, B. J. Epes, A. T. Powell, J. M. Townsend, and R. H. Gilliam, attorneys in attendance— all from Petersburg except the two Dinwiddie lawyers and Gravatt from Nottoway.

March 22. Night at J. Y. Harris's. Walked this evening to "Laurel Branch," the home of Winfield Scott on the slope overlooking Stony Creek about a mile south of Dinwiddie Court House. The old house was standing but unoccupied in 1854 when Judge [Branch J.] Epes came from Nottoway, and was then the property of John F. Young, who lived on the opposite side of the creek (Drury Young's place now) but was taken down after the War and some of the timber used to build a darkey house now belonging to William Mabry (colored).

March 23. Walked over to Judge [Branch J.] Epes's ("Gatewood") to spend the night. He told me there was a Gaines family which formerly lived at Dinwiddie Court House, at the place now owned by Stern. Marcus J. Gaines was sent before the War Minister to Tripoli and married and settled in that country. His brother Lucius Gaines went to Missouri and became, Judge Epes heard, a brigadier-general in the C. S. A. under Price and was killed in battle.

March 25. Court at Dinwiddie. Walked on the old Smith place this morning—the home of Dr. E. Harvie Smith and birth place of John Ambler Smith, M. C. The place is variously called "Village View," "Pea Ridge," etc. Some of the old people are buried there—one or two tombs.

March 26. Finish Court this A. M. and Cutler Galusha sends me by buggy to Church Road. A part of the Confederate earthworks at Five Forks—immediately on the north side of White Oak Road and east of the forks—still stand, after forty-five years. On the right of the road, going from Church Road, and south of Hatcher's Run are the chimneys of an old plantation house that is gone.

March 28. Forest Hill. Get up at 5:30 to start for Amelia Court. Hunter Watson, Louis C. Epes, Nottoway; Walter Sydnor, Hanover; Joseph P. Sadler, Chesterfield; Henry Lee, Nottoway, and the local Bar in attendance.

March 30. Spend night with John W. Vaughan on Beaver Pond Creek—one of the old Leath places, Jos. G. Leath I have heard, who was brother of Jesse and Edward Leath and had a sister who married a Marshall. "Fleetwood" near the Court House Fork of the road from Bridgforth's Mill to Dennisville—a few hundred yards east of the fork on north side—was I think the home of Jesse Leath.

April 3. Forest Hill. Richmond evacuation day (1865). Mrs. Tinsley says the fire swept the city from 14th Street to 7th Street, reaching Franklin Street in places on the north, and the river bank on the south. The Postoffice and National Exchange Bank[194] were the only buildings left on Main Street. The Yankees checked the fire east by blowing up some buildings: that he understood that our authorities set fire to the War and Commissary Department.

April 9. Woodland. James D. Fowlkes told me he had not remembered the day was the anniversary of Appomattox. Said he was with his company (Prince Edward Cavalry) and surrendered there staying until Tuesday evening. John Knight signed the paroles for the Co. (1st Lt. in charge I think). Jim Fowlkes said he did not cut through the lines or get away with any cavalry from Appomattox.

April 10. Went to Harris's Spring[195] for water today. Forest fires have done considerable damage during last week. Smyrna Church (Methodist) on Genito Road and Sandy Creek (Baptist) in Amelia both burned, though the first was thought possibly to have been set intentionally.

April 19. Forest Hill. J. E. Spatig, of Brunswick, here offering to support me for Congress two years hence.

May 1. Got a telegram announcing the death this morning of my old friend, Mr. Albert M. Orgain, Clerk of Dinwiddie. He had held office since the war and had been a member of the Legislature. He was a native of Brunswick County and his mother was a Powell. He was in the army (3rd Va. Cav.) and had carried a ball in his shoulder from the battle of Winchester—1864. A man of good sense, large popularity, an excellent companion and a good man.

May 2. Go to Dinwiddie to attend Mr. Orgain's burial—one of the honorary pallbearers. The burial at the home, about a mile and a half S. E. of Dinwiddie Court House. George Bernard, Alexander Hamilton, Wm. McIlwaine, George Mason and other lawyers in attendance and perhaps three hundred people of the county.

---

[194]No national banks were organized in Richmond prior to April 24th, 1865. Before that time the bank referred to above was known as the Exchange Bank, subsequently the National Exchange Bank, and stood on Main Street, between 11th and 12th (north side), and later the National Exchange Bank and the First National Bank consolidated and became the First National Bank. It occupied the same building—on Main between 11th and 12th—until 1912, when it moved into its new quarters on the south-west corner of Main at Ninth. It still exists (1925) under the name of the First National Bank. The old site on Main between 11th and 12th is now occupied by the Union Bank, which purchased it from the First National.

[195]This spring was within a few miles of "Woodland" and at one time the water was shipped for sale and was supposed to have possessed valuable qualities.

May 3. Dinwiddie. J. Y. Harris and George Mason examined the Clerk's Office in Dinwiddie and found its condition O. K. whereupon I appointed A. M. Orgain, Jr., Clerk of the Court to fill the unexpired term.

May 9. Begin May term at Chesterfield. J. M. Gregory, Jos. P. Sadler, J. Haskins Hobson, L. R. Poole, of Chesterfield; C. L. Page, D. L. and W. C. Pulliam, of Manchester; George Mason, Wilcox, Robert Bass, of Petersburg; Mitchell, Newport News; A. Boschen, E. R. Williams, E. P. Cox, C. R. Sands, J. Samuel Parrish, of Richmond, attys. on hand.

May 12. Did not go to Court House but held Court at Judge Gregory's house.

May 13. Chesterfield Court. Got through early and walked from Centralia to "Bellwood." In the grove there is the grave of Walden, a soldier of the Washington Artillery killed near there May 16th, 1864. Battle of Drewry's Bluff (Beauregard and Butler).

June 4. John Jackson, of Lunenburg Court House, and recently of Richmond, son of "Gen'l." Jackson, and, I believe, a kinsman of mine, was stricken with paralysis yesterday evening at Westmoreland Club and died at 2 A. M. today at Memorial Hospital. He was a man right much out of the ordinary but will be mourned perhaps by few people. He had friends but lived for himself.

June 5. John Jackson buried in Hollywood today.

June 6. Mrs. Dr. Southall, of "Selma," called to see my mother, ill at Johnston-Willis Hospital. E. H. Wells is holding Nottoway Court for me.

June 8. A phone message from Hunter early this morning advised me of my grandmother Horner's death about five A. M. She fell from her chamber window at "Woodland"—the particulars I have not learned, probably they were not known. She was in good health physically, but of late her mind has been wandering. She was in her 88th year; was born in Nottoway at William Jennings's old place near Bell's old field on the road between the Ordinary and Burkeville.

June 9. Went up to Nottoway on the 6:20 A. M. train. The pall bearers at my grandmother's funeral were the young men of the neighborhood. Rev. ——— Conrad of the M. E. Church conducted the services and at four o'clock P. M. she was buried at Ward's Chapel beside her second husband, who died nearly ten years ago. Her only surviving sister and brother— Mrs. Rebecca Vaughan, seventy-six years, of Nottoway, and Caswell F. Robertson, seventy-eight, of Appomattox, were present.

June 21. Dinwiddie. Visited old Sappony Church, the oldest in Dinwiddie. The remains of Parson Jarratt and his wife (who, I am told, was a Claiborne) are beside the chancel, taken, I am told, from Locust Grove, the old Grammar burial ground, since the War.

We spent the night at "Kingston," the old seat of the Walkers and Brodnaxes, founded before the Revolution by Dr. Walker, an English physician of means and large practice. The place now belongs to the Hunts. Two of the main dwelling houses stand and a few of the outbuildings, one of octagonal shape.

June 23. Dinwiddie. Spent last night with Judge Branch J. Epes at Gatewood. The Judge says when the great storm of 1837 passed through Nottoway some hats belonging to gentlemen visiting his father at "Fancy Hill" were afterwards found four miles away in the Cellar Creek neighborhood, east. Says in his younger days the older men in Nottoway were very sober and temperate, and there was no dancing, and this habit did not change until the next generation.

June 26. The Hunts at "Kingston" told me that in the Revolution there was a man of large possessions in that neighborhood by the name of Greenway, who was a Tory and his memory was for that reason not honored, that there was great animosity towards him in those days. They say the Walkers are buried in the graveyard southwest of the house at "Kingston"—some 200 yards—around which there is now the remains of a stone wall.

June 27. Forest Hill. Judge W. E. Homes, of Mecklenburg, spent the night here. I rose at five-thirty to get to Amelia Court. Toney Miller and James Fowlkes walk with me to Presbyterian Church cemetery. Toney went to school with my father at "Miller's Hill." Says my father whipped Jack Fowlkes in a fight at school one evening coming away; the latter was killed at Gettysburg.

June 30. Finished Amelia Court today. Maj. John W. Daniel died after long illness of paralysis last night at Lynchburg about 10:30. I had personal acquaintance, more or less intimate, with him since 1892. In the popular opinion he was the largest man in Virginia for the past twenty-five years and was near to being a great orator in many respects. He was given to periodic intemperance but was a man of high character otherwise.

July 8. Very hot at Court House yesterday (Nottoway). I saw the flag of the Nottoway Cavalry recently sent back to the Governor by some one in Chicago. The flag was given to the company May 15th or 16th, 1861, by the ladies of the county. It was presented by Rev. Edward Martin, the Presbyterian preacher, and accepted by Capt. John E. Jones on the day the company went away—so grandma Watson told me.

July 13. Forest Hill. Randolph Williams and H. W. Anderson, of Richmond, over to see me today to ask me to see Governor Mann and ascertain if there be any chance of his

being induced to appoint Alex. Hamilton, of Petersburg, to the
Senate in John W. Daniel's place. The Governor told me he
had decided to appoint Swanson.

July 14. Connie and I go to Richmond to carry a poor
darky girl to the Johnston-Willis Hospital for Dr. Willis to
examine for goitre. He offers with Dr. Johnston to operate on
her free at Memorial Hospital.[196]

Aug. 3. With County Surveyor, F. L. Dunn, all day on
land near Burkeville.

Aug. 4. Nottoway. Surveying "Buck's old field," formerly part of Mrs. Jeter's tract.

Aug. 6. Connie and I went down to "Old Homestead,"
Mrs. [Samuel] Burke's (formerly Mr. Crawley Jones's) this
evening. Find one of the linden trees and the old mimosa still
there, which I knew in my earlier days. The same quiet, un-
travelled road leading from Ward's Chapel, only wide enough
for one vehicle. They used to call it the "chair," or "chariot"
road, they say, from old Mrs. Ben Ward's (of "West Creek")
coach.

Aug. 21. Forest Hill. Go to funeral of Mrs. Schutte at
St. Mary's Church—first time I ever attended a Catholic ser-
vice save one over Dr. Robert Bruce Stover at the chapel in
Hollywood.

Aug. 24. Mr. [Peter] Tinsley tells me that years ago a
Mr. Goodman, a Jew, tried the manufacturing of matches in
Richmond, but failed and then tried brooms with no more suc-
cess.

Aug. 25. The afternoon paper gave me the first tidings of
the death at his home on Cellar Creek in Nottoway, in his 69th
year, of Hon. James Fletcher Epes—my father's friend and
mine.

Aug. 28. Gholson Robertson, son of John C., died at
Forest Hill today, twenty-two years old.

Sep. 1. Nottoway. Small crowd at Court, and no criminal
cases. A. D. Watkins and G. S. Wing and J. T. Thompson, of
Prince Edward, Thos. E. Watkins, Charlotte, lawyers outside
county in attendance. Robert Jones, son of Jack Jones, of
Lunenburg, who proposes to settle at Blackstone, qualified to
practice law today.

Sep. 2. Some fish beginning to bite at Nottoway Pond
(Fitzgerald's Pond), now called "Crystal Lake."

Sep. 6. Nottoway Court. Trying a civil case, Lee *vs.* Wilson. George E. Caskie and J. Taylor Thompson for plaintiff.
Caskie, of Lynchburg, a son of John S. Caskie, member of Congress from Richmond, whose mother was a daughter of Samuel
Pincham, one of the old magistrates of Nottoway, who lived in

---

[196]This was one of the most remarkable surgical cases of its kind
on record at that hospital.

the Deep Creek country, and whose daughter, I think, got the place known as "Caskie's" on Deep Creek above Spain's Bridge in the division of her father's estate. John S. Caskie's father came to Richmond from Scotland; so says George E. Caskie.

Sep. 13. Forest Hill. Execute several deeds to property in Nottoway—land near Burkeville sold for twenty dollars per acre and the last foot of land I own in Nottoway. This ought not to be, but I have been at great expense this year by reason of sickness in the family, etc., and it is next to impossible to save anything out of the salary of a Circuit Judge, which is $2500, and mileage probably amounting to $250. The price of everything is now very high.

Sep. 21. Dinwiddie. Nothing doing in Court today. Arthur Richardson, Dolly Boisseau and I go fishing in Stony Creek at Roney's Mill, formerly Hardaway's Mill. Caught very good string of pike and red-eye.

Oct. 3. Forest Hill. Left for Petersburg Circuit Court. Go with Dick Mann in evening to Lee's Pond in Prince George to fish. Catch a few and spend night. Prince George is nothing but sand, pines, gum and peanuts.

Oct. 5. Forest Hill. Connie and I go in evening to Petersburg to St. Paul's Church to marriage of Rev. Wm. B. McIlwaine, Jr., and Miss Martin.

Oct. 13. Have been at Forest Hill all week save one day spent at Gregory's Pond fishing with Flynn.

Oct. 16. Reach Forest Hill from fishing trip of two days to Cohoke, King William County, with Tom Owen. Give fish to Quarles, Smith, Gus Royall, and McRaes and Lyons. Did not like mine, cooked for dinner—too soft and swampy. Many say they are not as good as same fish of Piedmont.

Oct. 17. Tom Owen and I go fishing at the Association (Licking Creek) Pond in Chesterfield. No luck.

Oct. 21. Go to Blackstone Fair (the first one). The exhibits were good and the crowd estimated at 5000.

Oct. 31. Go to Petersburg and take 2 o'clock train for McKenney in Dinwiddie where Mr. C. M. Rives met me and we went to his home some three miles off, where I was joined that night by Rev. Reuben Meredith of the Episcopal Church.

Nov. 1. Clear and bright. Mr. Rives, Rev. Mr. Meredith and I start horseback on turkey hunt through old Grammar tract between Lew Jones's and the Plant Road, then at midday across Jones's Road to the north side and hunt on Rocky Run where about sunset we flush nice gang on old Bristow place and build our blinds.

Nov. 5. William S. Campbell, of Charles Town, West Va., formerly of Burkeville, and C. E. Downs, of Roanoke, here this A. M. in automobile from Burkeville—first automobile I ever saw at "Woodland."

Nov. 7. W. H. Verser, Willie Norfleet and I hunt turkey over Flat Creek—mostly at old Tom Overton's over the north side of Ellis's Fork. Some third of a mile, a little north of west, stands a ruined house, lonely and desolte. Verser told me Tazewell Robertson left here for the war and never returned. He was killed in service. I saw the place many years (10) ago and it has not changed in appearance.

Nov. 8. Went to Crewe to vote. Voted for Turnbull and against all constitutional amendments. My wish was to vote against the ineligibility of County Treasurer, but found the amendment tied up and inseparable from the Commissioners amendment, which I do not approve.

E. F. Slaughter ("Old Wheel") Co. E, 3rd Va. Cav., C. S. A., and a friend of my father, died at Nottoway Court House, where he had lived—a wheelright—ever since the war. His death leaves nobody but Judge Mann and E. S. Downs of those who began life at the Court House at the close of the war.

Nov. 9. Hunt with Willie Norfleet and Leon in "Barebones," where we got no birds and saw but few signs of deer and turkey. Saw a beech tree in Barebones Creek with "G. D. Horner, 1850" cut on it—plainly legible after sixty years. Mr. Horner (my step grandfather) lived at that time at the place just south of the creek, now owned by Hamm.

Nov. 16. In Court (Chesterfield) until 5:30. Connie came over from Richmond and we went by Salem Church on way back to see marriage of Mary Cogbill (daughter of N. H. Cogbill) and John Trueheart, of Amelia, son of Batt Trueheart.

Nov. 23. Chesterfield. Got through Court and attended marriage of Mabel Cogbill to Walter N. Perdue at the house of her father P. V. Cogbill just across the road, immediately in front of the Court House.

Dec. 2. Nottoway. Thornton Jeffress at Court—perhaps the last I shall see of "Old Sunday" at Court. He has been a familiar figure and face here at Court and on the bone-yard[197] since 1895. He has recently sold "Mountain Hall" for Mrs. Perkins, his mother-in-law, and I suppose has made his home at Rochester, N. Y.

Dec. 13. Came from Nottoway to Forest Hill. Jim Fowlkes told me at Jennings Ordinary that his father had three brothers: David, who settled in Kentucky near Hopkinsville and left descendants, some of whom went to Missouri; Asa, who lived and died in Petersburg unmarried; and Robert, who died in Petersburg, leaving female descendants. Think old Mot's mother was a Thompson of Lunenburg or Mecklenburg.

Dec. 14. Met Ben Andrews, of Lunenburg, now Capitol guide, in Richmond. He married a daughter of William Hamil-

---

[197] A name given at that period and previously to places to which horses were brought for sale.

ton, who lived overseer of Capt. Dick Irby and was killed at Gettysburg. William Hamilton was brother to Jim Hamilton and son of Davy who, Mr. Andrews says, was born in Powhatan and moved to Lunenburg, where his children were born in the neighborhood of Hungarytown (Hell's corner, I suspect). He says Miss Lucy Hamilton died at his house about three years ago.

Dec. 16. Forest Hill. Went to Manchester today to see several lawyers and visited Squire Cheatham's Court at Oak Grove—Jacobs sitting for him.

Dec. 17. At Court of Appeals Library, Richmond, and attended to some vacation matters in Chesterfield Court with Attorneys Poole, Smith (and Mimms, colored). Called at Auditor's office to see if Frank Ward's pension had been paid.

Dec. 19. Start early for Dinwiddie Court. Long day in Court. Morton Goode and J. C. Blackwell, of Lunenburg—young lawyers—qualified to practice law in Dinwiddie. The former is settled at the Court House and the latter at McKenney. The former is a son of Col. J. Thomas Goode and grandson of William O. Goode, M. C., until 1859. He seems to be well educated but not forceful in his first speech; has good manners. Blackwell, like so many Lunenburgers, is a fiddler.

Dec. 25. We attend Church of the Good Shepherd in the morning.

Dec. 27. Rev. and Mrs. Ben Dennis here to supper. Mr. Dennis tells me he as a ministerial student once supplied a church in Nottoway boarding with Mrs. Hallowell at Burkeville. Remembered and liked Dr. Pryor. Said Dr. Pryor told him his grandmother was a Dennis. Mrs. Dennis was a daughter of General William Terry, of Wytheville. Mr. Dennis has recently resigned his church [Meade Memorial P. E. Church] Manchester. He performed the marriage ceremony for Connie and me, Jan. 18, 1905.

Dec. 29. Connie and I went to "Dundee" to see the Carsons.[198]

1911

Jan. 8. Returned to Amelia from Forest Hill and took dinner with Bob Southall. He and I went in evening to call on Major Charles R Irving—he having moved to the Court House—the last surviving Regt. officer in Amelia. He was Major of 1st Va. Regt. Cavalry, C. S. A. and is disabled from a wound but right well preserved. Is now confined to the house. His mother was, I think, an Eggleston—afterwards Masters—and his wife a Cocke, a daughter of Richard Cocke, a very large planter of Mississippi, formerly of Amelia. His half sister was second wife of Col. William B. Tabb, C. S. A.

---

[198] J. Preston Carson's family.

Feb. 3. Forest Hill. Called on Mr. William E. Neblett, of Lunenburg, at St. Luke's Hospital, Richmond, today. Went to see Gov. Mann to get him to appoint Tom Arvin on Board of Agriculture.

Feb. 6. Nottoway. We had some talk yesterday about my mother's uncle, James C. Robertson—none of us knowing what had become of his family. W. H. Verser told me today (which is correct) that one of his daughters married J. Z. Brown, one Reese Cary, one John Jenkins and one William Tucker (now at Crewe). Jimmy and George, two of his sons, now in railway employment, Crewe; John, another, also in railway employment, married Spott Vaughan's daughter.

Feb. 8. Rev. T. P. Epes died today at Blackstone, after long illness. He was the son of the late Thos. Freeman Epes and ———— Hardaway his wife. He conducted the funeral service of my father and wrote the obituary notice in the *Central Presbyterian* and the *Christian Observer* of Louisville. He was a good man and pastor, and above average in intellect.

Feb. 10. Went to Blackstone to attend Mr. Epes's funeral in the Presbyterian Church; buried at town cemetery. Large crowd in attendance, filling the church and some standing.

Feb. 26. Forest Hill. Went to "Buck Hill" this morning to see Ben Owen and Squire Cheatham about appointing county policeman in place of P. L. Watts. He wants a man named Redford appointed. I will appoint A. T. Traylor.

Ned McGavock and Mrs. W. B. Wilson, of Lynchburg, here this evening and after they left we went down to Mrs. T. W. Wood's to see Mr. W. E. Neblitt, Commonwealth's Attorney of Lunenburg, who was well enough to come from the hospital to his sister's (Mrs. Wood) yesterday.

March 1. Left today for Nottoway Court. Ride from Petersburg with Wat. Dunnington as far as Nottoway Court House. Walk with Charley Deane down as far as "The Castle" now inhabited by Northern people.

March 9. Had long walk up to Capt. Frank Epes's ("Rittenhouse"), from which place I got a peep across Deep Creek about Mountain Hall and Hamm's—my old native heath. Had talk with Crawley Fitzgerald today, son of Jack Fitzgerald of "Walnut Hill." He said his grandfather was Dr. John Fitzgerald (educated in Europe) and that he lived at "Rose Hill," the Presbyterian Manse. William (Poney) Fitzgerald, of "Leinster," was his father's brother. Francis Fitzgerald, of "The Castle," married Catherine Ward and was the father of Benjamin W. Fitzgerald, of "Aspen Circle," and Robert Fitzgerald of "The Castle" and Miss Mary and Mrs. Pryor. Mr. Jack Fitzgerald lived at one time at Lallard's, now Jones's Mill, and east of Blackstone. He married a Scott.

March 18. Jim Wright came down on the train with me from Amelia. He told me he lived at "Winterham" (J. G. Jef-

ferson's) soon after the war and that as much as 3000 bushels
of wheat had been made there in a single crop.
March 19. Forest Hill. Have to go over to Petersburg
late this evening to meet Jim Mann and T. E. Chambers on
the matter of finding a way to have Madison Harris made Auditor. Present man wants to resign.
March 23. Got through Dinwiddie Court this evening and
made Forest Hill at night. Saw Eddie Lewis and Dr. Price, of
Brunswick, on the way. Maddy Harris spend night with us.
Burglars entered the houses of John C. Robertson and Harvey
Williams this night—the first visit I ever knew them to make
in this neighborhood.
April 9. The days of the week are the same as for the
year '65, and in imagination I have this week each day marched
with the Confederate Army on the retreat to Appomattox. It
is known that 24 officers of the grade of Brigadier-General and
above still survive and it may be a few individuals are unknown
and still living. The portraits of the 24 appear in this day's
[Richmond] *Times-Dispatch*. There are about 90 ex-Confederate soldiers living in Nottoway at this time. No country perhaps in history has undergone a more complete change in its
social, economic and political character than Southside Virginia
in the half century which closed today.
April 16. Went to Blackstone this morning. Took dinner
with Maddy Harris and went to "Woodland" in evening, riding
home from Crewe with Rob. Williams. Polk Wiley, Needham
Turnbull and Darrell Perry came in at night.
April 17. Take 8 o'clock morning train for Boydton to
visit my kinsman, Judge Homes. Rain. It has been 12 or 13
years since I was at Boydton. A picturesque old burg with several fine homes scattered about. Judge Chas. Alexander, son
of the late Hon. Nathaniel Alexander, brother of Hon. Mark
Alexander and C. J. Faulkner, Atty., were at Judge Homes's to
meet me at supper.
April 18. Judge Barksdale opened his court today. There
are 14 attorneys living in Mecklenburg. The population of the
county, 28,000. Saw the will of Field Jefferson in the clerk's
office—uncle of Thomas Jefferson.
Walked with Judge Alexander and Miss Homes up to old
Randolph-Macon College this evening. It is a duplication of the
old building at Hampden-Sidney, but less well-built, I think. The
Judge told me the founders incorporated the name of Randolph
in the expectation of getting old Jack's property, and they took
the name of Macon for the sake of patronage in North Carolina.
The building has been used as a negro institution by Northern
educators in recent years, but not much used of late. Two pic-
tures of Abraham Lincoln were the only signs of life I saw on
its walls. Judge Barksdale and quite a number of gentlemen
met me at Judge Homes's for supper tonight—a very well-con-

ducted entertainment. Mrs. Homes was a Puryear, a niece of Professor Bennett Puryear of Richmond College, and kinswoman of Hon. Richard Puryear, of North Carolina, a member of Congress.

Judge Alexander on Events of the Civil War. Judge Alexander told me that he understood, though he did not ascertain positively the truth of the report, that the night after the battle of Five Forks, Pickett, Anderson,[199] Bushrod Johnson, and perhaps others, held a kind of consultation, in which it was decided that they had as well give up and make no further efforts; that this got to General Lee and greatly displeased him, and he ordered Johnson to turn over his command to Wise, and had Anderson arrested. Judge Alexander did not hear of Pickett's arrest. Said he was thrown with General Lee in the West Virginia campaign and heard him tell one of his officers on one occasion that he was conscious of his years and that he was not able to accomplish all that he had been able to do as a younger man. Heard the general say in reply to the suggestion that artillery be placed on a certain mountain that the devil himself could not carry artillery to that mountain top. Never but on one occasion knew General Lee to be cheered by his troops—that was when he left a railroad station in company with President Davis; he was never cheered on the field. Toward the last Jackson was cheered whenever he appeared and sometimes orders had to be sent to prevent it.

He said President Davis was a cultured man of great powers of speech, but not fit for a revolutionary leader. Johnston and Beauregard he thought inefficient—the latter he knew to be so. R. M. T. Hunter knew all the routine business of government and could have conducted with ability any department, but had no backbone. John Seddon told him he subscribed three thousand dollars towards starting *The South* at Richmond, to be edited by Pryor and for the object of securing Hunter's nomination to the presidency. The paper failed. Seddon said Pryor was obliged to fail—that he had no discretion (judgment). Judge Alexander said Pryor wrote out carefully his speeches beforehand, but with this he never could make what you would call a speech.

He said Thomas F. Goode was not a highly educated man but grew mightily as he grew older. He was known as the bulldog of the Secession Convention, but made speeches there that, he supposed, he was ashamed of afterwards; that General Braxton Bragg was born in Warren, N. C. His father was a carpenter, and he, General Bragg, was a brother of U. S. Senator and Governor Bragg and also brother of Judge Bragg of the Supreme Court. The mother was a woman of strong mind who killed a negro once and was tried for murder but was acquitted

---

[199]General R. H. Anderson.

When her son, Captain Bragg, returned from the Mexican war, a great barbecue and welcome was given him and the speaker's stand was erected upon the spot where his mother had killed the negro.

He said Erasmus Kennon Harris had the sweetest voice he ever heard in Mecklenburg.

He said the little town of Helena, Ark. (some 5000 people), sent seven generals to the Confederate armies,[200] among them Tappan, Adams, Cleburne, Hindman (who at 16 commanded a company in the Mexican war, and killed three men in a single combat about politics before he was nominated for Congress at 28). He was a singular-looking man, his eyes so gray as to appear almost white. He was assassinated after the war.

Judge Alexander told me a portion of Sherman's army passed through Mecklenburg on way to Washington after the war ended—a division or so crossed at Taylor's Ferry south of Boydton. That Sheridan's cavalry was sent to Mecklenburg after the war was over to make the people feel the war and for no other object; that they took nearly every watch in the county.

May 6. Forest Hill. Mr. Tinsley says out where the [Catholic home of the] Little Sisters of the Poor [in Richmond] now stands was formerly a place owned by Mr. Anderson, called "Warsaw." John Harmer Gilmer, brother of T. W. Gilmer, he thought married Mr. A's daughter and lived there afterwards; then Andrew Stevenson, minister to Great Britain, lived there. In those days Monroe Park was an old field of blackberries and scrub pine, occupied by a negro woman, the manumitted slave of General Jacqueline Harvie.

May 11. Chesterfield Court. Attended burial of "Dr." Hill [colored], janitor at court for years.

May 14. Clear, the roses in bloom. Mr. Tinsley says he was married on May 13th, 1853, and the 14th there was an inch and a half of snow on the ground in the morning.

May 18. Saw two white women working in the field at Woodcock's Fork on my way to Chesterfield Court House this morning—a very uncommon sight in our country yet, though nearly fifty years since the War.

June 19. Go to Boydton to hold Mecklenburg Court for Judge Barksdale. Carter Glass spoke in the interest of his Senatorial canvass. Very dignified and strong speech, but to a small and unfriendly audience. He left them something to think about.

---

[200]Mr. Biscoe Hindman, of Chicago, Ill., son of General Thomas C. Hindman, states in a letter dated May 21, 1925: "Helena, when the war broke out, was a little city of about three or four thousand people, including, of course, a large number of negro slaves . . . The seven generals were . . . Major-General Thos. C. Hindman, Major-General Patrick R. Cleburne . . ., Brigadier-Generals James C. Tappan, Dan C. Govan, Lucius E. Polk, Chas. W. Adams and Arch. C. Dobbins."

June 22. Heard today from Dick Oliver of the death last Saturday near Mannboro in Amelia of Micajah J. Oliver, one of the best soldiers in the Nottoway cavalry—conspicuous for gallantry on every field, and a life-time friend of my father. He was buried at Salem Church in Amelia and the only member of Company E present was George Hawkes, of Nottoway, now of Amelia.

June 24. Jacqueline S. Epes, oldest daughter of Hon. Jas. F. and Rebekah Payne Epes, died at her home on Cellar Creek in Nottoway this day. She had been long in failing health and was a young woman of more than ordinary mind and culture. I knew her intimately in the life time of her brother and my schoolmate James P. Epes.

June 27. Amelia. Returned from Amelia Court with Mr. George K. Taylor to his home "Oak Grove" in Terrapin Neck.

June 28. Went with Mr. Taylor to see Mrs. "Cajah" Oliver and on our return met with Dick Oliver at Dixie Craddock's. Came back to Steger's, who recently lost his wife. Mr. Taylor told me his house was built by Seth Ward Jones. He emigrated to Miss., the place being bought by Captain Gregory, the father of W. T. C. and Crabb Gregory; that the Gregorys were originally King William people, as were their neighbors, the Quarleses, who were kin. Major W. T. C. Gregory married a daughter of Dr. Joseph B. Anderson, of Amelia.

June. 29. Back to Court House. The Taylors had breakfast at six and we reached Court House at 9:15. Mr. Taylor told me Major Irving was in command of the 1st Regiment of Cavalry at Appomattox; that the command was turned over to him at High Bridge, when their Col., Morgan of Loudoun, was put in charge of the brigade. Said Major Irving was riding one of the handsomest horses he ever saw on the retreat—was dressed well and was an exceedingly handsome man.

July 2. Forest Hill. We went over to Richmond to see the sick—Mr. Whiting, of Hampden-Sidney, my old school teacher, and Mrs. Dr. Garland, of New Kent, at the Johnston-Willis, and Marguerite Quarles at the Memorial.

1914

Jan. 3. Washington, D. C. *Reminiscences of Col. John S Mosby.* Col. Mosby lives at "The Alamo," a little apartment house a few squares from the Cochran, at which hotel we live and comes around quite frequently to see me at night. He has turned his eightieth year, but his mind is clear and his memory extraordinary. He has the lawyer's mind very highly developed. His ideas and language are clear-cut, his conversation very interesting, and his personal experience, of course, most varied. He dislikes, and does not tolerate, any questions while talking, but keeps the floor himself. On this account he is much less instructive than he would be if he would permit a question every now and then. I have jotted down in a disconnected way in the following memoranda some of the many things he said to me at different times of late:

THE LEES:

"General R. E. Lee's father was a Federalist of the strictest sort and he married into the Washington family, so his whole life had been spent in the Anti-States' rights school. Not long before Joe Johnston died I visited him in his home in Washington. In talking of 'Lighthorse' he told me that General Pendleton, who was raised in Louisa, told him an anecdote of an escapade of 'Lighthorse Harry's' while on a visit to that county. He sold the servant and two horses of a friend with whom he had spent the night and who had sent him to take the stage at some point on the road.

"One of his elder sons, Henry Lee, a very brilliant political writer, wrote, someone told me, a large number of 'Old Hickory's' best state papers. 'Old Hickory' gave him a foreign appointment somewhere in Europe; but John Tyler, who was then in the Senate from Virginia, prevented his confirmation.

"General Robert Lee was a poor talker and a poor writer. L. L. Lomax told me he was at West Point with him and he was then known as 'The Marble Model' in reference to his reticence and faultless figure. I never saw him inclined to be communicative but once. In December, 1864, I went to Petersburg to see him and he invited me to dinner with him. After dinner we retired to his room, and for half an hour he seemed inclined to unbosom himself on war matters generally. He was evidently not cheerful as to conditions. He said Johnston ought not to have left the line of the Rapidan, and if he had pushed on northward McClellan would never have occupied the James River Peninsula; and that after Johnston went to the Peninsula he ought to have made a stand in the vicinity of Williamsburg. It was a great mistake to fall back in front of Richmond.

"General Lee on this occasion paid me a very delicate and high compliment. I was on crutches from a recent wound, and as I got out of the ambulance in which I traveled, he, with Longstreet, was standing in the yard and seeing me approach came down the walk to meet me. After receiving me with great cordiality—almost affectionately—he turned to present me to General Longstreet, saying 'General, here is my good friend Col. Mosby; the only fault I find with him is that he too often gets wounded.'

"General Lee was the most combative officer I came in contact with during the war; he took a personal interest in and was always ready for any enterprise which held promise of results. I have great admiration and reverence for the memory of General Lee; he had great ability and was a splendid and well-rounded character, better rounded-out than Washington; but I am not a Hindu and do not worship his name in the fashion of present day Virginians. They seem to invest him with a sort of divinity. I think he was human."

STONEWALL JACKSON:

"I had no association with him in the war; saw him on several occasions and happened to be near him at Second Manassas and at Antietam and observed him somewhat, but without the opportunity to form a mental impression of his personality. In my opinion he was the only military genius on either side during the war. The only man whom the common soldier—who judges by instinct and whose judgment is pretty apt to be right—was inclined to follow in a spirit of fanaticism. He regarded Jackson as the Arab regarded Mahomet."

JOE JOHNSTON:

"I knew all the Johnstons in Southwest Virginia. They were people of fine literary talent and great lawyers. Old Joe was a good writer and a fine talker. He was a fine mathematical general; but took no account of moral and phychological forces in war. He was always complaining of lack of "transportation." He told me it was a great mistake to have held on to Richmond so long; it ought to have been evacuated. On one occasion he told me Longstreet was, in his opinion, an abler commander than Jackson. McClellan was the same kind of man as Johnston; but abler, for he was a good organizer of an army and I don't think Johnston was."

GENERAL GRANT:

"I became a close friend of General Grant after the war and saw much of him when he was President. I never heard him utter a word which could have wounded the feelings of any Confederate. I got him to appoint a good many Virginians to office —all of whom had voted against him—and among them Edward C. Marshall, last surviving son of the Chief Justice. Mr. Marshall had been wealthy, but after the war he had to go to teaching school for a livelihood and would walk to school with his dinner in a little tin bucket."

GENERAL WASHINGTON AND JUDGE MARSHALL:

"Mr. Edward Marshall told me his father told him General Washington got so alarmed at the opposition to the Alien and Sedition Acts he sent for him to come to Mount Vernon and urged him to run for Congress in the Richmond district. He did not want to do it, but the General urged so that after spending the night, he told him next morning he would run and went back and announced himself, beating Clopton in the election. Told me his father said Jefferson had broken up the Federalist party by adopting its principles."

JEFFERSON DAVIS:

"Dr. Fraser, late head of the State Normal School at Farmville, told me that Joshua Hill, of Georgia, a member of Congress in the C. S. A., told him he was riding with Jeff Davis while President on the lines out of Richmond, when they were halted by a picket who refused to let them pass. Davis told him who he was, but the man persisted and Davis started to pass and the man drew his gun upon him; whereupon Davis drew his sword cane and the officer of the day came up in time to prevent a collision. Davis afterwards had the man put under arrest and punished. I think this story improbable and cannot believe it."

GENERAL LEE:

"Only a few men in history deserve the name of great commanders in war. Lee and Jackson, I think, will stand the test, and they are the only ones of our time.

"Lee was cordial and almost affectionate in his treatment of me during the war. I did not see him again until 1868 at White Sulphur Springs, when I greeted him with great cordiality. His response was indifferent and cool. I mentioned the circumstance to General Magruder, who was there at the time, and he told me his conduct had been the same to all the Confederate officers there, and that when Lee met him, notwithstanding their former intimacy, he felt like he had been soused in a hogshead of ice water. [P. G. T.] Beauregard, Lindsay Walker, P. M. B. Young, [Matthew W.] Gary and [John B.] Magruder were there at the time, and during the two weeks I stayed there was no association between them and General Lee, and I was told that his reception of all of them had been the same. It was a matter of remark at the time. I have no explanation of this strange conduct. The last time I ever saw General Lee was about August 1870. He was in Alexandria at Mr. Frank Smith's, and was given some sort of reception, and I paid my respects. When I took leave of him he said (and they were the last words I ever heard him speak) : 'Colonel, I hope we shall have no more wars.'

"I never was able to discover anything which I could call a political principle or a military principle. War is not a science, it is an art. Napoleon made maxims, but broke them all. In war I always considered moral forces of more importance than physical ones."

Elkton, Va.,
July 2nd, 1913.

Hon. Walter A. Watson:

Dear Judge:—

Your letter just received. Thanks for adopting me as your constituent. I do not even know the member from my own district—8th—by sight. In *Virginia* I have been a political outcast. In reconstruction days I was what was then called a conservative. Ever since then I have always supported that party in State elections; because the personnel of the other was too bad. Blackstone would have defined me politically as *nullius filius*. Now I am writing to urge you to come here and spend a few days and bring with you my friend Major Steadman, of North Carolina. I believe I wrote you that this is an ideal spot—on the Shenandoah River—"daughter of the stars"—all that the Vale of Tempe ever was conceived by the poets to be and all that the vale "where the bright waters meet" was in the imagination of Tom Moore.

A member of Congress from Georgia, Mr. Howard, arrived last night with his family.

Stonewall Jackson's army once camped on this ground—on the map of his campaigns this is marked as Conrad's Store. From here he marched to fight the battles that made him immortal. I have been in the house here that was his headquarters. I am, however, thankful that I am not in the sad condition of the Greek, when gazing on the field of Marathon, who standing on the Persians' grave could not deem himself a slave. The spectacle of what is going on today at Gettysburg proves that we never enjoyed so much freedom before. Yet no man feels more pride than I do in the glory of the Southern arms. Now just run up here—bring Major Steadman with you—and refresh yourself in the lithia water and the mountain air.

My regards to Major Steadman.

Yours truly,
Jno. S. Mosby.[201]

Feb. 21. Connie and I dined with Senator and Mrs. Swanson on R Street, N. W., [Washington, D. C.] where Mr. & Mrs. [William Jennings] Bryan were guests of honor. The German Ambassador [Bernstoff] and his lady were present, as well as Admiral Peary. The North Pole discoverer is a rather queer looking specimen—wiry rather than robust. Seems to be a modest man with somewhat restless, downcast eyes. Looks

---

[201]The above is a copy of a letter written by Col. John S. Mosby to Judge Watson and illustrates the poetic and tender nature which lay latent in this unusual man, suspected by none but those who knew him well.

somewhat like Dick Lane of Amelia, though a larger man. He said the atmosphere at the pole was dry and still and he experienced no great discomfort from cold, though he had lost a part of each foot from freezing. Had suffered more in the States. He said the wiry man of average size who weighed not more than $2\frac{1}{2}$ pounds and not less than 2 to the inch of height had most endurance. We all went from the Swansons' to the reception of the British Ambassador, Sir Henry Spring-Rice.

Feb. 23. Saw in papers today notice of the recent death of Mrs. Harvey Wiley at Blackstone (I think she died Sunday). She was a daughter of the late Capt. Giles A. Miller and her mother was a Webster. She married first a Wilson and had a child or children. and then Harvey Wiley, son of Capt. John F. Wiley of Amelia. Until recently she lived at Flat Creek in our neighborhood.

Feb. 24. Mrs. R. T. Jeter, daughter of Harlo Cadwell (brother of Chester Cadwell), died at her husband's home near Lodore in Amelia County, Va.

Feb. 25. A. C. Finley, my old friend of Prince Edward days, helping me in my office.

March 1. Went to Flood's Committee[202] Room at Capitol this evening to confer with him and Hay and Swanson concerning the primary bills introduced in the Va. Legislature. It was decided that I go down tomorrow night to Richmond.

March 2. Leave for Richmond at 4:45 to confer with members of the Legislature respecting the primary bills now pending there. The dominant or "organization" element in the Legislature, though largely in the majority, is lacking in leadership and somewhat cowed by the Richmond press.

March 3. Spent day at Richmond Hotel conferring with friends in the Legislature, and succeed I think in having action of primary law postponed beyond the year 1914 so that our Congressional primaries may not be mixed up with liquor question submitted to people in September.

[Christian] McKinney told me last night that in his youth, after the war, he spent much time at "Saratoga" in Buckingham. Col. Edmund W. Hubard was then living and kept open house notwithstanding the ravages of war. He said the place was one of great comfort. He remembers that gas for lighting was made on the premises. The home of W. E. Gannaway near by was at that time even better kept but had not so much company.

March 4. Got up at 6:30 A. M. and took train for Washington. Connie and I dine with Christian McKinney, son of late Governor of Virginia. He and his wife live at the Cecil. His

---

[202]Henry D. Flood was Chairman of Foreign Relations Committee in the House of Representatives.

mother was a Christian of New Kent or Charles City and kin or connected with the Tylers—daughter of Robert Christian.

March 7. Spent the day at office writing letters and at the Post Office Department over Fourth Class Post Office appointments.

Col. B. O. James, Secretary of Commonwealth of Virginia, and Thos. E. Owen, of Chesterfield, lunched with me at Congress Hall Hotel.

Got P. O. Department to appoint Henry Jones postmaster at Green Bay over Snow, who stood some seventeen points ahead on the Civil Service examination. It was because of the strong local endorsement of the patrons.

March 9. E. B. Lewis, of Brunswick, and I went to the P. O. Department about Meredithville P. O. Found that his man Peterson had only second place on the examination list.

March 10. Judge Henry Wood, of Clarksville, here about the P. O. at Buffalo Junction. Paul McRae, of Cumberland, and Mr. Boatwright, of Buckingham, here to supper (dinner) with us.

March 23. Papers contain notice of the death of Allen Caperton Braxton on yesterday at Staunton. He was one of the best lawyers in Virginia and made more reputation in the Constitutional Convention of Virginia in 1901-02 than any other man in it. He was a genial, kind man of lovable character— a son of Dr. Tomlin Braxton, of King William County, and his mother was a daughter of Senator A. Caperton, of West Va. Braxton was a friend of mine and helped me in my fight for the judgship in the Legislature.

March 28. Arthur Richardson, Lewellyn Clarke, and W. M. Stern, from Dinwiddie, here today about Dinwiddie Court House P. O. I endorse Mrs. J. H. Clarke.

Col. John S. Mosby here to see me tonight (Cochran Hotel, Washington). Sat very late as he usually does. Said his great-great-grandfather, Daniel Mosby, lived at "Gibraltar," in Powhatan, and his grandfather, John H. Mosby, who went from there to Nelson. Dr. Montgomery Mosby lived there afterward, a kinsman and brother of Charles L. Mosby, of Lynchburg. Dr. Mosby's son was made postmaster of Louisville, Ky., by Lincoln. John Brown Tinsley was the owner of "Gibraltar" afterward and had a female school there. Col. Mosby said his father was at Hampden-Sidney. Charles L. Mosby's father was Wade Mosby, a horse racer, the owner of Duroc, sire of American Eclipse. He lost his property, and General John H. Cocke, of Fluvanna, loaned C. L. M. money to take law at the University of Virginia.

April 1. Knox Boisseau and Daniel Dunn, of Dinwiddie, here in the interest of P. O. at Ford. Mrs. Clarke was settled upon as applicant as P. M. at Dinwiddie. She stood second on the list, Mrs. Sterne first. This is the fourth place in the Congressional District in which the P. O. Department has turned down the party standing first in the examination list—Nottoway C. H., Green Bay, Stony Creek, Dinwiddie.

April 5. This day, 1865, the Yankees were at The Ordinary in great force, so the citizens said ("the fields were black with them in all directions"). My grandfather, with his private papers, had taken to the woods on Flat Creek, but was captured somewhere on "Bright Shadows," Mr. Beverley's place, and his papers taken from him. One of these, a Confederate bond, was carried over to Webster's (Harvey Wiley's) and picked up by some of the people on the place. Polk Miller returned this to me some forty odd years afterward. [This bond is now in the Virginia State Library, the gift of Mrs. Watson]. On the night of April 5, 1865, Generals Grant, Meade and Sheridan stayed at Jetersville. The next night Grant was at Burkeville, and the night of the 7th he spent at Farmville. The night of the 4th he spent at Wilson's and of the 3rd at Sutherland's. On the morning of the 6th, Dr. Joe Southall told me, he saw all three of the above at Al. Childress's house, where, he said, they spent the night, but Grant's "Memoirs" does not bear out the impression that they were together.

Robert Shore was born April 5th, 1865, at "Cedar Grove" (Col. R. B. Eggleston's old home).

April 9. Tidings came confirming the defeat of my friend Geo. W. Taylor, of Demopolis district, Ala., for re-nomination to Congress. He is a fine man and an ex-Confederate soldier—a great-grandson of Col. Thomas Taylor, of Amelia County, Va., who removed to South Carolina and owned much of the land on which Columbia is built; he lived to be very old and was called "the father of secession." Taylor was hit harder by the liquor vote than anything else.

April 11. Left office about four o'clock and spent most of the afternoon in Lowdermilk's book store near the Treasury Building. Found sketch of Judge [John W.] Nash in some large volumes published in 1853 by John Livingston of New York bar, under the title "Portraits of Eminent Americans now Living." It was quite extended—saying he was born in Fauquier County 1792, 3 or 4, and read law under John Love, of Prince William County, and settled in Cumberland Co. in 1813; later moved to Amelia, where he lived until about 1830; then moved to Powhatan, where he was then (1853) living. Represented Cumberland, Amelia and Powhatan in the House of Delegates and Powhatan in Senate, where he was speaker. Married three times. His grandson, Dr. Frank Nash,[203] told me one of his wives was Miss Mary Brackett, of Brackett's Bend, Amelia County; his second wife Miss Elizabeth Hatcher, of Cumberland County; and his third wife was Miss Mary Jones, of Caroline County. Dr. Frank Nash was the grandson of the second marriage.

---

[203]Dr. Francis Smith Nash, Medical Director, U. S. Navy, at that time.

April 17. Received tidings from Robert Gilliam, Chairman of the 4th Congressional District Committee, this evening that no other candidate for Congress had filed notice and that I would be declared the nominee without opposition and the primary called for the 18th of June, in case of a contest, would be called off. At one time (in fact ever since the last primary in which I won out by so slender a margin) it seemed likely I would have opposition; but by degrees the thing got further off. There are still many in the district not friendly to me, or rather indifferent. I hope to do enough here meanwhile to overcome this indifference. I have only moderate ability and have to make up in industry for lack of shining qualities.

April 18. Left Capitol at three to get ready for Hal Flood's marriage at All Soul's Church, 14th and L. Sts., N. W., at five o'clock. It is a Unitarian church. It was handsomely decorated with flowers. We had seat no. 5 from front. The President, Vice-President and Mr. Bryan (Secretary of State) sat in the left corner of the church, first bench. The reception at the Pan American Building, whither all went afterward, was very stylish, and agreeable despite the style. Miss Anna Portner, the bride, is a daughter of Robert Portner, of Alexandria, Va. There were perhaps over five hundred invited guests at the marriage; and as almost all officialdom was there, it was held to be and was a social event of the first magnitude.

May 1. Went to Richmond, where the Democratic Committee of the 4th Cong. Dist. met to call off primary and declared me nominee for Congress, which transaction took place in room at Murphy's Hotel.

May 9. Miss Nanny Taylor, daughter of late Dr. R. F. Taylor, died the first part of this week at her brother's home in Amelia (I think on last Sunday). She was buried at "Farm Hill." Also on Monday or Tuesday Maj. Charles R. Irving at Amelia Court House, the last prominent Confederate in my immediate locality. At Appomattox he was in command of 1st Regt. Va. Cavalry, C. S. A. Mr. Geo. K. Taylor told me he was dressed well on the retreat and riding a splendid horse and was a very handsome man. He was born in Terrapin Neck in 1835. Some dozen years ago I attended his wife's funeral at Grub Hill Church. The Major was not present. When I mentioned his death to Colonel Mosby, he said, "Irving was a good soldier."

May 17. We went to the Campbellite Church, where President Garfield used to worship, with Senator Thornton of La. who belongs there. He told me today his father's people came from Spottsylvania Co., Va., and his mother's from Nottoway and that he was a descendant of Judge Peter Randolph.

May 19. Col. Mosby has returned from Toronto, Canada, where he delivered an address on "Stuart's Cavalry at Gettysburg."

May 24. Senator Randolph Thornton, of La., stopped by on his way to church this morning. He tells me he is a grandson of Judge Peter Randolph, of Nottoway. His mother, who died when he was two years old, was Cornelia Virginia Randolph, and her mother was a Cocke. Judge Randolph's mother was Sarah Greenhill, and his father was Peter Randolph. He pronounced Greenhill "Grenle." His mother was born in Nottoway. He has a letter from Judge Randolph's father introducing him to Bishop Madison at William and Mary College. Judge Randolph went to Wilkerson County, Miss., and his son Col. John Hampden Randolph named his plantation "Nottoway." Sen. Thornton had never heard of the Wells trial at Nottoway. Judge Randolph went to Mississippi in 1824 and died in 1832. Senator Thornton's father went from Spottsylvania County to Miss. Judge Randolph was descended from Henry Randolph, who, according to the Senator, was a brother of William of "Turkey Island."

May 21. Saw "General" Coxey of Ohio drive up to Capitol today, with perhaps a dozen followers, in a buggy drawn by a mule, accompanied by his wife, and ascend front steps of Capitol, where he was soon surrounded by several hundred people and made quite a lengthy speech. He drove all the way from Ohio by private conveyance and was much heralded by the newspapers. Twenty-two years ago he came with an army of unemployed from the West and marched upon the Capitol with popular demands. Today he delivered similar demands to Congress. He seemed to me to be an earnest man, and he and his retinue excited my pity

June 8. Went to Hampden-Sidney College and qualified as trustee. Dr. Peter Winston, Dr. Paulus A. Irving, Dr. Chas. A. Blanton, Richmond, Rev. A. M. Fraser, Staunton, Rev. W. C. Campbell, Roanoke, Rev. J. B. Bittinger, W. Va., Rev. F. T. Mc-Faden, Richmond, A. B. Dickinson, Richmond, D. P. Halsey, Lynchburg, Joseph Stebbins, Halifax, A. B. Carrington, Danville, A. D. Watkins, Farmville, H. A. Stokes, Prince Edward, and myself, present.

Aug. 6. Washington. Mrs. Wilson, wife of the President, died this evening about five o'clock, and the House adjourned out of respect for her memory.

Aug. 8. Mrs. Wilson to be buried at Rome, Ga., her girlhood home and where her mother and father are buried. Her father was a Presbyterian preached named Axson.

Aug. 11. Col. Hughes, of Chase City, Mecklenburg Co., here—in trouble with "Pure Food and Drug Act." They don't want him to put "Blood Purifier and Liver Tonic" on the label of his calcium water at Chase City.

Marvin Smithey, of Brunswick, here.

Granville Sydnor, my old class-mate at Hampden-Sidney, is pastor of the Presbyterian church at Rome, Ga., and conducted the burial service of Mrs. Woodrow Wilson there this evening.

Aug. 14. Stayed in the House until about three today and left for Mecklenburg at 4:45 P. M. to speak at the Confederate Reunion at South Hill. Spent night at the Jefferson Hotel, Richmond.

Aug. 15. Took nine o'clock Seaboard Air Line train and was met at La Crosse by automobile party—machine decorated with Confederate flags—Sheriff Jones and Jamieson in the crowd. The former was in 3rd Regt. Va. Cavalry and the latter Cavalry also; Capt., Berryman Green. Had a large crowd in the grove at Methodist church—too large for all to hear my voice.

Aug. 16. Went with Gilbert Saunders to see his father, Archer Saunders, who is very sick in Lunenburg. His people came from upper end of Lunenburg and are kin to me—through the Towlers I reckon. He lives with his son Luther in Lochleven district. Drive to La Crosse with Hiram Wall and Norberne Smith to get 2:40 train for Washington.

Aug. 20. Washington. Dr. and Mrs. Lofton, of Emporia, to lunch with me at the Capitol. She was Miss Tiller, of Emporia; he came from Ga. some years ago.

Aug. 28. Mr. William Gaines, who lived at Gaines Mill in Hanover (the last of the old friends of Mrs. Tinsley) died there yesterday and will be buried at Hollywood in Richmond. He was a native of Charlotte, I think, but married Dr. Gaines's daughter and moved to his wife's father's at Gaines Mill.

Aug. 29. Gordon Vincent here to see me about post office at Emporia. I decide to recommend F. A. Lewis.

Aug. 31. Granville Sydnor, pastor of Presbyterian church at Rome, Ga., here today. I have not seen him since we graduated at Hampden-Sidney, June 1887. He said Ash White had married Abner Hopkins's sister; that Bob Anderson was at Montreat, N. C.; "Seminite" Moore, Tom Jones and Porter Holliday were the only members of our class who he knew were dead. He himself married a daughter of Chas. Lockett, Esq., of Lynchburg and has six children.

Sep. 4. Capt. [J. M.] Harris and W. G. Dunnington here yesterday. The latter said he had on hand about two millions value of tobacco waiting to ship to Europe.

The President read his message to Congress today on the War Tax, asking for one hundred millions of dollars. He looks as well as I ever saw him. The members of Congress always vie with one another in hand-clapping the President when he comes to Congress. They overdo the thing, and many of them, I think, are insincere.

Sep. 5. The House adjourned early till Tuesday, Monday being Labor Day. My father, were he living, would be seventy-three years old today and it has been forty-eight years this day since he and my mother were married at Powhatan Court House. They went to "Woodland" (Nottoway County) that night, where there was a supper and a dance after the custom of the day. Junius Lipscombe, a one-armed soldier of Gettysburg, called the figures. Lieut. Tyree G. Leath waited upon my father. He is long since dead. I can think of none now living who were at "Woodland" that night but my uncle Frank Watson's widow, and perhaps G. W. Leath, and Mrs. Rowlett Perkinson, of Blackstone.

Sep. 8.   G. Stanley Moore, of Prospect, here today.   E. S. Taylor will be appointed postmaster at Prospect.

Sep. 15.   John T. Lewis, of "Grassy Creek," Mecklenburg Co., here to spend the night with us.   Says he is going to vote Local Option and that there has been great change in this direction in Mecklenburg.   He says there are plenty of wild turkeys at "Grassy Creek."

Sep. 21.   Left for Crewe this evening.   Saw [Harry D.] Eichelberger, of Chesterfield, and J. Preston Carson, of "Dundee," Forest Hill, at Byrd St. Station.   Carson surprised me somewhat by telling me he expected to vote dry tomorrow.   Saw Sam Nicholson and Wilfred Epes and Judge Martin Williams and Dr. W. E. Anderson, of Farmville, on the way to Crewe.   I told them I should vote dry and was somewhat surprised when Dr. Anderson told me he would do the same.

Sep. 22.   As I was compelled to return to Washington as soon as possible, I went to the polls at Crewe as soon as I had breakfast, taking with me Haney Tunstall and Edgar Williams— one a leader of the Drys and the other of the Wets—and when I got into the voting room requested them to come into the booth and fix my ticket.   The judges said they would not allow this, and I then told them I had not wished any capital made out of my vote, but as I wanted it known how my vote had been cast I would prepare my ballot openly and for State Wide Prohibition.   Went back to the Ordinary to take the 10:30 train for Washington.   Talked with Tom Williams on the way to Richmond.   Saw Rev. J. S. Peters at Manchester and he said he was glad to hear I voted Dry, but had rather expected me to support Local Option.

Sep. 23.   Washington.   The papers show Va. went Dry by over 30,000—all the cities going that way but Richmond and Norfolk.   I thought the State would go that way by comparatively small majority, but never dreamed that Petersburg and the cities generally would turn up on that side.   Sen. Martin voted Local Option and so did Carlin and Montague; Jones did not vote at all; Swanson's father died that day and he may not have voted; the rest of the delegation voted Dry.   Glass jumped in at the eleventh hour and made a speech at Richmond in which he reflected upon all his colleagues for not having advertised their positions like himself in answer to the inquiries of the *Times-Dispatch.*   Before he made his speech, he told me he had answered the *Times-Dispatch* because some of the Wet people at home had started the report that he had abated in his attitude towards the saloon.

Sep. 24. Went to the White House this morning with the cotton people to see the President and confer with him as to the situation of the cotton crop, which has been knocked out of the foreign market by the war. They want the Government to make a loan of money directly to the cotton planters on the basis of warehouse certificates, etc. We have done many things to alter the character of the Federal Government since we came here a year ago and President Wilson is at bottom a Hamiltonian, but I don't think he will take this step. When I went to the White House, I did not know what would be the demand of the cotton people.

Oct. 4. Connie, Judge Bartlett, of Ga., and I go to hear Dr. McKim at Epiphany. Today was set apart by Presidential proclamation to pray for peace. The Doctor's sermon showed he did not want any peace until Germany was trodden out so she would be unable to put the world to war again. He said war was not always inconsistent with Christianity; that war in defense of country, home and the liberties of the people was justifiable. I went to hear him because I thought a good ex-Confederate soldier, if anybody, had a right to pray for peace.

Oct. 5. Connie and I take lunch with Senator Thornton at the Capitol. He said "Nottoway" was one of the handsomest places on the Mississippi River. It was the home of his uncle John Hampden Randolph, now dead, in Iberville Parish and had passed out of the family. His home at Alexandria, La., he named "Rabbit Foot."

Oct. 8. The cotton and tobacco people have agreed upon a bill to be introduced tomorrow by "Alfalfa Bill" Murray[204] making a direct loan to the cotton and tobacco planter. I attended the caucus. The Farmers' Union agitators are behind it, but there is no chance for it to pass. The war has put an end to cotton and dark tobacco market.

Oct. 9. W. S. Kennedy here from Lunenburg, also Lee Morris from Farmville. He wants the Post Office and had he come earlier would have been the most available candidate.

Philippine bill in the House, Jones[205] very slow in its management. His health is giving way. He is the oldest member of Congress in point of continuous service—24 years.

Oct. 23. Capt. Robert Lee, last surviving son of Genl. Lee, died last Monday night at the home of a relative in Fauquier Co. at the age of seventy. His home was at "Romancoke" in King William County. His sister, Miss Mary Lee, is the only member of the family left. She is in Europe and spends most of her time in travel.

---

[204] William H. Murray, of Oklahoma, familiarly known as "Alfalfa Bill."

[205] William Atkinson Jones.

Nov. 2. Connie managed to walk a few steps today after her long and desperate illness.

Tomorrow is election day and I think for the first time since my majority I will miss casting my ballot. Nobody stands against me for Congress but a man named Herzig claiming to be a Socialist. He lives at Meherrin and is a foreigner I suppose. I never saw him that I remember. I hope the Democratic majority in the House will be reduced to a small margin. It will be better for the party and for the country, and I think will curtail the domination of legislation by the President.

Nov. 6. It seems that I got nearly all the votes cast at the election in our District, though in the absence of contest only a small proportion of the voters attended the polls.

Nov. 10. Sidney Parham Epes, only son of Sidney P. Epes who died in Congress from our District in 1899, died of typhoid fever at Blackstone today nearly eighteen years old. His mother was Lucy Jones, daughter of Capt. A. B. Jones and Fanny Dyson his wife, whose father was Francis Dyson, and her mother ———— Vaughan, sister of Joseph N. Vaughan. Capt. Baxter [Jones's] (Capt. A. B. Jones) father was Capt. Dick Jones, of "Bellefont," an attorney of Nottoway Bar who died before the war. His grandfather was Major Dick Jones, of "Blendon" or "The Poplars," I don't know which. Capt. Baxter's mother was an Epes, sister of "old Freeman" and I remember her.

Nov. 15. Hunter having written me he would be married at Dinwiddie C. H. on the 24th, I wrote Mrs. Judge Epes, telling her Pattie would be an acceptable member of our family and that I trusted serious personal responsibility was the thing Hunter needed most. Pattie Epes's father was Branch Jones Epes, of "Gatewood," Dinwiddie Co., and her mother a daughter of Capt. Doyle of that county. Her grandfather on the father's side was Col. Francis H. Epes, of "Fancy Hill," Nottoway Co., and her grandmother on that side was ———— Jones.

Nov. 19. The Richmond papers contain notice of the death of W. Tazewell Fitzgerald, of Richmond. He was the son of Dr. George Fitzgerald, of "The Glebe"; his mother was a Tazewell. The papers say he was in Confederate Army; I doubt if his name is on the monument in the Court House yard. He was half brother to the late Lt. Col. J. P. Fitzgerald, of Farmville. He was grandson of old Francis Fitzgerald, clerk until 1852.

Nov. 21. We left for home (Nottoway) on the 4:45 train. I was gratified to feel that at last we were able to travel after so much delay. Spent night in Richmond.

Nov. 22. Leon, Hunter and Calva met us in the automobile which Hunter bought this year—the first one owned at home. They have come into use gradually in our county. In Nottoway County I suppose there are now forty machines privately owned and perhaps eight or ten more for public hire at Burkeville, Crewe and Blackstone.

Nov. 24. Hunter Watson and Pattie Epes married at Dinwiddie tonight.

Dec. 2. Leon and I went to "Grassy Creek" in Mecklenburg on Roanoke River to hunt turkeys—the home of John Taylor Lewis.

Dec. 5. Take train at Soudan for home, having tramped far and found no game.

Dec. 7. Go to Farmville to see if I can settle the very bitter post office contest. The opposition to Jim Hart threatens to assail his personal character. I found the town divided into five different factions and most difficult to deal with. Night at old Randolph Hotel.

Dec. 13. Take train at the Ordinary (Jennings) for Washington and reach there at nine P. M.

Dec. 23. Clem Dickinson, member of Congress from Clinton, Missouri, and I spend the night in Richmond at the Jefferson; he is on his way to Prince Edward to spend Xmas at his old home ("Springfield," Prince Edward County) and I, to Nottoway. Said he was at "Inverness" (J. P. Agnew's)[206] in July, 1864, and could distinctly hear the guns at the Crater fight. Said Col. Knight, who married his father's sister, carried him from "Wilton" to hear Jeff Davis's inaugural address in the Capitol Square, Richmond, 22nd February, 1862. Thos. S. Bocock told in his hearing, in a company at "Springfield" (his father's home in Prince Edward, that a woman (he thought a Mrs. Pollard) walked into the Confederate House one day just as he was about to open proceedings and attempted to cowhide Rep. Geo. C. Vest, of Missouri. The officers came up and he told the sgt. at arms to "show the lady the door" and called the House to order.

Dec. 31. Washington. I was awake when the city bells and horns announced the end of another year. The shadows of the great war in Europe have overcast our land for months past and the prosperity of our people has been greatly disturbed. I take leave of this little record with the wish that if I should begin another it may be under brighter skies and with fairer prospects.

1916

Jan. 1. We have been in Richmond for a few days at the Jefferson and have visited a few old friends who have fallen out of sight—Miss Cornelia H. Crutchfield, Connie's aunt, who is about to embark on a new expedition to King William County— an invalid and about eighty; Mrs. Stover, now Mrs. Wm. P. Marshall, who lives in great seclusion near Westhampton; Dolly,

---

[206]Near Burkeville, Va.

our Indian girl, who has married John Howell, an Indian, and recently moved out of New Kent to Fulton in this city; and Mrs. John P. Quarles who lives now on the Midlothian Turnpike in Chesterfield, just beyond the Belt Line Railroad. Went to Eppa Hunton's reception in his new house on Franklin Street just above Monroe Park. His little son is the grandson of two general officers of the Confederacy—Generals W. H. Payne and Eppa Hunton. General Pryor's grandson Walker (and grandson of General Lindsey Walker) is also grandson of two Confederate generals.

Jan. 3. We leave old Virginia for Washington this afternoon, where the Congress reconvenes tomorrow. The session will be long and troublous. "The times are out of joint" and the horrid tragedy now being enacted in all of Europe shows no sign of end.

Jan. 12. Went to see W. A. Jones. He says Senator Martin deserves the credit of being always loyal to his friends.

Richard A. Farrar, son of the late Judge F. R. Farrar,[207] died today aged about sixty years at Jetersville, they say of diphtheria. He will be buried at the home of his grandfather, Dr, R. A. Farrar, at "Mohican" near Deatonville.

C. D. Epes was found dead in his bed at Nottoway Court House this morning. He was son of "Long Dick" Epes, who was half brother to Dandridge [Epes].

Jan. 13. Went to White House with a delegation of Virginians to present Joseph L. Kelly, my old classmate, to President Wilson for Supreme Court appointment. The President looks thinner and older than when I saw him last. His face is one of striking intellectuality. Senator Martin made a strong and most effective statement for Kelly. A. J. McKelway, an old college mate of Hampden-Sidney, called this afternoon.

Jan. 30. Great and extensive disappointment felt in Congress over the President's nomination of Brandeis for Supreme Court. He is a German Jew of very radical and almost socialistic views. It is generally supposed his selection is a sop to the socialistic and labor vote of the country.

Feb. 4. Telegram saying Alexander Hamilton died in Petersburg early this morning. He was sixty-five years old and had been unwell some weeks. Born in Granville (now Vance) County, North Carolina; the grandson of Pat Hamilton, a Scotch immigrant, and son of Robert. His mother was daughter of Hon. Nat Alexander, of Mecklenburg, brother to Hon. Mark Alexander, of "Park Forest," that county. He was among the first men in Virginia, and altogether, I think, the finest gentleman in the State. He was my friend and I am proud of the relation.

[207]Judge Farrar wrote under the pseudonym of Johnny Reb.

Feb. 5. Got leave of absence to attend Alexander Hamilton's funeral. Was honorary pall-bearer and dropped the last flower in the grave at Blandford a little before sunset. There were fewer depressing circumstances than on any similar occasion I ever saw. The music at the church was cheerful, there was dignity but little form and ceremony; just as Hamilton would have had it.

Feb. 7. Sat up most of the night preparing some law references for my speech on child labor delivered on Jan. 26th, but withheld for revision.

Feb. 18. Constance, Madame Tournier and I go to the White House reception where I meet Mrs. Wilson (2d) for first time. Madame Tournier (a French Canadian) has spent much of her life in Paris. She said the French people regarded this war as something inevitable, that they believed they would in the end succeed, but that it would be at the sacrifice of the existing generation of French people—that life and all it held was gone for them—consequently, there was none of the gaiety or enthusiasm so characteristic of these people, but a quiet and resolute dedication of themselves to public sacrifice.

Feb. 22. Flood told me today he would not be surprised to see the country at war by the 15th of March. The President told him and Senators Kern and Stone last night that he thought the Allies' position as to armed merchant ships sound international law and if the Germans again destroyed American life by submarine, without warning and the opportunity to escape, he would end diplomatic relations with Germany; and that in that event he had been strongly advised by the German ambassador his country would declare war upon us. That if the U. S. took part, Germany would be beat by midsummer; that our war would be through navy and commerce.

Feb. 23. Great excitement in Congress among some people for fear of war, and there is strong sentiment for giving way to Germany on the submarine question. It is due to different motives. First, some have considerable German element in their constituencies. Second, some are of German blood themselves and sympathize with that cause. Third, by for the larger number do not think the country could be justified in going to war over what they consider a technical legal question—no matter what its merits.

Feb. 24. I have about come to feel that the cause of the Allies in Europe is the cause of democracy and free government in this age of the world and that if they be beaten America would be left single-handed and alone to confront the great military giant. I sent the President a letter this morning telling him I did not believe the American people wished him to recede in this controversy and that if war had to come I wished the destiny of this great free republic fixed on the side of accepted international law, of the faith of treaties, of the right of unarmed men and of women and children to live, and on the side of democracy against military autocracy.

Feb. 25. Went to Richmond to attend meeting of Hampden-Sidney Trustees. Met Harry Houston, Speaker of the House of Delegates, for first time. Like him very much. Dr. Peter Winston in a little talk gave us delightful reminiscences of the old president's house at Hampden-Sidney, now proposed to be converted into a gymnasium.

Feb. 27. Washington. Connie and I went to supper with Alf Thom. Miss Thom, his sister, told us an interesting story about Governor Tazewell, who was her kinsman, illustrating the change in political customs. The Governor came up late from his library one night to his chamber, and his wife asked him who the gentlemen were she heard come in after she had retired, and why he received them so late. He told her it was a committee of the Legislature which had come to inform him he had been elected by that body Governor of Va. This was the first he had heard of it.

March 3. Newspapers contain notice of the death in Norfolk, Va., of Col. Walter H. Taylor, Adj. General on the staff of General Lee. He was the last survivor of those closely associated with General Lee in life. I knew Col. Taylor, having served on the Board of the Asylum at Williamsburg, Va., with him. He was a rather small, good-looking, quick, active, well-knit man; with marked executive capacity, somewhat impatient of opposition, of high character and forceful. I never heard him talk about General Lee. He was a man of pleasant, but reserved manner, and somewhat high bearing—slightly military.

March 4. No vote in the House today on the McLemore resolution to warn American citizens off belligerant merchant ships, as the President had requested. I think the house will side-step, as the Senate did on the Gore resolution. The whole proceeding is the staging of a comedy in the face of a great national tragedy.

Mr. Harry St. George Tucker and Constance took lunch with me at the Capitol. He told me that George Tucker, once professor at the University of Va., was his kinsman and born in Bermuda. That Senator Aldrich told him he regarded Mr. Tucker as being a high authority on financial legislation.

March 5. Senator Clark, of Arkansas, told me tonight he thought a considerable majority of the Senate favored the exclusion of American citizens from the merchant ships of the belligerents.

I paid Bob Southall yesterday $616.87. The last debt I owe. I have had to be in debt most of my life, and it is a great relief to get out.

March 12. Mr. G. W. Taylor told me today that Dixon H. Lewis and Benjamin Fitzpatrick, senators from Alabama, were brothers-in-law, both having married Elmores of that State, who were his kinswomen. Their father, Mr. Elmore, went from South Carolina to Alabama—Calhoun having defeated him for the Senate in that State.

March 17. Debate began on Military preparedness bill in House. I had intended speaking but could get only fifteen minutes of the five hours allotted to Chairman Hay, and I did not care to work in such short harness, and I did not feel fully prepared—in fact, had expected the debate to begin next week and was preparing myself accordingly.

March 31. Paul McRae here from China. He is U. S. Marshall at Shanghai and brought prisoners here. His home is at Cumberland Court House.

Telegram from Arthur Richardson announcing the death of John Hargrave, Treasurer of Dinwiddie County.

April 2. Was called up before breakfast by Capt. A. R. Hobbs, of Prince George, who came to advise about Peter B. Halligan being appointed Treasurer of Dinwiddie County. I spent most of the day reading "A Diary from Dixie," by Mrs. General Chesnut of South Carolina. She was a clever woman and gives excellent glimpses of Confederate folks in South Carolina and at Richmond during the War.

April 9. Snow this morning. To show how far 51 years have taken us from the mighty events of the past, I have not heard a human being here speak of Lee's surrender today, nor any mention of it in a newspaper. Except for the student and occasionally the politician, the Civil War seems to be forgotten.

April 11. W. H. H. Stowell, who represented my district in Congress after the War and lived in Burkeville (a carpetbagger), came to see me this evening. Says he left before there was any very special bitterness in politics and had nothing but pleasant recollections of our people. Represented the Halifax district first, where he was first defeated by Booker, of Henry; he then beat W. L. Owen, of Halifax, who he says was a Union man. After he came to Nottoway he beat McKinney and next time Judge Mann. Says he and McKinney had joint discussions. He married a daughter of General Averill (M. C. from Minn.) and went from Nottoway to St. Paul. Now living with son, a prof. in Amherst College, Mass. Is a very prosperous and genteel man of some ability.

May 29. Col. Mosby, who has been sick at Garfield Hospital for a week or so and who had expressed a wish to see me last week, I called to see this evening but found he had been taken much worse and was *in extremis*. I instructed his daughter that should he appear well enough and desired to see me she should call me at any time during the night.

May 30. I called at Garfield Hospital to see Col. Mosby this morning, but he had passed away without pain about nine o'clock A. M. He was in possession of his faculties to the last. I think he had not the Christian's faith. He had become quite poor but don't think he was in actual want. He was perhaps the most conspicuous Confederate figure left and certainly the most picturesque. Roger A. Pryor is in the same category, but his Confederate record is said by some to have failed towards the end. He still lives in New York. Col. Mosby will be buried in Warrenton. I regret not being able to go on account of the State Convention at Roanoke.

June 2. State Convention at Roanoke concluded its work in a day. Ellyson, Flood and Glass got some political capital out of the convention. I don't think anybody else did. It was intended I should be chairman of the Platform Committee (Resolutions), but nobody had arranged beforehand for my nomination and others got ahead and put up Addison, of Lynchburg, and, of course, I was unwilling to contest for it. The platform, though, was my draft, so far as the rehash of trite political generalities could be said to be anybody's.

I am nominated the third time for Congress—the last without opposition. The time for entry in the primary expired today.

June 3. Left Roanoke at 12:10 for Lynchburg and return to Washington at midnight. Saw beautiful sunset over the Blue Ridge across the hills of Nelson.

APPENDIX II.

WALTER A. WATSON

A SKETCH

By Constance Tinsley Watson, "Woodland," Nottoway County, Va.

Walter Allen Watson was born November 25, 1867, and was the son of Meredith and Josephine Leonora (Robertson) Watson. His family for several generations had resided in the counties over which he was to preside as circuit judge, and later to represent in the halls of Congress. His earliest ancestors came from England and Wales. Colonel Jesse Watson, who was appointed by Thomas Jefferson in 1780 lieutenant of a company of militia of Prince Edward County, Virginia, who was raised to captain in 1782 and made colonel of Virginia militia in 1803 and who served at the battles of Camden and Guilford Courthouse under a Captain Allen, was his great-grandfather.

His infancy and childhood were passed on his father's plantation, "Woodland," near Jennings Ordinary, Nottoway County, Virginia, and in his early years he was seldom more than a few miles from that neighborhood.

His education began in a primary school taught by the estimable and beloved Mrs. Lelia Shore. After a few years at this school and up to thirteen years of age he attended what was known as "old field schools," where instruction was thorough and where the relations of master to pupil were so intimate and affectionate as to enable the master, both by example and precept, to inculcate those principles of conscientious attention to duty, of purity and honor, which made of the youth of that day the intellectual and incorruptible men of later years.

He was not reared in affluence but in the unpretentious though comfortable conditions common to farming communities at that time and in a section of the State upon which the losses incident to the Civil War had fallen hardest. It became inevitable, therefore, that work upon a farm should be a part of his training; and so far as such experience must have gone towards stimulating industry, independence and originality, doubtless a deep impress was left upon his future character and habits.

It is during this period he acquired that fondness for the open, that knowledge of the habits of the denizens of the forest, and that keen sympathy and understanding of the simpler folk which as a man led him to seek his recreation in the solitude of the woods, his labors in the service of mankind; and which gave to his conversation and writings unusual freshness and figurativeness. He thought in terms of broad humanity, he wrote and spoke poetic prose.

Tradition and local history were the themes which in his youth he heard most discussed around a fireside where gathered representatives of four generations:—his great grandmother, both his paternal and maternal grandparents, his own parents, and his brothers and sisters, eleven in number. Here he heard much of tradition, anecdote and personal experience covering more than a century of time; and here was laid the foundation for that passionate love for his community and State which ever characterized his utterances and largely influenced his every act.

His deep devotion to home at an age when usually the desire for adventure and outside contact is strongest is expressed touchingly in a letter written by him when only seventeen years of age to a relative who was traveling extensively. It says: "Now let us talk something of things nearer home, things which wherever we journey always appeal to our interest. For over every vicissitude or joy in life, beyond every ambitious dream, we love and can never forget the sweet white face of the angel that guards the door of home, and over every thought of self we hear the still small voice that whispers to the soul from the spot that gave it birth."

With unswerving fidelity to this feeling, he went through life in every change of circumstance, whether it were achievement which brought conspicuous honor, or discouragement and disappointment; even through outraged gratitude and broken confidence.

None of these; nor the offer of flattering business connections; nor the lure of financial benefits could break the chain which bound him to the place of his nativity. His fondest longing was for the time when he might retire to the quiet of the country and spend the evening of his life under the trees beneath whose spreading branches he had whispered the hopes and caught the visions of his boyhood. And to the day of his death he suffered many sacrifices to prevent the passing into alien hands of the old farm on which he first saw the light of day and which was endeared to him through tenderest memories.

At the old academy at Worsham, Prince Edward County, Virginia, a preparatory school for Hampden-Sidney, under the direction of the venerable Dr. Thomas Wharey, was continued the instruction which was to equip him for his place among the learned of his day; and he had often been heard to say that the high standards and uplifting influences of that wonderful old school, at this formative period of his life were among his most vivid recollections and among the strongest influences of his life.

Arriving at Worsham, he entered Prince Edward Academy

in the year 1880, at the tender age of thirteen years; a timid and unsophisticated country lad, he had much to learn besides what was contained in books, and he related many amusing incidents of his struggle to maintain himself without awkwardness, and even sometimes without tears, in this his first absence from home, among strangers.

He was a student in that school from 1880 to 1884. In 1884 he entered Hampden-Sidney College, from which he graduated in 1887 with the degree of A. B. His interest in his Alma Mater never lagged and he esteemed it a high honor when in 1913 he was elected a member of her Board of Trustees. He delighted in the gathering together of her former students, and among his papers were found an amusing illustration of this in what are probably the only minutes of the Hampden-Sidney Alumni Association of Nottoway County. They are in his handwriting, and read as follows:—

"At Nottoway Court House, June 21st, 1893, Hampden-Sidnew Alumni Association organized. Present, Hon. Chas. F. Goodwyn and Walter A. Watson.

"On motion of Walter A. Watson, Chas. F. Goodwyn elected President, and W. A. Watson authorized to act as Secretary *pro tem*. The following ex-students of the College were elected members: Dr. Jos. A. Jones, T. E. Epes, James F. Epes, Freeman Epes, R. W. Tuggle, Peter B. Epes, Emmet Robertson, F. W. Epes, T. F. Epes, A. B. Jones.

"Adjourned to meet on call of the President.

WALTER A, WATSON,
Secretary, *Pro Tem*."

Leaving Hampden-Sidney College in 1887, he taught school in Nottoway County for a year, and October 4, 1888, matriculated in law at the University of Virginia.

Returning to Nottoway in 1889, he began the practice of his profession.

At the age of twenty-four, in 1891, he was a member of the Virginia Senate. He was its youngest member, as he often was of bodies with which he was associated in large responsibilities.

The keynote of his character was unselfishness, and in no act of his life, private or public, did he disregard the rights, the necessities or the happiness of others. Without greed, without vanity, without ostentation, he sought only to render service, and counted sacrifice no loss.

In 1893, by reason of the death of his father, he became the responsible head of a large family, with the affairs of a hopelessly involved estate to settle. Unflinchingly he devoted himself to all the obligations and self-denials which such a situation involved, meeting this as he met every crisis of his life with undaunted courage and self-effacement. It was a crucible from which his nature came all the sweeter and finer for the test. On June 6, 1895, he qualified as commonwealth's attorney of Nottoway County and filled that office until 1904.

His was the privilege to have lived through the period which "tried men's souls"—the transition period immediately succeeding the War between the States—and his earliest ambition lay in the hope that some day he might aid in averting the dangers which menaced his people in the changed social and economic conditions, conditions such as only the highest courage and the best intelligence could meet without being destroyed in the contest. This ambition came to partial fruition in the part he was destined to take as a delegate to the State Constitutional Convention of 1901-02, in which his influence was in no small measure felt in the framing of a constitution which lifted for a time from Virginia a burden under which she had been stumbling and straining for many years, and which like a cancerous growth had threatened the very vitals of her body politic. Of his speech in that convention on the education and political status of the negro it was said, "It was universally regarded as a classic and is entitled to a high place in the records of American oratory."

The United States Department of Agriculture sent to each member of this convention a small oak tree (pin oak) with the request that it be planted as a souvenir of that epoch-making assembly; and the one sent Mr. Watson was not only planted, but kept well cultivated and trimmed, and still stands on the crest of a gently sloping eminence in front of the house at his old home in Nottoway, a fitting memorial to the labors and accomplishments of a loyal son of Virginia and of a noteworthy and distinguished gathering which performed for the State the most valuable service of any since the stifling curtain fell at Appomattox.

In 1904 upon the death of Judge Beverley A. Hancock he was elected judge of the fourth judicial circuit of Virginia. The *Times-Dispatch* of January 12, 1912, in referring to the close of a famous case in which he presided, said: "When he vacated his chair on that dramatic night in September, 1911, he ended a trial which demonstrated Virginia justice—a model and a marvel among the States of the Union."

On January 18, 1905, he found the fulfillment of a long delayed hope in his marriage to Miss Constance R. Tinsley, of Richmond, Va.

His serious mind was in strong contrast with his buoyant spirit and youthful appearance. With the zest of a boy he could enjoy a fox chase or a good story while with gravity and fine judgment he could meet the most trying and responsible situations.

Of none was he so exacting as of himself and he adhered rigidly to the old idea that a man's word should be as good as his bond, recognizing no difference between a moral obligation and a law-bound written contract. Avarice he condemned in no measured terms, and for political greed he had neither patience nor tolerance. Pursuant to this conception of right, and being unwilling to fill one public office while seeking another, he resigned from the bench in 1912 to offer for a seat in the Congress of the United States, and having conducted a successful campaign entered upon his duties as congressman from the fourth district of Virginia in March, 1913, serving through the sixty-third, sixty-fourth and sixty-fifth Congresses, and being re-elected to the sixty-sixth Congress without opposition.

In Congress his views on constitutional questions carried weight, and his argument against the constitutionality of the first child labor law was a conspicuous contribution to the House debates, his view being subsequently upheld by the Supreme Court of the United States in declaring the law invalid. He numbered among his friends in Congress those of opposing political faith as well as those whose views agreed with his own. Mr. James Mann, the then leader on the Republican side of the House, said of him: "Walter Watson was the most lovable man I ever knew. Sagacious, learned and courageous, he was upon the floor a formidable foe, but in the most heated arguments he was never led into a discourteous or inconsiderate remark—he had the power to argue without disputing, to differ without intolerence."

He belonged to no clubs or organizations except the Sons of Confederate Veterans and the order of Free Masons into which order he was initiated as a very young man July 8, 1891.

In 1906 he was elected a member of the Phi Beta Kappa fraternity of William and Mary College, and in 1912 honorary member of the newly-installed chapter of the Phi Alpha Delta Legal fraternity at Washington and Lee University. While deeply conscious of the honour conferred in neither case did he become a member, not having found time to attend for initiation.

Neither in political nor private life was he a reformer in the commonly accepted sense, but he was an uplifter through the quiet force of his example, and everyone who knew him was the better for having passed his way.

Reared by a faithful, intelligent and unselfish mother, and with the example of an upright father, there was no act of his life which brought them sorrow. He was a credit to their instruction and an honour to their memory.

He was brought up in the Presbyterian faith and early united with that denomination. While never conspicuous in the work of the church his religion was a vital reality and was reflected in his every act. He gave of his time and slender means freely and ungrudgingly to the relief of suffering and need wherever he found it, seeking no proof of deserving save the need itself He was a devout and unquestioning believer in the loving mercy and justice of God and no lateness of the hour, no weariness of the body nor fag of the mind made him neglect or forget, each night before he slept, to bend the knee in supplication and thanks to his Creator. Being asked by an old gentleman who had never found the consolation of faith to suggest a text which might help one groping for the light, he replied, "I have always found comfort in the words 'Lord, I believe, help Thou mine unbelief'."

He had many times expressed the opinion that the memorial exercises customarily held at the Capitol following the death of a member of Congress was a perfunctory and harrowing form which he thought had outgrown its day and should be abandoned. In conformity with what she knew would be his desire, his widow requested the omission of these formalities, the day for which had been set as Sunday, February the twentieth, nineteen hundred and twenty-one.

Few men ever rated themselves so modestly. Even to the one who knew him best and from whom he withheld no confidence he uttered no word of self-commendation at any time, considering, as he did, every honor conferred upon him, not so much a tribute to what he was, as to the standard he was endeavoring to maintain. Every height scaled was to him but a sight of a further and a worthier goal. His last words were, "So much to do and so little done."

When he entered into his great reward that Christmas Eve in the year 1919, it might deservedly be said of him:

"He scarce had need to doff his pride or slough the dross
     of earth—
E'en as he trod that day to God so walked he from his
     birth,
In simpleness, and gentleness and honor and clean mirth."

WALTER A. WATSON

As a School-Boy

By W. H. Whiting, Jr., Hampden-Sidney, Va.

The Prince Edward Academy was owned by a number of gentlemen in the vicinity of Worsham, Va., who had bought the old court house property when the people of the county voted to make Farmville the county seat. Of this corporation the late Joseph D. Eggleston, M. D., was the president and B. J. Worsham, Esq., was the secretary.

For some years the Academy was in charge of Professor James R. Thornton, and it attained an enviable reputation as a high-grade school. In 1881 Professor Thornton accepted a professorship in Central University, Ky., and the Rev. Thomas Wharey, D. D., was elected to succeed him as principal of Prince Edward Academy—assuming his new duties in September, 1881. He continued to be the head of the institution until June, 1885, when he resigned in order to accept a call to the First Presbyterian Church of Corsicana, Texas.

From the student body which assembled in the old court house in 1881 have come an unusually large number of prominent men. Without attempting an exhaustive list, I might mention the following:—Robert L. Blanton, scholar, teacher, editor; A. B. Dickinson, writer, lawyer, public spirited citizen; J. D. Eggleston, teacher, superintendent, college president; John B. Finley, business man and active in public affairs; P. Frank Price, D. D., prominent missionary; John M. Hart, lawyer, state senator, Federal collector; A. J. McKelway, preacher, editor, publicist; J. F. Rice, lawyer and Democratic leader in S. C.; Walter A. Watson, lawyer, orator, statesman.

To be a leader among boys like those in Prince Edward Academy required rare gifts of head and heart and a forceful personality. Though very young when he entered the school, Walter Watson was soon regarded as one of the leaders and so remained throughout the period of his residence as a pupil in the Academy.

I remember well the day he came and his first connected sentence on arriving. His father, Meredith Watson, Esq., drove up from his home near "Jennings Ordinary" in Nottoway County in a buggy with his son to see him safely started on his academic career. Walter was just thirteen years old at this time. After greeting the newcomers, Dr. Wharey turned to Walter and asked, "Did you find the ride a tiresome one?" The boy replied, "It was a lonely ride, and I was mighty glad to see the clump of locust trees in the distance, and I told papa that must be the place, for old court houses always have locust trees around them." He thus early evinced powers of observation which became one of the marked traits of his maturer years.

As his teacher, I was much impressed with the fact that he felt and expressed interest in everything. So many young people assume the *blasé* attitude, the I-know-it-all manner, that I felt it as a real inspiration to teach a boy of brains and intelligence who really enjoyed meeting new facts, who relished new ideas, who liked to face new combinations and adjustments of familiar things. This frame of mind and attitude towards his work made him a most interesting and successful pupil, albeit his active mind would often evolve curious and baffling questions. He was never willing to take things on faith but wished to have the why's and wherefore's carefully set forth. Thus leaving no enemies in his rear, his progress was rapid and his mastery of his subjects was unusual.

I do not remember that Walter took much part in the sports of the boys; but in those days athletics in our institutions of learning had not taken the centre of the stage as is the case today. The Academy had a literary society in which the pupils took great interest. On Friday nights the pupils and the public assembled in the school auditorium—the old court room—to hear declamations, orations and debates which were most creditable and much enjoyed. These exercises must have pleased the spirits of the old lawyers, one-time practitioners at this court,— Henry, Randolph, Anderson, Flournoy, Thornton, and the like— if spirits revisit the scenes of their earthly labors. Of this society Walter Watson was one of the moving spirits. He prepared himself with great care and put his best into ever exercise. Most of his fellow students were his seniors; but they all knew that in him they had a foeman worthy of their steel. Woe to the opponent who made an unskillful thrust or left a point unguarded!

The fence around the school yard had a flat top—a sort of board finish—and this was one of Walter's favorite places for the preparation of his speeches, and he often might have been seen walking around on this precarious path, utterly oblivious of the outside world, every now and then stopping to emphasize a point and to get a proper gesture.

For a part of the period of his stay at the Academy, he boarded at "Slate Hill," an ancestral home of the Venables, in the family of Mr. John Venable. Mrs. Venable tells me that it was a favorite practice of Walter's to take Mr. Venable's old dog out to the corn-house with him and to make the dog stand at attention while the youthful orator practiced some oration or debate. The dog seemed to enjoy the proceedings thoroughly, and would listen most attentively until the rehearsal was over. The Literary Society[208] offered a medal for excellence in debate, and I remember how Walter struggled to have the award made by a committee of gentlemen of the community rather than by a vote of the society itself. He thought, very properly, that young and immature boys would not be competent to pass on the merits of a debate; and, further, he realized that some might be swayed by personal feelings and that an impartial verdict might not be reached. The pupils of the school had done me

[208]This was known as the Academic Literary Society.

the honor to elect me the president of the society; and Walter came to me to bespeak my support for his plan and invoke my aid and influence. I agreed fully with his position—particularly as I had reason to suppose that we had some wily politicians among our members. A rather stormy meeting was held to decide the method of holding the election of medalist; the society voted down Walter's proposition, and the issue was decided by "popular vote." Walter was awarded the medal by a large majority; but I think he was disappointed that the award was not made in a different way. (This was the only medal ever awarded by the society and is now in the possession of Hampden-Sidney College, having been presented to that institution by Mrs. Watson after her husband's death).

The boy's interest in politics was remarkable and his grasp of the issues and his knowledge of the men who figured in State and National politics were unusual. It was a great delight to him to discuss these matters with the gentlemen with whom he met; and we were often amazed at his clear comprehension of the political situation and its causes. To those who knew him at this period of his development it was not surprising that later he was one to whom the State looked for guidance.

Thus early did he show industry, perseverance, enthusiasm, courage, love of justice and fair dealing—traits of mind and character which made him a marked man in later life. And besides, there was that sweetness of temper, that charm of manner, that winning smile, that poise and dignity, that purity of life, that steadfastness of purpose which made men trust him and bound them to him as with hooks of steel. I suppose no boy who ever attended Prince Edward Academy enjoyed in fuller measure than did Walter Watson the esteem and confidence of his fellows, of his teachers and of the community.

After three sessions at the Academy, he entered Hampden-Sidney College in the fall of 1884 and he graduated as a Bachelor of Arts in June, 1887. Of this period of his life I cannot speak from personal knowledge as I moved to a distant field of labor, and before my return, he, with all the boys of his class, had left Hampden-Sidney and taken up his life's work elsewhere. But I have heard Dr. Richard McIlwaine, late president of the college, time and again express his admiration for his old pupil as a man of wide reading, of trained intelligence, and of high character. So, I take it that we may assume that his development was steady and continuous and that the fine traits of mind and character, so prominent in the school-boy, matured during his life in college. Walter Watson impressed himself upon the friends of those early days, and they still remember him with the warmest feelings of affectionate regard.

WALTER A. WATSON

As a Student at Hampden-Sidney College

By J. D. Eggleston, Hampden-Sidney, Va.

The old proverb that "the boy is father to the man" was never truer than in the case of Walter Allen Watson. When one studies his career and personality after he reached years of maturity, it is easy to go back and see that the characteristics which distinguished him were in the germ in his school and college days.

His good humour; his alert mind; his deep interest in public affairs; his distinction as a speaker and debater; his rare gift for remembering names and faces; his unbounded devotion to Virginia, and especially to Southside Virginia; his fund of anecdotes about people and places—all these were developing in the days of his youth.

Even as a boy he attracted the attention of people of mature years, and it was universally predicted at college that he would enter public life, and distinguish himself. The prophet of his class, J. Cary Alderson, at the final exercises, humorously predicted for him a brilliant career in law and politics; but, as Mr. Alderson says in a recent letter, "it took no prophet to foresee this."

Full of interest and mischief himself, he always enjoyed a joke and delighted in pranks; but his teasing and his jokes had no sting in them. I remember one prank which Watson did not enjoy until it was over. The room of W. B. Hopkins and Hugh A. White, on first passage at Cushing Hall, was just over the recitation room of Professor Walter Blair, our teacher of Latin and German. Sometimes the boys that were gathered in this room were innocently forgetful of the noise they were making, and Professor Blair had to come upstairs to ask for quiet. At other times they were not so innocent. On this occasion Hopkins, Billy Wilson and I conspired against Watson: Hopkins and I got Walter into the former's room and we soon began to make much more noise than was necessary. Hopkins got Watson into a wrestling contest. In a few minutes a heavy step was heard coming up the stairway, and I called, "Look out for Professor Blair!" and dived under one of the beds. Hopkins, of course, dived under the other one, and we both called to Watson to get into the cuddy that was in the room. A heavy step was heard coming slowly up the stairway, and it slowly approached the door. A solemn knock was heard; silence within the room. Another solemn knock; painful silence. A third solemn knock; silence now very painful and intense. Then the door opened and the supposed professor walked in, stood a moment, and then marched slowly across the room toward the cuddy door, which Watson was trying to hold from the inside. Of course Billy Wilson was impersonating Professor Blair, and Hopkins and I had slipped from under the beds and were looking over Wilson's shoulder when he opened the cuddy door, and we beheld Watson's frightened face. It was a picture I shall never forget.

One of Walter's classmates writes me in humorous vein that he is sure that Walter must have given diligent study to Webster's Unabridged Dictionary, as he gloried, when an upper classman, in giving exhibitions of his large vocabulary to some of the green and callow freshmen. And he adds, "I remember him as genial, frank, and full of fun."

Rev. G. G. Sydnor, now of Charles Town, West Virginia, was a classmate of Watson's. He says in a recent letter: "I well remember that Walter was fond of a good joke, and enjoyed getting a good one on the fellows. I also recall the impression made upon me by him in our fellowship in college life—that he had distinct gifts pointing to a successful public career. He was a fluent speaker, and his efforts were characterized by careful preparation. While Watson was in Congress I was passing through Washington and met him. He had me to lunch with him. He showed all the college spirit as of yore. Speaking to me of one of the most conspicuous persons in the public eye at the time, he said, that while this man was a native of the South, he was not characteristically a Southern man, that he did not have the geniality and the temperament of the Southerner. This was not long before Watson was stricken with the illness that terminated his life."

One of Watson's classmates who took great interest in Literary Society Work, as did Watson, was T. Stanhope Henry, now living in Texas. Henry was an unusually fine debater and an attractive speaker. He writes me:

"Watson was well known to me as a student of unusual general knowledge gained from his love of history and literature, and the extensive course of reading that he pursued outside of his regular class work. Gifted with a genial and social temperament, a pleasing personal appearance, fluency of speech, and a good fund of information touching the men and the measures that made the political history of the Colonies, and later the United States, I thought him then one of the best conversationalists and speakers in college, and one of those delightful, companionable persons one is always glad to meet.

"During most of the summer of 1893, I was in Richmond visiting an uncle, William R. Gaines, who had prior to the Civil War attended Hampden-Sidney College, who during the Civil War was a Confederate officer in the Charlotte Cavalry, in which service he had been badly crippled and wounded, and who in 1893 was in charge of the Land Office of Virginia. Here at this time I often met Watson, and then had with him many conversations most pleasant and profitable. He had become attached to the old soldier at the head of the Land Office, and this, taken with the fact that he and I had been in college together, seemed to call forth a delightful freedom on his part in the expression of his views on political, social, and moral questions, from which I judged that his mind had developed along the lines of his early predilections, while his character had been moulded under the auspices of the best traditions and ideals of his native State and county, and withal sweetened and tempered by the immortal precept of the Golden Rule.

"He always met me with that cordial warmth and interest that the few of my college mates whom I have seen in the last thirty-five years have each and all evinced, and with that geniality of nature and sweet candor of conversation that perhaps more than any other gift makes us feel that life is worth living.

"He had become a democrat in a broader sense than that of the political partisan, and I then thought, and still think, that the unpretentious simplicity of his views of life, manners and morals, and the chaste and elevated purity of his ideals, were worthy of emulation by all American citizens who really desire to preserve for their posterity those liberties achieved for them by their ancestors.

"Our departed classmate neither at college nor thereafter, so far as I knew him, lacked in conviction or in the knowledge of those sound principles upon which conviction should be grounded for support, but I never at any time knew of anything he did or said that was discourteous, or dogmatic, or harsh, or ungenerous."

I cannot close this inadequate sketch without including some extracts from a letter written me by another of Watson's classmates, Rev. R. A. White now pastor of the Presbyterian church at Mooresville, N. C. He says:

"I loved and admired Watson. We were classmates, literary society mates. and fraternity mates. Therefore I had a good chance to know him well. He had a winsome personality, and attracted special notice as soon as you came into his presence. His face and form were pleasing, his manners and movements graceful. Much above the ordinary as a youth, he had the gifts of a conversationalist. Hence he was always the centre of a group of his companions, causing them great delight with his inexhaustible fund of anecdote, wit and humor. To get Walter Watson and Billy Wilson together was to assure the crowd that gathered 'a high old time.'

"Coupled with these social traits in his character he possessed the natural gifts of the debater to an unusual degree. It was this he loved above everything else, and it was this that in later life helped to give him the success he obtained as lawyer and statesman. He delighted in mock debates, which he used to start in the boys' rooms at any time, night or day. It made no difference to him which side of the question he was on. These debates were often very amusing. With his keen wit and humorous retorts, he was sure to raise a laugh on his opponents.

"Watson was fond of practical jokes at which he was an adept, and it was very rare that the victim of his fun ever escaped when his plans were once laid.

"This is the youth in lighter vein. But there was a more serious side to his nature. Withal he was a fine student. His brilliant mind grasped things quickly; thus he had more time for fun than slower boys that had to plod along. His knowledge was accurate, broad and full. He simply devoured books, and digested them as well.

"He was one of the best rounded scholars I ever knew. He seemed to grasp and master all branches alike. His mind was under perfect control and his powers of concentration were marvelous. The bent of his mind, however, was in the direction of history and literature. In these he delighted, and of these he was a master. A large part of his time was devoted to the work of the literary societies, for in these his finest natural gifts had ample scope for development. Here he carried off the honors while at the same time standing high in his regular college courses.

"He had a passion for teasing. I recall that he was specially fond of teasing 'Jim' Epes, another brilliant fellow and a great friend of both of us. 'Jim' didn't like to be teased, especially when he had an interesting book. It was under the latter condition that Walter was sure to happen around. He would begin by asking 'Jim' a question or affirming something that he knew the latter would deny. Then an argument would begin, with the usual result that Watson was run out of the room with a poker.

"Thus I might go on with these pleasant recollections of a very happy past, but time forbids. This, however, in closing: In picturing those days, no form stands out upon the canvas with a clearer outline and more pleasing impressions than that of Walter A. Watson."

I knew him when he was a school boy at old Prince Edward Academy. At college he was not my classmate, but he was my fraternity mate, we belonged to the same literary society, and he was my intimate friend. I always loved him, and his untimely death cut short the career of a pure and able statesman, and one of the most delightful personalities I have ever known.

WALTER A. WATSON

As a Student of Law at the University of Virginia

By Hugh Riddell, Irvine, Kentucky.

In the year 1888, he being then not quite twenty-one, Walter A. Watson entered the University of Virginia in the Law Department. The writer was possibly his most intimate friend, and they spent no little time together. He had the most profound knowledge of the political history of the world and had an outlook and vision that was most unusual. The bent of his mind indicated a public career in which his friends predicted that he would become a marked personage. He expressed always the highest altruistic sentiments and his extensive knowledge of men and affairs was such as one would expect to find only in men many years his senior. As a scholar he took the highest rank, and being a graduate of Hampden-Sidney College it goes without saying that he was well trained both in thought and in useful information. Besides this he had a profound knowledge of the history of the world, not only of mere dates and facts, but the philosophy of history as it might be termed; and coupled with that he had an intimate knowledge of the history of every distinguished Virginian as well as of other men of affairs. He possessed an unfailing sense of humor that also characterized his later life. In his manner and intercourse one was reminded of the old fashioned Virginia gentleman. His courtesy of manner and his conversation were typical of a former generation. He was attractive in person and, as stated, possessed a keen sense of humor. His inexhaustible fund of witty and humorous stories made him always interesting and any he told might have been repeated in the presence of any company. By reason of his deep study and wide range of information his opinions were always worth while. He understood the real reasons for things, delving deep into human motives. As a fraternity man he took an active interest in college life and had no little to do with shaping the activities of the student body. He was Acting Recording Secretary for Omicron Chapter of Beta Theta Pi Fraternity from Nov. 4th, 1888, to Jan. 4th, 1889.

"He loved people." They were interesting to him. His intense and passionate love for the South-land was noticeable but never obstrusive. Tenacious in his opinions, he was never dogmatic; clear in statement and profound in knowledge, he was never pedantic. As a companion and friend he was never dull and was always loyal to those for whom he professed attachment. Courageous and unwavering in convictions, he confirmed in his maturity the promise of his youth and vindicated the judgment of those who predicted that he would be wise in council, clear in thought and sound in reason. Through all this his modesty was apparent and he appeared unconscious of his gifts and of his many pleasing and entertaining accomplishments.

WALTER A. WATSON

AS NEIGHBOR, FRIEND, AND PUBLIC SERVANT

By J. M. Harris, Blackstone, Va.

The superior qualities of heart and mind of Walter Allen Watson were observed early in his childhood. His precocious mind, contrary to the inclination of most children, was restless for development. Before his age permitted him to go alone to the "old field" school, he attended his first school session mounted on the back of a faithful manservant. At this early period his first teacher saw in him character, ambition, a strong mind, and quick perception. Those natural endowments developed at private schools, Hampden-Sidney College and the University of Virginia. He was distinguished by high standing in each institution as he advanced to the completion of his education. In recent years no son of Nottoway has been more admired, more honored and more loved than Walter A. Watson. This esteem and confidence of the public were reflected in his faith in and regard for his countrymen, and mutual affection resulted.

Young Watson and his political associate and intimate friend, Sidney P. Epes (later Congressman), both under twenty-five years of age, joined their efforts to rescue their county from negro domination then flourishing under Republican rule. Their success was an example to the rest of the congressional district, which rallied to the leadership of these progressive young patriots, and democracy was safely enthroned in the "Black Belt" of Virginia.

Watson's qualities as a thinker, a speaker and a safe leader in public affairs were early recognized beyond his county limits, and as soon as his age would permit him to take a seat in the Senate of Virginia he was elected to that branch of the Legislature to represent the counties of Nottoway, Lunenburg and Brunswick. Watson's habit of thorough preparation for every service to be rendered caused him to spend the time between his election and the session of the Senate in the State Library reading Virginia political history, with the result that in all debates in the Legislature pertaining thereto he was regarded as authority. His brilliant record and faithful service as Senator made him a statewide figure and secured him friends and political influence, which he never lost but added to, until his untimely death while giving his services to the nation in the halls of Congress.

The first official service rendered his county was as commonwealth's attorney. This office brought him in close contact with practically every citizen of the county, and in this position his home people placed the highest value on his qualifications. The bar and citizens of Nottoway boasted that no similar office in the State was filled by his equal. His judgment in dismissing indictments which he decided were not in reality "true bills" was not less applauded than the vigor of his prosecutions when he detected guilt in the "defendant at the bar." The position of attorney for the commonwealth affords the best test of character, impartiality, justice, judgment and general ability. He who occupies it is a protector and adviser for all with right motives, and a deterrer and punisher of all evilmindedness. His duties are not influenced by fees. His obligation is to protect the innocent and prosecute the guilty. The Commonwealth expects his judgment and sense of justice to determine his course. If a lawyer successfully fills this position, he is equipped for the highest call of the people. The subject of this sketch possessed every requirement mentioned and also the courage to apply his talents impartially for the cause of right.

Later on while chairman of the Democratic Committee of his county, Walter Watson prepared for adoption by that committee the well-known "Nottoway County Resolutions." These resolutions forcibly and frankly declared the danger to the morals of young democracy should the political methods used to maintain white supremacy in Virginia be longer and unnecessarily continued; and, the State now being able to finance a convention for the framing of a new constitution, notice was served on the State in these resolutions that the young democracy of this district demanded of the Legislature a Constitutional Convention, in order to provide an organic law that would legalize the elimination of the illiterate and vicious voter. These resolutions deeply impressed the people of Virginia, and newspapers used them as a standing advertisement until public sentiment demanded a new constitution and the convention was called.

[In the Convention he took a very prominent part. He was especially interested, however, in the question of suffrage, which was discussed for a long time in the caucus of the Democratic members of the Convention, and it was here that he especially shone.

Mr. Harris wrote some account of this, which has been, however, omitted, because Mr. Alfred P. Thom has contributed a special chapter on Judge Watson in the Constitutional Convention].

Upon the death of Judge B. A. Hancock in 1904, Walter Watson was overwhelmingly elected by the Legislature of Virginia judge of the fourth judicial circuit. This extended his personal contact to citizens of adjoining and other counties, and he became as greatly esteemed throughout a large territory as he was in his home county. After a distinguished service on the bench for eight years, and presiding over the trial of some of the most noted cases in Virginia court records, he was elected to Congress from the Fourth District, which included, with one exception, the counties forming his judicial circuit, which counties gave him a large vote. Having served his constituents with ever increasing ability as State Senator, Commonwealth's Attorney, member of the Constitutional Convention, and Circuit Judge, he was re-elected to Congress for four consecutive terms. He died after three surgical operations for mastoiditis while a member of the House of Representatives in the Sixty-sixth Congress of the United States.

In this mere chronological recital of his public career, I cannot record his many qualities of heart and mind, nor his accomplishments in the many responsible positions to which he was called. I can only refer to his fitness and to his characteristics.

Walter Watson seemed never to forget the faces and names of people he met, and when they were first presented to him, he would usually be able to say of what family or from what county of the State they came.

As a student, a lawyer, or civilian Watson's remarkable memory enabled him to retain whatever he learned from books, conversation or testimony of witnesses before a trial court. So safe was his memory that he was seldom known to make other than mental notes. He was employed by the prosecution in a murder trial in Dinwiddie County, the people of which county were at the time strangers to him. As many as twenty negroes testified in this case. They were negroes who "looked alike" to most strangers, yet when Attorney Watson summed up their testimony in his speech to the jury, without a written memorandum, he not only readily recalled the full name of each witness and what he said, but did, as to many of them, tell how the witness expressed himself and how he appeared while testifying. So accurate was Watson in reproducing for the jury all the facts and phases of the testimony that opposing counsel did not secure a single contradiction by referring to court stenographers' records. His memory never failed him. The terms and conditions laid down by the young attorney in accepting this case were told to me by the gentleman who engaged his services. I will relate them to illustrate the humanity, the fairness, and the pricelessness of the motives that controlled him. When asked to take the case and name his fee, his reply was, "I will think the matter over and let you know tomorrow whether or not I can undertake the case for you, but I will say to you now that I will not accept a fee for prosecuting a man for his life." In a few days he agreed to conduct the prosecution upon the further condition that he reserve the right, after hearing the testimony of the witnesses, to ask the jury for an acquittal if in his judgment the evidence justified it. The result of the trial was a verdict of death, asked for in a strong appeal to the jury by this conscientious prosecutor.

Necessarily, the positions of honor and trust voted him by the people made him a conspicuous figure in the public eye. His real gratification, however, was not in public admiration and applause, but rather in the approval and affection of those who knew him well. He valued and enjoyed social intercourse with his friends, and among these were numbered the rich and the poor, the cultured and the plain people, and they in turn loved and enjoyed him. His sympathetic nature, his cordial manners, his high and noble purposes, his brilliant and cultivated mind, his lovable disposition, his attractive face, made friends of all who knew him, and retained them always.

While he zealously spent his life repaying in acceptable service the honors and confidence bestowed upon him by the people, he always looked forward to the time when he would return to private life among the people of his native county and join them in a manner of living more suited to his simple tastes. Shortly before his death he set a near-by date when he would enter this retirement in which to spend the evening of his life. He did not, however, contemplate a selfish retirement from public duty. The principal factor in reaching the decision to refuse further public service was that he might have ample time to serve his people by writing a history of Southside Virginia, for which history he had accumulated much data, but to which he had not applied the genius of his talent in preparing it for publication. His taste and capacity for acquiring such information were so generally known by the people of Nottoway and adjoining counties, that it had been for a long time a common wish of those people that he should complete the history he was preparing to write. He loved to learn of the generation that had passed away—people who had occupied the homes, cultivated the fields, traveled the roads, and rested in the cemeteries of his county. His vacations for rest and pleasure were mostly spent in searching the court records and tombstones for such information as to people and landmarks as could not be acquired from books or living persons. He was too much a servant of the public to become a "trained huntsman," but his fox and dog friends knew his fondness for "the chase," and there were invitations always from many places throughout his congressional district awaiting his opportunity to join in that sport for which he had a natural and cultivated fondness.

Judge Watson loved the rural life, with its old homes, log fires, private libraries, forest and field, and unceremonious neighbors. Rarely, if ever, were combined in one person such qualifications for public life and such a disposition to live a quiet and retired life. He was congenial with the most distinguished company and companionable with his less educated associates. He saw merit in his friends, whether they were public men of high rank or plain citizens of honest purposes, and he was alike appreciated and esteemed by all classes.

As a conversationalist Walter had few equals. His broad views, fund of information, splendid humor, attractive voice, and modest, yet forcible expression, made him the most agreeable and instructive person I ever knew. He was a good listener, patient, sympathetic, and attentive, showing interest in all with whom he conversed.

The most prominent characteristics of his heart and mind were honesty of purpose, accuracy of conclusions, indifference to personal gain, loyalty to friends, fondness for local genealogical and topographical research, a wonderful memory, consideration for humanity and reverence for God.

His county people only loaned him to the State and Nation, and great was their sorrow when his return was intercepted by the angel of death. His ashes rest in peace in his family cemetery at "Woodland," Nottoway County, his life-long legal residence—where he was born Nov. 25, 1867, and where he was buried December 26, 1919.

WALTER A. WATSON

IN THE CONSTITUTIONAL CONVENTION OF 1901-02

By Alfred P. Thom, Washington, D. C.

For a number of years prior to 1901 there has been a growing demand in Virginia for a convention to revise and amend the State Constitution. In common with the other States of the South, Virginia had for 45 years been confronted by a race problem of enormous and threatening proportions. To deal with it effectively, large abuses had grown up in the election methods in the State. These were justified in public opinion by the necessity of insuring Anglo-Saxon control of the State as a means of protecting its social life and of preserving the integrity of its civilization.

In order to guard their domestic institutions, the white people of the State, quite irrespective of their views on economic and general questions of government, had, for the most part, come to associate themselves together into a political party bearing a national name. Its policy and action, however, were determined almost entirely by considerations relating to the local race problem.

The newer generations, as they became removed further and further from the shadow of the Civil War, grew restive at the fact that a social and political menace was depriving them of all liberty of thought and action on the economic and governmental problems of their day, and was extending over them a system of intellectual slavery from which there seemed to be no escape so long as the great mass of the white people believed that any division among them meant black rule for their several home communities. Accordingly there arose an insistent demand for the intellectual and political emancipation of the white people of the State, so that the election abuses which they sincerely disapproved and deplored might cease forever, and they be able to act freely and independently on the economic and governmental problems which so intimately concerned their welfare and happiness. They longed to be restored to an opportunity for influence and leadership in national affairs.

It was believed that nothing could be accomplished in this respect except by a fundamental change in the State's organic law of suffrage, and the hope of securing this change was the dominant cause for calling together the Constitutional Convention, which assembled in Richmond June 12th, 1901.

In this Convention, Walter A. Watson represented the counties of Nottoway and Amelia. He was one of the youngest members of the body, being less than thirty-four years of age when he took his seat on the assembling of the Convention.

He was, however, even at that early age, no stranger to the people of Virginia, having served with marked distinction in the State Senate, and having, for a number of years, been prominently connected with the State organization of the Democratic Party and the trusted associate and adviser of its leaders.

Although thus young in years, he came to the Convention with rare equipment for the service—valuable legislative experience, great familiarity with public affairs, an extensive and thorough knowledge of the history and traditions of his State, a fine appreciation of its needs, both economic and social, and a useful acquaintance with its public men.

He at once took, and was cordially conceded, a commanding position among his associates of the Convention.

Its members were much divided in sentiment, not on the question of the need for a fundamental change in the suffrage laws, but as to the extent of the change which should be made. This divergence of opinion grew out of the difference in conditions in the several sections of the State in respect to social and race problems.

This difference in conditions as between the various sections of Virginia has always had an important influence upon the sentiment of the State and upon its history. During the Civil War, what is now West Virginia, having no race or slave problems, was, by that fact, separated largely in sympathy from the other States of the South and from other parts of Virginia, and, in consequence, became a separate State. The same conditions as to the race problem which obtained in West Virginia obtained also—although to a smaller but still to a substantial extent—in certain parts of what after the separation of West Virginia was left of Virginia, being the parts which were more or less contiguous in territory, and more or less similar in conditions, to West Virginia.

Race questions always arise out of the menace of numbers. They do not exist where the numbers of the different race are comparatively few. There is no race question involving the Japanese in Virginia, because the Japanese in Virginia are not sufficiently numerous. In California the Japanese question is a dominant issue, because of the large number of that race in the state.

In Tide-water and Southside Virginia—known as the Black-Belt—the number of the negro race, as compared with the number of the white, was very great and was preponderant, while in that part of the State West of the Blue Ridge Mountains, and that part along the borders of Maryland, there were few negroes as compared with the white population. This fact, as stated, made the problem different in different parts of the State, and, in a sense, sectional.

The counties of Nottoway and Amelia, represented by Watson in the Convention, were in the Black Belt. Because of the large preponderance of negroes in his section, his interest in the principles to be established in the State's fundamental law related more particularly to social than to economic questions. He became, as he desired to become, a member of the Committee on Suffrage and of the Committee on Education.

It was in connection with these two subjects—suffrage and education—that he hoped to secure results of enduring benefit to his immediate constituents and to the State at large. He was untiring in his efforts, and his comprehensive grasp and clear cut views soon made him an acknowledged leader among the men who were trying to work out a sound solution of this difficult and important problem.

Watson's convictions in respect to it were very deep and were in accordance with the views of the people of his section. He became an earnest advocate of a real solution of the problem—of a solution which in his opinion would be in the interest, and would promote the happiness, of both races and would establish the social and community life of the State upon a secure foundation.

He had little patience with those who, because their immediate surroundings were different, were out of sympathy with the effort of the "affected" district" to find what he conceived to be a real and lasting solution. Always kindly and courteous in debate, he could not refrain from referring to those who (because of the comparative security of their positions west of the Blue Ridge Mountains) could not give their full sympathy to the views of the inhabitants of the eastern part of the State, as "peeping at the burdened and anxious people in Eastern Virginia through and from the protected side of Rockfish Gap."

He was not given to personal display but was most assiduous and energetic in his attention to committee duties, to the performance of which he brought the results of deep study and earnest consideration of the problems to be dealt with. He was not a frequent speaker, but when he spoke he commanded universal attention and respect, for he stood well up, among the most conspicuous of the leaders, as a debater and as a polished orator. He left the indelible impress of his genius on several of the most noted and most important of the debates. His contributions to the discussions are distinguished for their rare and classical beauty and for their real power. They are entitled to endure as examples of forensic excellence.

He did not believe it a blessing to the negro to educate him out of his station and beyond his opportunities. He considered it an injustice to him to cultivate in him tastes which he could never gratify and capacities which he could never use. In his judgment, this would not result in the development of a happy and useful citizen, but would bring disappointment and unhappiness, and would stimulate the tendency to get by criminal methods the things he had been taught to covet but could not otherwise obtain.

In discussing the kind of education which, in his opinion, would be useful to the negro and the unwisdom of an effort to give him a high literary training, he thus depicted the negro's place in history:

"This man, sir, has been exposed to and has associated with nearly every civilization that has existed upon the face of the earth. He was in Egypt when the pyramids were built, and yet he learned no useful art. He was in contact with the Roman Empire when that great government was building up a policy which gave itself an eternal name in the history of mankind. He has been acquainted with all the civilizations of Asia and all which have flourished in Europe, and yet he has never absorbed enough to lift his head above that dead line of darkness which has hidden his face in all the history of the world * * *

"I say, sir, that there are problems confronting the American people as grave and as serious as ever pressed themselves upon the attention of thoughtful men. It will require all of the patriotism, all of the intelligence, all of the character, all of the courage of this great race to which we belong to maintain itself against the temptation and the evils which confront it at the present time. And unless it be so that we are stronger than the Greek and mightier than the Roman, unless it be so that there is some special providence that takes care of an American which never took care even of the Hebrew in his chosen land, we have no right to assume that we can preserve this civilization if we undertake to incorporate with it this great black problem which has dragged down everything that it has touched since the curse of Ham was pronounced by the Almighty."

He repudiated with deep and sincere earnestness the suggestion that the people of Virginia had not dealt generously with the negro race.

He said:

"Some people say he is here in our power and that he is not here by his own will, consequently we ought not to hold him to account. I would remind those gentlemen that if the negro is in the bosom of the Commonwealth of Virginia without his consent, he is also here without our consent, and that the white people of Virginia are no more responsible for his presence here than he is himself.

"When those distinguished apostles of the enlightened sense of this nation were hauling him to Jamestown in order to land him on the shores of this Commonwealth, what were the people of Virginia doing? Standing at Cape Charles, with open arms to welcome him? No, sir. Eighteen times by acts of their colonial legislature they petitioned that sovereign beyond the Atlantic to keep that man from these shores. While those pious people in New England, who represent the enlightened sense of this great republic at this day, were thanking God that his Providence had thrown more heathen in their way, so as to come under the influence of their benign gospel, the people of this Commonwealth and of the Carolinas to the South of us, were petitioning the King of Great Britain and petitioning Heaven that he might avert from our shores this great calamity.

"But, sir, having gotten him here, what have we done for him? We took him a savage from the heart of Africa, swinging like moneys from trees in the jungles of that dark continent. We gave him a home. We gave him our language. We gave him the opportunity of the Christian religion, and last there came along these people who gave him the ballot, gave him his freedom, gave him citizenship.

"But, Mr. Chairman, the record does not end here. A ruined and conquered Commonwealth went to work amid its desolated resources, and in thirty years it has taxed its people to the extent of $37,000,000., for public education, out of which it has given the negro a third. The Commonwealths to the South of us have supplemented that until nearly $100,000,000 have been expended to educate and civilize him. The people of the North have supplemented it, so that by National and State action, nearly $200,000,000 have been expended in educating and civilizing this man, who has never, sir, in the history of the world lifted his little finger to educate and civilize himself.

"But, Mr. Chairman, that is not all we have done for him. I say, sir, the white race of the United States of America has spent more money and shed more blood in undertaking to establish the rights and the privileges of the negro than the entire negro race of the world has expended and shed for its own liberty and its own rights in the history of mankind."

In view of the emphatic protest which he felt it his duty to utter against what he conceived to be the mistaken education of the negro, he explained his attitude toward the race as follows:

"I believe, and I believe all my people believe, that in all the domestic and private relations of life we must treat this man honestly. We must treat him generously, treat him with mercy, in compassion, and give him that degree of enlightenment which may make for his good and that of the community."

The same spirit of earnestness and the same power of eloquence were exhibited in his discussion of the several proposals for changes in the suffrage provisions of the Constitution. By conscientious convictions he felt obliged to withhold his approval from the plan of suffrage ultimately determined on by the Convention. In his opinion it was not adequate to meet the problem. The earnestness of his convictions, the elevation of his spirit, as well as his uniform courtesy and consideration for others, are illustrated in the opening paragraphs of his final statement on this subject:

"Mr. President," he said, "to review the work of the Convention on the important question now under debate, I have tried sincerely to weed from my heart whatever might yet remain of disappointment, of pride of opinion, or of personal ambition. To many of you, gentlemen of the Convention, I am bound by countless ties of courtesy and friendship; to most of you I owe the allegiance of a common political faith. About me are many older and wiser heads than my own, some grown gray in the public service in a trying period of their country's history.

"In such situation, Mr. President, no ordinary cause could impel me to separate myself from them and from you in the closing days of this assembly. Such a course is one of sadness and infinite regret—come to me only after anxious days and sleepless nights of thought. But, sir, in the life of men, as in the life of states, there are moments when the individual must resolve and act for himself alone. A grave public responsibility—duty to an unfortunate, though a brave and chivalric people—commands me to make the sacrifice, and to stand up, if need be alone, in behalf of the present peace and future security. In the month of January last, before the Democratic members of the Convention, I had the privilege of presenting at length and in detail the views entertained by my constituents and by myself on this important subject; and I hall not again reproduce the incidents of that discussion. But, I owe it to myself, to the judgment of this honorable body, to the people of Nottoway and of Amelia, who have a right to exact an account of my stewardship here, and to the opinion of mankind, to make a brief statement of the reasons which have induced me to withhold my approval of the remedy which you have prescribed for the evils which afflict this Commonwealth."

Beyond these subjects of commanding importance, a question arose in the closing days of the Convention as to whether the new Constitution should be proclaimed by the Convention or submitted to the people for ratification or rejection. No question before the Convention created a sharper difference of opinion than this. It was finally determined, over most earnest opposition, by a vote of 47 to 38 to proclaim, and not to submit the new Constitution to a vote of the people.

Watson was one of those voting against proclamation and in favor of submission. He explained that he never doubted the power to proclaim, but merely the wisdom and the good faith of the exercise of that power; his views of the Convention's power having been previously expressed by him in another connection when he said on the floor:

"We can do almost anything here except make a man a woman and a woman a man."

Undoubtedly in the Convention he was controlled by the conviction that the race question was of such enormous proportions and so full of menace that it called for a radical solution. He was disappointed in the result. In this opinion he was supported, for the most part, by the representatives of those sections of the State where the problem was best known and was most pressing. Whether or not this view was extreme and the fear exaggerated, the future alone can determine. Temporarily the convulsion of the Great War has diverted interest away from this and other important domestic questions. But the problem is still here—the problem of the relationship of the races and of their reciprocal influence upon one another. Does it still enslave the freedom of thought and of action on economic and governmental questions of the two races?

However this may be, Walter Watson made upon the Convention an indelible impression of his sincerity, his charm, his personality and his power. No difference of opinion, no matter how pronounced or how acute, left a single shadow between him and any of his associates. He laid down his duties at the Convention's end, more beloved, more respected and more admired— because he was better known—than when he entered it. He, of course, grew and developed under his responsibilities, as all capable men do. He brought to the performance of his duties a heart that was pure and undefiled, a consecrated purpose, a dauntless and unflinching courage, and a measure of ability that will rank him always among the honored and foremost leaders of his people.

WALTER A. WATSON

As Judge

By R. G. Southall, George Keith Taylor, Jr., and Stephen L. Farrar, Amelia, Va.

Judge Watson succeeded the lamented Beverley A. Hancock and was elected judge of the Fourth Judicial Circuit of Virginia during the year 1904, at which time he was a practicing lawyer and attorney for the commonwealth in his native county, as well as one of the recognized leaders in the matters of social and political betterment in his community and State. He was keenly alive to all things pertaining to the interest of Virginia.

He revered her history and traditions, and his able efforts were employed generously in her behalf. By temperament and attainments he was a typical product of the best thought, sentiment and life of the State, and, having a professional training of great thoroughness, he was admirably fitted to uphold the prestige of the Virginia bench.

Judge Watson was a man of liberal and sound education; cultured, refined and accomplished. His qualifications as a judge were almost ideal. He presided with grace and dignity, and yet he was always most approachable and considerate. He had a logical, penetrating and discriminating mind, an accurate and retentive memory. His highest object was to administer justice without fear or favor. He was loved for his courtesy and fair dealing, and his example of personal worth, ability and integrity should be an inspiration to all of his professional brethren.

In delivering his opinions and presenting instructions as to the law (which he did in a style peculiarly his own) he employed language that clearly and exactly expressed what was in his mind. He spared neither time nor labor to reach a right conclusion and render evenhanded justice between man and man. He happily blended mercy with justice, and was always conservative, prudent and faithful. He brought to the bench in Virginia a peculiar combination of brain and heart, gave it an atmosphere of fidelity and strength, of grace and candor, justice and dignity. He was considerate to the members of his bar, and especially kind and reassuring to the younger and less experienced members, exercising almost a parental patience and sympathy for them. Mindful as he was of their embarrassment and anxieties, his responsiveness and gracious aid brought to him loyal friends, who today recall his memory with feelings of abiding gratitude and affection.

Judge Watson was peculiarly thoughtful of and kind to the officials of his court, and when he discharged his juries, he would in his unique way, express his appreciation of their services; in fact, all who came within the influence of his judicial life felt his charm of manner, his rare refinement and his mental force. He was a man of pronounced personality, magnetic, gentle and gracious in his social intercourse, yet firm and fearless in giving expression to his convictions.

He was not only a student of books but a student of humanity and a votary of nature. When not engaged in public duties, he loved to roam through field and forest, the deep vein of poetry in his temperament finding satisfaction in such rambles—often long and solitary.

He was the presiding judge in the trial of the famous case of the Commonwealth *versus* Henry Beattie in 1911. Judge Watson was not well at this time, and at first thought that he would not be able to sit in the case. It is a singular testimony to his reputation for fair-mindedness and ability that the father of Henry C. Beattie sought him and requested him to preside if possible because of the confidence he felt in his impartiality and legal attainments. Judge Watson finally decided to sit and conducted the case with such extraordinary skill and such fine feeling that the attention of the whole country was called to the high quality of Virginia justice.

The *Baltimore Sun* said on September the 13th, 1911: "Few criminal trials in recent years have attracted more general attention than the recent trial of H. C. Beattie for the murder of his wife * * * The trial took place in a little country courthouse of the plainest and least imposing character; yet no trial in the Supreme Court of the United States, with all its solemn and striking environment and proceedings, could have been more impressive and dignified."

"The trial will be remembered," said the *New York Times,* in an editorial, "as one of the most impressive in our criminal annals. It was rendered impressive by Judge Watson, and the way he controlled and ordered it was an object-lesson to judges all over the land. He conducted the case with wonderful moderation and held the balances with an even hand * * * If criminal trials were patterned after this one, the complaint of miscarriage of justice and of the law's delays would cease."

A touching tribute was paid to the humanity and unbiased rulings of the presiding judge when the father of the condemned man, broken and aged by his sorrow, came to Judge Watson after the trial and said: "Judge, you have sentenced my son to be executed, but I want to say to you that had you been trying your own son you could not have been fairer or kinder, and I thank you."

It took a great heart to utter these words, and Judge Watson was so touched by this tribute that he declared it more than repaid him for any trouble he might have been put to or any sacrifice he might have made, even to the impairment of his health.

He will long be remembered as a just, merciful and able judge, a distinguished citizen, a faithful and affectionate friend, and one who by his many virtues, brilliancy and charming characteristics adorned his day and time.

As his friends, as the judge who succeeded him, as the clerk of one of the courts over which he presided, and as a practicing lawyer whose first case was tried before him, we submit this brief outline of the judicial services and the personality of Walter A. Watson.

WALTER A. WATSON

As a Member of the United States Congress

By Thomas W. Harrison, Winchester, Va.

On December 24, 1919, when the world stood ready to burst into the joyous song of the Christmas morn, the soul of Walter A. Watson passed through the clay portals of mortality and joined the angel choir in their immortal anthems. On this Christmas morning when the angels touched their harps of gold, and the tidings of humanity's immortal hope swelled in joyous strains over earth's wearied plains, amidst all the joy there was sorrow, but not without hope, in the loving Virginia home, of whose happiness he was the stay; there was sorrow in the hearts of the people of the Congressional District and great State whom he had so faithfully served; there was sorrow in the hearts of his colleagues in Congress, to whom he was endeared by many acts of courtesy and kindness.

There was no man in Congress more honored and respected than he for the purity of his motives in the consideration of all public questions. There was no one who exercised more painstaking investigation in reaching a sound decision. There was no one who brought to investigation a clearer judgment and wider general information. When he reached his conclusion he could express himself with wonderful facility and forceful exposition. A graceful and courteous bearing captivated the attention of his audience, which his classic diction and faultless logic carried to conviction.

It was not always that he carried the House with him. There are too many strings to Congressional action which defy an ideal conclusion. The interests of the district, the partisanship of politics, the political considerations peculiar to each congressman, would sometimes result in an adverse vote, but there was no resisting the logical force of his reasoning if his premises were conceded, because they were the result of patient and thorough investigation.

In the Sixty-third Congress he attracted wide attention by his attitude on the bill seeking to suppress the competition of convict labor with honest labor. He made a report in favor of the bill which clearly and concisely presented the legal aspects of this great question. As he well stated in his report, for years it had been a difficult question which Congress was called upon to solve. The conflicting jurisdictions of State and Federal Government made the legal question one of great difficulty. States, to their profit, had made use of convict labor, paying little regard to the destructive competition brought upon honest labor either in their own limits or in adjoining States. State laws were inadequate because of the interstate commerce provision of the Federal Constitution, and the jurisdiction of Congress was doubtful because it began and ended with interstate transportation. But Walter Watson's clear conception pointed the path which might be successfully pursued.

His report on this bill is a marvel of simplicity of statement and forceful reasoning. He was in charge of the debate on the bill in the House, and his discussion of the Constitutional provisions attracted widespread notice and attention. Every speaker paid his tribute to Walter Watson's thorough grasp of the Constitutional question involved. The bill was passed by the House with only two dissenting votes, but failed of passage in the Senate. The pitiful pecuniary interests involved were too strong to be overthrown.

For several sessions he was chairman of one of the election committees, and his reports and debates showed a freedom from politicial bias rarely evidenced in a contested election case. He sought to introduce in the adjudication of these cases a system of judicial precedent such as prevails in the judicial system of the State and Nation. Out of a tangled web of partisan decisions, he sought to evolve a code of Congressional adjudication which might become recognized as binding beyond partisan assault. As long as he presided over one of these committees the deliberations of the committee assumed the character of a court, and here his eight years of service on the bench served him well. His reports on the contested election cases reflected the pose of an upright judge rather than the unfair frothings of a ward leader. In giving a judicial tone to the decisions in contested election cases he has rendered a great service to the people of the entire country.

His versatility and wide information were exhibited not alone in matters with which the ordinary lawyer and legislator is supposed to be familiar, but he showed an equal familiarity with such far-flung problems as were involved in the Alaskan Railroad proposition and in the laws applicable to the title to the Creek Indian lands. His discussion of these matters was with his usual ability and clearness.

A lover of peace almost to idolatry, he never faltered when the time came to draw the sword in the vindication of the honor of his country and the security of her free institutions. He voiced the American ideals, when in an eloquent statement he pronounced for the declaration of war against Germany. No one better expressed these ideals than in the following:

"Mr. Speaker, in this world there are things dearer than peace, and some things worse than war. Peace is not an end in itself, but only a means to a higher and nobler national life. Honor is dearer than peace, liberty is more important, humanity is far nobler * * *

"Hence I lift my voice for war in the profound conviction that in this crisis, when liberty and law and humanity are all at stake, when the foundation for the future governments of the world are being laid, it is better for America and mankind that we should take our predestined place in the great conflict."

In all the important war legislation necessary to raise armies, to raise revenues, to transport fighting men and supplies over three thousand miles of sea, in fact to bring a speedy triumph to American arms, the same clear vision, the same unselfish patriotic instinct is manifested. The times were trying for the trimmer, who sought to follow popular breezes. The trimmers soon found that public opinion demanded every sacrifice to win the war. Public opinion would not tolerate demagogic measures. And one of the leaders of public opinion was Walter Watson. In this great national crisis his voice was always for the most effective measure, his unswerving influence always exerted to secure needed legislation, although it might appear unpopular at the time. He voted for the Selective Draft, for the heavy imposition of taxes, for enormous appropriations to carry the war forward. There was never any question with him as to the popularity of a measure, but only if it were the most effective.

In his quiet, unostentatious way he rendered to his district, his State and his country, loyal service which was a great factor in securing the most effective defensive legislation. And so his record during these trying and epochal times is the record of his country in her triumphant march to victory.

His public services came to their end by his untimely death, when the need of his country for patriotic devotion in the work of rehabilitation was the sorest.

He had served the State of Virginia in the [State] Senate, when he had rescued his people from the black curse of negro domination. He had served his State in the Constitutional Convention, which secured to the people of the State the maintenance of her ancient civilization, and which he had done so much to preserve. He had served his State on the bench with the ermine unblemished. Four times his people of the Fourth Congressional District had honored him with their confidence.

In the zenith of his prime, trusted and beloved by all his colleagues, with his armor on in the service of God and his country, he was called to his rest.

In the first heydey of youth we had served together in the General Assembly of Virginia, in later life we were brought together in the Constitutional Convention. We both left the bench to serve in Congress, and with these bonds of sympathy, my affection for him, when again we came together in the eventful years of our common service in Congress, deepened until it became a part of my being. I cannot dwell upon this.

Beloved comrade of many years, gallant Virginian chevalier, *sans peur et sans reproche,* hail and farewell. Hail to your memory, immortal in its beauty; farewell to earthly association, which has passed away with its sweetness.

INDEX

Brockenborough, William, 32.
Brodnax, Alexander, 14.
Brodnax, Anne, 157.
Brodnax, Mrs. Ann Holmes, 157.
Brodnax, Mrs. Ann Walker, 157.
Brodnax, Mrs. Ann Withers, 157.
Brodnax, Mrs. Cornelia, 157.
Brodnax, Elizabeth Power, 157.
Brodnax, Emily H., 117, 157.
Brodnax, Frances, 157.
Brodnax, Frances Holmes, 117.
Brodnax, Freeman, 157.
Brodnax, Henry, 157.
Brodnax, Jervis (Gervis), 117, 157.
Brodnax, (Dr.) John Wilkins, 157.
Brodnax, Louisa, 157.
Brodnax, Mrs. Margaret B., 157.
Brodnax, Mrs. Mary, 157.
Brodnax, Meriwether Bathurst, 157.
Brodnax, (Dr.) Robert Walker, 157.
Brodnax, Samuel, 157.
Brodnax, William, 157.
Brodnax, Mrs. William F., 174.
Brodnax, (Gen.) William H., 15, 157.
Brook, ———, 103.
Brook, Francis T., 82.
Brook, Thomas, 70.
Brooke, D. Tucker, 214, 215, 217.
Brooking, ———, 121.
Brooking, Amelia Sherwin, 146, 153.
Brooking, Mrs. Elizabeth Brodnax, 157.
Brooking, Elizabeth Thacker, 157.
Brooking, Thomas V., 78, 88, 153.
Brooking, Col. Vivian, 157.
Brooking, Vivian, 75, 88.
Brooks, Preston S., 176.
Brown, A. V., 7.
Brown, Bennett, 48.
Brown, George, 114.
Brown, Dr. George, 167.
Brown, J. Thompson, 40.
Brown, J. Z., 240.
Brown, Lawrence, 67, 88, 124.
Brown, Lodwick, 91.
Brown's Store, 205.
Bruce, Alexander, 108.
Bruce, B. K., 8.
Bruce, George, 188, 190.
Bruce, James C., 174, 183.
Bruce, Jane, 190.
Bruce, Jane C., 195.
Bruce, Lemuel, 110.
Bruce, Mrs. Martha Watson, 190.

Brunet, M. H., 57.
Brunswick County, 7, *passim* to 185.
Brunswick Courthouse, 176.
Bryan, ———, 88.
Bryan, William Jennings, 205, 248, 252.
Bryan, Mrs. William Jennings, 248.
Bryant, Dr. J. W., 203, 204.
Brydie's Store, 54.
Buchanan, Neil, 118.
"Buck Hill," 240.
Buckingham County, 9, 32, 36, 37, 42, 50, 159, 161, 209.
Buckingham Road, 49.
"Buckskin," 66, 106.
Buckskin Creek, 86, 142, 143, 144.
Buffalo, 188.
Buffalo Creek, 115.
Buffalo Junction, 250.
Buffalo River, 68, 128, 132, 134.
Buford, Abraham, 83.
Burfoot, Thomas, 116.
Burgess, 148.
Burke, ———, 20, 56, 62.
Burke, John, 48.
Burke, Richard F., 134.
Burke, Samuel, 203, 204, 219.
Burke, Mrs. Samuel, 236.
Burke, Samuel D., 33, 87, 219.
Burke County, 200.
Burkes, Charles, 67.
Burkeville, 12, 59, 60, 120, 202, 204, 206, 251.
Burnt Ordinary, 76, 79, 109.
"Burnt Quarter," 224.
Burnt Quarter Branch, 139.
Burruss, Charles, 88.
Burton, Abraham, 66, 67, 71, 88.
Burton, John, 69.
Burton, Mrs. Mary Oliver, 172.
Burton, Thomas, 71.
Burton, W. S., 172.
Burton's Bridge, 71, 72, 73.
Burton's Road, 69.
Burwell, Rev. ———, 52.
Bush River, 68, 73, 79, 125, 135, 145, 219.
Bush River Branch, 71.
Bush River Road, 71, 72.
Butcher's Creek, 105, 124.
Butler, William, 107.
"Butterwood," 66, 115, 169.
Butterwood Road, 66, 68, 72.
Butterwood Swamp, 140.
Byney's Hill, 202, 205.
Byrd, Col. William, 23, 155.

C

Cattail Run, 93, 139.
"Cattale (Cowtale) Quarter," 129.
"Causons," 93.
"Cedar Grove," 168, 201, 215, 251.
"The Cedars," 200.
Cellar Creek, 57, *passim* to 146, 235.
236, 244.
Cellar Creek Bridge, 80.
Cellar Fork, 137, 139, 141, 146.
Chaffin, Joshua, 48.
Chalmers, James Ronald, 7, 9.
Chamberlayn's (Chamberlain's
Chamberlayne's) Bed, 139, 224.
Chambers, ――――, 50, 63.
Chambers, Allen, 88, 129, 130.
Chambers, Betty Ann, 88.
Chambers, Judge E. C., 10.
Chambers, Elizabeth Allen, 88.
Chambers, Henry, 7.
Chambers, Henry C., 150.
Chambers, Dr. Henry H., 149.
Chambers, Hugh, 71, 81.
Chambers, James, 81, 101.
Chambers, John, 88.
Chambers, Josiah, 88, 128, 130.
Chambers, Mrs. Mary, 88, 130.
Chambers, Susannah, 88.
Chambers, T. E., 241.
Chambliss, Mrs. ――――, 185.
Chambliss, Mrs. C. C., 202, 204.
Chambliss, John R., 7.
Chandler, Claiborne, 80.
Chapman, W. B., 219.
Charles (free slave), 77.
Charles City County, 94, 95, 112,
138, 182.
Charleston, S. C., 177.
Charlotte County, 9, *passim* to 131,
156, 157, 183, 190.
Charlotte Courthouse, 175, 189.
Charlottesville, 45, 56, 154, 201,
202.
Chase City, 203.
Chatham County, 198.
"Chatsworth," 97, 178.
Cheatham, Squire ――――, 239, 240.
Cheatham, Mrs. Lucy Robertson,
119.
Chatham, Mrs. Martha Sherwin,
121.
Cheatham, Matthew, 121.
"Cheatman's," 95, 220.
Chesnut, Mrs. ――――, 262.
Chester, 179.
Chesterfield County, 7, *passim* to
185.
Chesterfield Court, 223, 226, 231,
234, 238, 243.

Chesterfield Court House, 94.
"Chestnut Hill" Church, 187.
Chicago Convention, 204.
Chickahominy River, 144.
Chickahominy Swamp, 127, 128,
129.
Chickasaw Bluff, 181.
Childress, Alfred, 251.
Childress's, 202.
Childrey, Jeremiah, 72.
Childrey, John, 71.
Chinquepin Church, 220.
"Christ in Camp," 175.
Christian, Frank W., 225.
Christian, Robert, 250.
Chula Depot, 163.
Church Road, 69, 72, 76, 82, 90,
98, 103, 123, 134, 232.
Church of the Good Shepherd, 226,
227, 229, 239.
Circuit Judge, salary of, 237.
Claiborne, Augustine, 95.
Claiborne, Elizabeth, 119.
Claiborne, J. F. H., 230.
Claiborne, John, 119.
Claiborne, N. C., 37.
Claiborne, Thomas, 9.
Claiborne, Wm. C. C., 10.
Clark, Senator ――――, 261.
Clark, Berry, 192.
Clark, Elizabeth, 192, 193.
Clark, Lewellyn, 250.
Clarke, Mrs. J. H., 250.
Clarke, James, 67.
Clarke, John, 72, 98.
Clarke, William, 68, 71.
Clarke County, 40, 195.
Clark's, 122.
Clay, Mrs. Amy Vaughan, 122.
Clay, C. C., Sr., 7.
Clay, Henry, 23, 30, 34, 35, 61.
Clay, John, 113, 141.
Clay, Thomas, 83.
"Clay Hill," 61, 216.
Clay *v.* Matthews, 204.
Clayton, Judge ――――, 57.
Cleburne, Patrick R., 243.
Clement's Mill, 72.
Cleveland, Grover, 40, 201, 202.
Clopton, ――――, 14, 247.
Clowes, E. H., 221.
Clyborne, Mrs. Elizabeth Robertson,
119.
Coalter, Judge John, 44.
Cobb, Seth Wallace, 9.
"Cobbs," 100.
Cobbs, ――――, 217.
Cobbs, Samuel, 108.

"Doolittle," 122.
Doswell, John, 75, 76, 77, 79, 81, 94.·
Doswell, Peyton, 82.
Doswell, William, 79, 154.
Double Bridge, 54.
Douglas, B. B., 209.
Douglas, Stephen A., 36, 209.
Dowdie's, 122.
Dowdy, Obediah, 80.
Downes, E. S., 238.
Downman, Agnes, 85.
Downman, Elizabeth Osborne, 86.
Downman, Martha Field, 86.
Downman, William, 85, 114.
Downs, ———, 180.
Downs, C. E., 204, 219, 237.
Doyle, Captain ———, 257.
Drewry, P. H., 224, 232.
Drewry's Bluff, Battle of, 234.
Drinkwater, 76, 113.
Dromgoole, Gen. ———, 176.
Dromgoole, Edward, 13, 14, 37.
Dromgoole, George Coke, 8, 13-19, 31, 44, 55, 176.
Dromgoole, Mrs. Rebecca Walker, 14.
Drury, Abner, 131.
Dry Creek, 103.
Dudley, ———, 88.
Dudley's Bridge, 80, 88.
Dudley's Road, 53.
Duels, 55, 56.
Duger, Daniel, 18, 55.
"Dundee," 239, 255.
Dunn, Daniel, 250.
Dunn, F. L., 236.
Dunn, Martha, 146.
Dunn, Thos. H., 105.
Dunn, William R. J., 105.
Dunnavant (Dunnivant), Samuel, 12, 58, 83.
Dunnavant (Dunifant), William, 12, 58, 70.
Dunnington, W. G., 254.
Dunnington, Watkins, 240.
Dunnivant, P., 99, 122.
Dunnivant, Phillip, Jr., 104.
Dupuy, ———, 83, 182.
Dupuy, Bartholomew, 92.
Dupuy, Alexander, 150.
Dupuy, Asa, 91.
Dupuy, Elvira, 91.
Dupuy, (Dupee), James, 75, 76, 81, 91, 92, 109, 111.
Dupuy, Capt. James, 84, 91, 150, 165.

Dupuy, James, Jr., 60, 76, 79, 82, 87, 99.
Dupuy, James, Sr., 79, 82.
Dupuy, James H., 91.
Dupuy, James P., 91.
Dupuy, Jane L., 51.
Dupuy, John, 91, 92.
Dupuy, John Bartholomew, 91, 92.
Dupuy, John James, 138.
Dupuy, John Purnell, 33, 34, 35, 84, 91, 150.
Dupuy, Joseph, 29, 84, 85, 91, 131.
Dupuy, Mrs. Judith, 92.
Dupuy, Mrs. Mary, 150.
Dupuy, Peter, 79, 91, 92, 97.
Dupuy, William J., 33, 52, 91, 150.
Dupuy, William P., 150.
Dupuy family, 150.
Duroc, (Race Horse), 250.
Dyer, David Patterson, 9.
Dyer, John, 145.
Dyersburg, 181.
"Dykeland," 162, 216.
Dyson, Daniel, 92.
Dyson, Elizabeth, 92.
Dyson, Francis, 83, 92, 257.
Dyson, Frank, Jr., 158, 159.
Dyson, Frank, Sr., 92, 158, 159.
Dyson, Harry, 181.
Dyson, John, 92, 159.
Dyson, Louisa, 92.
Dyson, Martha, 83.
Dyson, Mary, 92.
Dyson, Nancy J., 83.
Dyson, Tilman, 231.
Dyson, Thomas, 92, 159, 185.
Dyson, Thomas W., 83.
Dyson, Virginia, 180.
Dyson, William, 83, 92, 105.

E

Eanes, Thomas, 207.
Early, Gen. J. A., 7.
East Dereham, Norfolk, Eng., 199.
East Hanover Presbytery, 52, 174, 175.
East Lawn, 202.
Eastern State Hospital, 208, 217, 220.
Eby, ———, 223.
Eby, A. C., 224, 225.
Echols, William, 67.
Echols's Road, 71.
Edinburgh, 167.
Edinburgh University, 151.
Edmondson, ———, 223.
Edmondson's Old Ordinary, 109.

Goode, Col. Thomas F., 37, 176, 177, 242.
Goode, William O., 8, 14, 15, 36, 44, 177, 212, 239.
Goode's Bridge, 73, 75, 97, 207.
Goode's Creek, 221.
Goode's Store, 207.
Goodloe, Granville, 181.
Goodman, ——, 236.
Goodwyn, Albert Thweatt, 148.
Goodwyn, Alberta M., 148.
Goodwyn, Anny Eppes, 149.
Goodwyn, C. F., 225.
Goodwyn, Charles F., 266.
Goodwyn, Judge Charles F., 228.
Goodwyn, Elizabeth, 149.
Goodwyn, Joseph, 32.
Goodwyn, Mrs. Martha T., 148.
Goodwyn, Col. Peterson, 148, 149.
Goodwyn, Peterson, Jr., 148.
Goodwyn, Peterson, 8, 61.
"Goose Island," 117, 180.
Gordon, Alexander, 75.
Gordon, Basil B., 172.
Gordon, Mrs. Douglas, 172.
Gordon, R. L., 210, 211, 214.
Gordon's Bridge, 75.
Govan, Daniel C., 243.
Governors of other States than Virginia, born in Southside, Virginia, 10.
Governors of Virginia, from Southside, Virginia, 10.
Grace Church, Baltimore, 146.
Graham, ——, 20.
Graham, Miss Hartley, 20.
Graham, Lawrence Pike, 7, 20.
Graham, Mary, 134.
Granby, 184.
Granger's Path, 70.
Grant, Ulysses S., 246, 251.
Grant's "Memoirs," 251.
"Grassy Creek," 255, 258.
Gravatt, ——, 165, 223.
Gravatt, W. M., 224, 225, 228.
Graveley, Joseph J., 9.
Gravelly Run, 139, 140.
"Gravely Hill," 106, 221.
Graves, Anna R., 203.
Graves, Charles W., 32.
Graves, R. F., 196.
Gray, William, 128.
Grayson, John, 121.
"Great Lawn," 203.
Great Road, 123.
Green, ——, 71, 99.
Green, Abraham, 71, 72, 73.
Green, Col. Armstead, 183.

Green, Judge Berryman, 208, 210, 211, 214, 215, 217, 254.
Green, George, 75.
Green, Grief, 77, 78, 80, 81, 99, 110, 136.
Green, H. F., 230.
Green, Louisa, 99.
Green, Mrs. Lucy, 99.
Green, Martha Tabb, 99.
Green, Marston, 99.
Green, Maston, 99, 102.
Green, Rosalie Martha, 183.
Green, Thomas, 80, 127.
Green, William, 66.
Green, William B., 34.
Green Bay, 222, 250.
Green County, Ky., 186.
Green Creek, 143.
Green River, Ky., 86, 115.
Green, Nathaniel, 59, 154.
"Greenhill," 227.
Greenhill, Ann, 124.
Greenhill, Mrs. Catherine, 99, 100.
Greenhill, David, 99.
Greenhill, Mrs. Elizabeth, 99, 124.
Greenhill, Elizabeth Ward, 124.
Greenhill, Joseph, 99.
Greenhill, Lucy, 99.
Greenhill, Martha, 99.
Greenhill, Paschal, 99.
Greenhill, Phillip W., 99, 124.
Greenhill, Samuel, 99.
Greenhill, Sarah, 99.
Greenhill, William, 75, 76, 82, 84, 99, 124, 135.
Greenhill, William C., 32, 34, 56, 57, 83, 100.
Greenhill, William G. C., 82.
Green's Church, 50, 51, 76, 113.
Green's Road, 221, 222.
Greensville County, 9, 17, 31, 32, 148.
Greenway, ——, 235.
Gregg, James Madison, 9.
Gregory, Crabb, 244.
Gregory, J. M., 223, 231, 234.
Gregory, Mrs. Martha Robertson, 117.
Gregory, Robert, 215.
Gregory, Roger, 217.
Gregory, W. T. C., 244.
Gregory, William, 36, 216.
Gregory, William F. C., 37.
Gregory's Pond, 237.
Griffin, Anthony, 71, 72, 73.
Griffin's Road, 72.
Grigg, ——, 107.
Grigg, Agnes J., 100.

Jennings, Robert, 62, 101, 165.
Jennings, Sampson, 223, 226.
Jennings, Sarah, 163.
Jennings, William, 29, 86, 103, 104, 105, 163, 165, 234.
Jennings, William R., 34, 35, 84.
Jennings Family, 165.
Jennings Ordinary, 35, *passim* to 270.
"Jennings's Burial Ground," 165.
Jennings's Mill, 81, 99, 103.
Jennito. See Genito.
Jeter, ————, 12, 61, 62, 63, 76.
Jeter, J. R., 219.
Jeter, John, 63.
Jeter, Mrs. Mary W., 92.
Jeter, Presley, 117, 118.
Jeter, R. T., 13.
Jeter, Mrs. R. T., 249.
Jeter, Rodophil, 63.
Jeter, Samuel B., 33, 34, 84.
Jeter, Tilman E., 34, 63.
Jeter's Mill, 54.
Jetersville, 60, 62, 63, 202, 218, 251.
Johnny Reb (pseudonym of Judge F. R. Farrar), 45.
Johnny's Branch, 102, 113.
Johns, Stephen, 74, 99, 108, 111.
Johnson, Ann, 123.
Johnson, Benjamin, 193.
Johnson, Bradley T., 207, 212, 213, 222.
Johnson, Bushrod, 242.
Johnson, Chapman, 31, 35.
Johnson, Gen. Edward, 7.
Johnson, Elizabeth, 193.
Johnson, Mrs. Elizabeth, 193.
Johnson, Mrs. Emily Ann Watson, 193.
Johnson, Frances Jane, 105.
Johnson, Henry, 71.
Johnson, James S., 193.
Johnson, Marmaduke, 105, 212.
Johnson, Michael, 129.
Johnson, R. M., 29.
Johnson, Sell, 71.
Johnson, W. R., 212.
Johnson, Walter, 229.
Johnson, William R., 42, 43, 102, 105.
Johnston, Anne, 227.
Johnston, Dr. George Ben, 202, 227, 236.
Johnston, Gen. Joseph E., 7, 82, 242, 245.
Johnston, Peter, 82.
Johnston-Willis Hospital, 234, 236.

Jones, ————, 70, 151, 152, 158, 165, 182, 255, 257.
Jones, Capt. A. B., 203, 216, 257, 266.
Jones, Abraham, 66, 105.
Jones, Alexander, 41, 106.
Jones, Amy Cock, 108.
Jones, Ann, 170.
Jones, Mrs. Ann Ward, 169.
Jones, Archer, 169, 171.
Jones, B. C., 34, 35, 53, 152, 168, 219.
Jones, B. Cralle, 170.
Jones, Bartholomew, 107.
Jones, Batt, 107, 125, 169.
Jones, Betsy, 181.
Jones, Mrs. Betsy Fitzgerald, 161, 170.
Jones, Binns, 41.
Jones, Branch, 105, 125.
Jones, Branch Cralle, 106.
Jones, Branch Osborne, 169.
Jones, Caroline, 81, 117, 167.
Jones, Catherine, 24, 170.
Jones, Mrs. Catherine, 105, 151, 160, 167.
Jones, Catherine C., 106.
Jones, Mrs. Catherine Cralle Ward, 106, 170.
Jones, Mrs. Catherine Harris, 166.
Jones, Charles A., 47.
Jones, Claggett B., 215, 217.
Jones, Crawley, 236.
Jones, Daniel, 60, *passim* to 186.
Jones, David C., 169.
Jones, Major Dick, 257.
Jones, Mrs. Dorothy, 107.
Jones, Dorothy C., 106.
Jones, Dorothy Chamberlain, 167.
Jones, E. M., 225.
Jones, Edgar, 106.
Jones, Edward, 73, 79, 81, 105, 107, 133, 170.
Jones, Edward Henry, 169.
Jones, Elizabeth, 81, 105, 167, 169, 170.
Jones, Mrs. Elizabeth, 108, 119.
Jones, Mrs. Elizabeth A., 119.
Jones, Elizabeth B., 51, 107.
Jones, Mrs. Elizabeth Campbell, 166.
Jones, Mrs. Elizabeth Epes, 166.
Jones, Mrs. Elizabeth Fletcher, 166.
Jones, Elizabeth Royall, 169.
Jones, Fanny, 161, 170.
Jones, Mrs. Fanny Dyson, 257.
Jones, Frances, 105.
Jones, Frances A., 106.
Jones, Frances Scott, 169.

Mills, Henry, 116.
Mills, Mrs. Martha A. E., 123.
Mills, Robert, 49.
Millson, John S., 35.
Mimms, ———, (colored), 239.
Minor, John B., 201.
Minute Men, Amelia, 154.
Mississippi, 86, 150, 230.
Mitchell, William, 78.
"Mohican," 206, 259.
Mole, Jonathan, 101.
Mole, William, 141.
Mole's Path, 141.
Moncure, Thomas J., 214.
"Monksneck," 122.
Monroe, James, 26, 44, 230.
Monroe Park, 243.
Montague, [A. J.], 255.
Monticello House, 56.
Moody, Mrs. Elizabeth Robertson, 114.
Moody, Robert, 86, 101, 109, 142.
Moore, ———, 97, 101, 103, 122.
Moore, A., Jr., 40.
Moore, Andrew, 11.
Moore, George, 109.
Moore, Lygnol [?], 58.
Moore, G. Stanley, 255.
Moore, "Seminite," 254.
Moore, Susan, 53.
Moore, Thomas Patrick, 9.
Moore, Tom, 248.
Moore, R. Walton, 40, 215.
Moore's Ordinary, 54, 132, 191.
Morgan, Colonel ———, 244.
Morgan, Buck, 206.
Morgan, John, 82.
Morgan, John A., 47.
Morgan, Major John L., 53.
Morgan, Martha F., 193 (note).
Morgan, Samuel, 33, 71, 76, 78, 79, 80, 83, 84, 85, 109, 119.
Morgansville, 54, 83, 109.
Morley, Miss ———, 198.
Morris, Elizabeth, 118.
Morris, Dabney, 80, 81, 85.
Morris, Gouverneur, 178.
Morris, Lee, 256.
Morriss, Lucy, 92.
Morris, Richard, 44.
Morris, Robert Page Waller, 9.
Morrison, A. J., 175 (note).
Morton, ———, 128, 145.
Morton, John, 122.
Morton, Joseph, 68.
Mosby, Charles L., 250.
Mosby, Daniel, 250.
Mosby, John H., 250.

Mosby, Col. John S., 248, 252, 262, 263; reminiscenses, 244-48.
Mosby, Montgomery, 250.
Mosby, Wade, 250.
Moseley, Mrs. Elizabeth, 115.
Moseley, Frank L., 34.
Moseley, Martha, 86.
Moseley, Mrs. Elizabeth Archer, 85.
Moses, William, 67.
Mosely, Mrs. Elizabeth Archer, 85.
Motley, Jim, 203, 205.
Motley, Joel, 35.
Motley, John, 109.
Motley, Joseph, 123, 142.
Motley, Josiah, 71.
Motley, Thomas, 76.
Moulden, John, 73.
"Mount Airy," 60, 100, 106, 161, 170, 186.
Mount Carmel Church, 52.
"Mt. Vernon," 246.
"Mountain Hall," 24, 27, 50, 64, 120, 151, 182, 202, 203, 238, 240.
"Mouslen's," 122.
Muddy Creek, 48, 102.
Muir, Francis, 75.
Muir, Francis Adolphus, 57.
Mullins, John, 113.
Mullin's Spring Branch, 113.
Munford, ———, 112.
Munford, George W., 44.
Munford, James H., 82, 84.
Munford, Richard I., 123.
Munford, Robert B., 102.
Munford, T. T., 7.
Munford, William, 28.
Murkland, Dr. Sidney Smith, 212.
Murphy's Hotel, 252.
Murray, "Alfalfa Bill," 256.
Muse, ———, 111.
Musterfield Spring, 134.
"My Homestead," 169.

N

Namozine Bridge, 66, 70.
Namozine (Namozine, Namozain, Namozeen, Namozene, Nummisseen) Creek, 65, 66, 67, 68, 78, 82, 110, 137, 140.
Namozine Road, 19, *passim* to 230.
Nance, John, 66, 67.
Nansemond County, 40, 168, 216.
Nash, ———, 109, 133.
Nash, Abner, 9, 10.
Nash, Caroline, 197.
Nash, Mrs. Elizabeth Hatcher, 251.

Oliver, J. Collier, 171.
Oliver, James, 74, 86, 109, 110, 142, 171.
Oliver, Mrs. Jane Robertson, 171.
Oliver, John, 110.
Oliver, John B., 158.
Oliver, John Billups, 171.
Oliver, Joseph Thomas, 172.
Oliver, Mrs. Judith, 110.
Oliver, Mrs. Lucy, 110.
Oliver, Lucy Jane, 171.
Oliver, M. J., 172.
Oliver, Martha C., 147.
Oliver, Mary, 172.
Oliver, Mrs. Mary Jennings, 83, 104, 110, 172.
Oliver, Matilda, 110.
Oliver, Micajah J., 244.
Oliver, Mrs. Micajah J., 244.
Oliver, Nancy B., 172.
Oliver, Pattie B., 172.
Oliver, Polly, 110.
Oliver, R. B., 172.
Oliver, R. W., 13, 64, 171, 172.
Oliver, Rebecca, 110.
Oliver, Richard, 74, 77, 83, 104, 110, 171, 172, 244.
Oliver, Robert, 171.
Oliver, Robert B., 172.
Oliver, Sally, 110.
Oliver, Susan J., 172.
Oliver, Thomas B., 171, 172.
Oliver, William, 110.
Oliver, Yelverton, 171.
Oliver and Knight's Mill, 165.
Oliver Family, 171.
Orange, Mrs. ———, 220.
Orange, Lewis, 125.
Orgain, A. M., 224, 228, 233.
Orgain, A. M., Jr., 234.
"Original Lists of Persons of Quality," 193 (note).
Ornsby, John, 142.
Osborn, Ann, 167.
Osborne, ———, 83.
Osborne, Abner, 76, 110, 113, 120.
Osborne, Branch, 108.
Osborne, Mrs. Elizabeth, 110.
Osborne, Elizabeth C., 91.
Osborne, Elizabeth G., 91.
Osborne, John, 71, 73, 94.
"Osmore," 208, 216.
Ould, Eugene, 221.
Overby, Rev. John, 72.
Overby, Nicholas, 146.
Overstreet, John, 13, 58, 102.
Overton, Ben, 13.
Overton, Eliza, 81.

Overton, J. W., 206.
Overton, John, 13.
Overton, Mary, 92.
Overton, Mrs. Pattie Oliver, 172.
Overton, Thomas, 238.
Overton, William G., 172.
Owen, ———, 13.
Owen, Benjamin, 240.
Owen, Mary, 119.
Owen, Thomas E., 237, 250.
Owen, W. L., 262.

P

Pace, ———, 102.
Padgett, Mrs. Sarah Vaughan, 122.
Page, C. L., 234.
Page, Richard Channing Moore, 178 (note), 179 (note).
Page, Governor John, 189.
Paget, Lord ———, 199.
Paine, Thomas, 11, 24, 104, 111, 118, 134, 135.
Paine Club, 62.
Paineville, 20, 24, 50, 54, 62, 64, 219.
Pamplin, 205.
Pan American Building, 252.
Pan-Presbyterian Alliance, 212.
Panton, William, 124.
"Pantops," 94.
Parham, ———, 120.
Parham, Matthew Robertson, 90.
Parham's Bridge, 75.
Parish, J. S., 206.
"Park Forest," 259.
Parker, Col. R. E., 29.
Parrish, J. Samuel, 234.
Parrot, William, 77.
Parson's Road, 76.
Partridge, Thomas, 101.
Patrick County, 9, 35, 44.
Patrick Henry Society, 174.
Patterson, Archibald Campbell, 152.
Patterson, Hamlin E., 152.
Patterson, John, 106, 110, 167.
Patterson, Dr. John, 152, 167.
Patterson, Mrs. Martha Campbell, 51.
Patterson, Martha E., 152.
Patterson, Charles, 42.
Patteson, Jonathan, 41.
Patton, John M., 36.
Payne, Dr. ———, 199.
Payne, Mrs. Sarah Ann Womack, 199.
Payne, General W. H., 259.
Payne's Plantation 111.

Raine, W., 199.
Raine's Tavern, 31.
Raleigh Parish, 66, 73, 91, 96, 100, 112, 124.
Ramsey, Z., 136.
Randle, ——, 109.
Randolph, ——, 82, 145, 179, 271.
Randolph, Alfred Magill, 226.
Randolph, Beverley, 10, 188.
Randolph, Brett, 179.
Randolph, Mrs. Cornelia Virginia, 253.
Randolph, Edmund, 135, 136, 180.
Randolph, Elizabeth, 102.
Randolph, Mrs. Elizabeth Beverley, 178.
Randolph, Elizabeth Wormley, 112.
Randolph, Grief, 112.
Randolph, Henry, 102, 112, 142, 253.
Randolph, Dr. Jack, 178.
Randolph, "Possum Jack," 178.
Randolph, John, 7, 15, 21, 30, 32, 44, 61, 112, 157, 159, 173, 178, 179, 198, 241.
Randolph, John, Jr., 48.
Randolph, Col. John Hampden, 253, 256.
Randolph, Mrs. Lucy Bolling, 178.
Randolph, Mrs. Maria Ward, 178.
Randolph, Mary, 93, 102.
Randolph, Mrs. Mary Eppes, 112.
Randolph, Mrs. Mary Isham, 102, 178.
Randolph, Mrs. Nancy, 178.
Randolph, Peter, 10, 11, 13, 32, 48, 56, 57, 58, 61, 65, 75, 76, 79, 81, 82, 83, 84, 90, 96, 97, 112, 113, 120, 124, 136, 178, 179, 230, 252, 253.
Randolph, Peyton, 25, 28, 29, 94, 178.
Randolph, Richard, 68, 70, 73, 113, 143, 178, 179.
Randolph, Mrs. Sarah Greenhill, 113, 253.
Randolph, T. M., 61.
Randolph, Thomas, 48, 112, 113.
Randolph, William, 44, 93, 102, 112, 121, 143, 178, 253.
Randolph Hotel, 258.
Randolph-Macon College, 176, 241.
Randolph's Mill, 81.
Randolph's Road, 72.
Randolph's Tavern, 94.
Rany, Francis, 142.
Rappahannock County, 172.
Rather, Mrs. ——, 12.
Rather, Brightwell, 81, 83.
Rather, Dick, 12.

Rattle Snake Ford, 66.
Ray, Rev. George, 13.
Read, ——, 71.
Read, Calvin H., 44.
Read, Clement, 41, 68.
Read, Thomas, 41, 48.
Reams, Thomas, 71.
"Red," Dr., 201.
"Red Hill," 11.
Redd, C. E., 201.
Redford, ——, 240.
Redford, Edward, 100.
Redford, John, 100.
Reedy Creek, 102, 140.
Registrars, for Amelia, 218.
Registration Ordinance, 217.
"Regulators" of 1771, 181.
Reid, John W., 9.
Religious denominations, 48-53.
"Republican Church," 164.
Republican Convention at Burkeville, 202.
Rhodes, Holden, 168, 226.
Ribble, ——, 201.
Rice, J. F., 270.
Rice, Dr. John Holt, 49, 50, 52, 174, 176.
Richard, a servant, 144.
Richardson, ——, 98.
Richardson, Arthur, 237, 250, 262.
Richardson, Walter, 215.
Richardson, William, 81.
Richmond, 32, passim to 202; burning of, in 1865, 233; Shockoe Cemetery, 153.
Richmond County, 36, 168.
Richmond Enquirer, 8, passim to 173.
Richmond Road, 60, 82.
Richmond Whig, 17, 18.
Riddell, Hugh, Sketch of Walter A. Watson by, 277-8.
Ridge Road, The, 71.
Ridgeway (Ridgway), Robert, 87, 176.
Riely, Henry, 230.
Ritchie, John W., 197.
Ritchie, Thomas, 44, 172.
Ritchie, W. F., 195 (note).
"Rittenhouse," 89, 240.
River Bridge, 70, 71.
"River View," 227.
Rivers, Flournoy, 167.
Rives, C. M., 237.
Roan, Mrs. Polly Burrell, 121.
"Roan Oak Road," 109.
Roane, Spencer, 82.
Roane, William H., 35.

CPSIA information can be obtained at www.ICGtesting.com
Printed in the USA
BVOW021838040112

279779BV00005B/22/P